Piedmont College Library

A Gift From The

Claude L. Purcell
Memorial and Teacher
Education Collection Fund

Understanding
Educational Research

Understanding Educational Research

Richard C. Sprinthall

American International College

Gregory T. Schmutte

American International College

Lee Sirois

American International College

Prentice Hall,   Englewood Cliffs, New Jersey   07632

Library of Congress Cataloging-in-Publication Data

Sprinthall, Richard C.
    Understanding educational research / Richard C. Sprinthall,
Gregory T. Schmutte, Lee Sirois.
        p.   cm.
    Includes bibliographical references.
    ISBN 0-13-945973-1 :
    1. Education—Research.   I. Schmutte, Gregory T.   II. Sirois,
Lee.   III. Title.
    LB1028.S7   1990
370′.7′8—dc20   90-30793
                                                              CIP

Dedication to Teachers

"The whole art of teaching is . . . the art of awakening the natural curiosity of young minds for the purpose of satisfying it afterwards."

Anatole France

Editorial/production supervision and
    interior design: Cyndy Lyle Rymer
Cover design: 20/20 Services Inc.
Prepress buyer: Debra Kesar
Manufacturing buyer: Mary Ann Gloriande

Printed in the United States of America

10 9 8 7 6 5 4 3 2 1

ISBN 0-13-945973-1

Prentice-Hall International (UK) Limited, *London*
Prentice-Hall of Australia Pty. Limited, *Sydney*
Prentice-Hall Canada Inc., *Toronto*
Prentice-Hall Hispanoamericana, S.A., *Mexico*
Prentice-Hall of India Private Limited, *New Delhi*
Prentice-Hall of Japan, Inc., *Tokyo*
Simon & Schuster Asia Pte. Ltd., *Singapore*
Editora Prentice-Hall do Brasil, Ltda., *Rio de Janeiro*

Contents

Preface   *ix*

CHAPTER 1

An Introduction to the Scientific Method   *1*

    What Is Science?   *4*
    Science Today   *9*
    Summary   *18*
    Key Terms and Names   *18*
    References   *19*

CHAPTER 2

The Language of Research   *21*

    Variables and Constants   *23*
    Independent and Dependent Variables   *24*
    Sampling from Populations   *27*
    Measurement and Measurement Error   *31*
    Research Error   *40*
    Summary   *48*
    Key Terms   *49*
    References   *50*

CHAPTER 3

Research Strategies   *51*

Research: Two Major Types   *52*
The Experimental Method: The Case of Cause and Effect   *56*
Post-facto Research   *71*
Combination Research   *74*
Summary   *75*
Key Terms   *77*
References   *77*

CHAPTER 4

Additional Research Strategies   *79*

Variations of Experimental and Post-facto Designs   *80*
Strategies Using Small Samples   *87*
Research Approaches for Special Purposes   *93*
Qualitative Research   *100*
Evaluation Studies   *103*
The Use of Multiple Response Measures   *106*
Internal and External Validity Reconsidered   *107*
Summary   *110*
Key Terms   *111*
References   *111*

CHAPTER 5

Statistical Thinking   *113*

Descriptive Statistics   *114*
Inferential Statistics   *128*
The Major Statistical Tests   *134*
Summary   *156*

Key Terms   *158*
References   *159*

CHAPTER 6

Practical Considerations in Doing Research in Schools   *161*

Doing Research in Schools: Planning the Project   *163*
A Research Example   *175*
Summary   *190*
Key Terms   *191*
References   *191*

CHAPTER 7

Research Simulations and Errors   *193*

Getting Started   *194*
Simulations   *199*
Research Errors: Case Studies   *217*
Simulation Solutions   *223*
Research Errors: Evaluations and Comments   *239*
References   *243*

CHAPTER 8

The Anatomy of a Research Report   *245*

Caution Signs   *246*
Documenting Your Writing   *248*
The Format of the Research Report   *249*
Reading Reports Firsthand   *260*
Summary   *270*
Key Terms   *272*
References   *272*

CHAPTER 9

Case Studies I: Experimental Research *273*

Case 1: The True Experiment with Independently Selected Samples
(Between-Groups) *275*
Case 2: The Quasi Experiment *289*
Summary *302*
Key Terms *303*
References *303*

CHAPTER 10

Case Studies II: Post-Facto Research and Others *305*

Case 3: Post-Facto Research *306*
Case 4: Single-Subject Research *318*
Summary *334*
Key Terms *334*
References *335*

CHAPTER 11

Computers, Educational Research, and the 1990s *337*

Educational Applications of Computers *338*
A Look into the 1990s *349*
Causal Modeling: The Debate of the 1990s *353*
Path Analysis *356*
Where Do We Go from Here? *360*
Summary *361*
Key Terms *362*
References *362*

Glossary *365*

Index *385*

Preface

This book is about scientific research in education: how to read it, how to evaluate it, how to do it, and how to write it. Some research courses demand that the student do and write up a (sometimes original) piece of research, and this can be very instructive. But this can present a real problem to the student. It is far easier to talk about research than to do it. But if one really gets down to it, sleeves rolled up, hands dirty with the data, one can more fully appreciate what the research enterprise is really all about. Does this mean that we cannot understand research without actually doing it? Certainly not! We are, however, in a much better position to understand the research that has been conducted by others if we have learned the procedures necessary for conducting our own research. Therefore, much of the information presented in this text is designed to prepare the student to actually carry out research. Whether or not this is required of the student is not so important. By learning how to do research, the student will be in a far better position to understand and analyze the research carried out by others.

If the student is required to do an actual research project, where does he or she start? What in the world is there left to do? Haven't all the research hypotheses been tried by now? And even when an idea suddenly strikes, how does one go about designing a meaningful study?

These are the issues dealt with in this book, and dealt with in a non-threatening, yet direct, manner. The student will be taken by the hand and shown the necessary techniques, and the *reasons* for those techniques, for doing his or her first research project. It will be assumed that the student has had (or is concurrently taking) an elementary course in either tests and measurements or statistics, and has at least a nodding acquaintance with some of the basic statistical procedures. The statistical tests, however, will remain largely backstage. The spotlight will constantly fall on the methodology involved in scientific research, not on the intricacies entailed in doing a factorial ANOVA. Research conclusions, as will be pointed out over and over again, properly result from both the methodology employed and the specific statistical tests that have been utilized. This is not to understate the importance of the statistical test. After all, it is certainly of paramount importance to discover whether or not a result is significant. But it will be stressed that a significant statistic simply provides us with a probability estimate, not a justifiable research conclusion regarding the possibility of discovering a direct relationship between variables.

Some of the questions raised in this book will be those involved in variable analysis: have the relevant variables been controlled, what are the relevant variables, have the variables been adequately defined, has contamination occurred, has the appropriate statistical test been used, and most important, what conclusions can be drawn? To answer these questions, the research enterprise will be carefully scrutinized. Basic research strategies will be presented, and each of the basic experimental designs will be dissected and explained.

To keep the presentation meaningful and pragmatic, actual research studies, taken from the educational literature, will be provided. These research examples will be used to highlight most of the basic research strategies and some of the more popular experimental designs. And the student won't be left alone to read these articles in a state of wonder or despair. Each article will be carefully analyzed, and each technique fully explained. The student will be exposed to the backstage machinery in order to appreciate the logic and flow of the particular design being used. In this way, a sort of case-study approach will be woven into the text, allowing the student to make some personal inferences based on exposure to these selected research studies.

This isn't the same as simply announcing that students should "go to the library." The problem with that approach is that either the bewildered student doesn't know where to start or the research selections tend to be random. The studies chosen for this book are far from random. They are all very carefully selected to illustrate specific research tactics. Students are thus taken on a *guided* tour of research landmarks and sensitized to what to look for when later taking library tours of their own. This helps to allay anxiety and prevent the situation in which students simply throw up their hands in states of confused trauma, murmuring such things as "How did I get myself into this mess?" or "Who do they think I am, Einstein?"

The chapter format is as follows:

1 *An introduction to the scientific method* This chapter defines science and its method. A quick look at the fundamental epistemologies, rationalism and empiricism, is provided, showing how the scientific method culls the choice morsels from each approach. The logic of both deduction and induction is studied from the point of view of the hypothetico-deductive approach to theory. The probability model is examined, and there is a discussion of scientific proof and "truth."

2 *The language of research* This chapter provides an introduction to the vocabulary of research, introducing and explaining in detail such concepts as variables and constants, independent and dependent variables, and the important difference between treatment IVs and subject IVs. The important concepts involved in sampling are also covered, including populations, samples, representative sampling, random sampling, and bias. Included here is a discussion of the importance of equivalent groups in experimental research. Consideration of measurement scales, a well as the reliability and validity of these measures, is presented. The chapter ends with a discussion of the most common research errors, and focuses on the reliability of research results as well as the validity of research results (internal and external).

3 *Research strategies* In this chapter the student is introduced to the major types of research—experimental (both true and quasi) and post-facto—as well as to the types of statistical hypotheses being tested, that is, difference and association. Important research terms such as independent and dependent variables are clarified within the context of a large number of different research situations, and the student is alerted to the problems of confounding variables and of inadequate control groups, and to the special problems inherent in repeated measures (within subjects) designs.

4 *Additional research strategies* Chapter 4 involves the presentation of a number of research techniques popularly used in the field of education. Many of these strategies are shown as modifications of those presented in the previous chapter. Topics include single-subject research, small-*N* research, historical (archival) research, surveys, case studies, multiple measures, meta-analysis, and qualitative research. This chapter is replete with illustrative and at times entertaining examples.

5 *Statistical thinking* This chapter guides the student through what he or she may at first have thought of as a seemingly endless maze of statistical techniques. By focusing only on those analyses, however, whose common threads underlie the most popular methodological procedures, a general theme emerges that allows the student to place each test into a coherent research context. After reading the chapter, students may not remember the name of each and every statistical test, but they will remember and understand the general reasons for statistical testing and where to look up the names and outlines of the various tests.

Although no actual calculations are demanded in this chapter, the student is helped to discover when and under what conditions a given statistical test is most appropriate. Chapter coverage includes an introduction to inferential statistics, consideration of the null and alternative hypotheses, alpha and beta errors, the concept of power, and a discussion of one- versus two-tailed analyses. The parametric statistical tests presented in this chapter include the independent t, the paired t, one-way and factorial ANOVAs, MANOVA, ANCOVA, the Pearson r, the multiple R, and regression analysis. Nonparametric tests include chi square, the U test, the H test, the Friedman ANOVA, the Wilcoxon T and the Spearman r_S. The discussion of each test will be accompanied by a specific research example.

6 *Practical considerations in doing research in schools* The thrust of this chapter is to alert the student to the research problems involved when one leaves the laboratory and actually goes out into the real world, especially the real world of schools and school systems. The student will be shown that a variety of needs and constituencies must be satisfied, and although the problems are intertwined, most of them will be shown to revolve around the following issues and questions:

a. stating the problems in operational terms and defining all terms
b. gaining access to schools and classrooms (emphasizing the importance of gaining cooperation from school boards, principals, teachers, parents, and the pupils being used as subjects)
c. writing the proposal (in such a way as to convince the school department that the results could be important enough to science in general or could have such an impact on policy at the local level as to be worth the disruption)
d. ethics (obtaining parental-pupil consent, and other basic issues involved in research ethics)
e. costs (personnel time, training costs, materials, etc.)
f. the decision process (issues involved in designing the research around all the constraints imposed by any or all of the foregoing and by the nature of the problem itself. Given the constraints of design, access, resources, and so on, a reevaluation of whether or not the results might be so limited as to be unusable, especially to the local system.)

7 *Research simulations and errors* This chapter is a hands-on, workbook-style, student-centered compilation of research issues and problems that the student must address and solve. Here the student is placed squarely in the driver's seat and asked to make the critical decisions necessary to evaluate and conduct an adequate piece of research. Rather than being a passive recipient of research information, like the passenger in a chauffeur-driven limousine, the student is now forced to take the wheel and learn how to steer the correct course and avoid all the roadblocks and detours that may seem to lie ahead.

In the first section, a series of twenty-seven research simulations are provided, in most cases simulations that model actual research studies that can be found in the education literature. We say here model, since in some cases a few of the procedures actually used are modified for the sake of clarity, and in other cases, simplified (since, after all, this is an introductory course). In all cases, however, the actual results of the study are provided in a form that the student should find understandable. It will thus be a double experience because while wrestling with the critical decisions, the student is also being exposed to some of education's most provocative and important studies.

In the second section, called Research Errors, a dozen (the dirty dozen) actual studies will be presented, all having been published, but each with a major methodological flaw. In going through these summaries, the student will be using a case-study approach, that is, will be learning by example. For both parts of the chapter, simulations and research errors, a complete answer section is provided at the end of the chapter to provide the student with that crucial learning ingredient—immediate feedback.

8 *The anatomy of a research report* This chapter faces the issue of how the research paper should be written. The student will be instructed in the APA format, considerations of writing style, proper documentation, and the format of the research report. The format will include (a) title, (b) name and affiliation of author(s), (c) abstract, (d) introduction, (e) method, (f) results, (g) discussion, (h) references, and (i) appendix. A reprint of an actual article will be used with comments keyed to the text.

9 *Case studies I: Experimental research* In this chapter the student is shown two actual experimental reports, one true experiment and one quasi experiment. The reprinted studies will be thoroughly analyzed, with comments keyed to the text of the study and aimed at highlighting

   a. the sample used and how it was selected
   b. independent, dependent, and controlled variables
   c. the research strategy (design of the experiment)
   d. types of hypotheses and data
   e. the major statistical analyses
   f. the possible flaws in each study with suggestions for alternative approaches.

10 *Case studies II: Post-facto research and others* The outline and general approach in this chapter is the same as was used in the preceding chapter except that the post-facto and single-subject strategies will be shown. Again, two actual research articles are reprinted and analyzed. The post-facto study will represent the hypothesis of difference, and the second study will be used to illustrate single-subject research.

11 *Computers, educational research, and the 1990s* This chapter discusses the basic issues involved in the use of computers in the overall research enterprise, such as literature searches and computerized data analysis. Coverage includes the use of micros, mainframes, and software (with special attention paid to SPSS, Minitab, and SAS). The use of computers in the presentation of instructions to subjects, the displaying of stimuli, and computer simulations are also covered. This chapter addresses the use of computerized archival research, where large data bases such as ERIC are accessed. Educational applications such as computer-assisted instruction are also covered.

Finally, the chapter speaks to all the preceding research articles and strategies, integrating the various pieces into a coherent whole. Research combinations and overall "game plans" are discussed, as well as the pros and cons of the meta-analytic approach. This section ends with a balanced discussion of what is sure to be the great educational-research debate of the 1990s: the use of the causal-modeling approach.

We would like to acknowledge the great help we received from the reviewers: M. David Miller, University of Florida; Tom Clark, Director of Research and Evaluation for Charlotte-Mecklenburg Schools; Glen Nicholson, University of Arizona. They were extremely helpful with regard to topic sequencing as well as their opinion on general areas for inclusion, as well as exclusion. We would also like to thank our own teachers, especially those, years ago, who played significant roles in preparing us for our own college experiences, Celia Dillon, Kay Furio, and Dudley Cloud.

To our mentors in college, Nate Maccoby at Stanford, Joel Warm at the University of Cincinnati and William C. Wolf at the University of Massachusetts, we owe a warm debt of gratitude for their significant roles in shaping our professional lives. They were all both substantive and caring teachers.

We are extremely indebted to the staff at Prentice-Hall: Susan Willig for her willingness to initiate the project, Carol Wada for her generous time in overseeing the overall editing and production, and Cyndy Rymer, our day-to-day production supervisor. Cyndy was never too busy to lend a helping hand.

Here in Springfield we received valuable suggestions from George Grosser, Phil Faticanti, and Jim Brennan. At Mount Holyoke we thank Barry Wadsworth, and at North Carolina State we owe a great debt to Norm Sprinthall and his research methods students. Our typists, Kathy Pollard, Lori Gervais, Dinna Cassello, Lisa McLaughlin, and Sharon Thomas, who transformed the manuscript into readable prose, also deserve more credit than a single sentence can adequately express.

We are also especially indebted to our wives, Dianne, Ellen, and Barbara for their continued patience and loving support.

Understanding
Educational Research

CHAPTER

An Introduction to the Scientific Method

WHAT IS SCIENCE?

Epistemology
The Early Greeks: Plato and Aristotle
Deduction and Induction

SCIENCE TODAY

The Scientific Method
The Scientific Method in Practice
Science and Survival

Science and Truth
Operational Definitions
The Law of Parsimony
Scientific Proof
Shifting Theories

SUMMARY

KEY TERMS AND NAMES

REFERENCES

The study of research methods in education is based on the very basic notion of trying to discover the most appropriate techniques for gaining new knowledge. For countless centuries people have attempted to understand more and more about their universe, their world, and themselves. This urge to understand, to increase awareness, is rooted in the fact that through understanding comes control. A sense of mastery over both the environment and the inner self has provided the driving force for the human species in its quest for survival. To understand is, in effect, to take charge. To take charge is to survive. The human ability to learn by experience, to share this learning with others and then to pass it on to successive generations, has been the hallmark of civilization's advancement.

The advances we have seen in the physical sciences, or in biology or medicine, are obvious and have increased our longevity as well as the quality of our life. In education these advances have not always been as obvious, yet they have occurred. We now know more about the thinking-learning process than we did a hundred years ago, and this progress has largely resulted from the refinement of our research endeavors. Yet some critics have carped that we have spent altogether too much time worshiping at the altar of science, too much time researching and theorizing, and not enough time allowing the working professional to use plain old common sense when urgency demands it. These critics insist that a teacher, counselor, or school principal cannot withdraw in the middle of a class, counseling session, or budget meeting and say "Well, I need to research that point more thoroughly, so I'll stop now, dismiss the staff, and go back to the laboratory. School is closed for the next three years."

On the other side are those critics who, demanding a rigorous approach, blame education for not being scientific enough. They charge that education is being held captive by armchair philosophers and as a result has become too speculatively trendy. Woolly-headed theories not grounded in scientific precision are too quickly put into practice, to the detriment of the confused student.

In a sense both these types of criticisms have some validity. There will probably always be times when a teacher has to react instinctively and can't call time out to consult the latest journal for help. Knowing all the current findings in the area of metacognition, for example, may not be all that helpful when a teacher tells an unruly student to sit down and the student responds with the challenging "make me." However, to fully rely on "common sense" may also lead to serious failures. To say, for example, that every pupil from K through 12 needs a microcomputer on his or her desk because it is intuitively obvious that "computers make kids smart" is a classic example of leaping before you look. Without first establishing what the research says in a given area, expensive educational fads may be foisted on an unsuspecting school population. And when the grandiose predictions are not followed by the promised gains (even though some gains may have taken place), the whole program is stamped "Failed." The news media are then quick to trumpet our alleged failures: "DE-CLINE IN SAT SCORES BLAMED ON POOR HIGH SCHOOL PREPARA-TION," or "JUVENILE DELINQUENCY SEEN AS A RESULT OF A LACK OF DISCIPLINE IN THE CLASSROOM."

Our field, unlike, say, physics, is constantly being subjected to public scrutiny and is often vilified by a public and a press who feel that they already know most of the answers, while we, the professionals, don't even yet know what the questions are. Imagine a headline that said "PHYSICS CONFESSES TO A LACK OF FULL UNDERSTANDING OF APERIODIC CRYSTALS." The average reader would probably yawn and then turn to the sports section. In the long run it is probably both a blessing and a curse that the public feels so strongly about our field: a blessing, since it shows a basic concern about the academic life of our children, but a curse because there are so many self-proclaimed experts.

It is the solid contention of this book that an increase in genuine understanding in any field that is even remotely concerned with the scientific endeavor must be solidly grounded in the same basic strategies and knowledge-gathering techniques. And this, after all, should be the goal of all researchers in the field of education—to increase the size of our book of knowledge.

Before getting into the demands of today's research techniques, we must take a look backward to appreciate the various fits and starts that have occurred over the centuries with respect to different knowledge-gathering attempts. At times you may feel as though you are being led far away from the essentials of hypothesis testing and research design. However, to fully appreciate where we are today as well as to understand the logic of the research enterprise, some grounding·in the area of epistemology and the scientific method is absolutely essential. You have to know what the rules are before you can play the game, and to know the rules, you have to know where we've been. So, sit back, fasten your seat belt, watch the rearview mirror, and let's see how and *why* we got to where we are today.

WHAT IS SCIENCE?

What is this thing called *science*? In a very real sense, science is what science does, that is, science and the methods of science are really inseparable. People can accumulate scientific knowledge only by practicing science. Although the origin of the English word "science" comes from the Latin word *scientia,* which means knowledge, today's use of the term goes beyond that envisioned by the early Romans. Definitions of knowledge vary, and the techniques used to acquire knowledge also vary. It is one thing to set up a long list of guiding principles to live by, as the second-century Roman emperor Marcus Aurelius so thoughtfully did. But although these Stoic maxims were considered by the Romans to contain "truth and knowledge," and maybe they still do, they were not arrived at by the knowledge-gathering techniques that are today considered essential to scientific inquiry. In fact, Marcus Aurelius even titled his book after the method he used; he called it "Meditations." And although today's scientists may spend part of their day meditating, there is certainly more to the scientific method than that.

Even now in the twentieth century, there is no absolutely agreed-upon definition of science. To some, science is only the *method* of obtaining knowledge: "Science is a way of looking at the world" (Nash, 1963, p. 49). To others, science is the organized knowledge itself: "Science is the ordered knowledge of natural phenomena and the rational study of the relations between the concepts in which these phenomena are expressed" (Dampier, 1961, p. 19). The majority opinion, however, clearly sees science as *both* knowledge and a knowledge-gathering technique, or that the method of science is not separable from the scientific knowledge itself. For example, Einstein once said that "science is the attempt to make the chaotic diversity of our own sense experience correspond to a logically uniform system of thought" (Einstein, 1940, p. 487).

Epistemology

Before setting forth a more current definition of science, let's take a few minutes to review some of humankind's attempts to discover how knowledge has been acquired. The word *epistemology* refers to the study of how knowledge is obtained, and although there are a few minor variations on the themes, over the centuries there have been only two major epistemological currents: *rationalism* and *empiricism*. In answering the question, How do we know? the rationalists have answered, "We know because we have reasoned out the solution" or "We know because our thinking powers have given us the answer." The empiricists, on the other hand, also claim to "know," but their answer to the how-do-you-know question has been, "We know because we have seen it, or heard it, or touched it, or smelled it—in short, observed it." The roots of both these epistemologies, rationalism and empiricism, undoubtedly go back to the first person who ever inhabited the planet, but their clear articulation can be found in the writings of the early Greeks, especially Plato and Aristotle.

The Early Greeks: Plato and Aristotle

Plato (427–347 B.C.) argued that knowledge could be revealed to a person if that person would meditate, introspect (look within), and use his or her powers of reason. Plato went further and said that one's power of reason offers the only source of knowledge, that it is foolish to include sensory experience as a valid test of knowledge. Plato believed that our imperfect sense organs merely provide an imperfect copy of the external world. Plato felt that we are all like cave dwellers who discern reality only from the shadows that a fire projects on the wall. Aristotle (384–322 B.C.), who had been one of Plato's students, agreed with his mentor that knowledge could be obtained by using one's powers of reason, but he added that knowledge could also be obtained by using one's senses. Aristotle believed that sensory observation could be trusted. Thus, the origins of rationalism can clearly be seen in the writings of Plato, and empiricism in the writings of Aristotle.

It is alleged that in the late fifteenth century A.D. a group of monks had been endlessly discussing the question of how many teeth a horse had. They reasoned that since a horse was bigger than a human, it must have more than thirty-two teeth, and that since a horse is one of God's creations and since God is perfect, the horse must have the perfect number of teeth for its size, and on and on. One young novitiate, tired of this long-running debate, ran out of the monastery, found a horse, opened its mouth, and counted the teeth—an early example of the difference between the epistemological techniques of rationalism and empiricism.

Deduction and Induction

Rationalists and empiricists also differ with regard to the general logic of their arguments. The rationalists have tended over the years to rely on deductive logic, while the empiricists have favored inductive logic.

Deduction is based on arguing from a general premise to a specific conclusion. In deductive logic the conclusion is a necessary consequence of the premise, that is, *if the premise is true and the argument is valid,* so too will be the conclusion. For example, if one were to say that

EXAMPLE 1

(Premise A) all dogs bark, and
(Premise B) Fido is a dog, then
(Conclusion C) Fido barks,

the conclusion (C) must be true, since the premises (A and B) are true, *and the logic of the argument is legitimate.* The validity of the foregoing argument can be seen more clearly if we substitute letters for the terms.

x = all dogs
y = bark

Thus, the premise that all dogs bark is saying that "if x, then y." The second premise states that Fido is a dog, or that "Fido is an x." Then the conclusion that states that Fido barks is saying that since Fido is an x, Fido must y, or bark.

Obviously, one should not argue that

EXAMPLE 2

(Premise A) All dogs bark, and
(Premise B) Fido is a dog, then
(Conclusion C) cats bark.

This is a flagrantly illegitimate argument, since cats were never mentioned in either premise. In other words, cats were never equated with x; therefore, one cannot conclude that cats could imply y.

EXAMPLE 3

(Premise A) All dogs bark, and
(Premise B) Fido barks, then
(Conclusion C) Fido is a dog.

Although Example 3 appears to be superficially similar to Example 1, it is just as fallacious as was Example 2. In this case the premise that all dogs bark still sets up the condition that "if x, then y," but the second premise, instead of equating Fido with x, equates Fido with y (barks). In fact, what has happened is that the logic of the syllogism has suddenly been turned around to state that "if y, then x," a conclusion that was never implied in the premise. In fact, Fido might be the stage name of an animal impersonator, or the name of a trained seal at Sea World. Accepting this type of false conclusion is known by logicians as *the error of affirming the consequent.* In the last chapter of this book in the discussion of correlational techniques of causal inference, much more will be said on this subject.

Try this one:

(Premise A) All men are mortal, and
(Premise B) Socrates is a man, then
(Conclusion C) Socrates is mortal.

Since x (all men) are y (mortal), Socrates, who has been equated with x, must be y, or mortal. The conclusion is valid.

Now try this one:

(Premise A) All men are mortal, and
(Premise B) Socrates is mortal, then
(Conclusion C) Socrates is a man.

If you said this was true you have just committed the error of affirming the consequent, or the assumption that y implies x. After all, Socrates in this case might be the pet name for the cat we talked about in Example 2.

Now that you've got the general idea, assume for the moment that the research literature clearly indicates that dyslexic children consistently produce scoring patterns on the WISC-R (an intelligence test) that show a performance score that is higher than the verbal score, or that $P > V$. A valid logical statement could then say that

(Premise A) all dyslexic children have $P > V$, and
(Premise B) Joe is a dyslexic child, then
(Conclusion C) Joe has a $P > V$.

However, as has been shown, one cannot say that

(Premise A) all dyslexic children have $P > V$, and
(Premise B) Joe has a $P > V$, then
(Conclusion C) Joe is a dyslexic child.

In this case Joe may be an adult who has spent his life repairing carburetors and hasn't read a book since leaving public school.

Deductive proofs, then, are eternal—true today, true tomorrow, true forever, *only as long as the premises are true and the logic remains valid*. Mathematical statements are primarily deductive in nature, which means that they can be checked for logical accuracy. You can establish whether a mathematical statement is true or false. In the following syllogism, two plus three equals five, and this is true without having to check a probability table.

(Premise A) $4 + 1 = 5$, and
(Premise B) $2 + 3 = 4 + 1$, then
(Conclusion C) $2 + 3 = 5$

Induction, on the other hand, refers to the logical techniques of arguing from the specific to the general, or arguing from a few instances to a general rule. The general conclusion in this method is more or less *probably* true. Thus, induction makes no claim to eternal truth, but to a validity of presumed likelihood. Induction is the hallmark of inferential statistics. When sample measures are taken, the statistical analysis of these measures creates what is referred to as a statistical decision, or a decision about the likelihood that these sample values can be generalized to the population.

Philosophers refer to this step of generalizing from a few instances to a general rule as the inductive leap—leaping from the few to the many. Statisticians refer to it as the aforementioned statistical decision. Induction is, therefore, always *problematical* because all generalizations are somewhat "iffy." Perhaps you remember being warned about "leaping to conclusions," or the dangers inherent in overgeneralizing. These warnings should be constantly kept in mind whenever one engages in, or reads about, the inductive process.

René Descartes: The Perfect Rationalist

During the 1600s the great French philosopher and mathematician René Descartes (1596–1650) ushered in the so-called Age of Reason—the era of the 1700s when philosophers assumed that all humankind's problems could be solved through the use of the powers of reason. Descartes was a true genius, and his far-reaching interests have made him famous in several disciplines. In mathematics he is noted for the creation of analytical geometry, and for his invention of coordinate space (for translating algebraic terms into geometrical form). In fact, his coordinates—the abscissa being the x or horizontal axis and the ordinate being the y or vertical axis, are still referred to today as Cartesian coordinates. He is remembered in psychology as the father of the concept of the reflex arc, and in philosophy for his interactionist solution to the mind-body problem (Cartesian dualism).

Our interest in Descartes, however, is due to the precise and elegant epistemology that he presented in 1637 in his *Discourse on Method.* This is the famous work in which Descartes begins by doubting the existence of God, and continues to doubt everything else, *except* the fact that he is doubting. His own doubt, then, became an indisputable fact, a kernel of truth that could not be refuted. He chose to describe this obvious truth by using the Latin phrase "cogito ergo sum," or "I think, therefore, I am." He believed that he had thus proved his own existence by relying only on his powers of reason and his use of *deductive* logic. He didn't have to see anything, or touch anything, or infer any generalizations; he only had to think out, "cogitate," the solution. And he assumed that his solution, arrived at deductively, had the absolute certainty of a mathematical proof. His appeal for truth was not to experience, but to reason. As Descartes himself said, "I doubt that a sheet of paper is now before my eyes; I may even doubt that 2 and 3 are 5. But suppose I try to doubt my own existence; this doubt disproves itself. I must surely exist in order to doubt that I exist."

Bishop Berkeley: The Probable Empiricist

A few years later, and a few hundred miles to the west of continental Europe, George Berkeley (1685–1753), bishop and philosopher, pursued another form of epistemology: empiricism. Born and bred in Ireland, Berkeley became impressed with the work of John Locke, the English philosopher and political scientist. Locke had said that knowledge comes not through reason but through sensory observation. Locke had stated "nothing in the intellect not first in the senses,'' thereby advocating the primacy of the senses over the intellect. Further, Locke had put forth his famous "tabula rasa" (blank slate) argument, which stressed an extremely environmental view of human nature. According to Locke, the mind is a blank slate upon which experience writes.

With Locke's position in mind, then, Berkeley felt that Descartes had been in error in his attempt to prove his own existence through the use of reason, and that he, Berkeley, would show that all existence depended instead on observation. "Esse est percipi" (to be is to be perceived), said Bishop Berkeley in his 1710 work *Principles of Human Knowledge*. Events exist *only* when they are observed, asserted Berkeley—a clear and uncompromising statement of the empiricist's credo. Berkeley also wrote on the pure inductive method, even mentioning the concepts behind such ideas as the independent variable, the dependent variable, and control variables. Berkeley saw with steady clarity the probabilistic nature of the inductive process.

As an aside, consider for a moment that old problem in logic that you probably encountered at some point in your education: If a tree fell in Siberia, and there was nobody there to hear it, did it make any sound? A rationalist, such as Descartes, would have to answer in the affirmative; that since it is logical to assume that all falling trees, no matter where they are, and no matter whether or not an observer is present, create noise, then so too did the tree in Siberia. On the other side of the aisle, an empiricist, such as George Berkeley, would have to vote no. With no one there to perceive the event, the falling tree could not possibly create a sound. In fact, Berkeley would probably add that without an observer, we could not even conclude that the tree existed in the first place, and further, that we could not even be too sure about Siberia.

SCIENCE TODAY

You may be wondering what all this business about an old French philosopher feeling the need to prove his own existence, or an Irish bishop denying the existence of nonobserved events, or Siberian trees falling in solitary splendor has to do with science. The answer is: plenty. You weren't taken on a museum tour of dust-covered relics just to witness a few philosophical oddities. You were taken for an express purpose: to cite just a couple of examples of humankind's long struggle to determine what can legitimately be entered into the great book of knowledge. The scientific method wasn't a post–World War II creation, nor did it spring full-blown out of the head of Zeus. It has a long and noble, though not always serene, history, and as in many other areas, you really should look at the acorn to study the tree.

Earlier in the chapter it was stated that science is both a body of knowledge *and* a process of discovering what that knowledge is. Thus, science is defined as an organized and systematic accumulation of knowledge obtained primarily by methods based on *observation*. The scientific method is, both first and last, an empirical epistemology. It begins with and ends with observation. True, there may be a pinch of rationalistic deduction thrown into the mixture, but the litmus test of science remains observation.

Since knowledge in science depends on how that knowledge is obtained, let's next outline the formal steps involved in the scientific method. These steps are (1) observation, (2) induction, (3) theory, (4) deduction, and (5) observation. The whole procedure is often referred to as the hypothetico-deductive approach (Walker, 1963).

The Scientific Method

Observation

Events must first be observed—somehow perceived. Which events? All events into which scientific inquiry can be made. Certainly the scientist may use measuring devices and instruments to aid the naked senses, yet in the final analysis it is only through the sensory apparatus that the scientist has the ability to observe. The senses may be extended, as when an astronomer uses a telescope to observe the movement of the planets, or as when a psychologist uses a galvanometer to observe the galvanic skin response. Yet extended or not, there must always be an interaction between the observed event and the scientist's sensory receptors.

The observations must be measured in some way, that is, the data should be quantified. Measurement is simply the assigning of numbers to observations according to rules (more on this in the next chapter). Anything that varies and *has been measured* is called a variable. This process allows for observations being more directly repeatable, perhaps by other scientists, and also allows for statistical analysis.

Also, science doesn't rest its case on a single observation. The scientist makes repeated observations and reports these observations in as careful and precise a way as is humanly possible. This is done to help ensure the consistency of his or her own measures, and just as important, to allow other scientists to repeat these measures. Science must always remain open to replication. Thus, the final authority for the scientific method is the authority of observation.

Induction

Once the specific events have been observed, the scientist attempts to form some sort of generalization concerning these observations. The scientist searches for some regularities among the data and, when found, induces a tentative explanation. There is nothing hard or fast about this procedure, since the generalization is always couched in terms of probability. That is, the scientist makes an "educated guess" about some perceived relationship among the data. This is an important step, for without it science would simply consist of a raw listing or tabulation of perceived events. As stated by Royce and Powell (1983, p.

19), "Science is not just endlessly collected empirical data; it is an explicit attempt to understand and explain what it is that empirical observations yield."

Theory

The educated guess which the scientist induces is called the *hypothesis*, and a series of interrelated hypotheses is called a *theory*. The theory is, therefore, a tentative hunch or series of internally consistent hunches concerning the possible relationships among variables. That is, the scientist, after making specific observations, hypothesizes some regularity among the data. The theory should then be stated in such a way that it can be generally confirmed *or* disconfirmed. If the hypothesis is so broad and vague that it cannot be disconfirmed, it is probably too general to ever be validly confirmed. Hypotheses can be of two types: (1) the hypothesis of difference, in which an assumed difference between events is induced, and (2) the hypothesis of association, in which two or more variables are presumed to correlate. These types of hypotheses will be more fully explained in Chapter 3.

Deduction

Every hypothesis must be tested, and to accomplish this, the hypothesis must be *capable* of being tested—that is, testable predictions may be deducible from it. Thus, the hypothesis—the induced generalization—must be open to deduced predictions. Deduction is that step which takes the scientist from the general hypothetical level back to the arena of specific observations. In our earlier discussion of deduction it was mentioned that when the premise is true the deduced conclusion must also be true, but in the *scientific method* there is no way to be absolutely sure the premise is true. In science, the premise, in this case the hypothesis, is only inferred, and is thus a probability statement. Since the premise may or may not be true, so too the deduced predictions may or may not prove valid. Thus, in science, unlike in mathematics, the "truth" of a deduced conclusion is still only a probable proof. Deduction does, however, bring the scientist back to the level of observation and allow the hypothesis to be tested against these new observations. As stated by Kimble, the hypothesis cannot be taken seriously until evidence is produced that it is not false. And if the evidence is logically impossible to obtain, the hypothesis is simply not part of science (Kimble, 1989). In short, the scientist is saying at this point that *if* the hypothesis is true, it should logically follow that certain specific events should be observed.

Observation

The deduced predictions are then checked against another set of observations, and in this way the hypothesis is either confirmed or disconfirmed. Notice, then, that the scientific method is anchored at both ends in observation. It begins with observation, followed by three "thinking" steps, and finally ends in observation. Recall the two Latin phrases presented earlier, Berkeley's "esse est percipi'' and Descartes's "cogito ergo sum." Distorting the Latin badly, we can say that the scientist begins by "esse est percipiing," then does a little "cogito ergo summing," and finally returns to the "percipiing." Science today uses a blend of those two great epistemological approaches, empiricism and rationalism. We can learn about the world by using our powers of observation. We can then try to understand what these observations mean by using our powers of reason, and then test our reasoning powers against a new set of observations. In short, the scientist attempts to observe certain regularities in nature, then reasons out what predictions should follow, and finally, attempts to validate these predictions on the basis of new observations.

It must be strongly pointed out that the scientific endeavor does not end at the point of the fifth step, observation. In fact, science is a never-ending chain of these five steps, for the observation in the fifth step may be used to induce further generalizations, new hypotheses from which more predictions are deduced. The goal of science is to make predictions of ever-increasing accuracy.

The Scientific Method in Practice

After reading the aforementioned five methodological steps, it should not be assumed that the scientist greets each new day by setting up a rigid timetable of sequenced steps, like a pilot consulting a checklist before landing a plane. There's no sign on the laboratory wall that reads

1. 8 A.M.—Observe data
2. 9 A.M.—Induce
3. 10 A.M.—Hypothesize
4. 11 A.M.—Deduce a prediction
5. Noon—Test the prediction against new observations
6. 2 P.M.—Work completed, go play golf

In reality many of these steps are taken almost without conscious awareness. The original observations may occur through reading someone else's research late in the evening, and then, perhaps, just before falling asleep having a quick moment of insight, an "aha" experience in which a hypothesis might be semiformed. The point is, you don't have to be wearing a lab coat and surrounded by scientific instrumentation to pursue the scientific method. You might be contentedly lying on a beach, perhaps watching the flocking behavior of gulls, when an idea occurs, or driving alone in your car, your mind wandering in every direction when suddenly an "aha" moment presents itself.

In short, don't get so engrossed in memorizing the steps in the scientific method that you miss the big picture: the scientific game plan. Otherwise, you'll be like the ninth-grade algebra student who loved doing equations but then became traumatized "when we got to the word problems." In fact, all of you at one time or another have used the scientific approach in your daily lives. For example, you may have noticed that the head ends of car keys have either rounded or squared-off ends. The squared ends usually indicate that the key is for the ignition, and the rounded-end keys for the trunk. But you don't know for sure until you take this hypothesis back to observation, that is, attempt to insert the key. Or, in telephoning a friend the busy signal may produce a guess that the friend is at home and talking to someone else, yet without physically going to the friend's home and checking out each room, an alternative hypothesis may still be true: the friend went out and left the phone off the hook.

Science and Survival

Just as you have undoubtedly utilized features of the scientific method in guiding your own life—that is, learning from experience—so too did our earliest ancestors. Since time immemorial persons inhabiting this planet have made observations, formed hunches about the meaning of these observations, and then attempted to validate these hunches by comparing them with further observations. They did this for a very good reason: survival! As an example, an early human may have reacted positively to his first meal of tasty mushrooms. Later, he may have eaten some poisonous toadstools and become violently ill. The next day he probably refused to eat mushrooms until he could definitely be convinced that they would not harm him. Thus, although the term "scientific method" is usually only applied when it is used with full conscious awareness, persons have undoubtedly always used at least some aspects of scientific methodology just to stay alive.

As stated by Walker (1963, p. 15), "the scientific method is a survival technique that developed during the biological evolution of living things. Any organism or device that includes a suitably connected memory unit can learn by experience, and this learning by experience contains the basic elements of the scientific method."

Science and Truth

This word *truth* can have some very tricky connotations. Earlier, in our discussion of Aristotelian logic, truth referred to the pure logic of the deductive technique. That is, when the consequences of a deductive statement lead to the support of a premise, rather than a contradiction, the statement is judged to be true. Because of this, it can be said that deductive mathematical statements are open to this type of truth verification.

Also, a straightforward empirical observation may be labeled as true or false. One can say that a certain dog has barked simply by observing the dog. That is, truth or falsity can be applied to statements that are directly open to empirical verification, but that doesn't prove that the dog will bark in the future, nor does it prove any possible theory that has been contrived to explain why the dog has barked in the first place.

In science, then, the search for truth can be a rather chancy undertaking. Scientific truth occurs when it creates order out of past observations and also correctly predicts the outcome of future observations. As one expert in the philosophy of science states it, "The statement of a principle is true when it has been developed by the process of induction and has successfully been tested by the process of deduction in scientific methodology" (Fischer, 1971, p. 31). We see, then, that in science truth is not an all-or-none affair. The more accurate the hypothesized predictions, the greater the degree of scientific truth.

Because of its various definitions, the word *truth* is sometimes even disregarded by certain scientists. To some, there is no real truth in science until that last fact is in on Judgment Day. One never knows whether some future observation may put the lie to some principle assumed to carry "eternal truth."

Operational Definitions

To create good, solid, precise communication in the scientific world, the physicist Percy Bridgman announced that all scientific concepts and terms should be defined *only* on the basis of the operations involved in their observation. In Bridgman's words:

> We may illustrate by considering the concept of length: what do we mean by the length of an object? We evidently know what we mean by length if we can tell what the length of any and every object is, and for the physicist nothing more is required. To find the length of an object, we have to perform certain physical operations. The concept of length is therefore fixed when the operations by which length is measured are fixed: that is, the concept of length involves as much as and nothing more than a set of operations; the concept is synonymous with the corresponding set of operations. (Bridgman, 1927, p. 5)

And if this is the case in the extremely objective world of physics, it must certainly carry over to the realm of the behavioral sciences, where "fuzzy" definitions are more apt to intrude. *Operational definitions* spell out in detail the relationship between what is being defined and the operations used for measurement, a technique that helps prevent the inclusion of fuzzy, nonobjective concepts.

A researcher may talk of subjecting a group of students to the "rich, meaningful" teaching technique and because of the overtones of the English language leave vague the exact nature of what these students were objectively being treated to. As readers of the research literature we tend to fill in on the basis of our own frame of reference what the term may or may not be conveying. We may feel that if it sounds good, it must be good. In science, this is an extremely dangerous situation, since each reader may form a different impression of the concept.

For example, take the term "intelligence." We may vaguely feel that this has something to do with how quickly a person can learn new material, or how much a person remembers. But to arrive at a precise operational definition of intelligence, we would have to specify exactly how we measured it. For example, in a research study intelligence might be defined on the basis of an individual's IQ score on the WISC-R.

In the field of education many outcome variables are stated operationally in the form of behavioral objectives, which are solid, observable criteria that both measure and define the educational goal. Reading skills, for example, might be operationally defined as the ability to recognize the correct definitions for one hundred selected words. Music appreciation might be objectified as the ability to identify the composers of twenty musical compositions. (If critics were to argue that being able to recognize twenty composers "isn't what we mean by musical appreciation," the scientist would say that it is up to the critics to state clearly what they do mean so that these goals can be consistently measured.)

It is important in reading research to take special note of how the variables and concepts are being defined, and it is also important not to attach any greater meaning to the concept than that involved in the operations used to measure it. Don't assume that you know what an "innovative" teaching technique is, or when the "teachable moment" has arrived. Find out by examining how the researcher has operationally defined the terms. A nonoperationalized term is like a "glittering generality" that seems to explain everything but indeed may explain nothing. As was stated earlier, the use of operational definitions aids in sharpening the meaning of concepts, thus allowing for more precise communication among scientists, and helping to produce that key ingredient in scientific methodology, *objectivity*.

The Law of Parsimony

Science should also strive toward parsimonious explanations, an effort that is greatly enhanced when operational definitions are used. Known as Morgan's canon, or Occam's razor, the *law of parsimony* insists that a concept should always be described in its least complex form. When one has the choice of defining at an abstract level or at a simple level, choose the simple level. As an example, take the following two explanations of why a dog wags its tail before being fed:

1. It wags its tail as a signal of its profound loyalty, basic altruism, and as proof of its advanced state of social consciousness.
2. It wags its tail because it heard the can opener.

Lloyd Morgan's canon, the law of parsimony, urges you to opt for the second explanation; that is, you should use Occam's razor to shave off all the excess baggage and get right down to the nitty-gritty. The term "group cohesiveness" may be abstractly and metaphorically defined as the cement that holds the members of a group together, or the feeling of pressure to conform to group standards and ideals. A more parsimonious and obviously operational definition might simply be the number of times the group members say "we" as opposed to "I." Again, both operational definitions and parsimonious explanations aid in the scientist's pursuit of objectivity.

Scientific Proof

It may at first seem paradoxical, but scientific research can only lead to *proof without certainty*, which although not perfect is still far better than certainty without proof. Scientific proof rests on the shifting foundation of a probabilistic model, which means that in science proof statements must always eventually be couched in terms of "likelihood," that is, in terms of how likely it is that this or that event could have occurred on the basis of chance alone. If this seems risky, it's because it is. But risky doesn't necessarily imply a murky scene of blind groping in the dark. There are, after all, high-risk events and low-risk events and also all points in between. The fact is that scientific proof doesn't offer eternal truth, forever carved in immutable stone. It offers instead a kind of "beat-the-odds" proof, a proof, it is to be hoped, of extremely high likelihood. If you were playing poker and happened to be dealt four kings, you would not be 100 percent guaranteed of winning that hand, but at the same time, your risk of losing would be extremely small.

Shifting Theories

Since the structure of a scientific theory rests on a probabilistic foundation, it obviously may change over time. The history of science is replete with examples. Two of the most commonly cited instances are (1) the shift in theoretical orientation from the earth-centered Ptolemaic view of astronomy to the Copernican view, which placed the sun at the center of the solar system, and (2) the more recent shift from Newtonian mechanics to Einstein's space-time manifold.

In neither case was the shift totally serene. A scientific theory is difficult for its adherents to give up, and the possibility of any significant change is fraught with discord. Nor is a shift in the scientific theory an automatic consequence of disconfirming empirical evidence. Scientists often tenaciously hold on to a theoretical viewpoint, even in the face of contrary evidence. In fact, the contrary evidence is either denied or, if it's so compelling as to demand recognition, reevaluated in terms that seem consistent with the original theory. For example, it was difficult for the Ptolemaic theorists to account for the observed movements of the planets. To account for these movements and still remain true to their earth-centered orientation, they resorted to a series of sleight-of-hand interpretations—interpretations that were, in fact, composed of more sham than substance. Eventually another theory was generated, the Copernican, which predicted more and assumed less. This, then, is how theories have historically shifted. A theory does not simply fall of its own weight but only when a new viewpoint arises that has stronger predictive power.

Kuhn and Scientific Revolutions

This view of how science changes has been outlined by Thomas Kuhn (1973). Kuhn suggests that a scientific theory, or paradigm, has a certain life span, and its development conforms to certain predictable sequences. When a theory is fully accepted by the great majority of scientists, it is said to be in its *normal phase*. However, when a number of empirical inconsistencies begin cropping up, the theory eventually faces a *crisis phase*. Kuhn calls these inconsistencies *anomalies*, and during the crisis phase the adherents of the theory do everything they can to explain away these anomalies. If at that point a new theory is proposed, especially one based on fewer assumptions that more parsimoniously explains these anomalies, this new theory may simply overwhelm the previous one and go on to become the accepted viewpoint. Thus, the crisis phase does not in and of itself sound the theory's death knell. Change occurs only when a *new* theoretical formulation is presented to take its place.

The replacement of an older theory does not mean that the older theory was all wrong. The things it did predict well, it still predicts well. It's simply a matter of not predicting enough—its inability to handle the newly discovered anomalies. The replacement of Newton by Einstein doesn't suddenly erase the predictive value of Newton. As has been said many times, Newtonian theory is still very handy for doing the everyday jobs around the solar system. The key to this seeming paradox is simply that Einstein predicted *more* and assumed *less*. Kuhn's warning, then, is that we should never become slavish disciples of any particular theory, even Einstein's; for who knows what will be next?

Science and the Human Observer

In conclusion, then, science is a body of systematically organized knowledge that has been obtained by methods based on observation. Science is dynamic, active, constantly seeking more precise predictions. The job of science is never complete, for in science each new observation leads to further observation, and each new idea to an even more novel idea. Finally, science is a strictly human activity. Human beings do the observing. Human beings make the inductions and deductions. Science, with its sophisticated instrumentation and computer-printout analyses, may seem to the casual observer to be mechanically flawless in its precision and objectivity. But after all, people like you and I do the observing and feed the data into computers. Science may not be perfect, partly because people aren't perfect, but its results and techniques have gone an astonishingly long way in changing both the way we live and the quality of human life.

SUMMARY

Science is both a body of knowledge and a knowledge-gathering technique. Epistemology is concerned with the study of how knowledge is obtained, including scientific knowledge. Over the centuries there have been two major epistemological branches, rationalism and empiricism. Rationalists assume that knowledge results from the use of reason, whereas empiricists assert that knowledge is only acquired through sensory observation. Rationalists and empiricists also divide on the issue of the form of logic used to determine the proof of a conclusion. Rationalists rely on deductive logic, in which the argument is directed from a general premise to a specific conclusion. Empiricists, on the other hand, utilize inductive logic, arguing from the specific observation to a general conclusion. Whereas deductive proofs can be checked for logical certainty, inductive conclusions rest on a probabilistic model, a proof without certainty. A quick recap of the works of two famous philosophers, the rationalist René Descartes and the empiricist Bishop Berkeley, highlight the fundamental distinction between these opposing points of view.

The scientific method, a blend of both epistemological positions consists of five formal steps: (1) observation, (2) induction, (3) theory, (4) deduction, and (5) observation.

Scientists today demand increasingly precise definitions for their terms and concepts. The physicist Percy Bridgman has urged that scientific concepts be defined only on the basis of the actual operations involved in their observations. The use of such operational definitions thus reduces the possibility of the scientist using vague, nonobjective language. Science also attempts to abide by the law of parsimony, which insists that a concept should always be described in its least complex form.

The scientific method, since it is grounded at both ends in observation, offers an empirical, probabilistic proof, not eternal truth. Because of this, scientific theories undergo revolutionary shifts. As shown by Thomas Kuhn, scientific theories have predictable stages of development: (1) the normal phase, (2) the crisis phase, and (3) the revolutionary development of new theory.

Science, despite its seeming precision and objectivity, is still a human activity and open to human pitfalls. The results of science may not be perfect, but these results have gone a long way in changing the way we live and the quality of human life.

KEY TERMS AND NAMES

Anomaly	Crisis phase
Aristotle	Deduction
Berkeley, George	Descartes, René

Empiricism

Epistemology

Hypothesis

Induction

Kuhn, Thomas

Law of Parsimony

Normal phase

Objectivity

Observation

Operational definition

Plato

Rationalism

Science

Scientific method

Scientific revolution

Theory

REFERENCES

BRIDGMAN, P. W. (1927). *The logic of modern physics.* New York: Macmillan.

DAMPIER, W. C. (1961). *A history of science and its relation with philosophy and religion* (4th ed.). Cambridge, England: Cambridge University Press.

EINSTEIN, A. (1940). Considerations concerning the fundamentals of theoretical physics. *Science, 91,* 487–492.

FISCHER, R. B. (1971). *Science, man and society.* Philadelphia: W. B. Saunders.

KIMBLE, G. A. (1989). Psychology from the standpoint of a generalist. *American Psychologist, 44,* 491–499.

KUHN, T. S. (1973). *The structure of scientific revolutions* (3d ed.). Chicago: University of Chicago Press.

NASH, L. K. (1963). *The nature of the natural sciences.* Boston: Little, Brown & Company.

ROYCE, J. R., & POWELL, D. (1983). *Theory of personality and individual differences: Factors, systems, and processes.* Englewood Cliffs, N.J.: Simon & Schuster, Prentice-Hall.

WALKER, M. (1963). *The nature of scientific thought.* Englewood Cliffs, N.J.: Simon & Schuster, Prentice-Hall.

CHAPTER

2

The Language
of Research

VARIABLES AND CONSTANTS

**INDEPENDENT AND DEPENDENT
  VARIABLES**

  Active (or Treatment) Independent
    Variables: Causal IVs
  Subject (or Classification) Independent
    Variables: Predictive IVs

SAMPLING FROM POPULATIONS

  Populations
  Samples

**MEASUREMENT AND
  MEASUREMENT ERROR**

  Measurement Scales
  Measurement Error
  Reliability of Measurement
  Validity of Measurement

RESEARCH ERROR

  The Reliability of Research Findings
  Validity of Research

SUMMARY

KEY TERMS

REFERENCES

Most of you are going to feel a certain amount of dismay when first encountering the literature of educational research. The rigors of seemingly complex statistical and methodological procedures and the vast and mysterious body of research jargon can be both awe inspiring and intimidating to the uninitiated. You may feel that educational researchers spend far too much time fretting over the details of methodological issues, such as independent variables, adequate control groups, measurement theory (the list seems endless)—in short, issues that may seem trivial to the casual observer. However, this attention to detail, this obsession with precision, is all part of a self-conscious attempt to be exact in the communication of meaning. And this is especially important in the social sciences, where the concepts being measured are not always as solidly grounded in hard evidence as they might be in physics and chemistry.

In fact, students in every field must learn the vocabulary of that field, and, like it or not, researchers, alas, have developed a language that is all their own—a language, however, that is universally accepted within their field and allows for precise communication among colleagues. To a psychologist, for example, "reinforce" means to manage a stimulus so as to increase the strength of behavior. The engineer's use of "reinforce" refers to a strengthening of materials (as in reinforced concrete) or to strengthening a building or bridge. A tailor uses "reinforce" to indicate use of stronger seams at points in a garment that might wear quickly. The professional baseball coach may "reinforce" a weak pitching staff by hiring a new pitcher. Any time you have taken an "Introduction to" course (such as Introduction to Psychology, Sociology, or Education), you have been exposed to the lingo of a new field.

The preceding chapter introduced you to some of the history, logic, and language of science. This chapter describes some of the terms most often used in applying scientific methods to real-life problems in real-life settings. At the same time, more of the logic of research will continue to unfold. As this unfolding takes place, you will also find that some of the terminology will become "reinforced" as you read and reread these terms in the context of the research situation. So, on to some of the basic terminology used in the world of research.

VARIABLES AND CONSTANTS

A *variable* is anything that can be measured and, although it might seem to go without saying, that *varies*. A person's height, weight, shoe size, intelligence, and attitudes toward war may all be measured. In comparison with measures on other people, all have the potential to vary. Indeed, the fact that people differ on a whole host of personal measures gave rise in the late 1800s to the study of what Sir Francis Galton called "individual differences." No two people are exactly alike on all human measures (even identical twins reared together are not exactly personality clones), and thus, the study of individual differences became the theme song in both psychology and education.

The researcher must, however, be aware of a potential trap: just because people differ on certain characteristics doesn't mean that these differences will show through. In other words, potential variables are not always treated by the researcher as variables. This is, after all, the way it should be. Each single study should not be obliged to allow all possible measures to vary simultaneously. If too many things are allowed to vary, you don't know what may be causing the observed effect.

Therefore, some measures should be left as *constants*, or measures that are not allowed to vary. Here is an example. It is known to researchers in the area of growth and development that among elementary school boys there is a dependable relationship between height and strength; that is, taller boys tend to be stronger than shorter boys. Although this is a perfectly valid piece of research evidence that certainly allows the researcher to make better-than-chance strength predictions using height as the predictor, it can lead to some fuzzy interpretations if other variables are not controlled. For example, on the basis of the height-strength relationship alone, one might speculate that longer muscles produce more strength than shorter muscles.

The problem with this interpretation so far is that all other measures have been free to vary, and it may be that some of these other measures may be more directly related to strength than is height. One that comes quickly to mind is age. So far in this study, age is a variable, one that would certainly affect the outcome of this study. Certainly twelve-year-old boys tend to be both taller and stronger than six-year-old boys.

Let's see what would happen, then, if we were to hold age as a constant. Suppose that we were to select only boys of age ten years six months and then attempt to assess the height-strength relationship. When this is done (and it has been), the original relationship between height and strength drops dramatically. Speculation now might be concerned with the maturity of the muscle, not its length, as the important component in strength. The point of all this is that when, as in the foregoing example, only subjects of the same age are used, age, although certainly measurable, is *no longer a variable* because it has been held constant by the researcher.

In reading research articles, then, be especially careful in your review of how the subjects have been selected. If the selection process has been designed to ensure that the sample is identical on some measured trait, for that particular study the common trait is not a variable but a constant.

Similarly, there are constants in studies in which environmental conditions are under examination. For example, a researcher may suspect that warm-color room decors are more conducive to relaxation than are cool colors. To pursue that suspicion, the researcher selects two groups of high-school students, and one group is taken to a room with red-yellow decor and the other to a blue-green room. The subjects are then connected to some biofeedback equipment that is supposed to assess their levels of relaxation. Here again, certain potential environmental variables should be held constant if the researcher hopes to indeed get at the effects of room color. The groups should be tested at the same time of day and under the same conditions of illumination, temperature, noise level, and so on. That is, the researcher should make every effort to control as many potential environmental variables as possible; in short, these other variables should be converted into constants to minimize their possible influence on the outcome.

Of course, a study of this type should also be designed to control individual-difference variables as well. For example, one group should not be composed only of overweight, relaxed persons and the other, of underweight, tense persons. In this case, weight and temperament could be called confounding variables, since group differences could be explained by factors other than the variable of room color. More will be said about confounding variables later in this chapter under the heading Validity of Research: Internal Validity.

Thus we see the important interplay between variables and constants in a study. Certain factors (constants) must remain unchanged throughout the study in order to measure the potential impact of other factors that are purposefully designed to vary (variables).

INDEPENDENT AND DEPENDENT VARIABLES

Research variables can be divided into two major classes: *independent* and *dependent*. Every study must have at least one of each. Your ability to identify these variables is absolutely critical to your understanding of research methodology.

In any antecedent-consequent relationship, the independent variable is the antecedent variable, and the dependent variable is the consequent variable. That is, the independent variable precedes the dependent variable. In some studies, which, as we shall see later, are called experimental, the independent variable is truly antecedent in every sense of the word. In these studies the independent variable (IV) is assumed to be the causal half of the cause-and-effect relationship, whereas the dependent variable (DV) is the effect half. For example, in the study mentioned earlier on room color and relaxation, the room color (the presumed cause) would be the IV and the amount of resulting relaxation the DV.

In another type of study, which will be called post-facto, the IV is antecedent only to the extent that it has been chosen (sometimes arbitrarily) as the predictor variable, or the variable whose measures are used to make the prediction. The DV in this type of research is the consequent variable only to the extent that it is the variable being predicted. For example, a researcher might be interested in the relationship between school size and teacher job satisfaction. The IV would be school size, perhaps put in three categories: less than 200 students, 201 to 400 students, and more than 400 students. The DV is teacher's job satisfaction. The IV is not under the researcher's control, so the only conclusion in this case would be that school size can be used to *predict* teacher job satisfaction.

In general, then, the IV-DV relationship is similar to an input-output relationship, with the IV as the input and the DV as the output. Also, the DV is *always* some measure of the subject's behavior, and in this case, behavior is being defined in its broadest possible context. The DV might be a behavioral measure as obvious as the subject's performance on an IQ or attitude test, or as subtle as the subject's incidence of dental cavities, or even the measured amount of some hormone that has been secreted during a moment of stress.

Active (or Treatment) Independent Variables: Causal IVs

The distinction between two categories of IVs, manipulated and subject, is especially important to an understanding of research methodology. A decision regarding which type of IV is involved in turn helps determine which type of research is being conducted—and hence, the kinds of conclusions that are (or are not) permissible. A *manipulated IV* is one such that the researcher has actively changed the environmental conditions to which the sample groups are being subjected. That is, with a manipulated IV, the researcher determines which group of subjects is to be treated in which particular way. Perhaps one group of subjects is being tested under low-illumination conditions and the other group under high illumination. Illumination would thus be the IV, and notice that it does and must vary, in this case from low to high. (If all subjects had been tested under identical conditions of illumination, illumination could not be an independent or any other kind of variable; it would be a constant.) Or, if the researcher were attempting to show that computer-assisted instruction improves reading comprehension, the manipulated IV would be whether or not the students received the computer instruction (which was determined by the researcher), and a measure of reading comprehension would be the DV. Thus, whenever the experimenter is fully in charge of the environmental conditions (the stimulus situation in which the subjects work) and these conditions are *varied*, the IV is considered to have been manipulated.

Manipulated IVs are, thus, called *active variables*, since they are actively manipulated by the experimenter. Manipulated IVs are also called *treatment variables*, since they are always involved in subjecting the individuals under study to different treatment conditions. In the previous example, the groups of subjects were "treated" by being exposed to differing conditions of illumination. Remember, when subjects are actively treated differently by the experimenter, this type of IV has the potential for being a causal variable.

Subject (or Classification) Independent Variables: Predictive IVs

In contrast with manipulated IVs, if the subjects are assigned to different groups or are categorized in any way on the basis of measured trait differences that they *already possess*, the IV is considered to be a *subject IV*. Thus, we have a subject IV when the researcher sorts subjects on the basis of some existing measured characteristic and then attempts to discover whether these characteristics are related to some type of response by the subject, this response measure being the DV. For example, it might be hypothesized that women have higher IQs than do men. The subjects are selected and then categorized on the basis of gender, a subject IV. The two groups then both take IQ tests, and the IQ scores (the DV) are compared. Or a researcher might wish to establish whether college graduates earn more money than nongraduates. The researcher selects a large sample of thirty-five-year-old men, assigns them to categories on the basis of whether or not they graduated from college, and then obtains a measure of their incomes. Level of education would then be the subject IV, and income level the DV. Notice that in this example, neither age nor sex were allowed to vary and are thus constants. The important point is that the IV can only be used to *predict* DV values (therefore the term *predictive IV*). The IV should not be interpreted as a cause of the DV, since the IV was not manipulated by the researcher.

Subject IVs always represent some measured characteristic that the subject already possesses. Subject variables such as age, sex, race, socioeconomic status, height, and amount of education may only be subject IVs, since they are simply not open to active manipulation.

Some IVs, however, can go either way, depending on how the researcher operates. For example, it might be hypothesized that fluoridated toothpaste reduces dental cavities. The researcher might randomly select a large group of subjects and then provide half of them with fluoridated toothpaste, while providing the other half with identical-appearing, nonfluoridated toothpaste. Then perhaps a year later, the groups are compared regarding incidence of cavities. In this case the IV (whether or not the toothpaste contained fluoride) would have been actively manipulated. That is, the subjects would have been *differentially treated by the experimenter*, which of course defines the fluoride as a treatment variable. If, however, the researcher had simply asked the subjects what kind of toothpaste they usually used and categorized them according to whether the toothpaste did or did not contain fluoride, the IV would have been *assigned*. In this case, the fluoride would have been a subject variable, or a characteristic the subject already possessed. The DV, of course, would still be based on a comparison of the incidence of cavities between the two groups.

Subject IVs are often called *assigned IVs*, since subjects are generally assigned to groups on the basis of their already present traits. Thus, in the preceding example, the assignment to the fluoride or no-fluoride condition depends on the subject's personal habits. They are also called *classification IVs* because subjects are classified according to their group memberships.

With either type of IV, manipulated or subject, the researcher tends to focus on differences between the DV scores for each of the groups. For manipulated IVs the outcome (DV) measures of the subjects who have been treated with one level of the IV are compared with the DVs of those who have been given a different level of the IV. For classification or subject IVs the DV results for the subjects who have one characteristic are compared with the results for the subjects who have the other characteristic. For each type of IV the researcher examines differences between groups. Because of that similarity, novice researchers who have studied a classification or subject IV sometimes feel that it can be interpreted in the same way as a manipulated IV. But this isn't so. These researchers fall into what's called the *cause-and-effect trap*. The temptation is to decide that the IV somehow "caused" a change in the DV, when in fact the only legitimate conclusion is that the IV and DV are related. We'll say more about the cause-and-effect trap in the next chapter.

SAMPLING FROM POPULATIONS

The researcher always needs one or more groups of subjects for any research project. The methods used to obtain subjects and assign them to groups influence the kinds of conclusions that can be made when the research is completed. Groups of subjects are almost always drawn in some fashion from a larger group. The goal is to obtain groups of subjects who are representative of the larger group or, at the very least, groups that are equivalent to one another. If groups of subjects are truly equivalent at the beginning of the research study, differences between these groups at the end are likely to be due to the manipulation of the IV.

Populations

The term *population* (or universe) refers to the entire group of persons, things, or events that share at least one common trait. If you wished to identify the population of college students, the factor of being a college student would be the common trait, and you would then have to list each and every such student in the entire world—a modest little assignment. Or if you wished to add another trait, you might limit your population to U.S. college students, or by adding a third trait, to U.S. college students attending state universities. Obviously, the more traits you add, the more you limit the designated population, but as your population becomes increasingly limited so too does the group to which your findings can rightfully be extrapolated. Since we're typically interested in generalizing research results in order to apply them to a population larger than the sample group, it's important to know as much as possible about the population from which they were drawn.

Samples

A *sample* is a smaller number of observations taken from the total number making up a given population. Thus, the sample is a subset of the population. That is, if the entire population of first-year college students in the United States were to number one million, selecting any number of first-year college students from that population would constitute a sample; any number from 1 to 999,999 would, thus, be a sample in this example. The real problem, then, is how to select a sample that is representative of the population. Obviously, a large sample will more accurately reflect the characteristics of the entire population than a smaller one. The sample of size 1 has far less chance of accurate representation of a population than the sample size of 999,999. However, although the sample of size 1 may yield highly distorted predictions, the sample of size 999,999 is so unwieldly as to be very impractical. In fact, if you have a sample of this magnitude, you might as well find that last millionth person and, thus, have nothing left to predict. Therefore, two basic techniques are commonly used for achieving representative samples: random sampling and stratified sampling.

Random Sampling

The researcher needs to be able to use a procedure for selecting samples that are representative of the defined population. A *representative sample* is one that truly reflects all the various characteristics of the population. A good representative sample provides the researcher with a miniature mirror with which to view the entire population. There are several procedures used for insuring that samples are representative, but the most desirable by far is random sampling.

Random sampling demands that each member of the entire population must have an equal chance of being included, and that no members of the population may be systematically excluded. Thus, if you're trying to get a *random sample* of the population of students at your college, you can't simply select from those who are free enough in the afternoon to meet you at the social science laboratory at 3:00 P.M. This would exclude all those students who work in the afternoon, or who have their own labs to meet, or who are members of athletic teams. Nor can you create a random sample by selecting every ninth person entering the cafeteria at lunch time. Again, some students eat off campus, or have classes during the noon hour, or have cut classes that day to provide themselves with an instant minivacation—the reasons are endless. The point is that unless the entire population is available for selection, the sample cannot be random.

One way to obtain a random sample of your college's population would be to go to the registrar's office and get a list of the names of the entire student body. Then clip out each name individually, and place all the separate names in a receptacle from which you can, preferably blindfolded, select your sample. Then *you go out and find each person so selected*. This is extremely important, for a sample can never be random if the subjects are allowed to select themselves. For example, you might obtain the list of entering students, the population of incoming first-year students, and, correctly enough so far, select randomly from the population of names, say, fifty. You then place requests in each of their mail boxes to fill out an "attitude toward college" questionnaire, and finally, ten of those questionnaires are dutifully returned to you. Random sample? Absolutely not, since you allowed the subjects, in effect, to select themselves on the basis of which ones felt duty-bound enough to return those questionnaires. Those subjects who did comply may have systematically differed on a whole host of other traits from the subjects who simply ignored your request. This technique is really no more random than simply placing the questionnaire in the college newspaper and requesting that they be clipped, filled out, and returned to you. The students who exert the effort to cooperate with you, almost surely differ in important ways from those who do not.

Stratified Sampling

Another major technique for selecting a representative sample is known as stratified sampling. To obtain a *stratified sample*, the researcher must know beforehand what some of the major population characteristics are and then deliberately select a sample that shares these characteristics in the same proportions as in the population. For instance, if 35 percent of a student population are sophomores and, of those, 60 percent are majoring in business, a stratified sample of the population must reflect those same percentages.

Bias

Whenever the sample differs systematically from the population at large, we say that *bias* has occurred. Since researchers typically deal in averages, bias is technically defined as a constant difference, in one direction, between a measure of the sample and a measure of the population. For example, suppose that the mean verbal SAT score at your college is 460, yet you select samples for your particular study only from those students who, because of poor performance on an English placement test, have been assigned to remedial English courses. It is likely that the average verbal SAT scores among your samples are *consistently* lower than the average of the population as a whole. This biased selection would be especially devastating if your research involved anything in the way of reading comprehension or vocabulary measures. Your results would almost certainly underestimate the potential performance of the population at your college.

Equivalent Groups

Recall that this whole discussion of populations, samples, and random samples was provided in the context of the researcher's attempt to create *equivalent groups* of subjects. We now return to that discussion with these new definitions safely tucked in place. Since a random sample is designed to reflect accurately the characteristics of the population from which it was selected, selecting two random samples *from the same population* should give us confidence that these two samples are equivalent in all important respects. Since both samples share the same trait characteristics as the population (in an unbiased fashion), it seems safe to assume, at least on a probability basis, that they must also contain the same gradations of traits as each other (also in an unbiased fashion). Is this a 100 percent guarantee? No, since it is still possible, even with random sampling, that the groups might differ from each other purely because of chance factors that occur during the process of selecting the samples from the population. Nevertheless, on balance, we can expect that the random sampling process has probably ironed out any original differences that might have existed between the sample groups.

Random Assignments

Another technique, closely allied with the random sampling of groups from a population, is called *random assignment* of subjects. In this technique the sample is not originally selected randomly from a single population (since this is often a lot easier to talk about than to do) but is, instead, presented to you as a fact. For example, your professor says that you can use her nine o'clock section of Introduction to Education students or your fraternity volunteers as a group to participate in your study. This is not the ideal way to obtain a research sample, because your sample will not be representative of any defined population, but it is, alas, often the best that you're going to do. The solution is to divide the large group into two smaller samples, strictly by random assignment. This is random assignment, since although the original sample was not randomly selected, the random assignment process was still used to divide the whole group into two presumably equivalent groups. The theory here is that even though your original group may not truly represent the population, at least the two smaller randomly assigned groups do mirror each other and are therefore equivalent. You have created equivalent groups, but the problem with this procedure concerns the ability to generalize the results to a population—because you can't.

In passing, notice that in either the random sample or random assignment techniques, the sample groups are independent of each other. That is, the selection of one subject for one group in no way influences which subject is to be assigned to the other groups.

Sampling with Subject (or Classification) IVs

Whenever random sampling or random assignment is used as a technique for creating equivalent groups, each subject has an equal chance of ending up in any of the research groups. However, whenever a classification or subject IV is used, subjects are assigned to groups on the basis of one or more characteristics they already possess. If, for example, one is interested in the relationship between sex and attitudes toward school, the subjects *must* be assigned to groups on the basis of their gender. In fact, the researcher's hypothesis is that the groups *aren't* equivalent and that is the basis on which differences in attitude are expected. Nothing, however, prevents the researcher from randomly *selecting* the groups from a population. Thus, the group of males would be representative of the population of males and the same would be true for the sample of females, and the results could be generalized to the population from which the samples were drawn.

MEASUREMENT AND MEASUREMENT ERROR

From the beginning of this chapter we have frequently used the word *measure*. You probably have some idea what is meant by the term *measurement*, but in a formal sense the definition may contain elements with which you are not yet fully familiar. Educators, psychologists, and other scientists use the term to refer to the rules that have been used in assigning the numbers or values to persons, events, or things to represent differing amounts of whatever attributes are under study. Throughout your education, teachers have (perhaps all too often) used rules to assign numbers to the attribute of achievement. For example, your achievement might have been represented as a score of 85 out of a possible 100 points on an examination, yet using a slightly different scale, your performance on the same test might have been rated as a "B." The rule used by the researcher for assigning numbers determines the scale (or kind) of measurement being used. We will find (in Chapter 5) that the statistical procedures used to analyze the results of any study are determined by which measurement scale was used to generate the values.

Measurement Scales

The *nominal scale* is the simplest form of measurement. It involves assigning numbers to category labels according to the frequency with which members of the category can be observed. If you look around your classroom, for example, you can count the number of people who fall into the category of "male" and the number who fit into the category of "female." The measurement rule you used for assigning numbers is to count the number of items (people) that fit the defined categories ("male" and "female"). Notice that with classification IVs subjects are always assigned to groups defined nominally or by category. As another example, one might count the number of cars in a parking lot that are Fords, Chevrolets, Toyotas, and so on. The same group of cars might be recategorized and counted according to whether they were made in America, Japan, or Germany. In each case the categories should be independent; that is, each car can fit into only one category. Frequency-of-occurrence data tell us how many persons, events, or things fall into each group.

The second measurement method, the *ordinal scale,* indicates the rank order or the relative position of observations within a given group or category. For example, in the group of people with whom you graduated from high school, you might have ranked 91st in a class of 426 students. Your position tells you that your grade-point average was better than number 92, but not as high as number 90. The rank indicates greater than or less than, but not *how much* higher or lower. Distances or differences between ranks are thus left unknown. We don't know, for example, that the difference between ranks 1 and 2 has the same meaning as the difference between ranks 91 and 92. What we do know is the relative position each person has compared with everyone else in the group.

The *interval and ratio scales* indicate considerably more than relative position. The *amount* of difference between values in these scales is meaningful. Not only do we get information about greater than or less than but also how much greater than or how much less than. The Fahrenheit temperature scale is often given as a good example of an interval scale, since the temperatures on the scale are in equal intervals. The difference between 1 and 2 degrees on the Fahrenheit scale is equal to the difference between 91 and 92 degrees. The differences of 1 degree are equal in meaning regardless of whether you are at the "cold" end or the "hot" end of the scale.

Interval scales that contain an absolute zero point are called ratio scales. Lengths or weights are ratio scales because zero is the smallest possible amount of the attribute. Although the Fahrenheit scale does have a zero point, values less than zero are possible, as you would discover if you stepped outside your hotel in Oslo, Norway, in mid-January. Because they are based on an absolute zero point, ratio scales allow for ratio comparisons such as "6 feet is twice as long as 3 feet." Interval scales simply do not allow for such ratio statements. For example, it doesn't hold true for Fahrenheit temperatures that 60 degrees is twice as hot as 30 degrees. In general, the data obtained from many educational and psychological tests are treated as either interval or ratio data, and no distinction is usually made between interval and ratio scores for statistical purposes.

Measurement Error

Measurement error is introduced whenever a researcher uses any of the aforementioned methods to find out how much or how little of a characteristic research subjects may have. The measurement of attitudes, achievement, or even height and weight involves some error, no matter how small. Measurement error is a fact of life that researchers must both understand and learn to tolerate. This is not because researchers are especially error prone or sloppy but rather because even the most careful experimenters must use measures and procedures in which some degree of error is inherent. Even "exact" measures contain error; the incredibly accurate atomic clock had to have one second added to it in January of 1988 because of a *tiny* imperfection. To *minimize,* not eliminate, measurement error, it's important to select tests or instruments that measure with as much consistency as possible, and also those that have been shown to measure what they purport to measure.

Reliability and validity are two of the key aspects of measurement, and an understanding of these terms will allow you to appreciate how well your observations are representing reality. Research procedures that are based on reliable and valid measures are less prone to measurement error. Independent and dependent variables that are defined in reliable and valid ways should result in less error in the research findings. Conversely, research using unreliable and invalid measures will end up with conclusions so limited and equivocal as to be in extreme cases even useless.

Reliability of Measurement

Reliability of measurement refers to the consistency with which a test or instrument produces results. The basic question addressed by reliability is whether a test given at one time will give the same result if given at another time under the same conditions. Educational research often involves the use of standardized tests of achievement, aptitude, personality traits, and interests, as well as classroom tests, behavioral checklists, rating scales, and so on. It is a general rule of research that the reliability of any measure should be established and known to the researcher. All good standardized tests have reliability information in the test manual. When using these tests it's relatively easy to discover the reliability level of the instrument; just read the manual. However, if you have to use your own test or scale, you'll have to establish its reliability yourself.

There are several different methods used to evaluate or establish the reliability of any measuring instrument. *Test-retest reliability* is one method. Fortunately, it is pretty much what the name suggests. A test is given to a group, then at some later date and under similar circumstances it is readministered to the same group. If we can assume that the tested individuals have not changed very much over time, and if each person gets the same or similar scores on the two occasions, the test is considered to be reliable.

The indicator of the degree of reliability the test possesses is called the reliability coefficient, and is calculated on the basis of a correlation coefficient between the two sets of scores. The correlation coefficient is a number ranging from $+1$ to -1 that indicates the degree of association between two variables. A high and positive correlation indicates that there is a strong relationship between the test and the retest, and therefore that the test is reliable. The higher the correlation, the greater the reliability, and vice versa. The reliability coefficient may also be seen as an indicator of measurement error. High reliability implies low error, and the potential for error increases as the coefficient declines. The highest possible reliability coefficient of $+1$ indicates *no* error, since the results of the two tests are identical. A perfect correlation is virtually never achieved in practice, but many instruments have coefficients ranging from .85 to .95, and some even higher. In fact, we should not even expect a perfect correlation, since that might indicate that the test is so rigid as not to reflect any real-life changes that have occurred among the subjects.

If you think about it for a minute, you'll realize that test-retest reliability has at least one major problem. It's very possible that a subject's score on the retest may be influenced by having been exposed to the original test and therefore having remembered or practiced some of the items. To make it even worse, this practice effect is greater for some test takers than for others, resulting in a contaminated reliability coefficient. A second problem with test-retest reliability is that it samples the same domain on both testing occasions. Every test contains questions that are only a sample of the entire population of questions that could have been asked. An achievement test in U.S. history, for example, can't possibly contain every possible question that could be asked, only a group of questions that are presumably representative of the entire U.S. history domain. As with any sampling procedure, taking a sample of test items from a population of test items will result in a form of sampling error. Using test-retest reliability means that only one sample of questions will be asked. For these reasons, test-retest reliability must be used with great caution, and perhaps in many situations avoided altogether.

A second common approach to establishing reliability is the *alternate-form* method. In this procedure two parallel forms of the same test are constructed that are similar in format, content, question type, length, and so on, but which have different questions, still, of course, from the same domain. The results of the administration of these alternate forms to the same population are then correlated to establish reliability. Well-constructed tests with two or more forms often have reliability coefficients that are slightly lower than test-retest coefficients for similar tests, but these instruments may be especially useful in research designs that require the use of pretests and posttests. Since the parallel forms contain different questions, practice effects are minimized (though not entirely eliminated), and reliability coefficients may still exceed .90 for some tests.

Another method for establishing reliability is the *split-half* technique. With this method (usually considered to be a form of internal consistency reliability, to be discussed presently), a test is only administered once. The test is split into two halves, each of which is scored separately. The two sets of scores are then correlated. The two halves of the test are made up of different questions and therefore represent two different samples from the domain. To create the two halves, the test is sometimes split down the middle, with scores on the first half of the test correlated with the scores from the second half of the test. This generally is not the best procedure because the second-half score could improve as a result of practice, or it could suffer from test-taking fatigue or even the inability of some test takers to finish the test. A better procedure for assessing split-half reliability is to utilize the odd-even procedure. The score for the odd-numbered items is correlated with the score on the even-numbered items. This helps avoid the practice or fatigue effects, since a student reaching item number 96 will be just as practiced, or just as fatigued, as when reaching item 97.

In general, longer tests are more reliable than shorter ones, because larger samples of questions inherently produce greater score consistency. This creates a problem when using split-half reliability. When we give the test, we want to give the whole test, but the reliability coefficient has been calculated by using, in effect, two tests (the "odd test" versus the "even test"), each being only half as long as the original. Since shorter tests have lower reliability, the split-half result underestimates the true reliability of the whole test. However, a statistical method exists, the Spearman-Brown formula, that can be used to correct the split-half reliability coefficient. The result of the use of the formula is a reliability coefficient that is higher and therefore more appropriate to the length of the whole test, not just of half a test.

The final method for establishing the reliability of a test is *internal consistency*, or interitem consistency. Internal consistency is established by any one of several statistical methods, each of which results in a coefficient that indicates the extent to which the items on a test measure a common characteristic. These methods essentially compare a group's performance on each separate test item with that same group's performance on the whole test. The result is the same as if a researcher had divided the test into all possible combinations of split halves, then calculated a split-half reliability coefficient for each of these split halves, and then finally averaged out all the obtained coefficients. Tests composed of questions that are very similar to one another will, therefore, result in high internal consistency, since each test taker's response on individual items will closely resemble his or her total score.

Similarly, a homogeneous test—that is a test consisting of highly similar items—will result in split halves that will greatly resemble one another, and the averaged reliability coefficients will be very high. Consider, for example, a first-grade arithmetic test that consists of one hundred items, each of which is a simple one-digit addition problem (such as $4 + 6$). Students who know how to add will make few errors, and their results on single items will closely match their overall total scores. Conversely, students who are weak in addition will make many errors, which will closely match their total scores. In similar fashion, the split halves of such a test must always have similar scores, and the test will show a high degree of reliability.

Conversely, the most heterogeneous tests will have lower coefficients. The most common procedures used to calculate these coefficients are the Kuder-Richardson formulas (usually referred to as KR 20 and KR 21) or the coefficient alpha (for further discussion on these methods, see Anastasi, 1982). These reliability coefficients, however calculated, are interpreted in the same way as any correlation coefficient.

If you need to create your own test, checklist, or rating scale, there are some things you should keep in mind. Be sure to construct an instrument that is neither too easy nor too hard. If it is too easy, everyone will do well and a ceiling effect will develop. This will cause any differences between groups that you may be looking for to be obscured by the uniformly high performance of all your subjects. The same thing will happen in reverse if the test is too hard. Furthermore, if everyone gets uniformly high or uniformly low scores, the reliability of the test will be lowered because the variability among scores will be diminished.

Ideally the test should contain some difficult items and some easy items (for the population you're studying), and a number of items of moderate difficulty. This will maximize variability and enhance the reliability of the test. Once you have developed your own instrument, you should then calculate its reliability before using it in any form of research (by using one of the methods outlined previously).

Now that you have some idea of how to reduce error by selecting or creating instruments that are as reliable as possible, you next have to face the issue of validity. Combating the reliability problem in your research is only half the battle. What if your test is highly reliable but you don't know exactly what it is that the test measures? If you use the test as a dependent-variable measure and you find differences between your groups, without some knowledge of the validity of your measures you simply won't have any basis for understanding what those differences mean! The next step, then, is to examine the instrument in terms of what it actually measures.

Validity of Measurement

In addition to being reliable, good measuring instruments should be *valid*. That is, they should actually measure what they purport to measure. The test scores should represent with as little error as possible the real-world traits or characteristics they're supposed to represent. To the extent that tests are valid, errors in the representation of real-world characteristics are minimized. The main message here is that the use of instruments with high validity will allow more clearcut (less error-prone) conclusions about the effect an independent variable might have on a dependent measure, or about the possible relationship between two or more separate measures.

It is important to remember that instruments are valid only for a particular purpose. A test that has been validated for one purpose cannot be assumed to be necessarily valid for any other use unless it has also been proven to be valid for that purpose. For example, a language achievement test, validated as a measure of knowledge about language and language usage, cannot also be presumed to be useful as a diagnostic test of language strengths and weaknesses unless it has also been separately validated as a diagnostic test. A test may be useful for a number of purposes, but it must be independently validated for each new use to which it will be put.

Test validity is established through the use of one of three general approaches. Which validation method you choose depends on the purpose of the test and the uses that are planned for it.

The first validation procedure is *content validity*. In content validity, it is the actual test content and the procedures used to develop the test that are used in the validation procedure. This procedure, commonly used for achievement tests, involves several steps. First, the behavior domain to be tested should be analyzed for its content. If one is interested in fourth grade arithmetic knowledge, the arithmetic curricula through the fourth grade should be closely examined. In addition, arithmetic textbooks should be examined and arithmetic curriculum specialists consulted. From this information, a detailed subject-matter description can then be compiled. Second, based on these subject-matter descriptions, test specifications are drawn up and provided to writers of test items. The test specifications detail the information to be covered by the test, the instructional objectives to be tested, and the degree to which each topic covered by the test should be emphasized. For the arithmetic test, the specifications would indicate the proportion of questions for addition, subtraction, multiplication, and so on, as well as the difficulty levels for each item. Finally, the item writers construct the individual questions and compile the test in such a way as to fit the specifications as closely as possible. When constructed in this way, the test should contain a good sample of all the possible questions that could be asked about a given domain. Errors in measuring the domain should, therefore, be small.

In constructing your own tests, even classroom achievement tests, you should follow the same basic procedure. Analyze the material to be covered by the test, outline the test specifications, and write the items to fit those specifications. Be careful not to confuse content validity with *face validity*. A test with face validity looks on the surface as if it measures what it's supposed to measure. However, face validity isn't really validity at all in the technical sense, since there are no scientific procedures for establishing it; the test either appears to measure a particular domain or it doesn't. A test of musical aptitude may be high in face validity simply because it has a picture of a G clef on the cover, is packaged with a metronome, and asks the child to state which of two musical passages is more appealing. Although all this tinsel and fluff may make the test appear to be valid, there is no guarantee that it will pick out the child who may be a musical prodigy from the child who is tone deaf.

None of this is meant to imply that face validity isn't desirable, because it can be. Imagine, for example, taking a test that has questions that appear foolish, irrelevant, or childish. If you respond in ways influenced by your own perception of the test's face validity (which in this case appears to be poor), the test results probably won't be reliable or valid for any purpose.

The second type of validation procedure is known as *criterion-related validity*. The basic purpose of the criterion-related validity procedures is to compare test scores with actual performance on a *criterion*, an independent assessment of the behavior the test is supposed to be measuring. This independent assessment is some measurement of the characteristic under study that most people already accept as a good and valid indicator of the trait in question. There are actually two types of criterion-related validity, predictive validity and concurrent validity.

For *predictive validity* the purpose of the test scores is to predict a person's future performance. Aptitude tests are typically validated this way. The Scholastic Aptitude Test (SAT) scores that students receive in their junior or senior year of high school are used to predict the criterion of college success as indicated by college grade-point average. In this case the correlation between SAT scores and college grade-point average becomes the validity coefficient. Correlations that are high and positive indicate high validity, more accurate prediction of the criterion, and less error in the test as a measure of aptitude for college work.

Concurrent validity is the second type of criterion-related validity, and in this case the test scores are compared with some other assessment of the same behavior *currently* being measured. Diagnostic tests are usually concurrently validated, with the test score being correlated with an independent assessment of the present diagnostic category of the student (or client). Scores on a test designed to diagnose the reading strengths and weaknesses of a given group of students might, for example, be correlated with the criterion of a teacher's independent judgment of the observed strengths and weaknesses of those same students. As with predictive validity, the higher the concurrent validity coefficient, the less error in the test as an indicator of a particular characteristic.

The logic of predictive and concurrent validation is essentially the same— test scores are correlated with some behavioral criterion—thus the general label of criterion-related validity. The only difference is that in predictive validity a person's future behavior is predicted, whereas in concurrent validity it is the status of the person's present behavior that is of interest. In either case, test results could simply be correlated with the results of some other test that has already been validated for the same purpose. For example, scores on a new test designed to measure IQ might simply be correlated with scores obtained by the same group of subjects on the Stanford-Binet, a test for which a great deal of validation information is already available. This is a quick yet effective way of finding out what your test measures.

Criterion contamination is a potential problem with criterion-related validity. You'll note that a criterion was defined as an *independent* assessment of what a test is purported to measure. If the teacher in the preceding example had seen the test scores before evaluating the students' reading strengths and weaknesses, the evaluation would not be independent. This is because the teacher could have been influenced by the scores, and thus the criterion's independence is contaminated. The validity coefficient would, of course, be spuriously high if the teacher's evaluations had been influenced by the test scores.

Conversely, spuriously low validity coefficients can be the result of using test scores to select high-aptitude students before a predictive validity coefficient has been calculated for that test. For example, many colleges accept only students who have SAT scores above some cutoff point. The correlation between SAT scores and college grade-point average for this selected group will be lower than the correlation that would have been found had the SAT scores not been used as a basis for selection. The low variability in the group of selected SAT scores will result in a lower correlation coefficient, and the result is an underestimate of the test's real validity.

The final validation method is called *construct validity*. A *construct* (sometimes called a hypothetical or theoretical construct) is a broad and abstract concept that refers to an attribute, or cluster of attributes, that a person is assumed to possess. The theoretical construct may be thought of as having only a hypothetical existence, not an empirical or physical existence. The "existence" of the construct is hypothesized or inferred from observations of behavior. Examples of constructs that might be used in Education include anxiety, fear, honesty, intelligence, motivation, and a variety of other mental processes or personality traits. Each of these theoretical constructs is hypothesized to have certain characteristics. The construct of intelligence, for example, may refer to a collection of specific abilities, such as problem solving, adapting to changes in the environment, memory, language, and logic. A test designed to measure a construct (such as an intelligence test) must be assessed for its construct validity.

Although content validation is accomplished by properly constructing a test, and criterion-related validity may be established by a single correlational study, construct validity can usually be established only after a long series of studies. Each study has a hypothesis, based on the nature of the construct, that predicts group membership of high and low scorers. Imagine, for example, that you have constructed a test that you believe measures anxiety levels. Given what we understand the construct of anxiety to be, what kinds of differences might you expect between people who have high amounts of anxiety and people who have lower anxiety? Let's try out this hypothesis: in general, people who are receiving psychotherapy should have higher anxiety (therefore they have sought help) than people not in therapy. If the hypothesis is correct, your test scores should be higher for people receiving psychotherapy and lower for people not in therapy. When you test the hypothesis and it is confirmed, you have one piece of evidence that supports your contention that the test measures anxiety. This might not tell the whole story, however, since persons seeking therapy may also differ on other traits, such as intelligence for example. Thus, the construct validation of the test should consist of a lot of evidence gathered from the testing of a number of different hypotheses all focused on the same underlying trait.

RESEARCH ERROR

Each of the types of research you will be introduced to in the next two chapters is designed to create or make use of a set of circumstances in which observations can be made. In experimental research, the observations are presumed to be the result of an IV fully or at least partially manipulated by the experimenter. In post-facto research, the observations may be gathered from a group or groups defined on the basis of a subject IV, and relationships between variables examined. The conclusions drawn from research should represent the real world as closely as possible. That is, the application of the research results in a real-life setting should produce the same general outcome as the study. In short, research conclusions should be as free of error as possible.

Research error may occur in the form of inconsistent findings in different studies using the same IV and DV, a limited ability to come to conclusions about cause-and-effect relationships, or a limited ability to generalize results to other settings. These errors may be due to a lack of control, an inability to randomly assign subjects to groups, or the use of research designs that contain inherent limitations. Minimizing research error involves searching for circumstances in which control, random assignment, and a strong design are possible. Failing that, the weaknesses of the research must be recognized and the conclusions should be appropriately cautious. The concepts of reliability and validity can be applied to research error in much the same way that they were used to evaluate measurement error. Thus, it's just as important to examine the reliability and validity of our research findings as it is to establish the reliability and validity of our measure.

The Reliability of Research Findings

The most fundamental procedure for establishing the consistency of the results of research is similar to that of the test-retest procedure for establishing measurement reliability: the whole research project, from beginning to end, is replicated, or repeated using the same definitions for the independent and dependent variables, the same procedure, the same setting, and similar subject samples. Such a *replication* of the original research serves as a test of reliability by comparing the results of the two studies. Exact replications of prior research are not common. When they are done, however, it is usually because the research has a great deal of importance either from a theoretical or a practical standpoint. If a study "disproves" a theory, the adherents or opponents of the theory may replicate the study to "prove" their point. Similarly, a study that has important practical implications might be replicated by practitioners who might themselves be affected by the results.

Most often, replications do not exactly duplicate prior work. Instead, they use the same basic hypothesis, but with different samples, procedures, settings, and definitions for treatments and dependent measures. Replications of this type are sometimes called *systematic replications*. Over a long time period many studies might be done that relate to the same basic hypothesis, but each study has added some unique characteristics. Such systematic replications often influence not only the reliability but also the validity of the research results, since they call into question the ability to generalize the research to a variety of settings. We will return to this issue in Chapter 4 under the heading Internal and External Validity Reconsidered.

Validity of Research

The question of the validity of research results is similar to the question of the validity of measurement: does the observed effect of the independent variable on the dependent variable represent a real-world effect? This question actually contains two components. The first, which relates to *internal validity*, refers to the extent to which the change in the dependent variable in an experiment is clearly and unequivocally caused by the manipulation of the independent variable. The issue of internal validity refers specifically to the research situation itself, and the degree to which this experimental treatment caused a change in this dependent measure in this setting with these subjects. At least some degree of internal validity is an absolute requirement for experimental research, otherwise the results are useless and uninterpretable. The second part of the question refers to *external validity*, or the degree to which the results of the experiment can be generalized to other situations, especially other situations that are not constrained by laboratory artificiality. As every teacher knows, what works in the lab doesn't always work in the classroom. We will return to the problem of external validity in the next section.

Internal Validity

To the extent that internal validity is compromised, error or *confounding* creeps into the experimental situation, so that *rival hypotheses,* or explanations for an experimental result other than the one being hypothesized by the researcher, may exist. Confounding occurs when a variable other than the independent variable might have been the real cause of the change in the dependent variable, possibly even in an unknown way.

Assume, for example, that a researcher was interested in the effects of aspirin on headaches. Two groups of subjects were randomly selected. One group was given the pills, was asked to take the pills whenever a headache occurred and to record how long each headache lasted. The other group was not given any pills, was instructed not to take any medication, and was told to keep track of the length of time that each headache lasted. When all the data were in, the length of time that headaches lasted was much shorter for the group which had taken the pills. The researcher concluded that aspirin reduces the length of time that headaches persist.

Unfortunately, there is a possible confounding factor in this experiment as conducted by the researcher, and another rival hypothesis exists. It is possible that the two groups (which are supposed to differ on only one IV, aspirin) differ on a second variable not controlled by the experimenter. Each group may have different expectations about their headaches. The group that took the pills *expected* the headaches to be shorter, but the other group had no such expectation. The groups therefore differed on *two* factors, one of which (expectation) was not under the control of the experimenter and which could also explain the difference observed between the two groups.

It is now well established that expectations must be controlled in such a way as to be equalized between the groups being tested. This could be done by giving the second group a placebo (something that looks like the aspirin but has no physiological effect), which should produce expectations similar to those in the group actually receiving the drug.

In post-facto research there may be several explanations for any set of findings, whereas a strong experimental design that is well carried out and precisely controlled should result in the highest degree of internal validity obtainable and should therefore rule out virtually all other rival explanations. However, even a well-designed experiment if improperly carried out will result in other plausible explanations.

Unfortunately there are several threats to internal validity that may or may not be controllable in specific experimental circumstances. You should be aware of their possible existence and either try to control for them if possible or at the very least recognize that equivocal results and rival hypotheses may exist.

The first of the threats to internal validity is *history*. This refers to specific events that occur while carrying out the experiment that may influence the results. Imagine that you are doing an experiment in a college classroom, and while one of your groups is being tested a serious accident occurs on the street just outside. Error (a rival hypothesis) now potentially exists because you don't know whether any differences between that group and any other group are due to the independent variable or to the accident that occurred during the experiment.

Maturation is another threat to internal validity that occurs purely because of the time that passes while the experiment is in progress. The experimental subjects may change as the study progresses by getting more tired, older, bored, or by gaining knowledge—all of which may influence the outcome. The best way to eliminate confounding due to maturation is to have control groups composed of subjects of similar age, and so on, and who experience much the same sequence of events (except for treatment differences) during the experiment.

A third threat is *testing*, which refers to the effects of having taken a pretest on an individual's later performance on a posttest. Subjects may learn from their first exposure to a test and do better on a subsequent posttest for that reason alone. Whenever possible, it is preferable to use research designs that avoid the use of pretests. With randomly selected or randomly divided groups, pretests are usually not necessary, but studies that do not have random groups may require pretests and thus be subjected to the testing threat to internal validity. In addition, studies on the effect of "training" may require pretesting, again resulting in a possible internal validity threat.

Instrumentation as a threat to internal validity refers either to changes in the calibration or accuracy of measuring instruments during an experiment or to changes in the way that observers record behavior. Most mechanical or electronic instrumentation remains reliable and can be checked or calibrated before and after the experiment. Checking the "calibration" of raters, scorers, interviewers, or observers, however, is more difficult. Judges may become more proficient, tolerant, or stringent as the experiment progresses and rate subjects within groups differently at various times or rate different groups in different ways. It is quite possible that as a study progresses, researchers will find that they can improve their methods for collecting data. It is tempting to implement these "improvements," but in actuality, doing so will detract from the internal validity of the study.

To control for "instrumentation," scorers, raters, and interviewers should become fully practiced in the observational and rating methods they will use before the experiment begins, not as the experiment progresses. Several raters should be used whenever possible, and the degree of consistency among raters (interrater reliability) established. This is done by correlating the ratings of different observers of the same events. A high and positive interrater correlation indicates high consistency of ratings.

Another potential problem is that observers may consciously or unconsciously exhibit biases in favor of the experimental hypothesis. One way of combating such bias is to "blind" the observers, that is, make sure that they don't know the hypothesis being tested.

Just as observers or raters may be biased, experimenters or researchers may also have biases or expectations about research outcomes. Such bias or *expectancy* may occur if, consciously or not, the experimenters' behavior affects group performance in different ways. This is sometimes called the Rosenthal effect because of a study done by Rosenthal and Jacobson (1968) in which teacher's expectations about student performance resulted in student achievement that corresponded to those expectations. When teachers believed that certain students would go through a growth period during the year, the students' performances were considerably better than the performances of students when instructors did not have the higher expectations. Experimenter bias has even been demonstrated in psychological research on animals. The best way to neutralize experimenter biases is to use a blind procedure so that the person who actually interacts with the experimental subjects is unable to affect subject behavior.

Expectancy may also affect subjects and their responses. They form expectations and then behave during the experiment according to their perception of what the experiment is intended to demonstrate. This form of subject behavior is sometimes brought on by the *demand characteristics* of the study, because participating in an experiment can create self-imposed demands on the subjects, which they then try to carry out. Demand characteristics are hints or clues that tip the subject off to the true nature of the experiment. If subjects are genial persons or are in a particularly good mood, or are perhaps attracted to the researcher, they are likely to "go along" with what they perceive to be the researcher's expectations. On the other hand, if subjects are bored by the research, have better things to do with their time, or don't particularly like the looks of the researcher, they may be quite contrary and behave in ways designed to upset the researcher's expectations. This is an "I'm-not-going-to-be-a-guinea-pig-for-anyone!" attitude on the part of the subject. Blinding the subjects, called a *single-blind* procedure, is a way to combat demand characteristics. When the subjects and the experimenter are both unaware of the purpose of the experiment, the procedure is called *double blind*.

The *Hawthorne effect* is a threat to internal validity that may occur purely because subjects know that they are participating in an experiment. The effect is so named because of the results of a study done in the 1920s at the Western Electric Hawthorne Plant in Chicago (Rothlisberger & Dickson, 1939). The effects of several independent variables, including lighting, working hours, and rest periods, on the dependent variable of productivity were studied. All the changes in working conditions seemed to increase productivity (and morale), even when the change was back to a prior treatment condition! The conclusion was that because of the attention the subjects received during the research they became more motivated, tried harder, and produced more. This effect is similar to subject expectancy except that the Hawthorne effect may occur even when a single-blind procedure is used. The use of control groups is the simplest and best way to avoid the Hawthorne effect. Group differences should then reflect only the different treatments they have received, since the effect of participation in an experiment should be the same for all groups.

Another threat to internal validity is *experimental mortality*. This may occur when subjects leave the experiment while it is still in progress, especially if the number of subjects who leave is different for the various treatment groups. Such differential mortality among subjects may occur for natural reasons, such as parental refusal to allow student participation in an experiment. This raises the question of whether the children of parents who do not consent to participation are systematically different from the children of parents who do consent. Random division of subjects after participation has been agreed to should help to cure this problem. There may also be some natural mortality in longitudinal studies as the families of children move in or out of a school district. Is the more transient population somehow systematically different from the relatively stable one? Examination of mortality patterns among groups is wise, so that properly considered interpretation of results is possible, and rival hypotheses can be examined. Further, experimental subjects have a right to leave an experiment if they are uncomfortable with what's going on. If this happens, even when originally randomly divided, groups may ultimately differ systematically if different numbers of subjects leave different treatment groups.

When groups are chosen for participation in an experiment because of extreme scores on some variable, *statistical regression* can occur. Statistical regression refers to the tendency for extreme scores (either very high or very low scores) on a test to be closer to the average on a subsequent retest. For example, an experiment done with "poor" readers might be subject to statistical regression if subjects are chosen for the experiment on the basis of low scores on a reading test. If these same students were simply given the test a second time, their performance would tend to move upward toward the mean of the entire group, and the so-called improvement would, of course, be unrelated to any treatment or to harder work on the part of the students. Similarly, selecting "good" readers on the basis of high scores would result in a regression on a second reading test, but this time the regression would be downward toward the mean.

One of the reasons that extreme scores at either end of the distribution occur is because of chance factors. The absence of the same chance factors on the second testing naturally results in movement toward the center of the distribution, or regression toward the mean. If an experiment requires groups to be composed of extremes such as poor or good readers, several criteria for inclusion in the group might be used. These might include a test score, teacher evalua-tions of instructional level, achievement on exams, and report-card grades. Of course, random division of low scoring subjects (or high scoring subjects) to treatments will allow direct comparison of treatment effects, since any regres-sion should be the same for the randomly divided groups.

Selection becomes a threat to internal validity when there are differences between treatment groups that occur as a result of selection or assignment procedures that are not random. Groups may differ in achievement, aptitude, ability, age, grade level, experience, socioeconomic status, gender, or any other factor. The most obvious cure for selection as a threat to validity is to randomly assign subjects to groups. Any differences between groups should then be chance differences, rather than systematic ones. Whenever bias in selection occurs because of the use of intact groups, a necessity in some educational research, results should be carefully interpreted. Research designs that control for selection biases when randomization isn't possible will be discussed in Chap-ters 3 and 4. These usually involve designs in which subjects serve as their own controls, or designs which incorporate special statistical procedures.

The last threat to internal validity involves *interactions between factors*, most commonly interactions between selection and another factor such as maturation. The interactive effect of selection and maturation might be quite different for various groups, and this would definitely confound the results. Selection and maturation would each threaten the internal validity, and the combined selec-tion-maturation interaction would add even more error to the results of the experiment. Selection might interact with other factors, and several of the other factors might interact with each other. One possibility is an interaction of history with experimental mortality, which could occur if some specific event led to greater mortality in some experimental groups than in others. For example, one group of experimental subjects happens to overhear a loud argument between the experimenter and another subject. As a result of that unpleasant experience some of them refuse to participate. Since the subjects in the other group did not experience that specific event they all take part in the research without objection.

Such interactions among factors are often not obvious unless the re-searcher is careful to examine the research design and the events that occur during the research process. Each threat to internal validity should be consid-ered carefully and the possible influences examined when drawing conclusions about the results of the study. Interactive combinations of threats should also be considered as possible confounding factors, and rival explanations should then be provided for research outcomes. Because of its extreme importance, we will be returning to the problem of internal validity several times throughout the book. As different approaches to planning research are discussed, relevant threats to internal validity will be included.

External Validity

Once the degree of internal validity of research is established, the next question concerns the amount of error involved in applying the research to other times, places, and people. This is called the question of *external validity*, and just as there are several factors that affect internal validity, a number of possibilities exist as threats to the ability to generalize experimental results.

Selection bias is probably the most common external validity problem. If an experimental sample is not representative of a population, the results of the research can't be generalized to any population other than the sample used, and the results are therefore very limited in application. Random selection of subjects from a population (or some other sampling procedure such as stratified sampling designed to produce a representative sample) will result in the ability to generalize results to the population from which the sample was taken. Selection that is not representative or assignment to groups that is not random each produces a different threat to validity. Failure to randomly assign subjects results in a threat to internal validity, but nonrepresentative selection from a population threatens the ability to generalize. Selection bias is often called the *interaction of selection and the experimental variable* (Campbell & Stanley, 1963), since nonrepresentative samples might react to the treatment levels of the independent variable in ways that are different from random samples.

Educational research using subjects randomly selected from a population is actually done relatively rarely. Instead, studies might use subjects who are selected because they happen to be available or because they volunteered. Results from such research are, unfortunately, limited to the subjects who actually participated in the study and are thus purely descriptive of the sample. In other cases, subjects might be selected because they attend or work in schools that are considered in some way to be "typical." To the extent that they can be demonstrated to be typical, the results might be generalized to other schools, but external validity in these situations may be limited. When subjects are randomly selected, it's often from a limited population such as the fourth and fifth grades of a particular school district. The ability to generalize beyond the fourth and fifth grades of that district then becomes questionable.

A second external validity threat is the *reactive effects of experimental arrangements*. Experiments conducted in artificial environments, such as laboratories or research facilities, may suffer from this effect. The subjects may be responding more to the artificial experimental circumstances than to the independent variable. As a result, the treatments may only produce the effect (or may produce different effects) when they are applied in the experimental environment, whereas the application of the results in real-world settings may fail or produce unexpected results. The surest preventative for these reactive effects is to use a setting for the research that is as similar as possible to the environment to which the results will be applied. Studies done in natural settings are said to possess *ecological validity*.

The *reactive or interactive effects of testing* are a result of pretesting subjects. The interaction in this case is between the testing and the independent variable, since the pretested subjects are now sensitized to the treatment and respond accordingly. If, for example, you had been pretested on the first day or your educational research course, you would pay more attention to your instructor when the topics covered on the pretest were discussed in class. Your excellent performance on a posttest wouldn't be entirely a result of your instructor's brilliant teaching (treatment), but would also be because you had been sensitized to those topics—an interaction of testing and treatment. Note that this is not the same as the testing threat to internal validity, a purely practice effect that threatens the integrity of the experiment itself regardless of the IV being manipulated.

The final potential problem of external validity is sometimes called *time validity*. Educational research conducted in the 1970s or earlier might not still apply because of the ever-changing nature of student, teacher, and administration populations and of demands made on schools by society. Generalization of "old" research might have been warranted back when it was "new" research, but application in the schools of today might be totally inappropriate.

SUMMARY

Researchers have developed their own language out of necessity. In order to be precise, as well as concise, a vocabulary of research has been established that allows researchers and others to communicate effectively. Distinctions are made between variables (which may take on different values in a study) and constants (which are not permitted to vary) to more accurately assess the impact of one factor on another. The two major types of variables are independent variables (IVs) and dependent variables (DVs). Research is generally designed to identify the impact of the IV on the DV. Thus, the IV is thought of as preceding the DV. Further, IVs come in two varieties, active (or treatment) IVs, which are directly manipulated by the researcher to measure their effect on the DV, and subject (or classification) IVs, which are based on characteristics that the subjects already possess. With subject IVs, relationships between the IV and DV(s) may be established, but *causal* relationships cannot be definitively identified.

Most researchers must take a sample of subjects from a population to conduct their projects. Sampling should result in groups that are as representative of the population as possible. Otherwise, bias occurs, which may greatly hinder the researcher when attempting to generalize the results of the study. Generally, random sampling or stratified sampling is the procedure used to obtain representative samples.

The area of measurement is one in which an extensive vocabulary has developed. Empirical research involves measurement of some kind, ranging from relatively simple nominal and ordinal measures to interval and ratio measures containing more information. The reliability, or consistency, of measurement is important to establish, and there are a variety of techniques for doing so (test-retest, alternate form, split-half, and internal consistency). However, even if consistent, measures must also be valid; that is, they must measure what they are purported to measure, and several techniques are also available for determining this (content validity, criterion-related validity, and construct validity).

Just as measures must be reliable and valid, research should be examined for these same characteristics. The reliability of research findings is typically demonstrated by replication, or redoing the research in much the same way as originally conducted. Research validity, however, involves two areas of concern, internal and external validity. Internal validity answers the question of whether or not experimental conclusions are unequivocal. If the study has internal validity, the experimenter has a high degree of confidence when stating that the IV caused a change in a DV, and that no confounding occurred. External validity refers to the ability to generalize the results of the research to other subjects, settings, times, and IV and DV values.

KEY TERMS

Active variable

Alternate-form reliability

Assigned IV

Bias

Causal IV

Cause-and-effect trap

Classification IV

Concurrent validity

Confounding

Constant

Construct

Construct validity

Content validity

Criterion contamination

Criterion-related validity

Demand characteristics (internal validity threat)

Dependent variable (DV)

Double-blind procedure

Ecological validity

Equivalent groups

Expectancy (internal validity threat)

Experimental mortality (internal validity threat)

External validity

Face validity

Hawthorne effect

History (internal validity threat)

Independent variable (IV)

Instrumentation (internal validity threat)

Interaction of selection and the experimental variable (external validity threat)

Internal consistency reliability

Internal validity

Interval scale

Manipulated IV

Maturation (internal validity threat)

Measurement

Measurement error

Measurement scales

Nominal scale

Ordinal scale

Population

Predictive IV

Predictive validity

Random assignment

Random sample

Ratio scale

Reactive effect of testing (external validity threat)

Reactive effects of experimental arrangements (external validity threat)

Reliability of measurement

Replication

Representative sample

Research error
Research reliability
Rival hypothesis
Sample
Selection (internal validity threat)
Selection bias
Single-blind procedure
Split-half reliability
Statistical regression (internal validity threat)

Stratified sampling
Subject IV
Systematic replication
Test-Retest reliability
Testing (internal validity threat)
Time validity (external validity threat)
Treatment variable
Validity of measurement
Variable

REFERENCES

ANASTASI, A. (1982). *Psychological testing*. New York: Macmillan.

CAMPBELL, D. T., & STANLEY, J. C. (1963). *Experimental and quasi-experimental designs for research*. Skokie, Ill.: Rand McNally.

ROSENTHAL, R., & JACOBSON, L. (1968). *Pygmalion in the classroom*. New York: Holt, Rinehart & Winston.

ROTHLISBERGER, F. J., & DICKSON, W. J. (1939). *Management and the worker*. Cambridge, Mass.: Harvard University Press.

CHAPTER 3

Research Strategies

RESEARCH: TWO MAJOR TYPES

Pass-fail Grading: A Research Example
The Cause-and-Effect Trap
Independent and Dependent Variables
Comparing Scores on the DV
Research: Experimental versus
   Post-Facto

**THE EXPERIMENTAL METHOD:
THE CASE OF CAUSE AND EFFECT**

Creating Equivalent Groups: The True
   Experiment
Designing the True Experiment
Requirements for the True Experiment
Quasi-Experimental Designs

POST-FACTO RESEARCH

Researching via the Post-Facto Method
Post-Facto Research and the Question
   of Ethics

COMBINATION RESEARCH

Experimental and Post-Facto: A Final
   Comparison

SUMMARY

KEY TERMS

REFERENCES

RESEARCH: TWO MAJOR TYPES

The two major types of research strategies are called experimental and post-facto. Both are perfectly legitimate, when performed correctly, but they do lead to qualitatively different kinds of possible conclusions. Experimental research offers the opportunity for drawing direct cause-and-effect conclusions, whereas post-facto research typically does not. In fact, post-facto research does not fully address the issue of cause-and-effect; it can't prove causation, nor can it disprove it.

As we shall see later in the chapter, experimental methodology comes in two forms: the true experiment and the quasi experiment. Although the quasi experiment does not offer the same unambiguous analysis of possible causation that the true experiment provides, it does allow the researcher to make a stronger deductive argument regarding the possibility of causation than does the straight post-facto analysis.

Thus, the problem boils down to this: if the researchers have used experimental methodology, they are allowed to discuss the possibility of having isolated a direct causal factor, but if the research is post-facto, they may not. And as a person new to the field, you must keep in mind when reading research that it's not enough just to read the report's conclusions. You must examine the entire methodology to be sure that the author's conclusions are indeed justified. Unfortunately, you just can't take the author's word for it when it comes to the "conclusions" section of the report. You must bore in yourself and carefully read the "methods and procedures" sections with a critical eye. Above all, don't assume that something was done simply because it seems obvious to you that it should have been done. You'll soon learn that what ought to be isn't always what is.

Pass-Fail Grading: A Research Example

One long-running controversy in the field of education revolves around the issue of whether or not to adopt the pass-fail grading system. Proponents of pass-fail claim that students will actually learn more, that they will be more likely to explore different course areas, and that they will feel less anxiety when taking a course without the pressure of regular letter grades. The opponents, on the other hand, argue that students will be less motivated and therefore learn less if they are graded on the less precise pass-fail basis.

A large number of studies have been conducted at a wide variety of educational institutions, and the data are fairly consistent on the following point: when students who are taking a course for regular grades are compared with students who are taking the same course on a pass-fail basis, the graded students achieve higher grades (Stallings & Smock, 1971). The comparison is made possible by not telling the instructor which students are taking the course on the pass-fail basis and having him or her assign letter grades to all students. The registrar then converts these to pass-fail for those students who had previously elected this option. This provision is included to protect the pass-fail students from possible instructor bias.

The data clearly show that there is a difference in grades between the two groups of students in the same class, those electing to take the course for pass-fail and those taking the course for regular letter grades. The interpretations of this difference, however, vary widely. Some claim that this difference proves that pass-fail students simply don't work as hard or take the course as seriously as students taking the course for letter grades. Others claim that this difference proves that only the less competent students elect the pass-fail option. Others claim that this difference proves that students only take their most difficult (for them) courses under the pass-fail option and therefore are exploring areas they might otherwise attempt to avoid. Others claim that this difference proves that students use the pass-fail option only in courses where the teacher is so personally uninspiring as to need the threat of letter grades in order to goad the students into studying.

What, in fact, do the data really prove? Nothing, other than that a difference in grades does indeed exist between the two groups. All the previously mentioned explanations are really only hypotheses, that is, guesses about the possible reasons for this established difference. One or even several of these hypotheses might eventually be supported, but at present none of the studies really proves any of the hypotheses. Yet in the hands of a statistical charlatan, the data may seem to an unsophisticated audience to prove whatever he or she says they prove. So, again, when reading research studies, be alert. Think out the procedures carefully, and, above all, don't just read the conclusions.

The Cause-and-Effect Trap

The example just cited was provided to point out one of the most serious dangers lurking out there in the world of research: the cause-and-effect trap. Too often the unwary reader of research is seduced into assuming that a cause-and-effect relationship has been demonstrated when, in fact, the methodology simply doesn't support such a conclusion. For example, a study was conducted several years ago (which shall remain nameless, to protect both the innocent and the guilty) that purported to show that sleeping too long at night promoted heart attacks. Headlines throughout the country trumpeted this early-to-rise news, and America reset its collective alarm clocks. The message was stark: don't sleep too long or you'll die!

However, the study that led to all this sound and fury was done in the following way. A group of recent heart attack victims, all male, were questioned about, among other things, their recent sleeping habits. It was found that as a group they had been sleeping longer than had a comparison group of men of roughly the same age, weight, exercise patterns, and so on. That is, the independent variable, amount of sleep, was *assigned after the fact* as a subject variable. Because of this, the study does not prove a causal link between sleep time and heart attacks. In fact, it's just as likely that the reverse is true, that is, that the same physiological conditions that led to the heart attack might also have led to feelings of fatigue and, therefore, a desire to stay in bed longer in the morning. The point is that although both these explanations are possible, neither is proven by this study. When a cause-and-effect relationship is actually discovered, it must be unidirectional; that is, there must be a one-way relationship between the IV and the DV. When a light switch is flipped on, the bulb lights up, and this is unidirectional, since unscrewing the bulb doesn't move the light switch.

Independent and Dependent Variables

As was discussed in the previous chapter, there are generally two types of independent variables, active IVs and subject IVs. The active IV is under the full experimental control of the researcher and relies on the fact that the subjects in the study have in some way been *treated differently* by the experimenter. The subject IVs, on the other hand, are measures of various traits that the subjects already possess, and the researcher simply assigns the subjects to different categories on the basis of those measured traits. Dependent variables are the outcome variables, measures of the subjects' responses or traits. These are the measures that are then compared.

Comparing Scores on the DV

To assess whether or not the IV had any impact, it is necessary to compare the dependent variable scores between the groups. The analysis is thus focused on whether or not a *difference* can be detected between the DV measures found in the various groups. The two methods available for analyzing these differences are *between-groups comparisons* and *within-subjects comparisons*.

Between-Groups Comparisons

A between-groups comparison means exactly that: a comparison *between* separate and distinct groups. The DV scores of one (or more) experimental group(s) are compared with the DV measures obtained on the control group. The groups being compared must be completely *independent* of each other. That is, the selection of a subject to be a member of one group may in no way influence who is to be selected in a different group. Subjects are randomly selected or randomly assigned to membership in the experimental and control groups. Thus, there will be a separate DV score for each subject in the study, and in the statistical evaluation of the data the total number of scores being analyzed must equal the number of subjects in the study.

Within-Subjects Comparisons

A within-subjects comparison looks for differences, not between separate groups, but within each of the individual subjects. For example, a group of subjects may be randomly selected and each person then individually measured on some variable, say weight. Then all the people are placed in a steam room for thirty minutes and immediately weighed again. In this study, the IV (treatment) would be whether or not the steam was present (and it is a variable, since initially the subjects don't get the steam and then at a later time they do get the steam), and the DV (outcome measure) would be the weight. Notice that in this example, each subject's posttreatment weight is being compared with that same subject's pretreatment weight. In short, the focus of analysis is on the change taking place within the subjects. In this case, the number of scores no longer equals the number of subjects, since each subject is being measured twice. In some studies the subjects are measured many times (a repeated measure design), and the number of scores far exceeds the number of subjects.

Research: Experimental versus Post-Facto

Of all the possible research strategies, only the experimental method allows for isolating a direct causal factor, and in the true experiment this causal factor is even more unambiguously identified than in the quasi experiment. How do you tell the difference between experimental and post-facto? Closely examine the independent variable. If the IV has been actively manipulated, the research is experimental. If not, it's post-facto. In the experimental method, then, the researcher always actively manipulates the independent (causal) variable to see if doing so produces a resulting change in the dependent (effect) variable. In post-facto research, on the other hand, the researcher does not manipulate the independent variable. Rather, the independent variable is *assigned* after the fact. That is, the subjects are measured on some trait *they already possess* and then *assigned to categories on the basis of that trait*. These subject-variable differences (independent variable) are then compared with measures that the researcher takes on some other dimension (dependent variable).

Post-facto research precludes a direct cause-and-effect inference because by its very nature it cannot identify the direction of a given relationship. For example, suppose that a researcher discovers that among students there is a significant relationship between whether or not algebra is taken in the ninth grade and whether or not the student later attends college. Since taking algebra in the ninth grade was the student's own decision, or perhaps that of the parents, this IV was a subject variable and therefore had to have been assigned. The research strategy in this case, then, was post-facto. Perhaps parents or guidance counselors who view a student as college bound encourage that student to elect algebra but discourage the student whose professed goal is to become a garage mechanic from taking it. Or perhaps a highly intelligent student, knowing that he or she eventually wishes to attend college, is self-motivated enough to elect ninth-grade algebra. Since the direction of the relationship is so ambiguous in post-facto studies, isolating a causal factor becomes virtually impossible. Although post-facto research does not allow cause-and-effect inferences, it does provide the basis for better-than-chance predictions. (Correlational research is one form of post-facto research).

In both education and psychology, *experimental research* is sometimes called S/R research, since a stimulus (S, independent variable) is manipulated and a corresponding change in a response (R, dependent variable) is sought. Similarly, post-facto research is sometimes called R/R research, since the responses (R) of a group of subjects are measured on one variable and then compared with their measured responses (R) on another variable.

THE EXPERIMENTAL METHOD: THE CASE OF CAUSE AND EFFECT

In the experimental method the relationship between the independent and dependent variables is unidirectional, since a change in the independent variable is assumed to produce a change in the dependent variable. The key to establishing whether research is experimental lies in discovering whether or not the IV is a treatment variable and has been actively manipulated. If it has, the method is indeed experimental; if not, the method is post-facto.

In its simplest form, the experimental method requires at least two groups: an experimental group that is exposed to one level of the independent variable and a control or comparison group that is exposed to a different, or zero, level of the independent variable. The two groups, experimental and control, must be as much alike as it is humanly possible to make them. The two groups are then compared with regard to the outcome, or dependent variable, and if a significant difference exists between the two groups, the independent variable can be said to have caused the difference. This is because all the other potential variables existing among the subjects in the two groups are presumed to have been held constant, or to have been controlled.

For example, suppose that you have been perusing the physiological literature and notice that a certain drug, magnesium pemoline, causes an increase in the production of one type of RNA in the cerebral cortex. Other studies then come to mind that seem to suggest that cortical RNA may be linked to human memory (through its role in protein synthesis). From reading all these studies and meditating on possible relationships, you begin to induce the hypothesis that perhaps the drug, magnesium pemoline, might lead to an increase in human memory.

You decide to test the hypothesis by designing an experiment. First, you select a large group of students, and then by random assignment you deliberately attempt to create two groups that are as much alike as possible. Through this process of random assignment, you hope to control all those variables that might possibly relate to memory, such as IQ, age, and grade-point average. One of the groups, the experimental group, is then given the drug, whereas the other (control) group is not. It would also be important that both groups be situated in identical environmental conditions—the same type of room, the same illumination, temperature, and so on. That is, the two groups should be identical in every respect except that one receives the drug and the other does not. Ideally, the subjects should not be aware of which groups they are in, for it is possible that if subjects knew they were in the experimental group, that in itself might affect them, perhaps make them more motivated. For this reason, when the members of the experimental group are given a capsule containing the drug, the subjects in the control group are given a nonactive capsule, called a placebo. Actually, the person conducting the experiment shouldn't even know which group is which. This prevents any possible experimenter bias, such as unconsciously encouraging one group more than the other. As mentioned in Chapter 2, when neither subjects nor experimenter are aware of which group is which, the experiment is said to be double-blind. (Obviously someone has to know which group received the drug. Otherwise the results would be impossible to analyze). Finally, both groups would then be given a memory test of some sort, and if the scores of the subjects in the experimental group average out significantly higher than those in the control group, a cause-and-effect relationship may legitimately be claimed.

In this example, whether or not the subjects received the drug would be the independent variable. This would be a *manipulated* independent variable, since it was the experimenter who determined which subjects were to receive how much of the drug. The subjects were not already taking the drug, nor were they given the opportunity to volunteer to take the drug. They were, in effect, being *treated* differently by the experimenter. The dependent variable in this study would be the subjects' measured memory scores.

In experimental research, the independent variable

1. is actively manipulated by the experimenter
2. is the potential causal half of the cause-and-effect relationship
3. in the fields of education, sociology, and psychology, is always a stimulus, that is, some environmental change (treatment) that impinges on the subjects.

The dependent variable in experimental research

1. is always the potential effect half of the cause-and-effect relationship
2. in most social sciences is a measure of the subject's response

Creating Equivalent Groups: The True Experiment

In experimental research it is up to the researcher to keep the subjects in the experimental and control groups as nearly alike as possible. The reason is that if the groups of subjects were systematically different to begin with, significant differences with respect to the dependent variable would be difficult to interpret. One might not be able to tell if these differences with respect to the dependent variable resulted from the manipulation of the independent variable, or were merely due to the fact that the groups differed at the outset on some important dimension.

If one wished to study the effects of word training on reading speed, it obviously would be the height of folly to place all high-IQ subjects in one group and all low-IQ subjects in the other. As was mentioned in Chapter 2, an experiment that is tightly controlled, that has no systematic differences between the groups of subjects to begin with, is said to have internal validity. An experiment that is internally valid allows the researcher to examine the pure effects of the independent variable, uncontaminated by any extraneous variables.

We also attempt, as we saw in the previous chapter, to design an experiment that is externally valid. External validity asks the question: Can the results of this study be applied to organisms other than those participating in the study? One should not do a study on albino rats learning their way through a maze and then quickly extrapolate these findings to cover the population of U.S. college sophomores struggling through a first course in statistics. Such an extrapolation would violate the study's external validity.

Independent Selection

In the last chapter we learned that one way to attempt to create equivalent groups of subjects is to randomly select the subjects for the various sample groups from the same population. Groups formed in this way are said to be independent of each other, since the selection of a subject for one group in no way influences which subject is to be assigned to other groups. The random-sample procedure gives us a high degree of confidence that the samples will be generally equivalent to each other (helping to promote internal validity), and that the results of the study may be generalized to the population from which the groups were selected (helping to promote external validity). Similarly, we saw that a single, large group may be divided into smaller groups by this random-selection process, in this case, called random assignment. This technique also produces independent groupings of subjects, since again the placement of a subject in one group does not determine who is to be placed in other groups. Although the random-assignment technique aids us in preventing some of the threats to internal validity, it does pose a problem for external validity. The question becomes: To which population can these results be generalized?

Dependent (or Correlated) Selection

Another method of obtaining equivalent groups is simply to select one group and then use that group under the different treatment conditions. The theory here is that no one on the planet is more like you than you yourself; consequently, you are used in both the experimental and control conditions. This method, although seemingly both simple and pure, actually opens up a veritable Pandora's box of pitfalls and, as we shall see later, should be used sparingly, if at all. When groups are formed in this way, the subjects are obviously not independent of each other, since the same persons are used in each condition and the analysis focuses on the within-subjects differences.

Finally, the last major method of creating equivalent groups, again based on dependent selection, is to select one group (ideally by random selection) and then create a second group by matching the subjects, person-for-person, on some characteristics that might relate to the dependent variable. For example, if one were to test the hypothesis that the phonics reading system produces higher reading comprehension scores than does the look-say technique, you would first attempt to list other variables that might influence the dependent variable, or in this case, reading comprehension. Such variables as age, IQ, grade, previous reading habits, and gender are strong possibilities. If one of your subjects is six years six months of age, has a WISC-R verbal IQ of 120, is in the first grade and reads an average of two books a month, you would attempt to find another child who closely resembles this subject on these specific variables. The members of a given matched pair, of course, should always be assigned to separate groups. Notice that these groups will not be independent of each other, since the selection of one subject for one group totally determines who will be selected for the other group.

Designing the True Experiment

There are three major designs of *true experiment,* and each has as its primary goal the creation of equivalent groups of subjects. This does not mean that all the subjects in both groups will be absolute clones of each other. There will be individual differences *within* the groups, some subjects being taller or smarter, or whatever, than other subjects within the same group. It does mean, however, that on balance the two groups average out about equal on any characteristics that might influence the dependent variable.

The After-Only (Between-Groups) Experimental Design

In this design the subjects are either randomly selected from a single population or else are placed in the separate sample groups by random assignment, or both. In any case, the presumption is that chance will assure the equivalence of the groups. Further, the subjects in this design are measured on the dependent variable only *after* the independent variable has been manipulated. This is deliberately done to avoid the possibility of having the DV measures possibly affect each other.

For example, suppose that we wish to find out whether the showing of a certain motion picture might influence a child's racial attitudes. In the *after-only design,* we test the racial attitudes of the subjects only after the IV has been manipulated, in this case, after one group has seen the movie and the other group has not. The reasoning behind this procedure is that if racial attitudes had been tested before the showing of the movie, the pretest itself might have influenced the way the children perceived the film, perhaps heightening their awareness of the racial content or sensitizing them to the racial theme of the movie. As was mentioned in Chapter 2, when subjects are sensitized by the pretesting procedure, the problem of external validity becomes an important issue, since few experimenters would be willing to generalize their results only to pretested populations. Also, since the groups in the after-only design are set up on the basis of random selection or random assignment, the groups are known to be independent of each other.

Finally, although we have been dealing with the after-only design as thought it were always a two-group design, one experimental and one control group, this design can be utilized just as readily on multigroup designs. The number of groups involved is a direct function of the number of levels of the independent variable being manipulated in any given study. If the IV is manipulated at only two levels, one group receiving zero magnitude of the IV (control group) and the other some specified magnitude of the IV (experimental group), a two-group design is adequate. But as you will soon see when reviewing the research literature, many experiments are produced in which the IV is manipulated at three, four or, even five levels.

For example, a researcher may wish to know not just whether or not seeing a film about racial prejudice will reduce antiminority attitudes among children but whether increasing the number of racially intense scenes within the movie has even more impact on viewer prejudice. For each different version of the movie, then, another experimental group must be added. To be truly an after-only design, however, none of the groups, experimental or control, should be tested on the prejudice scale before seeing the movie.

The Before-After (Within-Subjects) Experimental Design: Repeated Measures on the Same Subjects

The *before-after design* was originally borrowed from the physical sciences, where it had a long and noble history. Physicists, for example, would measure something like the temperature of a piece of metal, then apply an electric current to the metal, and finally measure the metal's temperature a second time. If a significant difference occurred between the pre and post temperature readings, and all other variables had been held constant, the conclusion could be quickly drawn that the electric current caused an increase in the metal's temperature. Why not use the same approach in the social sciences? After all, what could be more basic?

On the surface, this design seems to be the most obvious from a common-sense point of view, and yet as we shall soon see, it is also the one most fraught with the potential for dangerous ambiguities. Let's see how it works in the social sciences. Equivalent groups of subjects are formed by the simple expedient of using the same people twice. Could anything be more straightforward? It may be straightforward, but it can sure make the data interpretation a risky venture. Although examples of this design can unfortunately still be found in the educational literature, it should now be more kindly thought of as a historical curio. Why should we spend time discussing this anachronistic design? Because no other design offers the student the advantage of discovering so many research errors in one setting. It's a question of learning by bad example.

Advertisers constantly bombard us with examples of this basic design. You've seen the pictures in a before-after ad for a new diet, the woman looking fat, puffy, stupid, and sad in the "before" picture and then, miraculously, looking slim, proud, and exhilarated in the "after" pose. Now look again at the pictures and count the number of variables that have changed other than body shape. The poses are entirely different, first slouched, then erect. The facial expressions vary, from pathetically depressed to joyously self-confident. The clothes differ, the lighting differs, the backgrounds differ, and on and on. In this example, trying to isolate the pure effects of the independent variable is like trying to find a needle in the proverbial haystack.

Let's look at how this design is presumed to work. In this design a single group of subjects is selected, usually randomly, and then measured on the dependent variable. At this stage the subjects are considered to be members of the control group. In this design the subjects are obviously *not independent of each other*, since both "groups" are composed of the same people. Then the independent variable is manipulated, and these same subjects are again measured on the

DV. At this point the subjects are considered to be members of the experimental group. If the DV scores in the "after" condition differ significantly from those in the "before" condition, the independent variable is assumed to have caused this difference. And this assumption, let us quickly add, is based on the allegation that nothing else (other than the IV) has changed in the lives of these people. It is this premise that often contains this design's fatal flaw.

Let's take an example. A researcher is interested in testing the hypothesis that teaching the "new" math increases math ability among sixth grade elementary-school children. A random sample of sixth graders is selected from the population of a large, metropolitan school district, and the chosen children are all given a standardized math ability test (measured on the DV). Then the IV is inserted, in the form of a twelve-week "new math" program, replete with Venn diagrams and set theory. Then the math ability test is given again (DV), and the two sets of scores are compared. Let's assume that the second math measure was significantly higher than the first, which would seem to substantiate the efficacy of the teaching program. But was that the only variable in the children's life that changed during that twelve-week time span? Of course not! First, the children had twelve weeks in which to grow, mature, and practice their math skills, perhaps using the new math during school time and the old math after school (when making subtractions from their allowance to see whether they could afford to buy a new toy, or adding the total minutes of their piano-practice time to prove to their mother that they could go outside to play). Also, the mere fact of having been selected for this new program may have caused the children to feel somehow special, therefore increasing their motivation.

As has been pointed out several times, another concern with the before-after design is the pretest problem, that is, that the very act of measuring the subjects on the DV the first time might influence how they respond to the DV the second time. For example, the subjects might become sensitized to the test, which would make the entire study overly artificial. In our example of the math ability test, the act of taking the standardized math test the first time might have made some of the children more aware of what they didn't know or had forgotten and might therefore have prodded them into reviewing the rules on adding fractions, for example. When subjects become sensitized to the first test, they become more responsive to the second test, even without the manipulation of the independent variable.

Sometimes, on the other hand, subjects become fatigued by the first test. To take an obvious example, assume that a researcher wishes to study the effects of drinking coffee on the behavior of hyperkinetic children. A sample of hyperkinetic children is selected and told to report to a local football field. They are then told to run eight laps and their running times are clocked. They are then given a cup of coffee to drink and told to run another eight laps. Their running times are again clocked and found to be significantly lower. Here we have the classic before-after design, running times being measured both before and after the introduction of the independent variable (coffee). However, the "before" measure so tired the children that the coffee probably had little to do with the lowered speed recorded in the "after" measure. This is the kind of study the results of which could have been written before the data were even collected.

Another hazard when using the before-after design results from the passage of time. Since some amount of time must elapse between the pre and post measures, the mere passage of time might change the subjects in some important way.

Returning again to the example of the math ability test, literally dozens of other variables may have affected the lives of the children, and their higher math scores may really have resulted from these uncontrolled variables and not from the independent variable. Suffice it to say here that whenever you come across a research study using a one-group, before-after design, be alert to the possibility of uncontrolled variables intruding on the results. When the subjects are measured on more than just two occasions, the design is typically called a repeated-measures or within-subjects design. Repeating the DV measures several times does to some extent alleviate a few of the problems inherent in the two-measure, pre-post design, and more will be said on this issue later in this chapter in the section on the time series approach.

The Hawthorne effect. Perhaps the best and certainly most well known example of the confounding effects that may occur in the one-group, before-after design can be found in the previously mentioned research study conducted many years ago at the Hawthorne Plant of the Western Electric Company (Roethlisberger & Dickson, 1939). It is such a key issue in spotting one of the inherent problems with the one-group, pre-post design that a quick review will be instructive. You may recall that the object of the study was simply to determine if increased illumination would increase worker productivity. The researchers went into one of the assembly rooms and measured the rate of worker productivity, increased the level of illumination, and then measured productivity rates a second time. Just as had been suspected, under conditions of increased illumination productivity did indeed go up. However, when the researchers later added a control group, that is, a room containing another group of workers whose illumination they only pretended to increase, they found to their dismay that productivity in this room also went up.

What they really had discovered was that subjects will often improve their behavior merely because someone of seeming importance is paying attention to them. If there is no separate control group, the researcher can never know whether the subjects' response has improved because of the manipulated IV or because the subjects were flattered by the researcher's attention. When the increase is due to the heightened motivation of subjects generated by experimental conditions of attention and flattery, the change in behavior is said to be the result of the Hawthorne effect.

Ambiguous results due to the Hawthorne effect are most common in studies in which the researcher has used the before-after experimental design without an adequate control group. One researcher in the field of learning disabilities has complained that "any idea or finding which is unacceptable to anyone today can be explained away on the basis of the Hawthorne Effect" (Kephart, 1971). In point of fact, the only time results can be explained away on the basis of the Hawthorne effect is when the researcher carelessly fails to use an adequate control group. The Hawthorne effect should be viewed as an important warning to the researcher, since it encourages extreme caution when assigning specific causes to observed changes in behavior, especially in training studies using the before-after design.

Before-after designs with separate control groups.   To correct for the obvious pitfalls inherent in the one-group, before-after design, researchers now use an especially powerful variation of this design in which completely separate control groups are used. In fact, the use of a separate control group greatly minimizes the dangers inherent in the traditional before-after design. For example, many of the problems we encountered with the new math research could have been alleviated or even eliminated had a separate control group been added. That is, instead of using a single group of sixth graders, the researcher could have (and should have) selected one large group and then created two equivalent groups through random assignment. Both groups would then be measured on the math ability test, and then both groups would also enjoy the heady pride of being placed in an apparently special math program. At this point, the experimental group gets the twelve-week new math course, and the other group, the control group, goes to a twelve-week math course that is taught in the traditional manner. This should help in controlling the previously described uncontrolled variables: maturation, practice, sensitization, fatigue, and motivation. Even here, however, there could still be a problem regarding the qualities of the teachers. If possible, to control for this variation the same teacher should be used for both groups, a teacher, incidentally, who must consistently exhibit the same degree of enthusiasm for both instructional techniques.

In a study such as this the analysis is based on discovering how much each subject changed from the pre to the post measures. If the members of the experimental group change significantly more than do the members of the control group, the independent variable is assumed to have caused this difference. One of the simplest and most effective ways to analyze the data from this design is to focus on the "change" scores, or the differences between the pre and post measures, since in many of these studies the control group can also be expected to show an increase. The question, then, can be: Which group changed *the most*? Although some researchers have challenged the use of change scores because of the possibility of lowered levels of reliability, statistical techniques have been devised (using ANCOVA, a method described in Chapter 5) to counter this possible threat (see Kerlinger, 1986, p. 311). One must keep in mind, however, that if one of the groups scores at the very high end of the scale during the pre condition, there may not be room for much more of an upward change for this particular group (see the section on the ceiling effect in Chapter 9).

When setting up the separate control group for this design, the researcher has two choices:

1. *Random assignment.* The control group may be independent of the experimental group, as when two separate random samples are selected from the targeted population, or when a nonrandom sample is divided into two groups by random assignment. The DV comparison in this situation is *between* the groups.

2. *Matched subjects.* The separate control group may depend on the experimental group, as when the subjects in the two groups are matched on the basis of some variable(s) deemed relevant to the dependent variable. In this case each of the subjects in the experimental group is equated person-for-person with another subject in the control group. The DV comparison in this design is *within* subjects, since ideally the matched subjects should be so closely correlated as to be virtually a single person. In fact Kerlinger suggests that the before-after design is really an extreme case of the matched-subjects design (Kerlinger, 1986). The matched-subjects technique is best used when the matching procedure takes place before the experiment begins and the yoked subjects are then randomly assigned to the experimental and control groups.

The Matched-Subjects Experimental Design as an After-Only Technique

The matched-subjects, after-only design makes use of the aforementioned matched-subjects technique for creating equivalent groups. The subjects in the control and experimental conditions are equated person-for-person on whatever variables the researcher assumes might possibly be related to the dependent variable. That is, each member of the experimental group has his or her counterpart in the control group. In other respects, however, this design is similar to the after-only technique in that the DV is only measured after the introduction of the IV. (Again, this is done to prevent the first DV measure from in any way influencing performance on the second DV measure.)

As an example of a matched-subjects design, a researcher may wish to assess the effects of a behavior-modification program on the responses of a group of disruptive school children. A random sample of children is selected from the population of names provided by the school department of children identified as having been disruptive in class. For each subject so selected, a matched subject is sought, also from the same population of names, who resembles the originally selected subject in a number of important respects, such as age, sex, severity of problem, and previous treatment history. Then, perhaps by a flip of the coin, the matched pairs of subjects are divided into two groups. One group is chosen to receive a six-week behavior modification program, whereas the other group is left to function on its own. At the end of the six-week period, a panel of experts visits the various schools and judges all the subjects *in both groups* with respect to the extent of disruptive behavior. If the experimental group displays significantly fewer disruptive responses than the control group, it may be concluded that the behavior modification program was indeed effective.

Any experiment using the matched-subjects technique is not easy to conduct. The matching process, especially when a large number of relevant variables is used, can become extremely difficult. It may even become virtually impossible to find a suitable matched pair who resemble each other closely on all the important variables. As a general rule, the more variables used in the matching process, the more difficult becomes the task of selecting the subjects' control counterpart. Another problem inherent in this design is caused by the fact that it is not always easy to know what the relevant matching variables should be.

Repeated Measures

A note of caution. The repeated-measures design should be used with great care, and ideally should be restricted to those situations in which the researcher is investigating the effects of several treatment conditions on behavior under subsequent conditions. The subjects are measured and then presented with tasks A, B, and C and measured again, usually after each task has been completed.

Sequencing effects. When subjects in repeated-measure designs are given several treatments or tasks to perform, it becomes obligatory to ferret out the various effects that may be produced by the sequencing of the tasks or treatments. This becomes particularly important when those twin villains, practice and fatigue, are involved. The problem here is that when subjects are given several tasks to perform, that is, are involved in several treatment conditions, *sequencing effects* can occur. The subjects may be just as affected by the sequence of experimental conditions as they are by the presumed independent variable. Sequencing effects are generally of two types: *order effects* and *carryover effects*.

Order effects occur when the subjects are influenced by the order in which the tasks or treatments are presented. The actual ordinal position (first, second, third, etc.) occupied by the treatment may be influencing the subject's response, *above and beyond any possible effects of the treatment itself*. For example, a researcher may wish to test whether retention of verbal material might be influenced by the amount of material to be learned. Subjects are presented with a fifty-word list, one word at a time, and then asked to write down as many words as can be remembered. The subjects are then given a separate ten-word list and again asked to write down the recalled words.

As would obviously be expected, subjects recall a greater percentage of words from the ten-word list, thus justifying the assumption that as the length of the list decreased, verbal retention increased. However, by the time the subjects receive the ten-word list, they have experienced a great deal of memorization practice from just having been through the fifty-word list. Thus, changes in performance may be due to order effects alone. That is, as in the previous study, it would not have mattered whether the subjects began with the fifty-word list or the ten-word list. They would have shown increments in performance on the second list *just because it was the second list*.

Sequencing effects may also occur as a result of the carryover effect. This happens when a subject's performance on a second task, task B, is at least partly a result of that subject's performance on the first task, task A. In other words, the task or treatment that precedes a given treatment may be leaving a residue that affects later performance. Because of this carryover influence, it becomes impossible to assess the pure effects of the independent variable. Carryover effects differ from order effects in that with the former the direction of the subject's performance difference is indeed influenced by the task order. That is, the carryover effect might produce an increase in performance when the sequence is task A followed by task B, but a decrease in performance when the sequence is reversed.

For example, suppose that subjects were offered a one-dollar reward for successfully completing task A, and a one-hundred-dollar reward for task B. If the tasks are similar in difficulty, and if the subjects are not totally fatigued from completing task A, we would expect an increase in performance on the second task. However, if the one-dollar prize came second in the sequence, the subjects' performance might decrease as a result of the dollar being seen as far less rewarding than it would have been had the previous prize of one-hundred dollars not been presented first.

In summary, order effects stem simply from the ordinal positioning of the task or treatment, whereas carryover effects are due to the direct influences on later behavior that may result from one of the earlier tasks or treatments. For instance, consider the two possible sequences of presenting three treatments, BAC or CAB. From the standpoint of order effects, treatment A occupies the second ordinal position in both sequences and therefore cannot be differentially affected. However, there still could be a definite carryover effect, since there could easily be a problem with treatment A. In the first instance, A is preceded by B, and in the second sequence A is preceded by C.

Counterbalancing. To control for sequencing effects, researchers have created a technique called *counterbalancing*. When two experimental conditions are involved, each subject is faced with two tasks that are sequenced in the order ABBA. That is, the subjects are given task A, then B, then B again, and finally A again. Although this technique does go a long way toward balancing out any possible sequencing effects, it is still suggested that a separate control group be used in which the order of presentation is BAAB. In short, counterbalancing techniques, when used properly, tend to even out many possible sequencing effects and help to prevent confounding the independent variable. Each experimental condition precedes and follows all other conditions the same number of times, and ideally, each condition occurs the same number of times at each position in the sequence.

However, counterbalancing is by no means a panacea. There are situations in which an ABBA sequence becomes highly inappropriate. Suppose that the A condition assumes no special training, whereas the B condition consists of a highly specialized training regimen. The last A condition thus becomes totally inadequate and even misleading, since subjects who have already been trained cannot suddenly be assumed to have become untrained.

Requirements for the True Experiment

The following, as set down by Kerlinger (1986), are considered to be the basic requirements for the true experiment.

1. *The design must be able to answer the research question.* When setting out to design a true experiment, the researcher must keep constantly in mind what it is that he or she is able to prove. This means basically that the researcher must be clear regarding what the eventual statistical analysis will look like, and that it be *appropriate* to the overall design of the study. This must be done early, before the data are collected. Don't wait until the study is completed and then march up to the computer lab with a big pile of collected data and plaintively ask, "What do I do with it now?" By that time it may be too late.

2. *The design must be internally valid.* The true experiment demands that extraneous variables be controlled and that the experimenter actively manipulate at least one IV. Further, the assignment of subjects to the various groups must be under the full control of the experimenter. In short, the true experiment must be designed in such a way as to ensure internal validity and the possibility of an unambiguous interpretation of the possible effects of the IV.

3. *The design should be as externally valid as possible.* The subjects in the study should be representative of the population to which the results are to be extrapolated, and the study should not be so artificially contrived as not to allow for any real-life translations. Of the three criteria, this is by far the most difficult to satisfy when using the true experiment, since by its very nature some artificiality must be introduced whenever the researcher is involved in randomly assigning subjects to the various groupings.

Quasi-Experimental Designs

Until now our discussion of the experimental method has focused on the true experiment, that is, the situation in which the researcher has complete control of both the IV and the assignment of subjects into equivalent groups. Although this is certainly the ideal research situation, unfortunately we live in an imperfect world, and there are times when this paragon of research virtue may only be approximated. A quasi-experimental design is one that applies "an experimental mode of analysis and interpretation to bodies of data not meeting the full requirements of experimental control" (Campbell, 1968, p. 259). Methodologists thus talk of the quasi-experimental method whenever the researcher still has full control over the IV but is not in total charge by creating that key ingredient of the true experiment, equivalent groups. Thus, the *quasi experiment* is an attempt to simulate the true experiment and is thus referred to by many researchers as a compromise design (Kerlinger, 1986). Although there are several variations on the techniques presented here, all the quasi-experimental designs take one of three forms: after-only, before-after, or time series.

After-Only: Intact Groups

This design is typically used when the researcher is faced with the situation of having to compare two or more *intact* groups. Intact groups are those that are not formed by the experimenter but already exist, usually on the basis of the natural setting. In this design the measurement of the DV occurs only after the manipulation of the IV. For example, perhaps the researcher wants to assess the possibility of establishing a difference in the amount a student retains and the mode of presentation of the material to be learned. By a flip of a coin it is decided that the students in Mrs. Smith's first-grade class will receive a visual mode of presentation, whereas the students in Mr. Shea's first-grade class (across the hall) will receive an auditory presentation of the same material. The measure of the DV, scores on the retention test, are only taken after the groups have been differentially treated. This is done to prevent any pretest sensitization to the material being learned. Notice that the IV is being actively manipulated by the researcher; that is, the researcher has chosen, in this case randomly, which first-grade class is going to receive which treatment. However, the researcher *did not create the groups* on the basis of random assignment but instead used groups that had already been formed. It is true that these two groups may have differed on a number of characteristics, some that may even have been related to the DV, but in many situations this is the best that one can do. School systems, clinics, even college deans, may not always allow groups to be artificially formed on the basis of random assignment.

Before-After: Matched Groups

In this variation of the true experiment's before-after design with a separate control group, the formation of the groups is not directly under the experimenter's control, and because of this, the groups cannot be assumed to be fully equivalent. The researcher, however, must make every effort to create as much equivalence as possible, given the fact that random assignment is no longer under experimental control. Thus, instead of matching at the individual level, the attempt here is to match on group averages. For example, if the matching criterion were IQ, and the experimental group showed a mean IQ of 105, the researcher must seek out a control group whose average IQ would also be about 105. It is also important to try to equate the groups with respect to variability, so that each group would have roughly the same standard deviation with respect to the matching measure(s). Analysis of the results of the matched-group design is typically done on the basis of a between-groups comparison. Since the individual subjects have not been yoked together, the groups are considered to be independent. The manipulation of the treatment IV, however, is still under experimental control.

This type of design is often used in nonlaboratory field studies. For example, each summer the NCAA (National Collegiate Athletic Association) sponsors a youth fitness program at the author's home college. To assess the possible impact of the program on the physical and personal development of the participating children, a quasi-experimental study might be conducted by the college's psychology department. Since the NCAA would not allow, nor should they, a given number of children to be randomly assigned to the youth program (while a like number would then have to be prevented from participating), the analysis should compare those children that did enroll with a control group of their peers who did not enroll. Both groups would be measured before the program started on a number of physical and psychological measures (the "before" measure), and then again when the program had finished (the "after" measure). Change scores (the difference between the before and after measures) would then be compared between the two groups.

The key to the success of this type of quasi-experimental design is in the selection of the control group. Families living in close proximity to those of the enrolled children would be canvassed, and children of the same approximate age would be asked to participate. From this list of children a control group would be created that matched the parameters of the experimental group as closely as possible—same age, sex, prescores on the physical and psychological tests, and so on. Although this control group might still differ in some systematic way from the experimental group, the procedure employed would go a long way toward eliminating a number of threats to internal validity. For example, pretest sensitization would be controlled, since both groups would be pretested. Growth and maturity over the course of the summer were controlled. The possibility of outside events contaminating the results (both groups came from the same neighborhoods) would be largely controlled, as would the family's socio-economic status. Now, although this would obviously not be a true experiment, the possibility of pointing in the direction of a cause-and-effect conclusion would be made more compelling by virtue of the number of internal validity threats which would be controlled.

Time Series: Repeated Measures on One Group

In this quasi-experimental design a single intact group (or in extreme cases, a single subject) is measured on the DV at least twice, both before and after the manipulation of the IV. The scores are compared, and the analysis looks for the possibility of concomitant changes between the pre and post DV measures. All the problems inherent in the before-after experimental design discussed earlier also pose a threat in this quasi-experimental variation. A host of extraneous variables may also have combined with the IV, or even worked apart from the

IV, to cause DV changes. The same kinds of things that plagued the experimental equivalent of this design—such as sequencing effects (both carryover and order effects)—have the potential for becoming major contaminating factors here. However, the more often the IV is introduced and the more often DV measures are taken, the less the likelihood of contaminating factors coincidentally impinging on the IV.

For example, suppose that a researcher is interested in the possible effects of the drug Ritalin on the behavior of hyperactive children. A group of children who are already being treated at a behavioral-psychology clinic are chosen for the sample. The children are all observed each day, and a baseline of each child's hyperactivity is charted. Ritalin is given daily to all the children, and then for the next six weeks the children are reevaluated each day regarding their hyperactivity. Although it is true that outside events could play a role in reducing the hyperactive behavior, it would be a rather surprising coincidence if all the children happened to have the same outside forces affecting them for the entire six-week period. The possibility of growth and maturation, however, would still pose a threat to the internal validity of the study. Notice that in this case the DV comparisons would be *within* the subjects.

In conclusion, quasi experiments may be carried out using any of the basic designs previously mentioned—between-groups after-only, between-groups repeated measures, within groups, and so on. The difference between the quasi experiment and the true experiment is solely a matter of whether the researcher creates the equivalent groups by random assignment (the true experiment) or takes groups that are already at least partially formed (the quasi experiment).

POST-FACTO RESEARCH

So far the discussion of the various experimental designs has focused on just that: experimental methodology (both true and quasi), in which the independent variable has been manipulated by the experimenter. In *post-facto research*, on the other hand, the independent variable is not manipulated but *assigned* on the basis of a trait measure *the subject already possesses*. That is, rather than attempting to place subjects in equivalent or (in the case of the quasi experiment) nearly equivalent groups and then doing something to one of the groups in hopes of causing a change in that group, the post-facto method deliberately places subjects in nonequivalent groups—groups that are known to differ on some behavioral or trait measure. For example, the subjects may be assigned to different groups on the basis of their socioeconomic class, sex, race, IQ scores, or whatever, and then the subjects are measured on some other variable. The researcher then attempts to ferret out either a correlation or a difference between these two variables. Thus, in the post-facto method the researcher does not treat groups of subjects differently but instead begins with a measure of the DV and then retroactively looks at preexisting subject IVs and their possible influence on the DV.

There is nothing wrong with this kind of research. It is especially common in the social sciences. The problem lies not in the use but in the misuse of the inferred conclusions. You simply can't do a post-facto study and then leap to a cause-and-effect conclusion. That type of conclusion commits what scientists call the *post-hoc fallacy*, which is written in Latin as "post hoc, ergo propter hoc" (translated as "because it came after this, therefore it was caused by this"). Many examples of this fallacy come readily to mind. We have all heard someone complain that it always rains right after the car is washed, as though washing the car caused it to rain. Or that the traffic is always especially heavy when you have an important meeting to go to, as though all the other drivers know when the meeting has been planned and gang up in a conspiracy to force you to be late. Or perhaps while watching a sporting event on TV you have to leave your TV set for a few minutes. When you return you discover that your favorite team has finally scored. You angrily hypothesize that the team deliberately held back until you weren't there to enjoy the moment. Some post-facto research conclusions have been very similar to these rather obvious examples.

For example, several years ago Arthur Jensen reported that race makes a difference regarding measured intelligence. Jensen compared large groups of black and white children and found that whites performed significantly higher on IQ tests (Jensen, 1969). This is obviously post-facto research, the IV (race) resulting from examining the children's skin color and then, on that basis, assigning them to the two groups. It should be obvious, however, that these two groups also differ on a myriad of other important variables—all of which are left uncontrolled. There are, in short, many systematic differences between white and black children other than skin color, any one of which could easily account for the IQ difference.

In another example of post-facto research, Jerome Bruner once did a study in which children were selected from differing socioeconomic backgrounds and then compared with respect to their ability to estimate the sizes of certain coins (Bruner & Goodman, 1947). It was found that poor children were more apt to overestimate the size of coins than were wealthier children. In this example, socioeconomic class was the independent variable, clearly a subject variable, and was *assigned*, not manipulated. Bruner assigned the children to the economic categories on the basis of subject traits they already possessed. The dependent variable was the child's estimate of the coin size.

What can be concluded from this study? Various explanations have been put forth. Bruner felt that the poorer children valued the coins more highly, and thus overestimated their size. Another suggestion was that wealthier children had more experience handling coins and were thus more accurate in estimating their size because of familiarity. The point is that no causal variable can be directly inferred from this study.

Of what use, then, is post-facto research? Prediction! Even though causal factors may be difficult to isolate, post-facto studies do allow the researcher to make better-than-chance predictions. That is, being provided with information about the independent variable puts the researcher in the position of making above-chance predictions about performance on the dependent variable. If, in a two-newspaper city, there is a dependable relationship between which newspaper a person buys (liberal or conservative) and the political voting habits of that person, one might predict the outcome of certain elections on the basis of the newspapers' circulation figures. We can make the prediction without ever getting into the issue of what causes what, that is, Did the liberal stance of the newspaper cause the reader to cast a liberal vote, or did the liberal attitudes of the reader cause the selection of the newspaper? We don't know, nor do we even have to speculate on causation to make the prediction. In short, accurate predictions of behavior do not depend on the isolation of a causal factor. One need not settle the chicken-egg riddle to predict that a certain individual might choose an omelet over a dish of cacciatore.

Researching via the Post-Facto Method

In the early stages of researching some new area, it is often necessary to use post-facto techniques and then, as information accumulates, follow up with the experimental method. Post-facto research is often quick and easy to do because the data may be already in hand, and it may also lead to educated speculation concerning independent variables that might then be manipulated in experimental fashion.

Post-Facto Research and the Question of Ethics

It is also important to realize that for many kinds of research studies, post-facto techniques are the only ones that don't violate ethical principles. Post-facto techniques allow a researcher to gather predictive evidence in areas that might be too sensitive to be handled experimentally, or that might be harmful to the subjects. Suppose, for example, that a researcher is interested in discovering whether the heavy use of alcohol lowers academic achievement. To test this experimentally, the researcher would have to select two groups of students randomly and then force one group to drink heavily on a daily basis, while preventing the other group from touching a drop. Then if after a term or two grade-average differences were found between the two groups, it could be legitimately claimed that the use of alcohol lowered academic performance. But in isolating a causal factor, the researcher might cause the subjects to suffer more than just low grades. Suppose that they developed liver problems or delirium tremens. Should a researcher be allowed to expose subjects to possible long-term damage merely for the sake of nailing down the causal factor? Of course not; the experimental method should be used only when the risks are minimal compared with the potential benefit to mankind.

A study of this type could be more ethically handled by the post-facto method. The researcher would simply identify students who are already known to be heavy drinkers and then compare their grades with a group of non-drinkers. In this case the subjects themselves have chosen whether or not to drink, and the researcher simply finds out whether the two groups also differ with respect to grade average.

Of course, no direct cause-and-effect statement would be possible, for even if a significant difference was found, one could not determine for certain the direction of the relationship. Perhaps *A* (drinking) caused *B* (lower grades). Perhaps *B* (lower grades) caused *A* (drinking). Or perhaps *X* (unknown variable) caused both *A* and *B*. The *X* variable might be a depressed state of mind that caused the student to both drink too much and also not do the work necessary for academic achievement. (For more on the problems of the "third variable," see Sprinthall, 1990).

COMBINATION RESEARCH

Sometimes, as you will quickly notice as soon as you turn to the research literature, both experimental and post-facto methods are combined in one study. This often occurs when the research involves more than just a single independent variable. When at least one IV is manipulated (active) and at least one other IV is assigned (subject), the study is said to be *combination research*.

For example, a researcher might wish to discover if there is any difference between previously expelled versus nonexpelled prep-school students with regard to the impact violence on TV has on their overt aggressive behavior. In this study, whether the student had been expelled is an assigned IV, whereas the amount of violence on TV (since the researcher will determine who gets to see which program) is a manipulated IV. Random samples of both previously expelled and nonexpelled students are selected from the prep-school population of a certain midwestern state. Then the samples are further divided, again randomly, so that half the expelled and half the nonexpelled must watch violent TV shows in their dorms for two hours each night and are not allowed to watch TV at any other time. The other groups of expelled and nonexpelled students are forced to watch only nonviolent TV during the same time period and of course cannot watch TV at any other time. The design would appear as follows:

	VIOLENT TV	NONVIOLENT TV
PREVIOUSLY EXPELLED		
PREVIOUSLY NONEXPELLED		

The students are subjected to this TV fare each night for six weeks, and all subjects are carefully monitored for overt acts of aggression. Analysis of these data must then be very carefully done. It might turn out that TV violence caused more overt aggression among both the expelled and nonexpelled groups, in which case a cause-and-effect statement could be made (but generalized only to the prep-school population from which the samples were drawn). Or it might be shown that the TV violence only had an effect on previously expelled students, in which case that's the only population to which the results should be extrapolated. Or perhaps the differences in overt aggression could only be shown between the previously expelled and the nonexpelled and would thus have nothing to do with their TV viewing. In this case the chicken-and-egg phenomenon would again be rearing its ugly head. Perhaps the reason these students had been expelled was their inherently greater aggressiveness. In any case, in this study only the type of TV viewing (manipulated IV) could be construed as possibly having a causal nature, whereas the expelled-nonexpelled IV (assigned) could only be regarded as predictive. (More will be said on this in the next chapter, especially regarding the possibility of interaction effects among IVs).

Experimental and Post-Facto: A Final Comparison

The fundamental difference between the two methods, experimental and post-facto, lies in whether a cause-and-effect relationship may be unequivocally claimed. This difference is so enormous, however, that great care should be taken in identifying which method has been used before evaluating research findings. The bottom-line difference is this: when the experimental method has been used the independent variable is a treatment variable and has been actively manipulated by the researcher. That is, when the independent variable has been actively manipulated, the researcher must have somehow *treated* the groups differently, somehow subjected them to different environmental conditions. If this has not been done, the research is post-facto.

In the experimental method, the researcher attempts to make the subjects as much alike as possible (equivalent groups) and then treats them differently. In the post-facto method, the researcher takes groups of individuals who are already different with respect to some measured variable and then treats them all the same (measures them all on some other variable).

SUMMARY

Two of the major types of research strategies are addressed in this chapter, experimental and post-facto. The difference between the two can best be established by identifying the IV(s) and noting the amount of control the researcher has over it. This issue is crucial, since when the researcher has full control over the IV the potential exists for drawing cause-and-effect conclusions. In the true experiment the researcher has absolute control over the IV, whereas in post-facto research this control is severely limited (since the IV is assigned after the fact). The pass-fail research example illustrates some of the problems that arise when post-facto research findings are used to draw causal conclusions. The cause-and-effect trap (inferring causation from post-facto studies) spotlights the extent of and the reasons for this type of fallacious analysis. The distinction between active IVs and subject IVs is stressed, the former identifying experimental research and the latter indicating post-facto research.

The researcher focuses the analysis of experimental data on the differences that may be found among the DVs, or outcome measures. These DV comparisons may be between groups, in which case the sample groups are independently selected, or within subjects, in which case the same group is measured under all experimental conditions. In post-facto research, the analysis may be focused on the differences among DV measures or on the possible association (correlation) between the IV and DV.

In the true experiment the researcher creates equivalent groups of subjects through the process of random assignment to the treatment conditions. Other methods used for providing sample-group equivalence are based either on using the same group under all conditions or on matching the subjects on some variable known to be related to the DV. When groups are created on the basis of random assignment, and are thus independent, the researcher may use the after-only experimental design, in which the DV measures are taken only after the IV has been manipulated. This technique helps to prevent subjects from being sensitized to the IV.

When the same group is used under all conditions, the design is called before-after (for two conditions) or repeated-measures (for more than two conditions). When only one group is used a number of possible research errors may intrude, including the famous Hawthorne effect. Whenever before-after or repeated-measure designs are used, the researcher must be alert to the possibility of threats to internal validity that result from sequencing effects, including both order effects and carryover effects. The use of counterbalancing techniques may often mitigate the effects of these potential dangers.

Problems inherent in matched-subjects designs are also pointed out, especially the problem of determining which variable(s) should be used to create the matching condition.

Above all, a good experimental design should be internally valid, to ensure that the pure effects of the IV may be unambiguously examined. Experimenters should also make every effort to produce a high degree of external validity, so that the results of the study may be extrapolated to real-world populations.

Quasi-experimental designs—those in which intact rather than randomly assigned groups are used—demand extremely careful interpretation. Although the researcher does actively manipulate the IV in the quasi-experimental design, caution must be exercised, since intact groups have the potential for systematic differences at the outset. Quasi experiments can be set up using the after-only, before-after, or matched-subjects designs. Repeated measures on one group (as in a time series) can be handled as a quasi experiment, but again, the researcher must be alert to the possibility of confounding variables.

Post-facto research, in which subjects are assigned to groups after the fact, does not offer the potential for direct cause-and-effect conclusions. Despite this, however, better-than-chance predictions can be made from carefully contrived post-facto studies. Post-facto studies are always open to the possibility of the post-hoc fallacy: "because it came after this, therefore it was caused by this."

Finally, combination research is research in which the researcher uses a mixture of both experimental and post-facto techniques. That is, combination research is used when there are at least two IVs, one a manipulated IV and the second a subject IV. Interpretations of causality should be confined to the differences produced by the manipulated IV, whereas conclusions based on the subject IV should be restricted to prediction.

KEY TERMS

After-only design	Order effects
Before-after design	Post-facto research
Between-groups comparison	Post-hoc fallacy
Carryover effects	Quasi experiment
Combination research	Sequencing effects
Counterbalancing	True experiment
Experimental research	Within-subjects comparison

REFERENCES

BRUNER, J. S., & GOODMAN, C. C. (1947). Value and need as organizing factors in perception. *Journal of Abnormal and Social Psychology, 12,* 33–44.

CAMPBELL, D. T. (1968). Quasi-experimental design. In D. L. Gills (ed.), *International encyclopedia of the social sciences, 5.* New York: Macmillan, Free Press.

JENSEN, A. R. (1969). How much can we boost IQ and scholastic achievement? *Harvard Educational Review, 39,* 1–123.

KEPHART, N. C. (1971). On the value of empirical data in learning disabilities. *Journal of Learning Disabilities, 1,* no. 7, 393–395.

KERLINGER, F. N. (1986). *Foundations of behavioral research* (3d ed.). New York: Holt, Rinehart & Winston.

ROETHLISBERGER, F. J., & DICKSON, W. J. (1939). *Management and the worker.* Cambridge, Mass.: Harvard University Press.

SPRINTHALL, R.C. (1990). *Basic statistical analysis* (3d ed.). Englewood Cliffs, N.J.: Simon & Schuster, Prentice-Hall.

STALLINGS, W. M., & SMOCK, H. R. (1971). The pass-fail grading option at a state university. *Journal of Educational Measurement, 8,* 153–160.

CHAPTER

4

Additional Research Strategies

VARIATIONS OF EXPERIMENTAL AND POST-FACTO DESIGNS

Factorial Designs
Interactions in Factorial Designs
Post-Facto Factorial Designs
Combination Research
Mixed Designs
The Solomon Four-Group Design

STRATEGIES USING SMALL SAMPLES

Small-N and Single-Subject Designs
Case Studies

RESEARCH APPROACHES FOR SPECIAL PURPOSES

Survey Research
Developmental Research

Historical or Archival Research
Naturalistic Observation
Descriptive Research
Action Research

QUALITATIVE RESEARCH

EVALUATION STUDIES

THE USE OF MULTIPLE RESPONSE MEASURES

INTERNAL AND EXTERNAL VALIDITY RECONSIDERED

Meta-Analysis

SUMMARY

KEY TERMS

REFERENCES

In Chapter 3 you were introduced to the "big two" of research: the experimental (true or quasi) and post-facto approaches. A good deal of the research you are likely to read or hear about will be some variation of one or the other of these two major themes. There are, however, several other types of research methods, some of which are simply altered versions of experimental or post-facto methods, and some new ones that don't really fit neatly into either of these two categories. As you will soon see, there are variations on themes and themes within themes. As you read this chapter, don't try to memorize each and every subtype. Instead, read the chapter for understanding, and keep it handy as a reference when you encounter (and you will) some of these variations. All the various types of research, however, do have one common element: they are designed to test a research hypothesis (or to answer a research question) by making *systematic observations*. Experiments, as we have seen, are powerful research tools precisely because, when properly designed, they represent the most rigorously systematic approach to research. Experiments are also important because causal inferences may be made from internally valid experiments. Although some of these other research strategies may not allow cause-and-effect statements and may not be as systematic as experimentation, they all require at least some degree of rigor and careful attention to detail and process.

VARIATIONS OF EXPERIMENTAL AND POST-FACTO DESIGNS

First, we will examine the *factorial design*, a type of research that is useful for studying several IVs simultaneously. We will also look at a very special (and useful, in education) version of the factorial design called the *Solomon four-group design*.

80

Factorial Designs

Factorial designs are those in which two or more independent variables are used in the same research study. Whether such studies are experimental, post-facto, or both depends on whether all the IVs are manipulated variables (experimental), subject or assigned variables (post-facto), or a combination of both manipulated and subject (a type of research we have referred to as combination research). Regardless of the types of IVs, factorial designs will always provide the researcher with several results. Perhaps the most obvious results are those having to do with whether or not there are differences between groups that have been either treated differently or classified differently. But factorials also give other results, called *interactions,* that illustrate the ways in which IVs combine to produce results that may be unexpected on the basis of the impact of each of the IVs alone (more on this shortly).

Factorial designs come in all shapes and sizes. The simplest would be labeled 2 × 2 (read as "2 by 2"), which indicates that there are two levels (treatments or classifications) for the first IV and two levels for the other IV. The total number of groups in the experiment would be four (literally, 2 times 2). A more complicated design might be labeled a 3 × 4 × 4, or three levels of the first IV, four levels of the second IV, and four levels of the third IV. In this case the number of groups would be 3 × 4 × 4, or 48.

Interactions in Factorial Designs

Let's imagine a hypothetical 2 × 2 experiment in which one of the two IVs is alcohol consumption and the other IV is the use of sleeping pills (barbiturates). The DV for the experiment might be the accuracy of solving algebraic equations. For ethical reasons, such an experiment should not be done, but it will serve as a good example of the nature of the possible interactions between IVs. Such an experiment might look like the one shown in Figure 4.1.

This would be a true experiment if both the IVs are manipulated by the researcher. The numbers in parentheses in Figure 4.1 are hypothetical results in the form of the average number of problems solved by each group out of a total of fifty problems. The overall averages are the means for all the subjects who received a given treatment. These overall averages are used to identify what are called *main effects.* Main effects refer to the effect of an IV on a DV in a factorial design. If one level of an IV produces significantly different effects than another level of the IV, a main effect is said to exist. In the foregoing example there was a main effect due to alcohol because those who were given alcohol (groups 1 and 3) solved fewer problems (18 versus 41) than those not given alcohol (groups 2 and 4).

Notice that group 1 received both the alcohol and the barbiturate, and that group 2 received the barbiturate but a placebo in place of the alcohol. Group 3

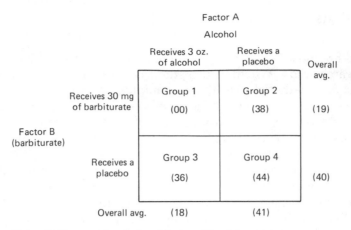

Figure 4.1 Diagram and results for a hypothetical 2 × 2 factorial design.

received the alcohol and a placebo, and group 4 got two placebos, one each for the alcohol and the barbiturate. Group 4, the no-drug group, got an average of forty-four problems right, and group 3 (the alcohol-only group) got thirty-six right, or eight less than the no-drug group. The barbiturate-only group (group 2) got thirty-eight right, or six less than the no-drug group (group 4). At this point, we know the effects of barbiturate on problem solving among those who received no alcohol (the average dropped by 6) and the effects of alcohol on problem solving among those who received no barbiturate (the average dropped by 8). Given these results, a reasonable prediction would be that the combined effect of the barbiturate and alcohol in group 1 should be a drop of 14 points (the 8 for alcohol and the 6 for barbiturate). Look at the score for group 1; they didn't get any right! The reason is that the subjects would all be unconscious, or possibly even dead, because alcohol and barbiturates interact to produce very different combined effects than would be expected either on the basis of the effects of each alone at that dosage level or on the basis of the added effects of the two IVs. Thus, the response to the presence or absence of alcohol in this example depended on whether the barbiturate was present. If the barbiturate was present, the effect of alcohol turned out to be very different than if the barbiturate had been absent. The druggist in your local pharmacy calls this effect drug potentiation. The last time you had a cold or the flu and you needed an antihistamine, it probably had a message attached that said, "This drug may cause drowsiness—alcohol may intensify this effect." Your druggist was warning you that this drug interacts with alcohol to produce greatly exaggerated effects. Note, as an aside, that since many drugs potentiate or interact with other drugs, you should pay careful attention to those little labels on prescription bottles.

Of course, such interactions occur not only in cases of the administration of drugs. *Any* two IVs may interact to produce an effect that could not have been

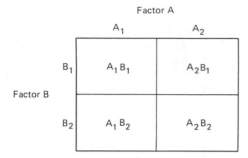

Figure 4.2 Diagram for a 2 × 2 factorial design

predicted by considering the effects of either of the two variables alone. For example, consider the more general case of the 2 × 2 factorial in Figure 4.2. The interaction between variables A and B would exist if, at a given level of A (say A_1), subjects were affected by variable B in one way (for example, $B_1 > B_2$) whereas those subjects who received the other level of A (A_2) were affected differently by variable B ($B_1 = B_2$, or $B_1 < B_2$).

When interactions are found in factorial studies, inferences and interpretations regarding the main effects should be made cautiously. It is possible that main effects exist *only* because of the presence of an interaction. In the alcohol and barbiturate study, for example, the main effects of alcohol are assessed by comparing *all* the subjects who had alcohol with *all* those who did not have alcohol, regardless of whether they had the barbiturate. Similarly, the main effects for barbiturate are found by comparing all the subjects who had no barbiturate with all those who did, regardless of whether they had alcohol. It is possible for those main effects to be misleading, since the unusual result produced by the interaction was included when figuring out the treatment effects.

As an example, assume that a researcher is interested in two IVs: anxiety levels of students and the amount of distracting noise. The DV is some measure of problem solving. Subjects would be assigned to two groups on the basis of scores obtained on an anxiety scale (either high or low anxiety). Each group would then be randomly divided into two groups and subjected to either a high noise level, in the form of music played loudly, or no noise. The DV might, once again, be the number of problems solved. Figure 4.3 shows this study in diagrammatic form with the average numbers of correctly solved problems in parentheses.

Based on a comparison of groups 1 plus 3 (the high-anxiety subjects with an overall average of 9) with groups 2 plus 4 (the low-anxiety subjects with an average of 13.5), one might conclude that low-anxiety groups solve more problems than do high-anxiety groups. Similarly, groups 1 plus 2 (the no-noise group with an average of 13.5) differ from groups 3 plus 4 (the high-noise group with an average of 9). But a close examination of the separate group averages reveals that an interaction clearly exists. At the no-noise level, the high- and low-anxiety subjects (groups 1 and 2, respectively) are very similar. The averages are also

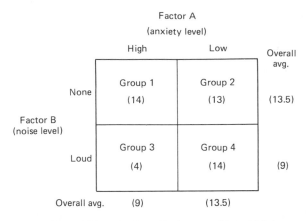

Figure 4.3 Diagram for a 2 × 2 combination research factorial design

similar in the no-noise and high-noise groups (2 and 4, respectively) for low-anxiety subjects. Group 3 appears to be an "oddball," showing considerably lower performance than any of the others. Something about the combination of high anxiety and loud noise seems to be different from any of the other IV combinations and is producing an interaction effect. This means that our conclusions about the differences between high and low anxiety and between no and loud noise must necessarily be drawn cautiously. The lower average for high-anxiety subjects might only be due to the combination result in group 3, and the same might be true about the low average for the group that received the loud noise.

One other comment about interactions should be made. The examples we have given may seem to be oversimplified in that the explanations for the interactions are fairly evident. In much factorial research, however, detecting the source(s) of an interaction is considerably more challenging. The group that appears to be producing the "oddball" result is not always the one in which the interaction is occurring.

Post-Facto Factorial Designs

As an example of a totally *post-facto factorial design*, consider a 2 × 4 factorial design in which the researcher is interested in the attitudes that students have about school athletic policy. Specifically, the DV is a score on a scale designed to measure whether students would drop out of school if their grades were so low as to exclude them from participation in interscholastic athletic competition. The IVs are the students' gender (male or female) and race (black, white, Hispanic, and other). Note, incidentally, that the choices of the number of racial groups and of which racial groups to include are somewhat arbitrary and might be influenced by the makeup of the local school district.

In this instance both IVs are clearly subject variables, and the study is therefore post-facto. No causal inferences should be made about student attitudes according to gender or race, since the study really only establishes the existence of relationships between the DV and each of the two IVs. Thus, knowing the results would allow school administrators to make better-than-chance predictions about the gender and race of students who might drop out if they were prevented from participating in sports, but they could not make inferences about race or gender as *causing* students to drop out. If an interaction between race and gender existed, it would mean that one or two of the eight groups (2 × 4) were more or less likely to consider dropping out than would be expected on the basis of the results for race and gender taken separately. Just as no cause-and-effect inferences can be made about the IVs in this design, none can be made about any possible interaction.

Combination Research

Our example of combination research will be a 2 × 2 factorial design with both a manipulated and a subject IV. The IVs in the study are the gender of tutors and the gender of low-achieving students, and the DV is achievement. The students are, obviously, assigned to groups based on gender, and then each group is randomly divided into two groups. Half of the now randomly divided males are helped by a male tutor, and the other half by a female tutor. The same procedure is used with the two groups of randomly divided female students. In this 2 × 2 design, the gender of the students is a subject variable, but the gender of the tutors is a *manipulated variable*, since the experimenter decided which of the randomly divided groups of students was to get the male or female tutors. Causal inferences might be made about the effects of the gender of the tutors, since this is a manipulated variable, but no causal inferences should be made for student gender or for the interaction. Predictive statements about the interactions, however, are still possible. Based on an interaction revealed in this study we may be able to predict, for example, that males will achieve more with a male tutor whereas females will achieve more with a female tutor.

As was pointed out in the last chapter, when examining research you must decide whether the IVs in the study are manipulated or subject variables. Failure to do this may lead directly to falling into the cause-and-effect trap. This is especially true of post-facto factorial designs and combination designs with several IVs present in the same study.

In some factorial designs the researcher's hypothesis might be an interactive one; that is, the researcher actually predicts that an interaction will exist between the IVs. In the example of male and female students getting help from male or female tutors, the researcher might have had the hypothesis that boys would achieve at higher levels with male tutors than with female tutors, and further, that girls would do better with female tutors than with male tutors. What the researcher is predicting is that the achievement for one level of the first IV (boys) will be different from the results for the other level of the first IV (girls) depending on the level of the second IV (male versus female tutor).

Mixed Designs

Just as factorial designs may use combinations of manipulated and subject IVs (combination research), they may also include repeated measurements taken on the same subjects as well as on different groups of subjects. Consider, for example, a mixed 2 × 2 factorial design in which one group is selected because they are strong visual learners and the other group is identified because they are strong auditory learners. Each group is then presented with a lesson that is primarily visual, and they are tested on how much they retained. They are then presented with an auditory lesson and are again tested. In this study we started out with two different groups classified on the basis of a subject variable: strength of sensory mode in learning. Differences between the groups, then, are just that: differences *between different groups*. Any differences between auditory and visual lesson presentations, however, are not between groups, since the subjects given the visual presentations were the *same subjects* as those given the auditory lesson. The measures are, thus, repeated for one IV (mode of presentation) and independent for the other IV (strength of mode). Designs that include both independent groups and repeated measures are often called *mixed* or *split-plot designs*.

All the cautions presented earlier about the internal-validity problems of repeated measures also apply in factorial designs, just as they did in single-IV studies. Of course, nothing can be said about internal validity for subject variables. In some repeated-measures factorial designs only a single group of subjects is used. In these cases each subject experiences all the levels of all the IVs, and the design is called a *fully repeated measures design*.

If you think about it for a minute, you'll realize that there are a tremendous number of possible variations of factorial designs. All the variations in numbers of IVs, numbers of levels of IVs, manipulated and classified IVs, and independent selection or repeated measures result in an impressive array of research tools. Imagine, for a moment, a 2 × 3 × 4 × 3 design with repeated measures on two of the four IVs, manipulation of three IVs, and subjects classified into groups for one IV. Such complicated designs become harrowing to contemplate, and the statistical calculations, although possible with a powerful computer program, become messy, time consuming, and not always possible to interpret. Computer programs have been designed to deal with data from highly complex designs such as this one. But just because the computer can handle complicated interactions is no reason to design such an unwieldy study.

		Pretest: No pretest	Pretest: Pretest
Workbook	Workbook A	Group 1	Group 2
	Workbook B	Group 3	Group 4

Figure 4.4 Example of a Solomon four-group design

The Solomon Four-Group Design

The Solomon four-group design is one that is particularly adapted to research in education. The design is always a 2 × 2 (four-group) factorial design in which one of the IVs is the presence or absence of a pretest. The other IV can be anything the researcher is interested in, but often it is a manipulated IV such as a teaching or training variable, and the DV is frequently an achievement variable. The typical design uses randomized groups and is similar to the one in Figure 4.4. In this case the second IV is the effect of two different reading workbooks on reading achievement.

In this design all groups are posttested to measure achievement, but only groups 2 and 4 are pretested. Note that both IVs are manipulated, and that cause-and-effect statements are possible. The results of a Solomon four-group study will allow the researcher to examine (1) the effects of pretests, (2) the effects of the second IV and, (3) the possible interaction effects between the two IVs. Recall that one of the threats to external validity mentioned in Chapter 2 was the reactive or interaction effects of testing. The Solomon four-group design speaks directly to this threat to external validity by allowing the researcher to see if such an interaction exists.

STRATEGIES USING SMALL SAMPLES

In some research situations the number of subjects available for use in the study is small, or in some cases may even be only one person. In such situations, one might be tempted to throw up one's hands and quit, especially in light of the often repeated statistician's and researcher's warning to use samples of adequate size. It is true that, all other things being equal, larger samples are always desirable. This is for three basic reasons. First, the conclusions from large studies tend to be more reliable (in much the same way that tests with more questions are more reliable). Second, large samples tend to be more representative of the population, thus enhancing external validity. Finally, larger samples produce greater statistical power; that is, if there are differences to be found among groups, statistical tests using larger samples are more likely to detect the differences (more on this in the next chapter).

Nevertheless, when all other things are *not* equal (as is so often the case in the real world), there may be good reasons to use small numbers of subjects in doing a research project. Dealing with a smaller number of subjects is less expensive because less time and money is required. This is especially important if the treatment is, by its very nature, expensive, as it would be if the study required intensive counseling by a high-cost professional. Smaller numbers of subjects are also more convenient to deal with than are larger numbers. Further, in some cases there may simply not be many subjects available who have a characteristic that is important to the research. This would be the case, for example, if the researcher is interested in a relatively rare form of learning disability. Finally, smaller numbers might allow for a kind of in-depth analysis not permitted with larger samples. Such areas of in-depth study might include college counseling procedures used on high-school students, or interviewing procedures used on prospective teacher employees.

Small-*N* and Single-Subject Designs

Whether for reasons of convenience or economy, limited availability of subjects, or the ability to do in-depth analysis, research using small samples has several characteristics that are very different from those of research involving larger samples. With large samples, the researcher typically measures one or more DVs on relatively large groups of subjects. The small-N researcher typically uses only a few subjects but measures their behavior frequently over a period of time (in a manner similar to the approach used in the time-series design discussed in the last chapter). Incidentally, the N in *small-N research* refers to the number of subjects used in the research project, and the number of subjects in such research is typically five or fewer. A second difference between large-N and small-N research is that large studies may be either experimental or post-facto, but small-N research always involves a manipulated IV (since, for example, one obviously cannot "classify" a single subject). Finally, since a small number of subjects is used, small-N research usually requires that all factors other than the IV be tightly and rigorously controlled. That is not to say that tight control isn't desirable in large-N research, because it is. However, the small numbers of subjects involved in small-N research leave the experimenter with literally no margin for error.

Designs for small-N research fall into two basic categories: *reversal* and *nonreversal designs*. Some nonreversal designs are called *multiple-baseline designs*.

Reversal designs involve at least three steps, with some designs requiring many more steps. The first step in the design is to establish a *baseline* for the behavior that will be used as the DV in the study. The baseline is the ongoing level of the subject's behavior or performance without any application of the IV by the experimenter. These observations of the subject's behavior are recorded over a period of time and may involve measuring frequencies, durations, time samples or product measures. *Frequency* indicates the number of times the behavior is exhibited during a given time unit. A teacher might count the number of times an aggressive child attacks other children each day. *Duration* refers to the length of time the person spends engaging in a behavior. A researcher might observe the length of time in each hour that a child spends on-task as opposed to off-task. *Time sampling* results in information about when, during a given time interval, the behavior occurs. A parent with a bed-wetting child might check every half hour during the night to discover the time when the wetting occurs. *Product measures* involve establishing a baseline level of performance in completing a task. A teacher might measure the "product" of reading speed for a student each day. These observations might be carried out for ten or fifteen time intervals, providing the researcher with information about "typical" or ongoing DV values over time.

Once the baseline is established, the second step in the study is to apply the IV. For example, a researcher attempting to find a way to alter children's behavior might reinforce a child with a gold star each time the child stays on-task for at least a five-minute time period. During this second phase, observation of the DV continues in exactly the same way as during the baseline phase.

The third phase of the study is the reversal phase; that is, the IV is removed and the observation of the DV continues for a period of time. This most basic form of reversal study is often referred to as an *ABA design*, where each "A" in "ABA" refers to measurement periods during which the IV is not applied, and the B refers to the time during which the IV is present. The reversal is done to examine the lasting or residual effects of the IV, and also to determine if it really was the IV that produced the effect. For example, Will any change in the on-task time continue after the reinforcers are removed? The only way to find out is to reverse the IV back to the non-IV phase. The results for this hypothetical experiment might look like those in Figure 4.5.

The child's typical on-task time was about ten to fifteen minutes per hour during the baseline phase, and quickly rose to thirty-five to forty minutes during the phase when the gold stars were used as rewards. As soon as the rewards were removed during the reversal phase, the performance quickly dropped again, showing that the results of applying the IV were, in this case, not permanent. It does, however, strongly suggest that the IV made a difference while being applied.

There are many types of reversal designs, some of which begin to resemble alphabet soup. All the reversal designs follow somewhat the same pattern as the ABA design except that several IV phases or several reversals might be done (such as ABAB or ABABA designs). In some cases more than one level of an IV might be used (such as an AB_1AB_2A design in which the 1 and 2 refer to different treatment levels of the IV). In still other cases two different IVs might be used (as

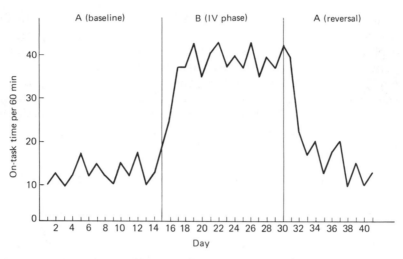

Figure 4.5 Results for a hypothetical ABA design used to increase a student's on-task time

in, for example, the ABACA design in which "B" and "C" refer to two different IVs). As we said, alphabet soup.

Nonreversal designs, some forms of which may be called multiple-baseline designs, do not involve a reversal phase in which the IV is removed. In some cases it would not be ethical to remove an IV. This, for example, would be the case if the IV was a medical treatment being provided to a sick person. In other cases the effects of an IV *cannot* be removed. Removal of an IV designed to improve a child's spelling cannot magically erase the knowledge the child has already gained while the IV was applied. For situations in which the IV cannot be removed or in which the IV effects are irreversible, a design with no reversals must be used. The most basic nonreversal design is the AB design. As you might expect, the AB design consists of the same first two phases as the ABA design, but without the reversal. The AB design is not as powerful as a reversal design, primarily because of the added support given by the second A in the ABA design. Note that an AB design is just a small-N version of a before-after design, and that internal validity is, therefore, threatened in many of the same ways. On the other hand, internal validity tends to be strengthened by the presence of the reversal(s) in ABA, ABAB, or other reversal approaches.

Multiple-baseline designs, as the name suggests, are designs in which two or more baselines are established. These designs are actually different versions of the basic AB design, with different baselines established for different behaviors, subjects, or settings. Baselines could be established for several different behaviors exhibited by the same subject in a given situation. A child who spits out food, eats with her fingers, and throws food on the floor at mealtimes might have a baseline established for each of these behaviors. Baselines might also be established for the same behavior for two different subjects. This approach could be used with identical twins who both exhibit spitting out at mealtimes. Finally, baselines might be established for the same behavior in the same subject, but in different settings. A disruptive ninth grader might, for example, have baselines established for his behavior in each of his school classes.

Regardless of the method used to establish baselines, the multiple-baseline design introduces the IV at different times for the different behaviors, subjects, or settings. For example, the child who eats with her fingers, spits out, and throws food on the floor would be observed over a period of time, and three baselines would be established. After, say, ten days, the IV, a verbal reprimand, is applied, but only for throwing food. After twenty days verbal reprimands might also be added for spitting out while continuing the reprimands for throwing food. After thirty days reprimands might be added for eating with the fingers. In effect, we have a mini-AB design for each of the designated behaviors, but the IV is applied at different times for the different behaviors. Notice that if one started reprimanding all three behaviors at the same time it would become difficult to determine if the IV is really responsible for any observed changes. Perhaps some other event in the child's life that is unrelated to the experiment is responsible for these changes. By staggering the introduction of the IV and watching for corresponding changes in the various behaviors, such coincidences can be more safely ruled out. Furthermore, the experimenter can alter the schedule if the IV is less (or more) effective than expected. If, for example, the introduction of the verbal reprimand had been only partially effective in eliminating food throwing after ten days, the experimenter might decide to delay the start of reprimanding for spitting out until some later time.

Some of these small-N designs might seem vaguely familiar. In educational psychology or other courses, you might have learned about a variety of behavioral management techniques based on operant conditioning methods. Some of these methods for controlling behavior are simply AB or multiple-baseline designs in which the IV is a reinforcement (or punishment) designed to increase (or decrease) the strength of a certain behavior. Most of these methods were originally developed in laboratory studies as "pure" research to answer a question or test a hypothesis, out of scientific curiosity, with no practical purpose or application in mind. After many replications the methods became well-established scientific phenomena, and researchers began doing more "applied" research to test hypotheses regarding the practical usefulness of a given technique. These methods are commonly used because they have been tried in a variety of laboratory and applied (including educational) settings, have often been successful in managing behavior, and the research results have been published, making them more available to a wider audience.

Case Studies

If a psychologist, psychiatrist, teacher, or other professional does an intensive in-depth study of one person, the research process and the resulting written description are often called *case studies*. The case study contains a thorough review of the subject's background and current status, including relevant diagnostic information and living (and other environmental) circumstances.

Consider, for example, a teacher who has observed a change in a student in one of his classes. The student had been performing well on exams, was consistent about turning in homework, interacted normally with teachers and other students, and dressed neatly when in school. More recently, the student has been doing poorly on exams, rarely turns in required work, has become sullen, quiet, and uncommunicative, and constantly appears sloppy. The student is simply not "with it" any longer. Concerned, the teacher approaches the school psychologist and discusses the problem with her. Thus alerted, the school psychologist conducts a thorough study, designed in this case to gather information useful in dealing with a student who may have a serious problem. The process would include (1) checking the student's academic record, behavioral history, and test scores, (2) talking with the student's friends, parents, and other teachers, and (3) talking with the student. The purpose of all of this, of course, is to find out anything and everything that might be useful in helping the student with whatever problem may exist.

Many such case studies are conducted, but only a few find their way into the scientific literature, primarily because the case study is conducted by a practitioner whose purpose is to help a student, not by a researcher whose purpose is to add to the scientific literature. When case studies are published they include the relevant background, diagnostic information, and current circumstances but, in addition, also include explanations for behavior (attempts at understanding causation) and a description of the outcome of whatever treatment was applied. A case study is essentially a form of post-facto research in which the subject's background and circumstances are thoroughly researched. As we have said many times, such research does not lead to cause-and-effect interpretations, but the writers of case study material sometimes provide the reader with behavioral explanations that may, for example, be based on a theory of personality (such as Freud's psychodynamic theory). The "effects" of intervention such as counseling might be included, since such treatment represents a kind of before-after IV manipulation. Some case studies are so unusual or spectacular that they even find their way into the popular media, including books, magazines, or movies. This was the case with *Sybil* (Schreiber, 1974), the story of a woman who was said to have sixteen distinctly different personalities.

Case studies don't have to be done on a single person. They may also be done on a single *unit*, such as a group, institution, or community. Such research projects are sometimes called *field studies*, but that term can also be used to refer to any study not conducted in a controlled laboratory setting. An in-depth study might be done on a group, such as a class of students, to gain a complete picture of the group in terms of student friendships, teacher-student interactions, and so on. The focus of a case study could also be on an institution, such as an elementary school or a college. The unit examined in a case study could also be an entire city or town. Such studies require a great deal of time and money, but sociologists have done a number of such studies, including research on social class, ethnic groups, socioeconomic status, family structure, educational institutions, and government. One such study is *Yankee City* (Warner, Low, Lunt & Srole, 1963), in which a coastal New England city of more than fifteen thousand people was studied intensively for five years, and less intensively for an additional twenty years.

RESEARCH APPROACHES FOR SPECIAL PURPOSES

A number of other types of research approaches appear in the educational literature. In some cases they are closely related to methods already discussed. In other cases, however, they represent entirely different approaches that have been designed for specific purposes or for particular circumstances. If you start reading the educational journals, you are sure to find one or more of these types of research.

Although it may appear to be stating the obvious, it should be noted that a research study may use more than one approach. Earlier in this chapter, for example, we described factorial designs of several types. In some designs one of the IVs may be manipulated (and that part of the research is, therefore, experimental), but the other IV may be classified (and that part of the research is postfacto). Such combinations of different approaches to research are not uncommon and may involve one or more of the research strategies described earlier as well as some of those discussed presently.

Survey Research

Surveys are designed to gather information from samples (occasionally, even from populations) by using questionnaires or, sometimes, interviews. The questionnaire contains questions (or interviewers ask questions) about behavior, opinions, attitudes, beliefs, or any of a number of other psychological or sociological qualities. Surveys may be used to investigate virtually anything that people do or think. The famous Kinsey studies (Kinsey, Pomeroy, & Martin, 1948; Kinsey, Pomeroy, Martin, & Gebhard, 1953), for example, described the sexual behavior of Americans. Surveys can be (and have been) used to obtain information about what people think about capital punishment, affirmative action, teacher effectiveness, corruption in government, and a myriad of other things. When sample information is gathered, one of the uses of survey information is to generalize the results to the population from which the sample has been selected. An important purpose of *survey research*, whether the survey is done on samples or populations, is to examine the interrelationships between the variables measured or the differences between samples in their response patterns.

The political polls that have become so familiar to us are one form of survey research. Early in the process of electing U.S. presidents, pollsters begin asking their samples a wide variety of questions designed to estimate the voting population's opinions about candidates or potential candidates. Questions used early in the process often involve "if-then" items such as "If Bill Frick was the Republican candidate and John Frack was the Democratic candidate and the election was to be held today, which would you vote for?" or "If the primary in your state was to be held tomorrow, which of the Democratic candidates would you vote for?" Items such as these help to identify stronger or weaker candidates early in the election process. Candidates often hire their own pollsters to help them decide how to run their campaign. These private polls (as opposed to the ones published in magazines or newspapers) might involve a question such as "What is the most important issue that the next president of the United States will have to face?" If the voters sampled consider the state of the economy as the most important issue, the candidate's campaign literature and speeches would stress that point. Later in the campaign, when the primaries and political conventions are over and the candidates for each party are selected, the polls become more specific about attempting to predict the election winner. We are constantly bombarded with poll results, so much so in fact, that many political scientists worry about the possibility that the polls may actually influence rather than predict the outcome of elections.

Surveys such as political polls or the Kinsey reports are only designed to provide information about the status quo—the existing state of affairs with respect to the attitudes, beliefs, opinions, or behavior of those surveyed. In a sense, then, the information gathered portrays the sample as it is, and the research is purely descriptive in nature. Note, however, that the descriptive information gathered might be used to make predictions about future population behavior.

As was indicated earlier in this section, surveys are often used to examine relationships between variables or differences between samples. A researcher might design and carry out a survey of teachers', principals', and school superintendents' attitudes about professional labor unions. The survey might contain, as one of the questions, the following item: "Do you believe that school principals should belong to a union?" The results of this hypothetical survey might look like those shown in Figure 4.6.

The data in the table describe the attitudes of each of the three groups, but the relationship between the position held and the attitude can also be examined. Principals and, to a greater extent, teachers believe that principals should be union members, whereas the superintendents are heavily opposed. Such

GROUP	RESPONSE		
	Yes	*No*	*No Opinion*
Superintendents	4%	89%	7%
Principals	65%	24%	11%
Teachers	81%	11%	8%

Figure 4.6 Results of a hypothetical survey question about whether school principals should belong to a union

relationships may or may not be explainable. One possible explanation is that superintendents believe that principals have a major role in setting educational policy, and that as policymakers (and supervisors of teachers) they should not be in unions. On the other hand, the teachers and principals might believe that union membership is the only way for principals to achieve higher salaries and better working conditions. In the absence of any other information, such explanations or explanatory hypotheses can only be tentative. The discovery of the relationship between position and attitude might give rise to another research survey designed to test possible explanations or hypotheses about relationships discovered earlier.

Developmental Research

Developmental research is used to examine changes in subjects that occur over time. The term is most often used to refer to research conducted by developmental psychologists on maturation and other human characteristics that change (or develop) as a result of the passage of time. For example, Piaget wrote mostly about cognitive development, Kohlberg about moral development, and Erikson about life-span personality development. In a more general sense, the term can be used to refer to any research that examines changes that occur over time. A researcher might, for example, be interested in the development of reading ability in school-age children from the time they enter the first grade to the end of the eighth grade. The research would examine not only the *kinds* of changes that occur over time but *when* those changes take place.

Developmental researchers typically use one of two basic approaches: *longitudinal* or *cross-sectional*. In the foregoing example, the researcher could either track the progress of the same group of students over the entire eight-year period (a longitudinal approach) or examine different groups based on the eight grade levels all at the same time (a cross-sectional approach). Each approach has advantages and disadvantages.

The strength of the longitudinal approach is that the same subjects are studied over a long period of time. The researcher is, therefore, comparing apples with apples—a subject's performance at one time with the same subject's performance at later times. This is more important as the length of time encompassed by the study increases, primarily because different samples at different stages might have been different to begin with.

Imagine, for example, that you were interested in changes in teaching effectiveness that occur during a teaching career. The time span might include thirty-five or forty years. If you simply took groups of teachers at different points in their careers, you run the risk of contaminating your results because of inherent differences between the samples at each age level. Examine a group of twenty-five-year-old teachers and a group of sixty-year-old teachers and ask yourself the question of whether they were the same when they began their careers. Their education and training were different when they attended college, and their attitudes were shaped by having grown up in entirely different cultural eras. Perhaps most important is the fact that the sixty-year-old teachers are survivors! How many of the teachers whom they started with thirty-five years before have left teaching, and why did they leave? Did, for example, the effective teachers stay because they found it rewarding, or did the others leave because they weren't effective? The point, here, is that these "survivors" are now a highly selected group who chose to stay in the classroom for whatever reasons. The question becomes, of course, Are the differences in effectiveness between the younger and older teachers because of "development", self-selection, or because they were different to begin with? If you compare a group of teachers' performance at age twenty-five with the same teachers' performance at sixty, that problem is avoided, but therein also lies the problem with the longitudinal approach. In this case you would have to take thirty-five years to do the study, and you might not live to see the project finished!

It simply takes too long to answer some research questions using longitudinal research, and the cross-sectional approach must be used for practical reasons. Thus, the advantage of cross-sectional research is that the entire study can be completed in a relatively short time span, and the disadvantage is that comparing different groups might result in unwarranted conclusions. It should be noted that despite the time and effort that go into them, longitudinal research studies conducted over long time spans have been done. Terman (1925) began a study of fifteen hundred gifted children (defined in terms of high IQ) in the early 1920s. Terman himself continued to direct follow-ups on the group (Terman & Oden, 1947, 1959) until his death in 1956. The study still goes on, however, being carried on by co-workers who promise to continue the work right up until the death of the last member of the original sample.

Historical or Archival Research

Research that is categorized as *historical* or *archival* uses available records as a source of observations about the behavior of interest. The records examined may be either public or private, and the search and data-gathering process are conducted as systematically and objectively as possible. Obviously, the researcher does not manipulate an IV, as is the case in most of these alternative strategies. Instead, the researcher simply gathers the information about variables of interest from available records. Notice that there is no control over any of the variables of interest—the records must be allowed to "speak for themselves."

The list of records that might be used by archival researchers may include elementary, secondary, or college files, birth, baptismal, marriage, or death records, library or government documents, hospital files, phonograph, tape, or compact disc recordings, clinical files, court or police records, or virtually any source containing permanent documents. Think about the kinds of records that you would need to examine if, for example, you were to do a genealogical study of your own family. Or consider the sources you would need if you really had to have a complete set of records about a child in one of your classes.

Recall that the major problem in the longitudinal research approach was that the time needed to complete the research could be unacceptably long. Cross-sectional research might, therefore, be preferable in spite of the fact that such a study could end up contrasting noncomparable groups. In some cases longitudinal research might be done either partially or completely by using the archival approach. For example, there is currently a great deal of concern about the school dropout problem. Many students simply do not complete high school and thus enter life without a diploma or the skills necessary to be able to compete effectively in the job market. If we could predict which students would drop out on the basis of variables that have been identified much earlier—say, when they were in the third or fourth grade—programs might be put in place that might alleviate this tragic problem. If one were to use the longitudinal approach, a group of children just starting out in school would have to be identified and apparently relevant variables tracked throughout their school years. As a straight longitudinal study, it would take more than twelve years to complete.

Instead, the researcher might use an approach that is essentially archival. The researcher would start with two groups of persons of similar age, one of which had graduated from high school and the other which had not. School and other relevant records would then be examined for both groups. Grades, teacher evaluations, family information, and so on, would be systematically gathered. In some ways this might seem like going on a "fishing expedition" in the hope of finding consistent differences between the graduates and nongraduates on one or more of the variables recorded. In a way, it is a fishing expedition, but keep in mind that the purpose of the research is to find factors that might help to predict an important social phenomenon. In deciding which variables to record, the researcher is hypothesizing about the nature of the factors that might be used to predict the future behavior of students long before these students have even entered high school. This kind of after-the-fact approach has elements of post-facto studies (a subject IV—graduates and nongraduates), longitudinal studies (long-term tracking of the same individuals), and archival research (a retrospective view based on gathering data from available records).

Naturalistic Observation

The *naturalistic observation* approach to research involves systematic observations of behaviors as those behaviors occur in a natural or normal setting. For example, a researcher might be interested in the degree to which first graders exhibit aggressive behavior patterns during recess periods. If the children were brought into a laboratory, the setting would not resemble the regular school playground and any observations made would lack generalizability to a natural setting. In effect, the artificial setting might prod the children into behaving in rather artificial ways. In the naturalistic study, the observations would be made while children play on the playground during actual recess periods.

The observations made should be systematic and are most often guided by the use of a checklist of behaviors, which in the case of the foregoing example would be defined as "aggressive." The behaviors operationally defined as aggressive might include such acts as punching, pushing, kicking, and more subtle aggressions such as name-calling and teasing. Each time the observer saw a child engaging in one of the behaviors defined as aggressive, a check mark would be placed beside the defined behavior. Often, several observers are used so that the reliability of observations can be assessed.

It is important that the observers *not interfere* in the natural processes occurring in the setting. If, for example, the observer became involved with the children on the playground, the setting would no longer be "natural" because of the changes that might be produced by the intervention of the observer. The important thing to keep in mind about naturalistic observation is that the behavior examined should be observed in the context of its normal, daily circumstances. The observer, therefore, should be as unobtrusive as possible so as to avoid influencing those being observed. In fact, the ideal situation would be one in which the observers could be concealed (without, of course, reducing the accuracy of their observations). Sometimes, for example, observers might be concealed behind a two-way mirror, thus reducing or eliminating the effect of the mere presence of the observers.

Descriptive Research

When researchers first begin to do research on particular types of populations, especially populations about which little is known, the first type of research done is frequently *descriptive*. The purpose of this approach is to measure one or more variables that can be used to describe the group of interest. Nearly all research studies involve at least some amount of description. In experiments and post-facto studies, each of the samples may, for example, be described in terms of composition (such as 24 males and 35 females, or 18 freshmen and 23 sophomores) or in terms of their average levels of performance.

Research is typically called descriptive when the primary purpose of the research is description, rather than some other basic goal such as looking for differences between groups or relationships among variables. As an example, Spafford (1987) identified a group of sixty students that had all been diagnosed as dyslexic. The basic purpose of her study was to examine the characteristics of this well-defined, large, and relatively homogeneous group of students. Since a number of prior studies had already described groups of students labeled as learning disabled, including dyslexic subjects as well as subjects with a variety of other learning disabilities, the groups so defined were relatively heterogeneous. Other studies had described the characteristics of very small samples, in which the subjects were described solely on the basis of dyslexia, a more homogeneous grouping. The description of the subjects in this study included average performance on the WISC-R Verbal and Performance Scales (particularly the discrepancy between the two scales) and each of the WISC-R subscales (especially the Digit Span). Such descriptive information can be useful to others doing research involving dyslexic subjects, and might also be of interest to teachers or diagnosticians. Although Spafford's research also included comparisons of the dyslexic group's performance with the performance of nondyslexic children, the primary purpose of the research was descriptive.

Several of the types of research mentioned in earlier sections of this chapter could be included under the category of descriptive research. These include archival research, naturalistic observation, surveys, and case studies. Each of these may be descriptive to the extent that they yield objective and, it is to be hoped, accurate information about the status quo, or what *is* (or *was*, in archival research). These descriptions may then provide information about relationships between variables. Since none of these methods gives the researcher the opportunity of controlling the environment or manipulating IVs, they cannot (by definition) contain any degree of internal validity. Hence, no inferences about causal factors should be made.

Action Research

Strictly speaking, *action research* isn't a type of research approach in the way that those discussed earlier are. It is, rather, research designed to solve problems that have a *direct application* in the setting in which the research is conducted. For most research a primary consideration is the degree to which the results can be generalized, but the person conducting action research doesn't care a whit about external validity, only about the usefulness of the results in the setting in which the research is conducted.

The action researcher may use any approach (or combination of approaches) that is presumed to solve a practical problem. The research is often somewhat informally conducted, and not much attention is paid to controlling the surrounding circumstances. Since this is the case, internal validity is, at best, poor even when an IV is manipulated and, of course, is nonexistent in research without a manipulated IV. Measurement is also frequently informal and may involve questionnaires or surveys constructed by the research workers themselves. The subjects used are rarely randomly selected but are instead students who happen to be available or staff members in the school or district who volunteer. Further, comparison groups are usually lacking, making it sometimes difficult to know how much of an effect a given treatment has really had.

The sources of hypotheses or research questions (and, incidentally, the persons who will carry out the research) are typically the teachers or administrators who identify a problem that they feel needs an immediate solution. For example, a high school principal is concerned about the ability of teachers to deal with students from bilingual homes. The principal feels that an in-service program designed to help teachers understand the special needs of these students would be helpful. A person who is skilled and well-informed in the area(s) of concern is engaged to provide the in-service program, and teachers are encouraged to attend. At the end of the program, a questionnaire is circulated among the attending teachers, and they are asked whether they thought the program was helpful. Note the informality of this type of "research" process. There is no random selection, no comparison, no control (it's hard to mandate attendance), and the measurement of the "effects" of the program are usually imprecise. The project has been conducted by the person concerned about the problem, and it was designed to help solve that problem.

The in-service programs initiated or conducted in schools (and there are many) fall into the action research category. They may involve surveys designed to pinpoint the sources of low faculty morale, information programs designed to increase parent involvement with schools, attempts to decrease school vandalism, drug and alcohol prevention programs (for staff or students), efforts to help teachers identify students with substance-abuse problems, and tryouts of new or innovative teaching methods or instructional materials. The majority of teachers and administrators will never conduct or be involved in a formal research study, but virtually all will be participants in action research projects during their careers—probably many times.

A great deal of action research is conducted, but most of it is never published, precisely because the results rarely possess external validity. The results of action projects are often communicated to others, but only in the school or district within which they will be used, or in casual or informal contacts with other professionals (at regional teachers' or administrators' meetings, for example). A description of an action research project that appears to be unusually effective might find its way into a professional publication, but as stated earlier, this is rare.

QUALITATIVE RESEARCH

A fundamental distinction is made between *qualitative research* and *quantitative research*. Although the basic difference is in the nature of the data-gathering techniques and the actual data gathered, there are several other philosophical and procedural differences between them. Most of the methods we have described are considered quantitative methods because they are used to gather numerical data. Qualitative methods, on the other hand, are approaches used to systematically gather data, but the data are purely *descriptive* and therefore not numerical.

The data in qualitative research are made up of written descriptions of people, events, opinions, attitudes, and environments, or combinations of these. The data may be derived from direct observations of an individual's behavior, from interviews, from written opinions, or from public documents. If, for example, there was interest in the general attitudes of college professors about how students of the nineties are different from those of the seventies, the qualitative researcher might interview twenty-five or fifty professors who have been teaching for at least twenty years. The researcher would record their responses to all the questions, either in writing or on tape. The data, then, are the interviewer's written notes or the tape recording. The result is a nonstatistical written description that helps us to understand what changes professors have perceived in students over the past twenty years. This is similar to the way cultural anthropologists describe the group norms of some remote society.

We could, of course, attempt to describe the same phenomenon in quantitative terms. We might, for example, create a survey of professors' attitudes on student change. A series of statements might be created that professors rate on a scale representing degree of agreement with each statement. The statement "Students' writing skills are similar to those of twenty years ago" might be responded to on a scale of 1 to 5, with 1 equaling "strongly disagree," 2 "disagree," 3 "neither agree nor disagree," 4 "agree," and 5 "strongly agree." The numbers are tabulated and would be dealt with statistically. The results might be descriptive ("68 percent of professors agree or strongly agree with this statement") or could be used to test hypotheses ("Social sciences professors were more likely to disagree or strongly disagree with this statement than were business school professors"). Thus, the data are derived objectively from the scientist's perspective using numerical definitions of terms.

Notice that there are several implicit differences between the qualitative and quantitative approaches. The quantitative researcher must begin with "hypotheses" about student change, from which the statements to be rated are then derived. The responder to the questionnaire is in turn limited to just those statements. On the other hand, the qualitative researcher begins only with a *general question* about the nature of student change and the data are generated by those interviewed. The data are derived subjectively from the interviewees' own perspective, not from the scientist-observer's perspective.

In some cases both qualitative and quantitative data might be combined in a single study. Qualitative data might be based on what people write in response to an open-ended questionnaire question as well as what is said to an interviewer. Many surveys contain both statements that can be numerically rated in some way, and more global, open-ended questions. The numerical ratings are quantitative data, and the answers to the global questions are qualitative data, both having been gathered from the same instrument. In such cases the written responses might be influenced by the statements to be rated, and a bias might thus be introduced into the qualitative portion of the data. A purely qualitative approach could avoid that bias.

There are other differences between the qualitative and quantitative approaches. One important difference is that the reliability of qualitative data is more difficult to establish and may of course be affected by the biases of the researcher-observer-interviewer. Even when it is established it is usually lower than the reliability of quantitative measures. Qualitative researchers are very conscious of these problems and pay a good deal of attention to them when conducting research.

Another difference is that the quantitative scientist's philosophical point of view is neutral. Data are gathered objectively from the perspective of a hypothesis or question that is deductively derived from theory or other observation (as was described in Chapter 1). The viewpoint of the persons observed or whose behavior is measured is not considered. The standpoint of the qualitative researcher is more typically humanistic, as reflected in the importance given to the observed persons' own perspective as it exists in their circumstances and environment. It is a holistic approach that is usually inductive and designed to answer general questions. In a sense, the human experience or point of view is seen as more important than the scientific point of view. Further, quantitative research hypotheses are often deduced from theory, and the research designed to lead to knowledge of *facts and causes*. On the other hand, qualitative descriptions may lead to general statements or theories designed to *understand* phenomena. The difference between the quantitative focus on facts and causes and the qualitative stress on understanding is also based on the neutral-versus-humanistic underpinnings of the two approaches. Figure 4.7 represents an attempt to summarize briefly the differences between the qualitative and quantitative approaches.

An *ethnography* is a qualitative study in which the researcher provides for the reader a pure or "true-to-life" description of the observations made during the research. It includes as accurate a representation as possible of the things that people say, write, and do in their own environments. The study typically

	QUANTITATIVE RESEARCH	QUALITATIVE RESEARCH
Basic approach	Deductive: theory leads to hypothesis reduced to measured variables (occasionally inductive)	Inductive: descriptions are holistic, yet detailed, and may lead to generalization or theory
Philosophical approach	Neutral	Humanistic
Starting point	Hypothesis or specific question: "If A then B," or "If A, what does B do?"	Nonspecific research question: "What is the nature of A?"
Purpose	To discover facts and causes objectively derived from data gathered; based on the scientist's perspective	To subjectively derive understanding from the perspective of observed persons in their own milieu
Data	Numerical; derived from surveys, questionnaires, and other objective measures	Descriptive; derived from observation, interviews, and a person's written or spoken words
Analysis	Statistical	Descriptive
Outcome	Decision with respect to hypothesis; may relate to practice or theory	Description, but may involve analysis or theory development

Figure 4.7 Summary of differences between quantitative and qualitative approaches to research

contains little or no interpretation on the part of the researcher. Instead, the readers are left to draw their own conclusions and generalizations.

Whenever possible, the qualitative research tries to gather data *unobtrusively*, or in ways that keep the observed people from knowing that they are being observed. As was mentioned earlier, this is designed to reduce the potential bias that could be introduced by the observation process itself. Of course, that isn't always possible, and the qualitative researcher may, as indicated previously, do interviews or gather data *obtrusively*, or in ways that may be known to the subjects in the research.

Sometimes the researcher may act as a *participant observer*, actually participating and socially interacting with research subjects in the setting normally occupied by the subjects. During these interactions, the participant observer tries to gather data in a systematic and unobtrusive way. The researcher keeps notes in as detailed a fashion as possible, frequently writing observations from memory between observation periods to keep the observation unobtrusive yet accurate.

Several of the other research approaches described in this chapter might be entirely, or at least partially, qualitative in nature. Case studies, field studies, historical or archival research, descriptive research, and naturalistic observation could result fully or partially in verbal descriptions based on qualitative data. Case studies on psychiatric patients, observation of animals in the wild, and research done on historical documents are, for example, heavily or entirely qualitative. Developmental and survey research, as well as evaluation studies (to be described in the next section), may have significant qualitative components. One thing you might keep in mind is that conclusions drawn in research that has both qualitative and quantitative components should refer to the data-gathering technique, numerical or descriptive, from which they were derived.

In this book our focus is admittedly on quantitative methods, since a substantial percentage of educational research is measurement based. Recent interest in qualitative methods has, however, been growing, and a fairly lively debate has been going on between advocates of each of the two perspectives. There are several works available that describe qualitative methods in great detail (see, for example, Agar, 1980; Taylor & Bogdan, 1984). It is expected that the debate will continue, and qualitative methodology will develop further as interest in its methods persists.

EVALUATION STUDIES

Evaluation studies do not represent an approach to research in the same sense as do the other research approaches thus far discussed. In fact, although most evaluation studies tend to use some of the strategies described previously, the purpose of evaluation studies is quite different. All the types of research discussed so far are designed to produce a result that in some way provides new information. The new knowledge produced may support (or contradict) a hypothesis deduced from a theory (thus enhancing scientific explanatory and predictive power), or it may be applied in real-life settings. In either case—whether pure or applied research—it is desirable for the research to possess high levels of internal validity (whenever at least one IV is manipulated) and external validity (except, of course, in the case of action research).

The purpose of evaluation studies is to provide information about whether a program or service is in fact being conducted as it should be, and whether progress toward the program or service objectives is being made. The results of the evaluation are designed to be used by program directors in making decisions about the worth of the program in terms of how the program is delivered and what the program does for those for whom it is being conducted. The results may be used to manage and adjust the delivery of services.

In short, whereas research studies are designed to *prove* that a particular relationship (often of the cause-and-effect type) exists between an IV and a DV, evaluation studies are designed to *improve* the delivery of services both in terms of *how* the service is delivered (the program delivery process) and *what* the service delivers (the result or product delivered). The accomplishment of the goal of improving programs may require the application of several research approaches, including rigorous experimental studies designed to identify cause-and-effect relationships. This is always done from the standpoint of whether the results produced will be useful from a program decision-making point of view.

Think about how you would go about developing a program to serve a particular purpose or set of purposes, say, for example, the development of study skills among eighth-grade children. From this basic purpose you would need to derive or develop a list of objectives for the program. You might want students to avoid procrastination and turn in neatly done homework on time, study every day rather than only before tests, plan work carefully, plan study time at specific hours of the day, and so on. Of course, improved classroom performance is also an important goal. Each goal should be defined carefully and in measurable or observable terms. Once the goals have been clearly defined, the means for attaining the goals—the program—is developed. The program plan includes a description of who delivers the service, the procedures, materials, and activities that will be used, the schedule of service delivery, and so on. Once these goals and strategies are developed, the next step is implementation, that is, running the program. Now it's time for the program evaluation to begin, but keep in mind that the evaluation should be planned just as carefully as the program itself. The evaluation should not be a mere afterthought.

Formative or *process evaluation* involves two possible elements, both having to do with events that occur as the program is being delivered to the students. One of these involves making observations of the delivery process itself. This is the evaluation of program implementation, and its purpose is to determine whether the program plan is being carried out as planned. For example, are the procedures and activities being used in the program the same as they were in the program plan? If so, the delivery is being carried out as planned; if not, adjustments in the running of the program may need to be done.

The second element of process evaluation requires monitoring student progress as the program is being implemented. This is the evaluation of progress, and the goal here is to determine the degree to which the students' behavior actually changes in the direction that is consistent with the program's objectives. For example, one question might be whether or not the students in the program are improving in submitting their homework assignments neatly and on time. If so, they are progressing toward those program goals. The purpose of the evaluation at this stage is to provide information that can be used by the program administrator to make changes in the program that will improve both delivery and progress. This might involve both examining the program materials as well as changing the timing, especially if some goals are achieved more quickly (or more slowly) than originally estimated. Such formative evaluation, whether of program implementation or of progress, is particularly important in the development of new programs (as the program is being formed) but may, of course, also be done with ongoing, established programs.

Although data are likely to be gathered along the way, *summative* or *product evaluation* is conducted after a program has been developed and completed. At this point the question asked in the evaluation process is whether the program objectives have really been met. This could be called *outcome evaluation* and might include a comparison of the students' current behavior with their behavior before the program was implemented. This, of course, is a form of before-after study, in which the IV is the training provided by the program. There are obviously many threats to internal validity in these studies, including maturation, testing, selection, and expectancy. These threats can sometimes be dealt with by using comparison groups, random assignment, or other research controls. Evaluation studies often contain descriptions of program strengths and weaknesses and recommendations for future changes. It should be noted that changes made in a program as a result of the formative process might easily threaten the summative evaluation because the final results are a product of the *entire* program, including the parts of the program conducted both before and after any changes.

Some evaluation studies are considerable in scope. For example, most colleges and universities, and many public and private secondary schools, are accredited by a regional agency. The agency grants accreditation for specific periods of time (such as a ten-year accreditation) only after a large-scale evaluation has been conducted. Virtually all the components of the colleges are examined, including course offerings, student competencies, dormitory policies, student activities, financial-aid services, library collections, classroom facilities, and faculty credentials. The college first prepares an extensive document (the "self-study") that contains information about the mission that the institution serves and the goals it attempts to accomplish. A team of experts assembled by the accreditation agency then visits the campus, pokes into every nook and cranny, examines each educational area, interviews administrators, faculty, staff, and students, and compares their observations and findings with the goals described in the self-study prepared by the institution. The visiting team then assembles an evaluation report that contains a set of conclusions about the college and whether it should be granted accreditation. The evaluation reports also contains a description of strengths and weaknesses that have been observed and usually includes recommendations for change and improvement. Such evaluation projects are, indeed, extensive, even for small colleges, but they are especially complicated for universities with hundreds of programs, several thousand employees, and twenty or thirty thousand undergraduate and graduate students.

THE USE OF MULTIPLE RESPONSE MEASURES

Thus far we have tended to describe research in which there is only one DV, but nothing prevents the researcher from being interested in the effects of one IV (or several IVs, as in factorial studies) on two, three, or fifty-one different DVs. Studies that use multiple response measures (more than one DV) are useful because a number of IV-DV relationships can be established within the framework of a single study. The use of multiple response measures has become quite common in educational research, perhaps even more common than single DV studies, especially when research is conducted in real-life educational settings. The reason for this is, of course, that many of the IVs manipulated by researchers can have effects on a whole host of behavioral variables. Post-facto research, case studies, surveys, and evaluation research may all use several DVs.

A researcher might, for example, be interested in the effects of computer assisted instruction (CAI) on achievement in arithmetic. Students would be randomly assigned to either a group that would be taught in a traditional way or a group that would receive CAI. In this experiment the researcher would be interested in achievement, but achievement in arithmetic might be operationally defined in many ways. Those measures could include achievement in addition, subtraction, multiplication, division, and the solving of word problems. The research worker might select only one of these as a DV, but several of them could also be measured. It is possible that the IV could affect some of the DVs but not all of them. In this example, it is possible that CAI might produce gains in number skills, yet not show any effect on word problems. Depending on the IV and the combination of DVs measured, almost any combination of differences might be possible.

From the standpoint of statistics, studies with more than one DV (often called *multivariate studies*) are more complicated to analyze than studies that have only one DV. However, with computer statistical programs these analyses can now be performed in only a few seconds. Despite the power and elegance of these programs, however, it still takes a trained researcher to interpret these analyses. Some of the types of multivariate statistics will be briefly described in Chapter 5 and discussed further in Chapter 11.

INTERNAL AND EXTERNAL VALIDITY RECONSIDERED

In the previous chapter and in this one, we've discussed a wide variety of strategies, methods, and designs that might be used in conducting educational research. The concepts of internal and external validity have been referred to again and again, and that is as it should be, since research results are of real value only if the effects of a manipulated IV are clear and can be generalized to a variety of circumstances. Some types of research (experimental) offer better opportunities for high internal validity than others (quasi-experimental). Other approaches offer no internal validity at all (post-facto or archival research, for example), since an IV is not manipulated. External validity also varies with the type of research, and in some instances (such as action research) may not even be relevant.

It is important to recognize that good internal validity and external validity are difficult to obtain in the same research study. Usually, high internal validity can only be achieved in controlled situations, such as in laboratories, but under these circumstances high levels of external validity become more difficult to obtain. Conversely, studies conducted in the most natural settings usually lack the opportunity for the control necessary for high internal validity. Compromises or trade-offs must be arrived at in making research decisions. The compromises made are usually a result of a variety of practical considerations in doing the project, but every compromise must be carefully considered when interpreting the results of the research.

More about the decision-making process will be presented in Chapter 6 under the heading Decisions, Decisions, but consider, for example, the following hypothesis: smaller class sizes will result in greater achievement by students. The decisions that have to be made begin with IV and DV specifications. What size classes will be compared, five students versus fifteen students, or perhaps ten students versus twenty-eight students? What measure of achievement will be used, teacher-made tests or published standardized tests? Beyond these specifications, the students' grade levels) must be chosen. These decisions are influenced by still other considerations, including the availability of a sample or samples of students that can be randomly assigned to classes of the chosen sizes. If randomization is not possible, a compromise might be to work with two intact classes that are already of different sizes, or better still, to set the class sizes but not the assignment of students to them. Each decision may influence either the internal validity or the external validity of the study, or both.

The issue of internal validity versus external validity is particularly important in educational research. One important goal of educational research is, after all, to be able to generalize the results of research to applied settings. Highly controlled laboratory research may result in clear and unequivocal (internally valid) conclusions about the influence of an IV on a DV, but great caution might have to be taken in generalizing the results to other IV levels, dependent measures, subjects, and settings. On the other hand, a strong design may be compromised by conducting research in school settings in which control is limited. In this case conclusions may be equivocal but may be more applicable to children in real classrooms.

A laboratory study of class size and achievement might be conducted with college students randomly assigned to different classes of fifteen or two hundred students each, with curriculum, classroom, instructor, time, and other variables tightly controlled. Under these carefully controlled conditions, the unequivocal conclusion might be that smaller classes result in higher achievement. Does that conclusion apply to second graders in classes of sixteen or twenty-five who are studying spelling in a public school? Maybe, but such a generalization is probably unwarranted. An in-school study using nonrandomized groups of sixteen or twenty-five students in different classrooms with different teachers might result in higher achievement for the students in the smaller classes, but the result would be equivocal because of the potential for confounding. Still, the result was obtained in a setting similar to those in which the results would be applied, and that lends credibility to the usefulness of the result in similar classrooms.

Meta-analysis

When a hypothesis is of sufficient importance, many research studies may be done that all address the same problem. These systematic replications may be done with different treatment levels, dependent measures, and subjects, and in different settings. When this happens, a *research review* is often conducted. In this review the researcher attempts to obtain a large number of studies related to the same subject and then summarize and integrate their results and conclusions.

Assume, for example, that ten studies have been done on the class size and achievement problem. The reviewer would obtain the ten studies, carefully read and digest the results and conclusions, and write a review that attempts to summarize the results. The ten studies might use different research designs, subjects, settings, treatment levels, and dependent measures. If the conclusion of all ten studies was that smaller classes produced better achievement, there would be a strong argument for smaller class sizes. This strong argument would be based on the ability to generalize the results of all ten of these studies. The idea is that if the phenomenon occurs consistently in a variety of settings, it probably generalizes to all settings. This obviously speaks to the issue of external validity. Even though each of the individual studies might not have particularly good external validity, the *group* of studies taken together do have a form of external validity in that they consistently produce the same result.

Unfortunately, research reviews have rarely provided results as unequivocal as the foregoing example might imply. Several reviewers may look at the same body of research on the same topic but come to different conclusions. This happens for a variety of reasons. First, of course, is that all studies rarely agree completely. In addition, reviewers may be biased in favor of one conclusion over another. Teachers, for example, might be biased in favor of small classes; but administrators, in favor of larger classes. Reviewers might differ in their theoretical orientations on some issues. Reviewers might experience "cognitive overload" and be unable to keep all the facts and information in their heads at once, particularly if the number of studies is large. Finally, the overemphasis or underemphasis of particular studies would result in different conclusions.

Some reviewers have used a vote-taking approach, in which the number of pros, no differences, and cons are tallied and compared. Thirty studies of class size and achievement might result in twenty-one pro votes (smaller classes better), six no-difference votes, and three con votes (larger classes better). The pro votes "win," but at least two issues emerge. First is the issue of whether the no-difference and con votes occurred in research circumstances that had elements different from the pro votes (all the con studies might have been conducted in college classrooms, for example). Second is the question of how much the results tell us about the *amount of the effect* produced by smaller classes.

One relatively new approach to the research review is called *meta-analysis*. Meta-analysis involves a statistical summarizing or integration of the results of a number of studies on the same topic. The most important result of conducting a meta-analysis is a statistic called the *effect size,* sometimes symbolized as d. A d of 0 indicates no effect of the IV on the DV. A positive value for d indicates an effect in favor of the hypothesis. A positive d for class size and achievement means that smaller classes improve achievement, and the size of d indicates the strength of the effect that smaller classes have. A d of 0.2 is considered a small effect, 0.5 is considered a moderate effect, and 0.8 is considered large. A negative d indicates an effect that is the opposite of that hypothesized.

The very topic we have used as an example in this section—class size and achievement—has been subjected to a meta-analysis (Glass & Smith, 1979). Reviewers had often looked at the voluminous literature on class size and achievement, but no clear consensus ever emerged. Many educational psychology books simply stated that a clear answer to the question had just not yet been found. Glass and Smith statistically integrated the results of more than seventy-five studies, and a clear relationship between class size and achievement did emerge. Smaller classes result in better achievement, with the size of d a function of the size difference between classes. A reduction in size from twenty-five to twenty students results in a small d, but a reduction from twenty-five to only one results in a large d.

Many meta-analyses have been conducted on educational literature since the late 1970s. These include such topics as the effects of ability grouping of classes on achievement, the effects of class size on teacher and student attitudes, the effects of the mainstreaming of handicapped students on achievement, the effects of retention in grade on both achievement and self-esteem, and the relationship of socioeconomic status to achievement. Meta-analytic methods have not been without critics (more about this in Chapter 11). Most researchers and reviewers agree, however, that the statistical integration of research results can be a useful indicator of experimental reliability and the degree to which research results may be generalized.

SUMMARY

After lengthy discussion in the previous chapter of the two most common approaches to research—experiments and post-facto research—this chapter has presented a number of other types of research that are commonly found in the educational literature. Variations of experimental and post-facto designs include factorial approaches, in which the design involves more than one IV. Factorial designs are often used, and powerful statistical analyses are available for examining each IV as well as the interactions or combined effects of the IVs.

Several approaches to research can be used when a study involves a small number of subjects or even a single subject. These rigorously controlled experiments are convenient, timesaving, and inexpensive ways to do research on a topic. ABA, ABAB and other reversal designs, as well as case studies and other approaches, result in in-depth analyses of behavior.

Research is also done for a variety of special purposes. Survey research is used to gather information from any defined group about their behavior, attitudes, opinions, beliefs, or other psychological or sociological characteristics. Developmental research is used to examine changes in the subjects that occur over time. Historical researchers examine past documents or archival material to draw conclusions about past trends or circumstances. Studies involving an examination of behavior in natural settings are called naturalistic observation, and descriptive research is used to gather descriptive information about a sample or a population. Action research involves doing studies in the school setting in which the results will be applied.

Most, if not all, educators will at some point in their careers be a part of an evaluation study. These research projects are designed to provide formative or summative information useful in conducting in-school programs or in examining the effects of a program so that it can be improved.

Reviews of research, and particularly meta-analysis of bodies of research, speak clearly to the issues of experimental reliability and external validity. If all the studies on a topic come to the same conclusions, the IV-DV relationship is a reliable one. The research projects were probably conducted in a variety of settings, with a number of different types of subjects, and at various times, and consistent results under these circumstances indicate not only the reliability of the phenomenon but that it has external validity as well.

KEY TERMS

ABA design	Mixed design
Action research	Multiple-baseline design
Archival research	Multivariate study
Baseline	Naturalistic observation
Case study	Nonreversal design
Cross-sectional approach	Outcome evaluation
Descriptive research	Participant observer
Developmental research	Post-facto factorial design
Duration	Process evaluation
Effect size	Product evaluation
Ethnography	Product measure
Evaluation study	Qualitative research
Factorial design	Quantitative research
Field study	Research review
Formative evaluation	Reversal design
Frequency	Single-subject design
Fully repeated measures design	Small-N research
Historical research	Solomon four-group design
Interaction	Split-plot design
Longitudinal approach	Summative evaluation
Main effect	Survey research
Meta-analysis	Time sampling

REFERENCES

AGAR, M. H. (1980). *The professional stranger: An informal introduction to ethnography*. Homewood, Ill.: Irwin, Dorsey.

GLASS, G. V., & SMITH, M. L. (1979). Meta-analysis of research on the relationship of class-size and achievement. *Educational Evaluation & Policy Analysis, 1*, 2–16.

KINSEY, A. C., POMEROY, W. B., & MARTIN, C. E. (1948). *Sexual behavior in the human male*. Philadelphia: W. B. Saunders.

KINSEY, A. C., POMEROY, W. B., MARTIN, C. E., & GEBHARD, P. H. (1953). *Sexual behavior in the human female*. Philadelphia: W. B. Saunders.

SCHREIBER, F. (1974). *Sybil*. New York: Warner.

SPAFFORD, C. S. (1987). WISC-R pattern categorization—persiflage or predictor? An examination of the usefulness of verbal-performance discrepancies and the Digit Span subtest as assessment tools in differential diagnosis of 9–12 year old dyslexics. *Dissertation Abstracts International, 46a*.

TAYLOR, S. J., & BOGDAN, R. (1984). *Introduction to qualitative research methods.* New York: John Wiley & Sons.

TERMAN, L. M. (1925). *Mental and physical traits of a thousand gifted children.* Vol. 1 of *Genetic studies of genius.* Stanford, Calif.: Stanford University Press.

TERMAN, L. M., & ODEN, M. H. (1947). *The gifted child grows up: Twenty-five years' follow-up of a supe-*

rior group. Vol. 4 of *Genetic studies of genius.* Stanford, Calif.: Stanford University Press.

TERMAN, L. M., & ODEN, M. H. (1959). *The gifted group at mid-life.* Vol. 5 of *Genetic studies of genius.* Stanford, Calif.: Stanford University Press.

WARNER, W. L., LOW, J. O., LUNT, P. S., & SROLE, L. (1963). *Yankee city.* New Haven: Yale University Press.

CHAPTER 5

Statistical Thinking

DESCRIPTIVE STATISTICS

Measures of Central Tendency
Measures of Variability
Measures of Relationship (Correlation)
Graphs and Tables
Skewness
Kurtosis
Transformed Scores

INFERENTIAL STATISTICS

Inferential Statistics and Standard
  Deviation
The Null Hypothesis: Ho
The Alternative Hypothesis: Ha
Alpha Error: Type-1 Error
Beta Error: Type-2 Error

Significance
The Two Basic Research Hypotheses
Scales of Measurement

THE MAJOR STATISTICAL TESTS

Statistical Tests and Power
Interval-Ratio (Parametric) Tests of
  Difference
Interval-Ratio Tests of Association
Nonparametric Statistical Tests
The Importance of Methodology

SUMMARY

KEY TERMS

REFERENCES

Although this book is about methodology, some discussion of statistical analysis is absolutely essential to an understanding of the various research strategies. Without any mention of the major statistical techniques, methodology alone too often becomes a sort of sterile philosophical inquiry—interesting to read about but difficult to nail down. In this chapter we are not going to outline all the calculations involved in producing solutions to the various statistical tests (the assumption is that you already have a statistics book), but we are going to point out when, and under what conditions, a given test is most appropriate. In this chapter the focus will be on *when to do a particular test*.

Before beginning our discussion of specific statistical tests, we must first look at some of the underpinnings of statistical analysis, some of the assumptions and concepts that drive the statistical engine. In general terms, statistical methods can be categorized under two major headings, descriptive and inferential.

DESCRIPTIVE STATISTICS

Descriptive statistics involve those techniques used for literally *describing* the characteristics of a given set or sets of scores. (The term may also be used to designate the measures used for such descriptions.) Descriptive statistics typically include the following:

1. measures of central tendency
2. measures of variability
3. measures of relationships
4. graphs and tables used to display the various measures of group characteristics

5. measures of skewness
6. measures of kurtosis
7. transformed scores, such as percentiles, stanines, and z- and T-scores

Measures of Central Tendency

The three major measures of *central tendency*—mean, median, and mode—are all used generally to describe the average or typical performance among a group of scores. The measures of central tendency are designed to allow the researcher to quickly identify the focal point around which the sample scores are distributed.

The most popular of these is the *mean,* or the arithmetic average. The mean is found simply by adding all the scores and dividing by the number of cases, as illustrated in Table 5.1. If the scores in the distribution are fairly evenly balanced, or not skewed (a term we will look at in a moment), the mean is an appropriate and accurate measure of centrality.

The *median* is the midpoint of any ordered set of scores, that is, the point below which half the scores fall and above which the other half fall. If there aren't too many scores (with a large data base you should use a computer), the median is easily arrived at by first arranging the scores from highest to lowest and then counting down until the halfway point is reached. (If there doesn't happen to be an actual score at that point, simply interpolate between the two midmost scores, as in Table 5.2, in which the median is 9.50.)

Notice that had we eliminated the score of 4, there would only have been 7 scores, with 6 as the lowest, and the median would then have been equal to 10. For reasons that will become apparent, the median becomes the appropriate measure of central tendency when the set of scores is not evenly distributed.

The *mode* is defined as the most frequently occurring score, and can usually be quickly spotted by simply eyeballing the data set. In the previous example the

Table 5.1   Calculating the Mean

X
12
11
10
10
9
8
6
4

$\Sigma X = 70$

The mean, or $\bar{X}$, equals the sum of Xs divided by N (the number of scores):

$$\bar{X} = \frac{\Sigma X}{N} = \frac{70}{8} = 8.75$$

Table 5.2 Finding the Median

X
12
11
10
10
Mdn = 9.50
9
8
6
4

mode, of course, is 10. Distributions may have one mode (*unimodal*), two modes (*bimodal*), or several modes (*multimodal*). When a distribution has more than one mode, the suspicion arises that perhaps the group under study is really composed of several subgroups. A sample of men and women, for example, might produce two modes if the groups were being measured on some variable that typically shows a gender difference, such as weight.

Measures of Variability

Just as data sets can differ with regard to centrality, so too can they differ with respect to *variability*. Variability accounts for the degree to which the scores cluster together in the distribution, usually around the mean. The less the variability, the more homogeneous the scores, and the greater the variability, the more heterogeneous the scores. A quick look at the following two distributions in Table 5.3 makes this point clear.

Although the two distributions X_1 and X_2 have identical means, the amount of variability displayed differs markedly. Distribution X_2, with most of its scores clustering tightly around the center, is far more homogeneous than is X_1.

Table 5.3 Distributions with Differing Variability

X_1	X_2
25	17
20	16
19	15
17	14
15	14
15	14
13	14
11	13
3	12
2	11
$\Sigma X_1 = 140$	$\Sigma X_2 = 140$

The three most common measures of variability are range, standard deviation, and variance.

The *range* (R) is the measure of the entire width of the distribution and is equal to the highest score minus the lowest score. Distribution X_1 has a range of $25 - 2 = 23$, which shows more variability than the range in distribution X_2, which is only $17 - 11 = 6$. Although the range is certainly quick and easy to calculate, it does have a major drawback: it is based on only two scores. The standard deviation, on the other hand, is a measure of variability that takes every score into account and thus provides an overall measure of how far all the scores vary from the mean. The simplest equation for obtaining the true standard deviation *as a purely descriptive measure* is

$$SD = \sqrt{\frac{\Sigma X^2}{N} - \bar{X}^2}$$

Table 5.4 shows the calculation of the true standard deviation for distribution X_1.

$$SD = \sqrt{\frac{2428}{10} - 14^2} = \sqrt{242.80 - 196} = \sqrt{46.80} = 6.84$$

The reader may wish to calculate the standard deviation of distribution X_2 (which should yield the far smaller value of 1.67). Later in the chapter we will show a slightly different version of the standard deviation, a version that is used when trying to estimate the population standard deviation on the basis of a set of sample scores.

The final measure of variability is called the *variance* and is equal to SD^2. The variance in distribution X_1 is equal to 46.80; and for distribution X_2, 2.80. Since variance and standard deviation are so closely related ($V = SD^2$, $SD = \sqrt{V}$) variance, like standard deviation, also measures how far all the scores deviate from the mean.

Table 5.4 Calculating the Standard Deviation

X_1	X_1^2
25	625
20	400
19	361
17	289
15	225
15	225
13	169
11	121
3	9
2	4
140	2428

VS Hixson

"Nothing correlates with anything. That'll be $4,000."

Measures of Relationship (Correlation)

Relationships, or correlations, indicate the degree to which two or more variables might be associated. A positive correlation, as in height and weight distributions, would tell us that taller people tend to be heavier and also that shorter people tend to be lighter. A negative correlation (or inverse relationship), as in grade-point average and number-of-absences distributions, would indicate that people with high GPAs tend to have fewer absences, whereas those with lower GPAs have higher levels of absence. Although, as will be shown later, correlational techniques may also be used to infer population characteristics, they are also, as shown here, perfectly valid descriptive measures of the particular group under study. Correlation values range from +1.00 (a perfect positive relationship) to −1.00 (a perfect negative relationship). Correlation values of zero indicate a complete lack of any relationship between the variables, or that the variables are independent of each other.

Graphs and Tables

Data can be described very effectively through the use of graphs and tables. In statistical analysis, the picture can often be well worth the proverbial thousand words. Tables are usually set up as summary statements and provide a visual recap of what the data are showing. In comparing two sample groups, A and B, with respect to performance on the verbal section of the Scholastic Aptitude Test, group A having been coached, the tabled values might look like those in Table 5.5:

Table 5.5   Breakdown Values

GROUP A (COACHED)	GROUP B (NOT COACHED)
$N = 420$	$N = 434$
$\bar{X} = 490.05$	$\bar{X} = 470.86$
$SD = 87.01$	$SD = 84.99$
$R = 522$	$R = 510$

* $R = Range$

The table immediately informs us that the coached group did perform at a somewhat higher level, and further, that both groups are displaying similar amounts of variability and were of similar size.

Tables may also be set up within tables to show various breakdowns of the data. Returning to the SAT example, we might like to make comparisons within the two groups, say, on the basis of whether or not the students in the samples were taking a college prep program.

Table 5.6   Complex Breakdown Values

GROUP A (COACHED)		GROUP B (NOT COACHED)	
$N = 420$		$N = 434$	
$\bar{X} = 490.05$		$\bar{X} = 470.86$	
$SD = 87.01$		$SD = 84.99$	
$R = 522$		$R = 510$	
COLLEGE PREP	NOT COLLEGE PREP	COLLEGE PREP	NOT COLLEGE PREP
$N = 210$	$N = 210$	$N = 217$	$N = 217$
$\bar{X} = 495.10$	$\bar{X} = 485.00$	$\bar{X} = 476.00$	$\bar{X} = 465.72$
$SD = 86.99$	$SD = 87.03$	$SD = 85.01$	$SD = 84.97$
$R = 522$	$R = 522$	$R = 510$	$R = 510$

This breakdown in Table 5.6 now tells us that the college-prep students scored higher than the non-college-prep students, and further, that the coaching apparently produced a difference among both the college-prep and non-college prep groups.

When graphing data, the two most popular approaches involve the *frequency histogram* and the *frequency polygon*. Before using either of these, however, you must first list all the scores and then indicate how many (frequency) of the subjects in the study received each score. Assume that the values in Table 5.7 came from a group of first graders being evaluated on the arithmetic subtest of the WISC-R.

Table 5.7 Frequency Distribution
              of Math Scores

SCORE (X)	FREQUENCY OF X (f)
15	1
14	0
13	4
12	11
11	16
10	20
9	15
8	12
7	5
6	1
5	1

Total N = 86 students

Place all the scores on the x-axis (horizontal; abscissa) at equal intervals, and run the scores from the lowest on the left to the highest on the right. Then indicate all the frequencies on the y-axis (vertical; ordinate), again using equal intervals and beginning with zero.

For the histogram, place a rectangular bar over each score up to the point where the score intersects the frequency. The resulting series of adjacent bars represents the histogram as shown in Figure 5.1.

For the frequency polygon, place a dot over each score, again at the point where the score intersects the frequency. Then, connect all the dots with a series of straight lines as in Figure 5.2.

Figure 5.1 Histogram of math scores

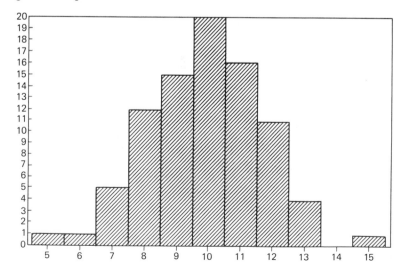

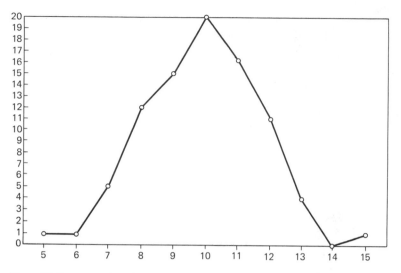

Figure 5.2 Frequency polygon for math scores

As we shall soon see, these graphs can be invaluable in providing a visual description of the shape of any distribution, and on the basis of that, aid in determining which measure of central tendency, or even which inferential test, might be most appropriate.

Another method for displaying histograms that has become increasingly popular, especially among statistical computer programs, is to express the frequencies horizontally rather than vertically, with each asterisk representing an individual score. (See Figure 5.3)

Finally, a very economical way of graphing data, called the *stem-and-leaf display*, presents only the first digit in the stem column, while in the leaf column we find the trailing digits. For example, if we were to graph the scores on a certain reading test, which range from a low score of 60 to a high score of 95, the

Score	Frequency
15	*
14	
13	****
12	**********
11	****************
10	*********************
9	***************
8	************
7	*****
6	*
5	*

Figure 5.3 Horizontal histogram

stem column would present the digits 6 through 9, with the 6 representing scores in the sixties, and so on. The leaf column would then include the trailing digit, so that a 0 next to the 6 would indicate a score of 60, the 3 a score of 63 and the 5 a score of 65.

Table 5.8 Stem and Leaf Display

STEM	LEAF
6	035
7	13578
8	04455569
9	00145

Note that in Table 5.8, most of the scores were in the eighties and were specifically 80, 84, 84, 85, 85, 85, 86, and 89.

Skewness

Skewness describes the extent to which a unimodal distribution of scores deviates from symmetry. In Figure 5.4, a positively skewed distribution (Sk+) shows the long tail pointed to the right and indicates that there are a few extremely high scores even though the majority of scores are fairly closely bunched together at the other end. A negatively skewed distribution (Sk−) shows the long tail pointing to the left and indicates that there are a few extremely low scores.

As we will discover later in the chapter, skewed distributions violate the assumptions of normality and usually should not be subjected to parametric statistical analysis. Also, with skewed distributions the median, not the mean, becomes the best measure of central tendency. Notice that with the positively skewed distribution, the mean lies to the right of the median, causing the mean to give an inflated picture of centrality. This situation, of course, is reversed with a negative skew, causing the mean in this case to understate where the typical scores are clustering.

A quick, but somewhat rough, estimate of skewness can be obtained by comparing the mean with the median for a given distribution. When the mean is higher than the median (lies to the right of the median), the skew is positive; when the mean is lower than the median (falls to the left of the median), the skew is negative. (For a technique to evaluate skewness as a single value, see Sprinthall, 1990.)

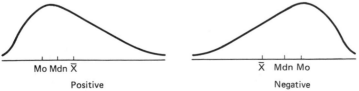

Mo Mdn X̄   X̄ Mdn Mo

Positive   Negative   **Figure 5.4** Skewed curves

EXAMPLE: A given distribution of test scores shows a mean of 50, a mode of 45, and a median of 47. The distribution is skewed to the right, since the mean of 50 is higher than the median of 47.

Kurtosis

Kurtosis is a term that describes the amount of variability shown in the graph of a unimodal distribution. When there is little variability, the graph shows a *leptokurtic* shape, and when there is a high degree of variability, the graph is *platykurtic*, as seen in Figure 5.5.

When kurtosis takes on a standard value, which as we shall see is the case with a normal distribution, the graph is said to be *mesokurtic*. A quick method of assessing kurtosis is to divide the range by the constant value, 6, and compare this value with the standard deviation. If the two values correspond, the curve may be mesokurtic. If the standard deviation is smaller than $R/6$, the distribution's graph is leptokurtic; and if the standard deviation is larger than $R/6$, the curve is platykurtic. (To evaluate kurtosis as a standard value, see Sprinthall 1990.)

EXAMPLE: A distribution of IQ scores has a mean of 100, a range of 90, and a standard deviation of 10. Since $R/6$ (90/6) yields the standard value of 15, the standard deviation of only 10 (which is, of course, less than 15) shows the curve to be leptokurtic.

When doing inferential tests on the possible significance of the difference between sample means, it is well to check whether all the sample distributions have a similar degree of kurtosis.

Transformed Scores

Transformed scores are typically used to identify an individual's performance with reference to the entire group being tested. Someone getting a score of 90 on a history test may feel extremely proud until being told that the average score on

Figure 5.5 Graphs of differing variability. The graph on the left is platykurtic; the one on the right is leptokurtic.

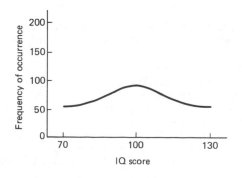
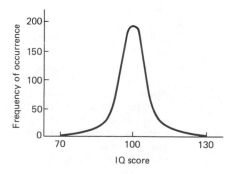

Table 5.9 Percentiles, Deciles, and Quartiles

Percentiles	0	10	20	30	40	50	60	70	80	90	100
Deciles		D_1	D_2	D_3	D_4	D_5	D_6	D_7	D_8	D_9	
Quartiles				Q_1			Q_2			Q_3	

that test was 150. Therefore, raw scores, those not yet transformed, often convey little, if any, information about relative performance. The easiest transformation to understand, and one of the most informative, is called the *percentile*. The percentile defines the percentage of cases scoring at or below the given raw score. That aforementioned history score of 90 may only be at the second percentile (meaning that only 2 percent of the group were at or below that score, and that 98 percent were above it). Remember, however, that percentiles refer to the percentage of cases, *not the number of cases*. (The only time those values will agree is when the entire group happens to be composed of exactly 100 persons.)

Other variations on the percentile theme include *deciles*, each worth ten percentile units, and *quartiles*, each worth twenty-five percentile units. Table 5.9 illustrates the comparison, where D_1 = the first decile and Q_1 = the first quartile.

Before looking at three other important transformations—z, T, and stanines—we must spend a little time reviewing the highlights of the normal distribution curve. (See Figure 5.6)

The *normal curve* is of extreme importance in the field of education, since so many measures of human characteristics approximate this general shape. In fact, most measures of students—physical, psychological, and educational—form normal distributions if the sizes of the groups being measured are large enough.

The normal curve is a unimodal frequency distribution curve with scores plotted on the x-axis and frequency of occurrence on the y-axis. However, it does have at least five key features that set it apart from other frequency distribution curves:

1. In a normal curve most of the scores cluster around the middle of the distribution (where the curve is at its highest). As the distance from the middle increases, in either direction, there are fewer and fewer scores (the curve drops down and levels out on both sides).
2. The normal curve is symmetrical. Its two halves are identical mirror images of one another, making it perfectly balanced.
3. In a normal curve all three measures of central tendency, the mean, the median and the mode, fall at precisely the same point, the exact center or midpoint of the distribution.
4. The area under the normal curve has a constant relationship with the standard deviation. When the abscissa of the curve is marked off in units of standard deviations, a series of constant percentage areas under the curve are formed. This relationship holds true for all normal curves, meaning that if a certain percentage of scores is found between one and two standard deviation units above the mean, the same percentage is always found in that specific area of any normal curve. Also, because of the symmetry of the curve, that exact percentage is always found in the same part of the lower half of the curve, that is, between one and two standard

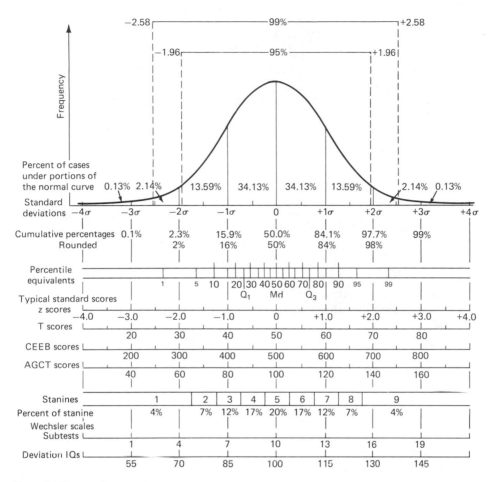

Figure 5.6 The normal curve

deviation units below the mean. This constancy of the percentage area under the curve is crucial to your understanding of the curve. Once the curve is plotted according to standard-deviation units, it is called the *standard normal curve* (see Figure 5.6).

5. The normal curve is asymptotic to the abscissa. No matter how far out the tails are extended, they will never touch the x-axis.

The standard normal curve has a mean of 0 and a standard deviation of 1.00. The standard deviation units have been marked off in unit lengths of 1.00 on the abscissa, and the area under the curve above these units always remains the same. Further, the area under the curve between the mean and a point that is one standard deviation unit above the mean always includes 34.13 percent of the cases. Because of the symmetry of the curve, 34.13 percent of the cases also fall in the area under the curve between the mean and a point one standard deviation unit below the mean. Thus, under the standard normal curve, between two points each located one standard-deviation unit away from the mean, there are always 68.26 percent of the cases.

As we go farther away from the mean, between one and two standard-deviation units, another 13.59 percent of the distribution falls on either side. Even though we have gone another full standard deviation away from the mean, only 13.59 percent of the cases are being added. This is because as we go farther from the mean the height of the curve, reflecting frequency, is getting even lower. Between the mean and a point two full standard-deviation units away from the mean, a total of 47.72 percent (34.13 + 13.59) of the cases will be found. Also, between points that are two standard deviations below the mean and two standard deviations above the mean, there will be 95.44 percent of the cases (twice 47.72).

Finally, the area under the curve between two and three standard-deviation units away from the mean only holds 2.15 percent of the cases on each side. There are, then, 49.87 percent (47.72 + 2.15) of the cases between the mean and a point three standard-deviation units away from the mean. And between points that are both three-standard deviation units away from the mean, 99.74 percent (virtually the entire distribution) of the cases can be found. Since almost the entire distribution of scores falls between three standard deviations below the mean and three standard deviations above the mean, we must expect that each standard-deviation unit as marked off on the abscissa will be equal to roughly one sixth of the range. It is for this reason that we earlier suggested that when a distribution is mesokurtic (normal), its standard deviation will approximate the value of $R/6$.

z Scores

The z distribution is a normally distributed set of scaled scores whose mean is always equal to zero and whose standard deviation must equal 1.00. Knowing the value of a particular *z score* allows us to know exactly what percentage of the cases fall below it (percentile), and also gives us a reference for gaining an understanding of an individual's relative performance compared with the performance of the entire group being measured. Also, we can compare an individual's relative performance on two separate normally distributed sets of scores.

For example, if a student were to get a score of 72 on a certain math test and 64 on an English test, you wouldn't know on which test the performance level was higher. The mean on the math test might have been 85, and the mean on the English test might have been 50, in which case the performance on the English test was higher, even though the raw score was lower. The point is that information about the distribution of scores must be obtained to compare and interpret raw scores. For this reason, z scores are especially meaningful, since they take the entire distribution into account. If a set of raw scores are known to be normally distributed, any specific raw score can easily be transformed into a z score.

$$z = \frac{X - \bar{X}}{SD}$$

EXAMPLE: It is known that the distribution of individual IQ scores is normally distributed around a mean of 100, with a standard deviation of 15. A certain individual has an IQ of 130. What is that person's z score?

$$z = \frac{130 - 100}{15}$$

$$z = 2.00$$

From our previous discussion, we now know that a z-score of 2.00 (two standard deviation units above the mean) must be at a point below which 97.72 percent of the entire distribution must fall.

T Scores

T scores are also based on the normal curve and are converted z scores, with a mean always set at 50 and the standard deviation at 10. This ensures that virtually all T scores have positive values (unlike z scores, which are negative whenever found below the mean). To calculate a T score, simply multiply the z score by 10 and add 50. Like the z score, the T score can be used as a measure of an individual's performance relative to the mean, and, of course, to the rest of the distribution. When raw scores are converted into T scores, they give us a measure of how far the raw score is from the mean of 50 in standard deviation units of 10. Thus, a T score of 60 is one full standard deviation above the mean, and a T score of 40 is one standard-deviation unit below the mean. T scores run from a low value of 20 (three standard deviations below the mean) to a high of 80 (three standard deviations above the mean). Thus, the range of T-score values is 80 to 20, which is equal to 60. Note too, that when the T range of 60 is divided by 6, we obtain 10, which is the fixed value for the standard deviation of the T distribution. Since the T distribution is normal, we must expect that its standard deviation will fulfill the R/6 criterion.

EXAMPLE: A certain student has a z score of 1.00 on a standardized reading test. What is that student's T score and its equivalent percentile? By multiplying the z of 1.00 by 10, we get 10.00, and adding that to 50 produces a T score of 60. The z percentage areas then show this T score to be 34.13 percent above the mean, yielding a percentile of 50 + 34.13, or 84.13 (which would be rounded to the eighty-fourth percentile).

Stanines

Stanines, like z and T scores, are also based on the normal curve, but unlike the z and T, stanines divide the distribution into units of nine intervals (whereas z divided the distribution into six intervals). The mean of the stanine distribution must equal 5 and the standard deviation must equal approximately 2. By examining Figure 5.6, one can see that stanine 5 (the midmost interval) contains 20 percent of the cases, stanines 4 and 6 contain 17 percent, stanines 3 and 7 contain 12 percent, stanines 2 and 8 contain 7 percent, and finally, stanines 1 and 9 contain 4 percent. A child who scored in the sixth stanine, for example, would have performed better than 60 percent of those taking the same test. Many standardized tests in the field of education report scores on the basis of stanines.

INFERENTIAL STATISTICS

Statistical analysis is a prime example of the inductive logic described in Chapter 1. Induction, you may recall, is based on arguing from the specific case to the general rule. Statistical tests of significance do precisely that: the researcher measures a small group, the specific cases, and then hopes to generalize these findings to a much larger group; that is, a sample is measured, and the resulting findings are then extrapolated to the entire population that the sample is assumed to represent.

Any measurement of a sample is technically called a *statistic*, whereas any measure of a population is called a *parameter*. That branch of statistics involved in using sample measures to estimate population parameters is called *inferential statistics*. Thus, the sample measures (statistics) are used to *infer* the measured characteristics of the population (parameters).

For example, we might select a sample of five thousand male high-school seniors and measure all their heights. The mean sample measure might turn out to be 5 feet 9 inches tall, and then through a process of inferential statistics, we would attempt to determine the likelihood of that sample value also being the parameter mean for the entire population of millions of senior males. We must, however, keep uppermost in mind that any time we make that inductive leap, from sample statistic to population parameter, we can *never* be absolutely sure that the generalization is valid. Inferential statistics are grounded in a probabilistic model. All we can ever hope to do is assess the likelihood that the generalization is accurate. We may be able to say that we are 95 percent certain, or even 99 percent certain, that a given sample finding will hold true in the population, but inferential statistics never allow for 100 percent certainty. No generalizations are always true—even that one!

Inferential Statistics and the Standard Deviation

Earlier, in our discussion of the standard deviation, the equation given was for the true standard deviation of the particular set of scores under study. When attempting to estimate the population standard deviation on the basis of a set of sample scores, an important correction must be made. The true standard deviation of the sample tends to underestimate the population standard deviation, thus producing a biased estimate of this important parameter. To correct for this, statisticians have generated an equation for an unbiased estimate of a population's standard deviation, which when applied to small samples tends to increase the value of the sample's standard deviation. (For a discussion of how this works, see Sprinthall, 1990.)

The equation is as follows (where we use s to indicate the unbiased estimate, rather than SD, which signifies the sample's true standard deviation):

$$s = \sqrt{\frac{\Sigma X^2 - \frac{(\Sigma X)^2}{N}}{N - 1}}$$

Table 5.10 shows the application of this equation to the distribution found in Table 5.4, in which the true standard deviation was found to be 6.84.

$$s = \sqrt{\frac{\Sigma X^2 - \frac{(\Sigma X)^2}{N}}{N - 1}} = \sqrt{\frac{2428 - \frac{(140)^2}{10}}{10 - 1}} = \sqrt{\frac{2428 - 1960}{9}} = \sqrt{\frac{468}{9}}$$

$$s = \sqrt{52} = 7.21$$

(With large samples, the difference between the values of SD and s becomes negligible.)

The Null Hypothesis: Ho

Because inferential statistical tests are based on a probabilistic model, it follows that any sample finding might simply be the result of blind chance. For example, suppose that we were to select two random samples from a single population and then give all the subjects in one group (the experimental group) a certain magical "smart pill," and all the subjects in the other (control) group a placebo.

Table 5.10 Calculating Unbiased Standard Deviation

X	X²
25	625
20	400
19	361
17	289
15	225
15	225
13	169
11	121
3	9
2	4
$\Sigma X = 140$	$\Sigma X^2 = 2428$

A few hours later we measure the IQs in both groups and discover an average difference of 15 IQ points in favor of the experimental group. Does this automatically prove the efficacy of the smart pill? No. Even a difference as large as this one still could conceivably be the result of chance factors.

The statement that any sample result is due to chance is called the *null hypothesis,* symbolized as Ho, and it is an ever-present reminder of the fragility of statistical inference. Although this may sound severe, it is not an indictment of statistical testing. It is meant, instead, to loudly proclaim a blatant empirical fact: that statistical proof is a probabilistic proof, not a statement of eternal etched-in-stone truth. Also, as we will see later, the statement of the null hypothesis may come in different forms, but underlying these various disguises is one basic, common message: the null hypothesis always insists that your sample results are strictly due to the vagaries of chance.

The Alternative Hypothesis: Ha

Any time a statistical test is performed on sample data, two, and only two, results are theoretically possible. Either these results are due to chance, or they're not. Returning to our smart-pill example, that difference of 15 IQ points might, of course, be the result of chance, *or* it might really be due to the ingestion of the smart pills. Just as the null hypothesis insists that the sample results are due to chance, the *alternative hypothesis,* symbolized by Ha, asserts that the sample results are *not due to chance.* In the case of the smart pills, the alternative hypothesis (sometimes called the research hypothesis) states that this 15-point difference between the control and experimental groups is, in fact, a "real" difference, or one that indeed does exist in the population at large.

Therefore, in any statistical proof the researchers will make a declaration regarding whether the null hypothesis is accepted or rejected. And if Ho is rejected, by deduction, the researchers are stating their agreement with the alternative hypothesis. Remember, this is typically a black-and-white issue. Either you accept Ho and reject Ha, or you reject Ho and accept Ha. There are no shades of gray here. You never "barely" reject or "almost" accept. You either do or you don't. The researcher's statement regarding the acceptance or rejection of the null hypothesis is called the *statistical decision.*

Alpha Error: Type-I Error

Since the statistical world is a world ruled by chance, it follows that even the statistical decision to accept or reject Ho is a chancy decision. A given statistical test might lead the researcher to reject the null hypothesis when, in fact, it should have been accepted. The *alpha,* or *type-1, error* is defined as the probability of being wrong whenever the null hypothesis is rejected. Note that the alpha error only becomes relevant when Ho is rejected. One cannot commit the alpha error when accepting Ho.

The alpha error is typically set at probability values of either .05 or .01. If the alpha error is set at .05, and the decision is to reject Ho, we conclude that there are five chances out of a hundred that the statistical decision is incorrect. If alpha is set at .01, there is only one chance in a hundred that the decision to reject Ho is erroneous. Note that although the alpha error keeps the door open to the possibility that the decision to reject is incorrect, limiting alpha to probability levels of .05 or .01 makes this an unlikely prospect. With an alpha error of .05 it is certainly true that there are five chances in a hundred of making an incorrect decision to reject, but it also means that the chances are ninety-five out of a hundred that "reject" was the appropriate decision. Remember, whenever you reject the chance explanation you may be extremely confident that your decision is the right one, but you can never be absolutely certain.

Beta Error: Type-2 Error

Since chance can never be totally ruled out of any statistical decision, it is also possible that a decision to accept null is incorrect. This is called the *beta,* or *type-2, error,* and it defines the probability of being wrong whenever the null hypothesis is accepted. After all, it is entirely possible that there really is a significant correlation or difference occurring out there in the population, even though the researcher fails to detect it in the sample. Some researchers are so concerned about this that they dislike ever stating that the null hypothesis has been accepted. Instead, they prefer to state that they have *failed to reject* the null hypothesis. As long as you keep clearly in mind that accepting null is just as much a probability estimate as rejecting null, the phrase "accept null" will carry its intended meaning.

In a very practical sense, the beta error is often a more private error than is alpha. After all, when you accept null, and that is the only time the beta error can occur, you are announcing that your hard-won results are merely due to the vagaries of chance—hardly the kind of announcement that gains headlines. It is often the case, then, that when you accept null, only you, your professor, or your journal editor ever know about it. Studies have shown that journal editors are far more likely to select an article for publication if the statistical decision is to reject rather than accept null (Greenwald, 1975). It has also been discovered that when researchers have to accept the null hypothesis, they rarely even bother to send their results to a journal. (There are exceptions to this, however, as when some cultural myth is exploded when subjected to rigorous examination.)

Private or not, the beta error is still of major importance to the statistical analyst. When you accept the null hypothesis when it should have been rejected, you are, in effect, throwing away a perfectly good alternative hypothesis. And as every researcher knows, good alternative hypotheses are not all that easy to come by.

Significance

Whenever the null hypothesis is rejected, we say that our statistical test has attained *significance*. A significant result is, therefore, assumed to be a nonchance result. It could still be chance, of course, and that's what the alpha error is all about. It is important that you not read any more into the term "significance" than the fact that the results are being explained on a nonchance basis. Because of the rich overtones of the English language, students new to the field of research sometimes mistakenly assume that significant results must necessarily be dramatic or profound results. In fact, significant results may even be trivial—maybe not due to chance, but still trivial.

It is true, however, that when a result is shown to be significant it *can be generalized to the population at large assuming that the samples were randomly selected.* When a correlation or a difference is found to exist within a sample, it of course does exist in the sample. We don't need tests of significance to determine that very obvious fact. The problem is, however, that information that is solely descriptive of the sample is only that: a description of the particular sample being studied. The key question in inferential statistics is whether the sample information can be generalized to the population. If the sample results are shown to be significant, they may safely be so generalized, but if not, they can't.

The Two Basic Research Hypotheses

All statistical tests of significance eventually boil down to the testing of only two basic research hypotheses, the *hypothesis of difference* and the *hypothesis of association*. The hypothesis of difference claims that the sample groups *differ* with respect to their dependent variable measures, that is, that the experimental group differs from the control group on the response measures under investigation (is smarter, quicker, healthier, etc.). The hypothesis of association, on the other hand, states that within a given group there is a dependable association, or *correlation*, between the independent and dependent variables.

The Hypothesis of Difference and Experimental Methodology

It is important to keep in mind that the hypothesis of difference is *always* at stake when experimental or quasi-experimental methodology is being employed. Thus, whenever the IV is being manipulated, we look for some concomitant variation on the DV, and hence, some *difference* between the control and experimental groups on these DV measures. The basic assumption is that the control and experimental groups are the same (represent a single population) before the IV is manipulated, but that they differ (represent *different* populations) after the IV has been manipulated. If, for example, we were studying the effects of frustration on aggression, we would randomly select two groups of subjects representing a single population of aggressiveness. Then we would frustrate one group (by blocking some goal), and we would not block that goal in the second group. Finally, we would evaluate their aggressive responses to see whether the groups then differed—then represented different populations of aggressiveness; and if the experimental group could then be shown to represent a different population than it was originally selected to represent, we might assume that the IV *caused* this difference.

The Hypothesis of Difference and Post-Facto Research

In post-facto research the hypothesis of difference may be, but isn't neces- sarily, the issue at hand. We may want to show that there is a difference be- tween the starting salaries of education- versus business-school graduates, or that there is a difference in years of life expectancy between men and women. In such cases, however, the groups were not originally selected to represent a common population. In fact the group selections were based on the fact that they originally represented different populations, and it was this very difference that determined the IV assignment. In this type of research, then, we take groups that are known to represent different populations (the subject IV) and then discover whether they also differ on some other variable, as measured by the DV. Although, of course, cause-and-effect cannot be directly determined by this technique, the fact that there are corresponding differences does set the stage for better-than-chance predictions. That is, although we cannot say that having two X chromosomes (being a woman) causes greater longevity, we can make the prediction that an average woman of a certain age will outlive an average man of the same age.

The Hypothesis of Association

The other major research hypothesis is the hypothesis of association, and is aimed at assessing the degree of *correlation* between at least two variables. In most instances the tested correlation is assumed to exist between the IV (the predictor variable) and the DV (the criterion variable).

Correlational research, as all post-facto research, does not directly address the issue of causation. It simply assesses the degree of relationship between the IV and the DV measures. If persons who have high scores on the IV also have high scores on the DV, and persons who have low scores on the IV also have low scores on the DV, the correlation is said to be positive. To use an earlier example, if we're trying to predict height (DV) from weight (IV), the correlation is positive when taller people are heavier and shorter people are lighter. If the relationship is inverse, however—that is, when people who score high on the IV tend to score low on the DV (or vice versa)—the correlation is said to be negative. In either case, positive or negative, when a correlation is found to be significant, it allows the researcher to make better-than-chance predictions.

Suppose that a researcher found a correlation between the amount of exer- cise a person indulged in and the amount of money that person had in the bank. The correlation would probably be negative, that is, people who are involved in heavy exercise programs tend to have smaller bank accounts. This would not necessarily mean that persons who exercise regularly don't have enough time left over to earn and save money, since it may well be that another variable, age, is being overlooked. Elderly persons who have had a lifetime in which to acquire money are probably less apt to jog five miles a day than a high school student who is still on a family allowance. Regardless of the reason, however, a significant negative correlation between exercise and bank account still allows for a better-than-chance prediction of bank-account value (DV) on the basis of exercise patterns (IV): the more the exercise, the smaller the bank account.

Scales of Measurement

The choice of which statistical test is most appropriate for the data analysis depends not just on whether the hypothesis of difference or association is involved but also on the kind of measures being investigated. Measurement is defined as the assigning of a number to an observation, and the technique used in assigning that number determines the measurement scale being used. Measurement scales can be rank ordered in terms of the amount of information contained in each, and the ordering from least to most is nominal, ordinal, interval, and ratio (Stevens, 1946). You should spend a little time reviewing these scales (see Chapter 2) before making any judgment regarding which statistical test to use.

THE MAJOR STATISTICAL TESTS

In this section we will present the major statistical tests, when they are appropriate, and how they may be interpreted. It is well to recall that interpretation depends on *both* the research methodology involved *and* the statistical analysis. The two are inseparable. Without keeping a special focus on methodology as these statistical tests are being reviewed, we can never come to understand or appreciate the research endeavor. We don't pretend to present all the possible tests or strategies, but we will give you the big ones, the top-of-the-marquee procedures that will allow you to analyze the majority of the studies in your discipline.

Statistical Tests and Power

We have been talking rather glibly of the importance of choosing the appropriate statistical test for a given research situation. By appropriate, we technically mean the statistical test that produces the most power for a given scale of measurement.

This term *power* has a very precise meaning in statistics. It is defined as

Power = 1 − B

or 1 minus the beta error. Since power is determined by subtracting the beta error from 1, anything that can be done to reduce the beta value automatically increases power. We've already seen that the beta error can only occur when the null hypothesis is accepted. Hence, a powerful test is one in which the beta error is rarely committed; that is, when there is significance, a powerful test detects that significance. The more powerful a test is, therefore, the higher the likelihood of rejecting null when null really should be rejected. Now let's look at the techniques that can be used to increase a test's power.

Increasing the Sample Size

A quick look at most tables of statistical-significance values confirms the fact that the likelihood of rejecting null increases as sample size increases. For example, as you can see in Table 5.11 with the Pearson *r*, a test of correlation, when the degrees of freedom are 5 (7 pairs of values), an *r* of .874 is needed to reject null at the .01 level, or .754 at the .05 level. However, with 100 degrees of freedom (102 pairs of scores), an *r* of only .254 is needed to reject at .01. Degrees of freedom are directly related in this table to sample size. The message: Always use the largest sample available to you under the constraints of practicality, of course.

Increasing the Alpha Error

A test's power is also increased by increasing the alpha error from .01 to .05. The significance tables again confirm the fact that with a given number of degrees of freedom, the statistical value needed to reject Ho at .05 is smaller than the value needed at .01. The researcher should rarely slavishly insist on .01 significance, for by so doing the beta error has to be increased. *Do not*, however, increase the alpha error above .05. A line has to be drawn somewhere, and by convention, it is .05.

Table 5.11 Selected Pearson *r* Values of Significance

df	$\alpha = .05$	$\alpha = .01$
1	.997	.9999
2	.950	.990
3	.878	.959
4	.811	.917
5	.754	.874
.	.	.
.	.	.
.	.	.
100	.195	.254

Using All the Information the Data Provide

When you have the opportunity to use interval-ratio data, use those data, and also use the statistical tests that have been designed to take advantage of that level of data. Interval measures provide more information than do ordinal or nominal measures, and the more information contained in the measurement, the more sensitive the statistical analysis. For example, both the Pearson r and the rank-order *Spearman* r_s can be used to assess the possibility of a linear correlation between two sets of measures. Although the r_s is a direct, ordinal derivation of the Pearson r, it is still a less powerful test. Again, look at the tables. For a given sample size, the Pearson r value can be consistently lower than the r_s value, and *still attain significance*. With a sample of, say, seven pairs of scores (5 degrees of freedom for the Pearson r), a Pearson r value of .75 reaches significance at the .05 level. The r_s value needed for .05 significance for that sample of size 7 is a larger .786. Thus, for the same sample size the Pearson r value reaches significance, whereas the same r_s value does not.

Fitting the Statistical Test to the Research Design

Your chances of rejecting null, and of thereby increasing test power, can be greatly increased by being extremely careful in fitting the statistical analysis to the research design. Let's compare the workings of the *independent* and *paired* (*correlated*) *t* tests. On the surface they seem to be very similar; both use interval-ratio data, both test for the possibility of a difference between two sample means, and both require a normal distribution of scores in the underlying population. However, they differ dramatically in both the procedures involved and the kind of results each may be expected to give. The independent *t* demands that the two sample measures be absolutely independent of each other, or that the selection of one sample in no way influences the selection of the second sample. An example of an experimental design in which this holds true is the between-subjects, after-only design. The paired *t*, on the other hand, demands that the two samples be somehow related to each other; the selection of a subject for one sample group helps determine who will be selected for the second group. An example of an experimental design in which this holds true would be the matched-subjects design, in which the subjects are paired off on the basis of some variable known or assumed to be related to the DV.

Although we promised you that few calculations would be involved in this book, a quick look at the *t*-test equation is now in order. (For a complete discussion of the independent and paired *t* tests, see Sprinthall, 1990.) Remember, the *t* is a ratio between the difference between the two sample means (in the numerator) and the standard error of difference (in the denominator). As with any ratio, the smaller the denominator for a given size numerator, the larger the resulting ratio. Thus, anything that reduces the value of the standard error of difference will increase the value of the *t* ratio.

$$\text{Paired } t = \frac{\bar{X}_1 - \bar{X}_2}{\sqrt{s_{\bar{X}_1}^2 + s_{\bar{X}_2}^2 - (2r_{1,2}s_{\bar{X}_1}s_{\bar{X}_2})}}$$

Notice here that the standard error of difference includes a subtracted term $(2r_{1,2}s_{\bar{X}_1}s_{\bar{X}_2})$, whose value is a direct function of the size of the Pearson r value. The larger the correlation, the more that is being subtracted, and of course, the more that is being subtracted, the smaller the overall value of the standard error of difference. Thus, when there is a significant correlation between the dependent value measures, as there *should be* when subjects are deliberately matched, the standard error of difference is

1. reduced in value, which
2. increases the t ratio, which
3. increases the likelihood of rejecting null, which in turn
4. increases the test's power.

This is all meant to show that if the statistical test and the research design are not in sync, the researcher is more apt to commit the beta error and thereby reduce the power of the test. In the foregoing case, if one were to mismatch the test and methodology—that is, use the independent t on the correlated data of a matched-subjects design—the opportunity of rejecting null might simply be thrown away. That is, since the independent t looks like

$$\frac{\bar{X}_1 - \bar{X}_2}{\sqrt{s_{\bar{X}_1}^2 + s_{\bar{X}_2}^2 - 0}}$$

with no correlation term to subtract, the use of the independent t on a matched-subjects design would mask the possible significance. There can be no correlation term in the independent t, since there is no way even to calculate a correlation between independent measures. It would be utterly impossible to know even how to pair off the scores, a necessary procedure in calculating r.

In summary, then, using the appropriate statistical analysis for a given research design means using the statistical test that provides the most power.

Interval-Ratio (Parametric) Tests of Difference

This section will summarize those tests of significance that attempt to establish differences between sets of interval-ratio scores.

The Independent *t*

The independent t is used whenever two sample means are being compared for possible differences, and the samples have been independently selected. When the research is experimental, the independent t becomes appropriate when the design is after-only, and there are two independent samples, one experimental group and one control group. The comparison to be made is *between* the groups. For example, a researcher wishes to test the hypothesis that the discovery teaching technique leads to higher levels of pupil learning than does the more traditional presentation. Two groups of sixth-grade students are randomly selected and presented with a geography lesson unit. Group A, the control group, is taught in a fairly traditional manner. The subject area is covered, and although the teacher does ask a series of rhetorical questions, she quickly answers them herself. Group B, the experimental group, is exposed to the same material by the same teacher, but in this case, she does not answer the rhetorical questions in the hope that this will stimulate pupil thinking and allow the pupils to discover for themselves certain basic relationships. Both groups are then tested, and their retention scores are shown in Table 5.12.

The statistical theory behind the use of the *t* test in analyzing experimental research is simple and straightforward. Since the two samples are assumed to represent a single population when originally selected, if they are later found to differ significantly, the assumption is made that they now represent different populations. And the cause of this difference is further assumed to result from the manipulation of the independent variable.

The independent *t* has also been used for post-facto analyses, again, as long as the samples are independently selected from population groups that are known to differ on some measure. For example, a researcher hypothesizes that boys and girls differ with respect to the personality trait of "need dependence." Random samples of ten boys and ten girls are selected and each subject is given the Edwards Personal Preference Schedule (EPPS). The scores on the scale for need dependence are then compared via the independent *t*. In this case, if the two sample means were to differ significantly, we could not, of course, make a cause-and-effect inference. We could *not* say that the two samples, originally selected from a single population, now represent different populations, for the very obvious reason that these two samples were selected from two different populations to begin with. We *could* say, however, that the two samples, which are known to differ in gender, have also been found to differ in need dependence.

Predicting the direction of the difference. One final *t*-test distinction is that which occurs between the one-tail and two-tail comparisons. The general rule on this issue is that if the researcher is simply hypothesizing that the two groups will differ, without regard to the direction of the difference, the two-tail analysis

Table 5.12 Comparison of Retention Scores

GROUP A (CONTROL GROUP)	GROUP B (EXPERIMENTAL GROUP)
X	X
8	13
8	12
5	12
3	9
3	8
2	8
$\bar{X} = 4.83$	$\bar{X} = 10.33$

should be used. If, however, the hypothesis does specify the direction of the difference (that one set of sample scores will be higher than the other), the one-tail evaluation is usually preferred. For example, if a researcher selects two random samples and hypothesizes that the average scores between the groups will differ (but doesn't say which group will have the higher scores), the two-tail *t* is appropriate. If, however, on the basis of some prior research or theoretical supposition, the researcher states beforehand that one of the group means will not merely be different from but will be higher than the other group mean, the one-tail *t* can be selected.

This is really an important issue, since, as a quick look at a *t* table will show, a one-tail analysis allows a lower *t* value to reach significance. For example, with, say, 10 degrees of freedom, a two-tail *t* value of 2.228 is needed to reach .05 significance, whereas a one-tail *t* value of only 1.812 produces the same significance level. Using the one-tail *t*, then, when it's appropriate, provides the researcher with a more powerful test of significance than does two-tail analysis.

ANOVA

The analysis-of-variance technique (ANOVA), or *F* ratio, is used for comparing two or more interval-ratio distributions. Thus, when the independent variable is being set at several different levels, resulting in a number of experimental groups, the *F* ratio becomes the statistical test of choice.

When the research involves *one independent variable* being set at various levels, the one-way ANOVA is used.

$$F = \frac{MS_{between}}{MS_{within}}$$

In this equation, the $MS_{between}$ represents the amount of variability that exists *between* the groups, and is typically assumed to result from the action of the independent variable. The MS_{within} describes the amount of variability occurring *within* the groups, and usually represents individual differences originally occurring within the groups or random error, or both. Thus, the more variability found to occur between the groups relative to the variability occurring within the groups, the greater the likelihood of rejecting Ho.

Unlike the *t* ratio, which has a one-tail version, the *F* ratio cannot be used to predict the direction of a given difference. Nor can the *F* ratio itself identify which of the various sample groups are deviating significantly from chance. There are techniques available, however, such as the Duncan-Range, the Tukey HSD, the Sheffe, or the Newman-Kuels, for making such precise identifications. These are all called *multiple comparison tests*.

For experimental research, the one-way ANOVA can only be used when the experimental design is after-only (between-groups). The sample groups must be completely independent of each other. For example, a researcher selects four independent random samples from the population of seventh graders in a large metropolitan school district. The hypothesis to be tested is that time of day influences the retention of learned material. Each of the groups is presented with the same material on the history of the stamp tax on colonial Americans just prior to the Revolutionary War. Group A is given the lesson between 9:00 and 9:30 A.M., Group B between 11:00 and 11:30 A.M., Group C between 1:00 and 1:30 P.M., and Group D between 3:00 and 3:30 P.M. All groups are tested immediately following the lesson. The retention scores are as shown in Table 5.13.

Table 5.13   Data for One-Way ANOVA

A	B	C	D
10	10	9	6
9	7	6	5
9	7	5	5
7	4	2	4

A one-way ANOVA can then be performed to assess the possibility of significant differences among the four groups, and if differences are established, they may be attributed to the independent variable (time at which lesson is presented).

The one-way ANOVA may also be applied to post-facto research, as long as there is only one subject IV and the subjects are independent of each other. For example, a researcher suspects that percentage of body fat among ten-year-old boys is related to metabolic rate. A group of subjects are randomly selected from a population of ten-year-old boys, and each subject is assigned to one of three groups on the basis of metabolic rate. All subjects are then measured for body-fat percentages. The data might look like those in Table 5.14.

The one-way ANOVA can then tell us whether boys who are known to differ with respect to metabolic rate also differ on percentage of body fat. Since the IV in this case is a subject variable and not manipulated, no cause-and-effect statements can be made, regardless of the size of the *F* ratio. It could be that some other variable might be producing *both* a low metabolic rate *and* an increased body-fat percentage.

Factorial ANOVA.   When the research involves two or more independent variables, the interval-data test for differences becomes the *factorial ANOVA*. With this technique the researcher can discover whether each of the independent variables, taken separately (main effects), is producing a significant difference, *and also* whether the independent variables have combined with each other to provide an interaction effect.

Table 5.14   Post-facto Data for One-Way ANOVA

GROUP A (LOW METABOLISM)	GROUP B (NORMAL METABOLISM)	GROUP C (HIGH METABOLISM)
24	20	16
30	18	14
25	22	12
24	20	15
20	17	16

The factorial ANOVA requires a minimum of four cells, or four separate treatment conditions, based on the bare minimum of two independent variables, each set at two levels. Further, the four cells must be kept independent of one another. As an example, a researcher wonders what effect both diet and exercise have on resting pulse rates. A random sample of 24 junior-high students is selected, and randomly assigned, six subjects each, to four separate treatment conditions. Then, six weeks later, the resting pulse rates of all subjects are recorded. (See Table 5.15.)

Three *F* ratios can then be calculated, one for diet (rows going across), one for exercise (columns going vertically) and one for the interaction of diet and exercise (rows and columns combined).

$$F \text{ rows} = \frac{MS_r}{MS_w}$$

$$F \text{ cols.} = \frac{MS_c}{MS_w}$$

$$F \text{ rows} \times \text{cols.} = \frac{MS_{rxc}}{MS_w}$$

The factorial ANOVA may also be used for post-facto analyses in which both IVs have been assigned on the basis of subject differences. For example, one might wish to test whether reaction times differ on the basis of both age and gender. A four-cell factorial design could be set up according to both of these subject IVs.

	FACTOR A (GENDER)	
	MALE	FEMALE
FACTOR B (AGE) Age 6		
Age 12		

Table 5.15 Data for Factorial ANOVA

	FACTOR A	
	NO EXERCISE	EXERCISE
NO DIET	98	90
	95	85
	85	80
	87	75
	85	80
	90	85
FACTOR B		
DIET	85	75
	75	65
	70	60
	80	70
	82	65
	80	75

Table 5.16 Combination Research via ANOVA

	IQ		
	85–100	101–116	116 AND ABOVE
	x	x	x
SPECIAL	x	x	x
TRAINING	x	x	x
	x	x	x
	x	x	x
NO SPECIAL	x	x	x
TRAINING	x	x	x
	x	x	x

Even combination research designs—that is, situations in which some IVs are manipulated and others are assigned—can be handled via the factorial ANOVA. It might be that high-IQ children profit more from a reading enrichment program than do average- or low-IQ children. We could select a random sample of ten-year-old school children and assign them to three categories according to IQ, 85 to 100, 101 to 115, and 116 and above. Half the children in each IQ category could then be given special, reading-enrichment training, while for the others such training would be withheld. After a certain period of time all subjects might then be given a standardized reading-achievement test and their scores compared.

This analysis would require a six-cell design as in Table 5.16, since the IQ independent variable is a subject variable and is being assigned at three different levels. Research of this type, although easily handled by the factorial ANOVA, does require great care when it comes to interpretation. Since the IQ variable has not been manipulated, nor could it be, the researcher must avoid the trap, regardless of how the F ratios come out, of imputing causality to IQ. Although the manipulated training IV is open to causal interpretation, neither IQ, nor any possible interactions, may be seen as anything other than predictive.

The importance of interaction: The paradox of Ritalin. Analysis of the interaction term in the factorial ANOVA is of extreme importance even when neither of the main effects appears to be significant. As an example of this, assume that a researcher wishes to discover if the drug Ritalin has any effect on reducing the activity levels of hyperactive boys. Further, the researcher wants to learn whether the drug effect is similar despite age differences among the subjects. A random sample of forty subjects is selected from the population of hyperactive boys. Of these, twenty are over age sixteen and twenty are under age sixteen. Each of the two age groupings are further divided into two groups of ten subjects each and randomly assigned to either the Ritalin condition or the placebo condition. The boys are then measured on their activity levels on a scale of 0 to 50, with high scores indicating higher levels of activity. The results are as shown in Table 5.17.

Table 5.17 The Paradox of Ritalin

		FACTOR A (DRUG)	
		PLACEBO a	RITALIN b
FACTOR B (AGE)	UNDER 16	mean = 35	mean = 27
	OVER 16	c mean = 33	d mean = 37

CELL	AGE GROUP	DRUG	MEAN
a	under 16	placebo	35
b	under 16	Ritalin	27
c	over 16	placebo	33
d	over 16	Ritalin	37

Calculation of the F ratios shows that

Age (in rows)	$F = 3.90$	Accept Ho
Drug (in columns)	$F = 3.80$	Accept Ho
Interaction ($r \times c$)	$F = 15.20$	Reject Ho: significant at $p < .01$

Thus, the F ratios tell us that the drug appears to have no effect, and that the age variable has no effect, but that the interaction between the two factors is clearly significant. To more fully understand this situation, a graph of these results is drawn by connecting the means from the same age grouping. (See Figure 5.7.)

Thus, it becomes clear that since the over-sixteen boys who were given the drug were more active, whereas the under-sixteen boys who were given the drug were less active, the effects of the drug were canceled out. That is why the F ratio for the drug (in the columns) is only 3.80 and produced an acceptance of the null hypothesis. This finding, that Ritalin appears to increase the activity levels of older children yet at the same time decreases the activity levels of younger children, is known as the paradoxical effect.

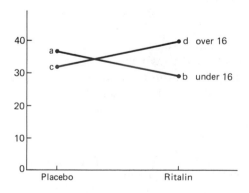

Figure 5.7 Graphing the interaction

Within-subjects (repeated-measures) ANOVA. Like the paired *t*, the *F* ratio is also capable of handling data from nonindependent research designs. When the selection of the subjects is not independent, either because of matching or using the same subjects in all conditions, the within-subjects or correlated *F* should be used. The paired *t*, as we saw in the analysis of the before-after design, can also be used for repeated measures, but in that case there can be only *two* measures, one before and one after. With the *F* ratio, we can have three or more different measures of the dependent variable, in a kind of before-after-after-after design. Similarly, just as the paired *t* handled matching designs in which the subjects were *paired* off, the *F* can be used on matched threesomes, or even foursomes and fivesomes. In short, the within-subjects *F* can do everything the paired *t* can do, and also a lot more. The within-subjects *F* can evaluate differences among three or more repeated measures *and* among three or more groups of matched subjects. Also, as with the paired *t*, the within-subjects *F* is a more powerful test of differences than is its independent counterpart, *when all its assumptions are met*. Thus, if the sample groups are not independent, the within-subjects *F* is more likely to show significant differences than is the independent *F*. The size of the *F* is increased by a factor associated with the strength of the correlation across the rows; the higher the correlation, the higher the *F* ratio.

Finally, as with the paired *t*, the *F* is a less powerful test when the samples are really independent. The message, as always, is that using the statistical test that is appropriate to the particular research design increases your chances of reaching significance.

Mixed Designs

Mixed designs, sometimes called split-plot designs, are those in which there are two or more independent variables, but at least one of the variables is between groups and at least one is within subjects. That is, although on at least one IV the groups are independent of each other, there is also at least one IV on which the same subjects are measured across all the conditions (as in a repeated-measures design). Typically the between-groups variable is indicated first, so that a 2×3 mixed design means that there are two independent groups, both being measured under three conditions.

For example, suppose that a researcher wishes to establish whether both mode of presentation and number of trials affect the retention of learned material. Two groups of subjects are randomly selected and assigned to either a visual or an auditory condition. That is, the two independent groups either receive the stimuli visually or through an auditory mode of presentation. All subjects then receive three retention trials (which produces three times as many scores as there are subjects). See Table 5.18 as an example.

The *F* ratios may then tell us

1. whether mode of presentation produced a significant difference regarding how much the subjects retained (a between-subjects *F* ratio)

Table 5.18 Example of Mixed Design

SUBJECT	TRIAL 1	GROUP A (VISUAL) TRIAL 2	TRIAL 3
1	x	x	x
2	x	x	x
3	x	x	x
4	x	x	x
5	x	x	x
		GROUP B (AUDITORY)	
6	x	x	x
7	x	x	x
8	x	x	x
9	x	x	x
10	x	x	x

2. whether increasing the number of trials influenced retention (a within-subjects F ratio)
3. whether the increase in trials had a different effect on retention as a function of which mode of presentation was being employed (an interaction F ratio)

MANOVA

Another variation of ANOVA that you may encounter is called *MANOVA*, or multivariate analysis of variance. With the MANOVA technique a researcher can test for group differences on not just one dependent variable but on two or more such measures. For example, when discussing the factorial ANOVA we illustrated the use of F ratios by testing whether the two independent variables, diet and exercise, had any effect on resting pulse rates, which was the lone DV. With MANOVA we could increase the number of DVs, perhaps measuring the subjects not only on pulse rates but also on, say, weight loss and blood pressure. Thus, with MANOVA the researcher is in a position to observe the possible effect of the independent variable(s) on two or more dependent variables.

Note that with repeated-measures ANOVAs, mixed designs, and MANOVA, the subjects (or at least some of the subjects) are measured more than once. In some cases they are measured repeatedly on the same DV (repeated-measures designs) and in others they are measured on several different DVs (basic MANOVA). In either case these designs are often considered multivariate in the sense that several measures are obtained from some or all subjects. In some computer statistical packages (SPSS, for example), these approaches are all done using the MANOVA model.

ANCOVA

The analysis of covariance, or *ANCOVA*, is used by researchers in an attempt to create equivalent groups of subjects *after the fact*. The groups of subjects are thus presumed to be statistically controlled. ANCOVA can be used in a variety of research situations, since it attempts to even out any possible differences that may have occurred between the groups *before* the independent variable had been manipulated. For example, as often happens, a researcher may not be able to select random samples, or assign subjects randomly to the different groups, or even match the subjects on some relevant variable. In such situations, ANCOVA is probably the best solution, and it is often used when groups have not been randomly divided, although technically, ANCOVA assumes that the groups were, in fact, randomly divided.

To take an extreme example, suppose that a researcher wishes to find out whether a new speed-reading teaching technique really improves reading speed. A quasi-experimental design is set up, using two intact groups of sixth-grade classes, Mr. Smith's class in room 201 and Ms. Shea's class in room 208. Mr. Smith's class becomes the experimental group and is given the speed-reading course each day. Ms. Shea's class receives the traditional reading program for the same length of time. To control for teacher personality, the same person is used to teach both classes, and also the times of day are counterbalanced by alternating the morning and afternoon sessions for both groups.

Finally, after six weeks the groups are compared with respect to reading speed, and the experimental group is found to be superior. It is then suggested that perhaps the two groups originally differed regarding their IQs, that Mr. Smith had a smarter class to begin with and should therefore be expected to have faster readers. The ANCOVA technique is then applied, after the fact, to discover whether there were differences in reading speeds between the two groups that were over and above any differences that might be accounted for by their possible preexisting differences in IQ. In short, the groups were made statistically equivalent by controlling IQ as the covariate. The researcher may attempt to use a statistical control using one, two, or several covariates.

Earlier, in discussing the *t* test, we suggested that there is another method for comparing experimental and control group change scores using *t*. One way to do that is to consider the pretest scores as covariates when comparing posttest scores. Thus, using the ANCOVA procedure, the researcher may look for differences in the posttest scores that exist after the pretest scores have been taken into consideration.

MANCOVA

Finally, *MANCOVA,* or multivariate analysis of covariance, is a method of statistical control in which groups are presumably made equivalent on one or more variables, when two or more DVs are also being measured. In the previous example, the two classroom groups were statistically controlled on one variable, IQ, and tested on one DV, reading speed, but with MANCOVA two or more DVs might have been tested. In addition to reading speed, for example, reading comprehension might also have been measured. Like ANCOVA, MANCOVA assumes that the groups were randomly divided at the outset, but it's often used even when that assumption is violated.

Neither ANCOVA nor MANCOVA can be considered perfect solutions to the problem of nonequivalent groups, especially when used with groups that were not randomly assigned at the outset. They are, however, powerful tools for the researcher who has no other choice. As has been stated many times, it is far better to create equivalent groups methodologically, and then apply the appropriate statistical technique, than to use a statistical control after the fact.

Interval-Ratio Tests of Association

We shift the focus now, from testing for differences to testing for *correlation*. This puts us squarely into the post-facto arena—an area of prediction but no direct evaluation of causation. Although correlation was mentioned during the description of one of the difference tests (the paired *t*), correlation was in that case only used as a vehicle for calculating a *t* test of differences. That is, the Pearson *r* was only a means to an end, not an end in itself. In this section, correlation will be viewed as the final goal of the researcher's efforts, not a brief stopping point along the way. With very few exceptions, most of the direct tests of association involve a comparison between the IV (predictor) and the DV (criterion), and not a correlation between DV measures as was used in the paired *t*.

The Pearson *r* (Product Moment Correlation)

When looking for the possible linear relationship between two interval-ratio-measure variables (bivariate analysis), the Pearson *r*, or product-moment, correlation is the appropriate statistical test. The Pearson *r* allows the researcher to investigate relationships between qualitatively different measures, like height and weight, or high-school grades and college grades, or reading speed and verbal retention. The correlation technique therefore allows us to make comparisons between the proverbial apples and oranges. Whether positive or negative, the closer the correlation is to unity (+1.00), the stronger is the association and the greater is its predictive accuracy. Thus, a correlation of $-.90$ shows a stronger linear relationship than does a $+.85$. In correlation studies, the variable we predict from (the predictor) is usually called the X variable, and the variable we predict to (the criterion) is usually called the Y variable. The correlation between high-school grades and college grades would thus be set up so that high-school grades would form the X distribution and college grades the Y distribution. This correlation, which has been shown to be $+.52$, then represents an index of about how much information about Y (college grades) is contained in X (high-school grades). The precise value designating how much information about Y is being contained in X can be found very easily by simply squaring the r value, which yields the coefficient of determination. In the previous example, then, $r = .52$, and $r^2 = .27$. Multiplying r by 100 provides a percentage value, which in this case tells us that 27% of the information regarding college grades is contained in the high-school grades. Had r been equal to 1.00, r^2 would equal 1.00, telling us that 100% of the information about Y is contained in X; hence, a perfect, error-free prediction could be generated.

To predict specific Y values for each given X value, r can be used in calculating the regression equation. This equation would allow us to take a high-school grade average of, say, 3.00 and predict a college grade-point average of, say, 2.71. Finally, the standard error of estimate could be calculated, providing us with an estimate of how accurate that 2.71 value really is. Other examples of research situations in which the Pearson r might be used will be found in later chapters.

The Pearson r may not imply causation, but neither does it rule it out. After all, whenever the experimental method isolates a cause-and-effect relationship between a manipulated IV and a DV, there is also a correlation between those variables. Many times the idea for an experimental evaluation of some relationship originated with a correlation study.

Multiple Correlations

The correlations so far discussed have all been bivariate, or two-variable, correlations. Many correlation studies, however, involved assessing the relationships between three or more variables. Instead of simply attempting to find out how much information about Y is contained in X, which is the goal of the Pearson r, a *multiple correlation* could establish how much information about Y is contained in X_1, X_2, X_3, and so on. Suppose, for example, that your job is to predict the height of the very next person to enter your room. Knowing that you're to predict the height of a *person* helps you somewhat: you wouldn't guess 3 inches or 60 feet. Next, we add some information and tell you that the person in question is an adult male. You know that gender correlates to some extent with height, and that the adult-male height distribution tends to have a higher average value than the female distribution. You might now guess a value of 5 feet 9 inches, the actual mean of the adult male distribution. Next, we provide even more information and tell you that the person weighs 230 pounds. Again, since you know that height and weight tend to correlate positively, you might now increase your estimate to 6 feet or 6 feet 1 inch. Finally, we give one last bit of information and tell you that the person plays center on a professional basketball team. You now jump your estimate to 6 feet 10 inches or 7 feet. The point is, your prediction becomes increasingly more accurate as more and more predictor variables are supplied. Although the foregoing example is based partly on nominal variables (male versus female), the same sort of results can be obtained when all the correlated measures are in the form of interval-ratio data, and the appropriate statistical test then becomes the *multiple R*.

Let's take an example using real data. When a university admissions office attempts to predict the college grade-point average (Y variable) for a given applicant, they use among other things, at least two predictor variables, high-school grades (X_1) and SAT performance (X_2). Each of these variables, taken separately, does correlate significantly with college grades:

X_1 (high-school grades) correlates at .52 with Y (college grades).
X_2 (SAT scores) correlates at .41 with Y (college grades).

Thus, although the correlations are far from perfect, each does produce a better-than-chance prediction. When the two are combined together in the multiple R however, the multiple correlation increases to a value of .58, a considerable statistical increase over the correlation found for the single best predictor, high-school grades (Turnbull, 1980).

As with the Pearson r, the multiple R also allows for specific predictions via the use of the multiple-regression equation. Further, by using the standard error of multiple estimate, the accuracy range of each predicted value may also be found.

Nonparametric Statistical Tests

All the tests shown thus far use interval-ratio data and are called *parametric tests;* that is, each makes certain population- or parameter-measure assumptions, such as the placement of the population mean. Also, each of the interval-ratio tests assumes that the underlying population measures distribute normally (even though each sample distribution isn't necessarily normal). The parametric statistics all test a null hypothesis that concerns some relevant aspect of the population, such as its mean or its variance. In the sections to follow the focus will be on *nonparametric statistical tests*, tests that use ordinal or nominal data and that make no assumptions regarding the population characteristics. Nonparametric tests, for example, can be used in situations in which it is clearly evident that the underlying population distribution of some measure is decidedly not normal.

Ordinal Tests of Significance

All the tests presented in this section have one thing in common: they have all been designed to handle ordinal data. This may involve two approaches:

1. The data are originally presented in the form of ranks, such as a group of students in which each student is ranked by a panel of judges on the basis of the amount of extraversion displayed.
2. The data are originally in interval-ratio form, but the distribution of these measures is known to violate the assumption of normality. For example, it is known that distributions of family income levels are not normal in that they are typically skewed to the right. The researcher simply takes the income measures and rank orders them from highest to lowest, allowing an ordinal test of significance to then be performed. As stated previously, however, all these nonparametric tests are less powerful than their parametric counterparts. The reason: ordinal and nominal data contain less information than is contained in the interval-ratio measures.

The following tests have all been designed to test the hypothesis of difference, that is, that one set of ranks is higher than another set (Siegel, 1988).

The Mann-Whitney U test. The ordinal counterpart of the independent *t* is the *Mann-Whitney U test*, a test that attempts to establish a significant difference between two sets of independently selected ordinal distributions.

In experimental research, the *U* test is appropriate when the after-only design has been used and the data are in ordinal form. For example, a study of the effects of a preschool counseling program on the social-maturity levels of a group of four-year-old children is conducted. Two groups of children are randomly selected from the population of a large day-care center, one group receiving the counseling and the other not. Three months later all subjects in both groups are rank ordered by a panel of judges (who are not informed as to which children have been counseled) with regard to their social-maturity levels. The two sets of ordered ranks are then compared via the *U* test.

The *U* test may also be used for post-facto analyses, again, as long as the two groups are independent of each other. For example, a researcher wishes to establish whether a difference in family income exists between children whose parents encouraged them to opt for a college-prep high-school program and children whose parents did not. Random samples of both populations are obtained and the annual income level of each family is measured. When it became obvious that the income measures are badly skewed to the right, the researcher decides to rank order the family income and then compare the two distributions via the *U* test.

The Kruskal-Wallis H test. The ordinal equivalent of the one-way ANOVA is the *Kruskal-Wallis H test*. *H* is used to compare three or more ordinal distributions when each sample has been independently selected. In experimental methodology, *H* is appropriate, therefore, when three or more independent groups are being compared for differences in an after-only design. For example, suppose that a researcher were interested in discovering whether differing amounts of vitamin E had differential effects on skin acne among teenage boys. Four groups of sixteen-year-old boys would be selected from a large metropolitan school district. One group would receive only a daily placebo; a second group would receive 50 IUs (international units) of vitamin E each day; a third group would receive 100 IUs, and the final group 150 IUs. At the end of six months all boys would be rank ordered with respect to acne severity, and the four distributions would be compared via the *H* test.

As an example of a post-facto analysis, a study is conducted to find out whether acne severity among teenage boys is a function of how much vitamin E they are already taking *on their own*. A large, random sample of sixteen-year-old boys is selected, but this time rather than providing varying dose levels of vitamin E, the researcher simply contacts each boy's family and finds out *after the fact* whether the boys have already been taking vitamin E (and if so, how much). The boys are then assigned to groups according to their parents' estimates of each boy's vitamin E consumption and then rank ordered on the basis of acne severity. Statistical comparisons are made using the *H* test.

The Wilcoxon T *test.* The ordinal counterpart of the paired-*t* test is the *Wilcoxon T test.* Using this test, the researcher is able to test whether two sets of correlated ranks might differ significantly. Experimentally, then, the Wilcoxon *T* handles ordinal data from either the matched-subjects or before-after designs. For example, a researcher wishes to discover if competency-test scores for high-school teachers can be increased by the introduction of a three-day in-service workshop in the teachers' own specialty area. A random sample of high-school teachers is selected. Each subject is given the competency test, sent to the workshop, and then given the competency test again. The Wilcoxon *T* test is selected for the analysis when it is discovered that the distribution of test scores is severely skewed to the left. (This study could have been better handled by having a separate control group that took the competency test both times but did not attend the in-service training.)

A post-facto example of the Wilcoxon *T* is research on whether differences in perceived leadership are a function of height among female high-school students. A large sample of female high-school students was selected and divided into two groups, according to height—those under 5 feet 5 inches versus those 5 feet 5 inches and above. In an attempt to control for maturity, the subjects were then matched with respect to age. All subjects then took part in a leadership group situation and were then rank ordered with respect to the amount of leadership each exhibited. The ranks of the taller students were then compared with the ranks of the age-matched, shorter students via the Wilcoxon *T*.

The Friedman ANOVA by ranks. The ordinal counterpart of the within-subjects (correlated) *F* ratio is the *Friedman ANOVA by ranks.* This test allows the researcher to compare three or more ordinal distributions when the various samples are *not* independent of each other, as in repeated-measures or matched-subjects designs.

As an experimental example of the Friedman, assume that a researcher wishes to establish whether differences exist among the Breathalyzer readings from a group of high-school students suspected of drunken driving as a function of the time elapsed between apprehension and the onset of the testing procedure. A random sample of suspected drunken drivers are tested on the Breathalyzer under three conditions: first, twenty minutes after being stopped; second, after one hour and twenty minutes; third, after two hours and twenty minutes. Although the Breathalyzer scores are originally in interval-ratio form, ranging from 0 to .40 (and allegedly indicating the percentage of alcohol in the bloodstream), the distribution is typically badly skewed to the right. Since a score of .35 is usually associated with a comatose condition, few subjects score that high. All scores are thus converted to ranks, and the comparison made via the Friedman.

As an example of post-facto research using the Friedman, a researcher wishes to establish whether perceived alcohol dysfunction is related to body weight, holding gender and amount of alcohol consumed as a constant. A random sample of adult males is selected and divided into three groups, according to weight: below 150 lbs, 151 to 180, and 181 and above. All subjects are then given the *same amount* of alcohol (6 ounces), which keeps alcohol a constant and *not* an independent variable (the subject IV in this study is body weight). The subjects in each weight category are matched on the basis of previous drinking habits, and the subjects are then all ranked on the basis of their induced dysfunction, as judged by their ability, or lack of ability, to perform simple coordination exercises. The ranks of the matched trios are then compared via the Friedman.

The Spearman r_S. The ordinal counterpart of the Pearson r is the Spearman r_S, sometimes called the Spearman rho (ρ). In fact, the r_S is a direct derivation of the Pearson r, and unless there are tied ranks, it yields precisely the same numerical value. Like all nonparametrics, however, it is still a less powerful test than the Pearson r, since it takes a higher r_S value to reach significance for a given sample size. The r_S can be used in a wide variety of correlation studies, including the following:

1. When both distributions are originally in ordinal form.
2. When one distribution is in interval-ratio form and the other is ordinal. Since interval-ratio scores can always be rank ordered, the interval distribution is converted to ordinal form, and the r_S then calculated. It could not be done the other way around and a Pearson r calculated, since ordinal scores cannot be converted to interval measures. (Remember, we don't know the distances between successive scale points on an ordinal distribution).
3. When both distributions are in interval-ratio form, but the distributions are so badly skewed that the Pearson r assumptions would be violated.

An example of an r_S situation would be when a researcher attempts to discover whether a significant correlation exists between the amount of money contributed to a university by an alumnus and the age of the alumnus. It becomes obvious to the researcher that the distribution of alumni donations is skewed. Although the mean donation was over $100, the median was $40, and the mode only $20. Thus, a few large donors jacked up the mean and skewed the entire distribution to the right. The age distribution is also found to be positively skewed, with most of the alumni less than forty years old but a few in their eighties and even nineties. Both sets of scores, then, must be translated into ranks, and the ordinal test of correlation, the r_S, should be used.

Nominal Tests of Significance

When the data come in the form of classified frequencies, nominal tests of significance must be used. Perhaps the most important message to keep in mind when dealing with the nominal case is that the cell entries must be absolutely

Table 5.19 Chi Square for Experimental Data

	SYMPTOM IMPROVEMENT	NO SYMPTOM IMPROVEMENT
DRUG	X	X
PLACEBO	X	X

independent of each other. That is, although the frequency count of observations within each category must share a common trait, they *may not share that trait* with observations appearing in any other category.

Chi square.   Far and away the most important statistical test for nominal data is the *chi square*. It can test for trends, for group differences, and even, in conjunction with other tests, for correlation. Also, it can be used for both experimental and post-facto research. For nominal data, chi square is a veritable workhorse. Like the ordinal tests, chi square makes no parameter or distribution assumptions and is thus called a nonparametric or distribution-free statistical test.

When testing for frequency differences between two or more groups, the appropriate statistical test is chi square. Because of its independent cell restriction, chi square is ideal for experimental research of the after-only variety. For example, a major pharmaceutical company wishes to test the effectiveness of a certain new antimononucleosis drug. A large random sample of recently diagnosed mono patients is selected and randomly divided into two groups. One group (experimental) is treated daily with the new drug, while the other group (control) receives a placebo. After three weeks, the two groups are compared with respect to either "symptom improvement" or "no improvement." That is, the groups are compared regarding *the numbers of students* reporting relief versus no relief. The appropriate test of significance would of course be chi square as outlined in Table 5.19.

Chi square may also be used for post-facto analysis if the groups are independently selected. For example, a researcher wishes to determine if enrollment in a typing class differs on the basis of gender. A random sample of high-school students is selected and categorized on the basis of gender. The numbers of males and females who are, or are not, taking typing is then determined, and analyzed via the chi-square test. (See Table 5.20)

Although the two previous examples drew comparisons between only two groups, the chi square can also handle multigroup comparisons. In the study of the mono drug, for example, the independent variable could have been manipu-

Table 5.20 Chi Square for Post-facto Data

	IN TYPING CLASS	NOT IN TYPING CLASS
MEN	X	X
WOMEN	X	X

Table 5.21 Chi Square with IV at Four Levels

	SYMPTOM IMPROVEMENT	NO SYMPTOM IMPROVEMENT
Placebo group	X	X
10-mg group	X	X
20-mg group	X	X
30-mg group	X	X

lated at, say, four levels: placebo, 10 mg of the drug, 20 mg of the drug, and 30 mg of the drug. (See Table 5.21)

Because of the independence rule, the researcher must be especially careful when handling nominal data studies involving matched-group or repeated-measures techniques. With correlated selection of samples, it's only too easy to fall into the trap of violating this rule.

For example, a researcher wishes to know whether an assertiveness-training course will produce more aggressive responses among ninth-grade girls. A random sample of one hundred ninth-grade girls is selected and measured on overt aggressiveness both before and after an assertiveness-training course. The data are as follows:

Table 5.22 Chi Square with Violation of Independence

	SHOWED AGGRESSION	DID NOT SHOW AGGRESSION
Before training	30	70
After training	70	30

At this point the researcher realizes that something has gone awry: adding the frequencies in all the cells yields 200, not the 100 total number of subjects that were involved. What went wrong? The basic independence rule for chi square has been violated, and the data are simply not testable in this form. That is, in this four-cell design, the same subjects are being counted in the "after" categories as had been counted in the "before" categories.

The McNemar test for correlated samples. The solution to the seeming dilemma in the foregoing example is to use a chi-square variation, called the *McNemar test*, for correlated samples. With this test the categories are set up on the basis of change scores. That is, instead of categorizing the same group of subjects, before and after, on the basis of whether they showed aggression, the subjects should have been categorized on the basis of whether they *changed* from not having shown aggression to later having exhibited aggressive responses. The change scores will thus be totally independent of each other.

The data should be set up as follows:

Table 5.23 McNemar Test Design

		AFTER	
		NO AGGRESSION (−)	AGGRESSION (+)
BEFORE	AGGRESSION (+)	10	20
	NO AGGRESSION (−)	20	50

The cells now contain only those subjects who changed from either having shown aggression in the before condition to not having shown aggression in the after condition, *or* who did not show aggression in the before condition but did show it in the after condition (as well as those subjects who did not change at all.) Notice, too, that the total of all the cell frequencies now equals 100, the actual size of the sample.

The McNemar test can be used, as just shown, for handling before-after experimental data, and also for the analysis of matched-subjects data.

Like the chi square, the McNemar test can be used for post-facto studies, but with the McNemar test the groups must be correlated through some sort of matching procedure. After the matching is completed, only the change-score frequencies are used (Sprinthall, 1990).

The coefficient of contingency. Correlation coefficients can also be calculated on nominal measures, usually, but not always, by first calculating the chi-square value. The most flexible of these is the *coefficient of contingency*, or C. The only values needed to calculate C are the value of the chi square and the size of the sample. For a two-by-two contingency table, however, C cannot exceed a value of .87. The maximum value of C depends on the number of categories, and even with eight cells in the contingency table, C can reach a value no higher than .97. Thus, C consistently yields lower estimates of correlational strength than does the interval-ratio, Pearson r, or the ordinal Spearman r_S.

An example of C would come from research attempting to show a correlation between eye color and hair color. A random sample of subjects is selected and categorized on the basis of both hair and eye color, and the numbers of subjects in each group are indicated as in Table 5.24.

Table 5.24 Chi Square and Correlation

		EYE COLOR	
		BROWN	BLUE
HAIR COLOR	BLONDE	X	X
	BRUNETTE	X	X
	RED	X	X

The chi-square value is then calculated, and this value is then plugged into the C equation.

$$C = \sqrt{\frac{\chi^2}{N + \chi^2}}$$

Other nominal tests of correlation are available, such as phi or Cramer's V. Each of these has certain assumptions and each requires a different contingency-cell size.

The Importance of Methodology

In this chapter a large number of statistical techniques have been outlined. It is absolutely critical, however, to remember that drawing logically derived research conclusions does not depend solely on which statistical test has been applied; it also depends on which type of research methodology has been used. Also, the particular research methodology must be evaluated with great care before any legitimate conclusions can be extrapolated. It is not enough to say that cause-and-effect has been demonstrated in a certain study simply because an independent variable was manipulated and the t ratio found to be significant. The exact methodology must be scrutinized for possible flaws. Was the control group adequate? Were other possible variables really controlled? Were the pure effects of the independent variable unambiguously clear, or was the IV possibly confounded?

The most powerful of statistical analyses cannot rescue a flawed design. Finding the appropriate statistical test is important, but it's not an end in itself. Good research demands a hand-in-hand coupling of methodology and statistical analysis. Like the motor and the fuel, the research vehicle just won't go without both—an all-cylinders methodology and a high-octane analysis.

SUMMARY

Descriptive statistics involves those techniques used for describing the characteristics of a given set or sets of measures. Descriptive statistics include the following:

1. measures of central tendency (the mean, the median, and the mode): describe the centrality of, or typical values among, a group of scores
2. measures of variability (range, standard deviation, and variance): describe the degree to which scores deviate from the middle of a distribution
3. measures of relationship: describe the degree to which two or more variables might be correlated

4. graphs and tables: visually describe the various measures of group characteristics
5. measures of skewness: describe the extent to which a distribution of scores deviates from symmetry
6. measures of kurtosis: describe the amount of variability shown in the graph of a distribution of scores
7. transformed scores (percentiles, stanines, and z and T scores): describe individual performance relative to the performance of the entire comparison group

Inferential statistics involves the use of sample measures (statistics) to infer the characteristics of a population (parameter). These inferential techniques are all based on the inductive model, that is, extrapolating from specific observations to an overall generalization. The various statistical tests all provide an estimate of the accuracy of these generalizations.

The statistical decision regarding whether the sample results are significant is based on the acceptance or rejection of the null hypothesis. To reject the null hypothesis implies that the results are indeed significant, and that in all likelihood they are not merely the result of blind chance. To accept the null hypothesis implies that the sample measures do not show significance, that is, that they could readily be explained on the basis of chance.

Since both these decisions are, in effect, chance decisions, it must be kept clearly in mind that either decision could be in error. If we reject chance when we should have accepted it, it is called the alpha or type-1 error, whereas if we accept chance when we should have rejected it, it is called the beta or type-2 error.

The opposite of the null hypothesis is called the alternative hypothesis, or, sometimes, the research hypothesis. The alternative hypothesis supports either differences or associations. The difference hypothesis can be tested in either experimental or post-facto research situations, whereas the hypothesis of association (correlation) is primarily tested when the research is post-facto.

The power of any inferential test is based on that test's ability to detect significance among the samples when the results are indeed generalizable to the population. A powerful test rejects the null hypothesis when the null hypothesis should indeed be rejected. Methods for increasing power include using interval-ratio data when possible, using as large a sample as possible, using an alpha error of .05 rather than .01, and fitting the statistical test to the research methodology.

The interval-ratio (parametric) tests of difference include

1. The independent t test: for examining the difference between the means of two sets of independent measures.
2. The paired t for examining the difference between the means of two sets of measures taken from correlated samples.
3. ANOVA (analysis of variance): the F ratio used for examining differences between two or more sets of independent measures. The one-way ANOVA is used when there is only a single IV, whereas the factorial ANOVA becomes appropriate when there are two or more IVs, whose interactions must also be analyzed.

4. The within-subjects ANOVA: used when a comparison is being made between sets of scores obtained from subjects who have experienced all the various IV conditions (as in a repeated-measures design), or from subjects who have been carefully equated on some measure(s) known to relate to the DV.
5. MANOVA: used when testing for differences on two or more DV measures as a function of two or more IV conditions.
6. ANCOVA: used to create a statistical control among the groups being tested with respect to one more variables (called the covariates). Adjusting for the covariate helps to prevent any systematic differences among the groups from acting as a confounding variable.
7. MANCOVA: used for essentially the same purpose as ANCOVA, but with MANCOVA more than one DV is involved in the study.

The interval-ratio tests of association include

1. The Pearson r: for assessing the degree of linear association (correlation) between two variables, X and Y.
2. Multiple correlation: used when three or more variables are being judged for possible association and an overall correlation among them is needed.

Nonparametric ordinal tests of difference include

1. The Mann-Whitney U test: used for assessing possible differences between two sets of independent measures.
2. The Kruskal-Wallis H test: used for comparing three or more distributions when each of the sample groups is independent of the others.
3. The Wilcoxon T test: used for establishing whether differences are occurring between two sets of correlated measures.
4. The Friedman ANOVA by ranks: used for identifying differences from within-subjects studies, that is, where one group has been subjected to three or more conditions or three groups have been equated on the basis of subject matching.

An ordinal test of association is the Spearman r_s correlation coefficient.

A nominal test of difference, chi square, is appropriate in both independent and correlated situations (the McNemar adjustment being applied in the latter case). Variations on the chi-square theme are also useful for handling situations in which correlations are needed among nominal measures.

KEY TERMS

Alpha error	Bimodal
Alternative hypothesis	Central tendency
ANCOVA	Chi square
ANOVA (between groups)	Coefficient of contingency
ANOVA (within groups)	Correlation
Beta error	Decile

Descriptive statistics
Factorial ANOVA
F ratio
Frequency histogram
Frequency polygon
Friedman ANOVA by ranks
Independent *t*
Inferential statistics
Kruskal-Wallis *II* test
Kurtosis
Leptokurtic
MANCOVA
Mann-Whitney *U* test
MANOVA
McNemar test
Mean
Median
Mesokurtic
Mixed design
Mode
Multimodal
Multiple comparison test
Multiple correlation
Multiple *R*
Nonparametric test
Normal curve

Null hypothesis
Paired *t*
Parameter
Parametric test
Pearson *r*
Percentile
Platykurtic
Power
Quartile
Range
Significance
Skewness
Spearman r_S
Standard deviation
Standard normal curve
Stanine
Statistic
Statistical decision
Stem-and-leaf display
T score
Transformed scores
Unimodal
Variability
Variance
Wilcoxon *T*
z score

REFERENCES

GREENWALD, A. (1975). Consequences of prejudice against the null hypothesis. *Psychological Bulletin*, *82*, 1–20.

SIEGEL, S. (1988). *Nonparametric statistics* (2d ed.). New York: McGraw-Hill.

SPRINTHALL, R. C. (1990). *Basic statistical analysis* (3d ed.). Englewood Cliffs, N.J.: Simon & Schuster, Prentice-Hall.

STEVENS, S. S. (1946). On the theory of scales of measurement. *Science, 103*, 677–680.

TURNBULL, W. W. (1980). *Test use and validity*. Princeton, N.J.: Educational Testing Service.

CHAPTER

6

Practical Considerations in Doing Research in Schools

DOING RESEARCH IN SCHOOLS: PLANNING THE PROJECT

A Basic Rule of Research
A Corollary to the Rule
Decisions, Decisions
A Final Note on Planning Research

A RESEARCH EXAMPLE

Will Teachers Alter Their Teaching
  Behavior Based on Research Results
  on Good Teaching Practices?
A Real-Life Example
Brief Comments on Griffin and Barnes
  1986

SUMMARY

KEY TERMS

REFERENCES

Is research in the schools any different from research in a laboratory or other highly controlled environment? In a great many ways, the answer is yes. Much of the discussion so far may seem to be based on the premise that the researcher always has a high degree of control over most aspects of the test situation. Although the experimental laboratory may be neat, aseptic, and totally controlled, what happens to the researcher who wishes to do a real-life study in a real-life school? It's like the dilemma faced by a new teacher, imbued with all the latest theoretical notions of motivation and learning theory, who suddenly faces an unruly student for the very first time. The teacher tells this student to stop being disruptive, to be fair to the other pupils, and to *please* sit down, only to be faced with a threatening pose and the challenge, "Make me." Thus, the ideal world of research and the world of research in practice may at times be very different places. In this chapter you will become acquainted with the kinds of considerations researchers face when planning and conducting research "out there" in the land of schools, where things may not always be fully controllable, and where, unlike the docile white rat, a subject may even say "Make me."

The list of practical considerations may at times seem almost endless but at a minimum would have to include ethical and legal restrictions, access to schools and classrooms, definitions of terms, cooperation from school personnel, and project costs. Careful and conscious consideration while the research is being planned is an absolute must. What makes the planning especially difficult is that the problems can't simply be considered one by one. The issues are sometimes intertwined and must be considered together, and furthermore, each decision influences what may be decided later on. Each set of considerations may impose a variety of constraints on the project and therefore influence the usefulness of the results from either an applied or theoretical standpoint. This last point, that is, whether the study has any potential practical or theoretical value, must be kept clearly in mind as all the other problems are being considered.

DOING RESEARCH IN SCHOOLS: PLANNING THE PROJECT

Now that you have some background in the nature of research thinking and basic research methodology and statistics, it's time to examine some of the problems and practicalities of conducting research in the real world of the school setting. In Chapter 4 it was pointed out that high levels of internal and external validity are not always easy to obtain in the same research study. This means that there are usually two ways to conduct research.

The first is the "best" way, the one in which the researcher has total control over the full range of conditions: subjects are randomly assigned, the IV(s) are carefully manipulated, and confounding factors are effectively dealt with. This will obviously produce experimental results with high levels of internal validity—a kind of experimental ideal which is, unfortunately, unlikely to be reached when research is actually being conducted in the schools. It was also indicated in Chapter 4, however, that these "ideal" studies may not have a high degree of external validity. In some situations, however, a high level of external validity is not the top priority. High internal validity is, of course, desirable (that's why we labeled this approach the best), especially when the research is to be used for theory testing and when application of the research results is not the primary purpose of the experiment. In planning that type of project, the decisions the researcher makes about manipulation of the IV, randomization, amount of control, and so on, are in favor of unequivocal results as opposed to their usefulness in an applied setting.

The second way to conduct research is the "practical" way, the compromise that the researcher often must settle for, especially if the purpose of the research is application to real-life situations. A wag once observed that since so much psychological research is done on college campuses, the definition of psychology should be changed from "the scientific study of the behavior of living organisms" to "the scientific study of the behavior of white rats and college freshmen." Actually, psychologists don't want to do their research exclusively in college laboratories using rats and college freshmen, because the results of these studies, although they may have high internal validity and might be very useful from a scientific or a theoretical standpoint, may not be applicable outside the lab.

The same issue is probably even more relevant when it comes to educational research. As educational researchers, we certainly hope to apply our research findings in a way that will benefit students, teachers, and administrators. As an aside, note that a good deal of psychological research is also educational research because the results may have educational value or at least potential educational application. When B. F. Skinner spent all those countless hours watching his rats press levers in experimental chambers, he wasn't just interested in rodent behavior. He hoped to apply his findings to the child in the classroom, as he did when he developed the teaching machine, or when he applied behavior modification programs to classroom management. And the reverse is also true, since many studies that were originally designed to test specific educational hypotheses were later found to provide psychologists with important theoretical knowledge about such things as the thinking process itself.

A Basic Rule of Research

There's an old proverb that says that one should believe none of what one hears and only half of what one reads. Though we tend to have a good deal of faith in the research we read, this warning should be heeded. Just because a study and the conclusions drawn from it are published does not guarantee its accuracy or importance. In fact, many errors in research design, analysis, control, and conclusions can be found in published articles, in spite of the fact that journal editors and reviewers do spend long hours carefully examining manuscripts prior to printing.

More on this issue will be found in the next chapter, but three of the most common errors to be found in published research include (1) failure to state the limitations of the study, (2) drawing conclusions that are not substantiated by the evidence, and (3) overgeneralization of results. In each case, the author of the research article has probably failed to remember the compromises and trade-offs made when the research was conducted. Researchers should carefully examine the research they have planned and conducted, and then provide a clear statement of the possible *limitations* to their conclusions. Given these limitations, the results should be interpreted cautiously, and the generalizations applied only to the appropriate populations and settings. Better still, when the researcher is planning the research, all these compromises and trade-offs should be kept in mind when later drawing conclusions. In other words, when the researcher is planning the study, decisions are made that will influence both its internal and external validity. Thus, any concessions that are made should be included in the discussion of the results.

Out of this discussion emerges a *basic rule of research:* when planning a research study (1) look for a natural research setting, (2) optimize control by using the strongest method and design that the situation allows and (3) consider threats to internal validity that may make interpretations equivocal and rival hypotheses reasonable.

The idea of looking for a natural research setting emphasizes the importance of external validity. The usefulness of the results in educational settings is, especially for practitioners, the primary issue.

The next point clearly speaks to the issue of internal validity. Certainly we want external validity, but we cannot ignore the importance of being able to come to clear and unequivocal conclusions about the effects of an IV on a DV. Given that we want to have a natural setting, we should try for the highest degree of control and the best method and design possible, within the constraints that may be imposed by that setting. Certainly we need to make decisions about how the research will be conducted in a natural research setting, while considering the degree to which control may still be possible. Doing research in natural settings will almost certainly limit the researcher in gaining total control over the circumstances. What is important about that is that as the researcher defines the IV and DV, and plans the project and carries it out, the decisions, compromises, and trade-offs made in planning must be kept clearly in mind.

The third point in this basic rule addresses the researcher's thinking when the project is completed and conclusions are being drawn. If, at each planning phase, the researcher carefully keeps track of every decision and the effect that each decision might have on the amount of control, the interpretation is more likely to be appropriate.

To keep these needs in perspective, however, it's necessary to have a bit of a split personality. The researcher part of you has to try to develop a project plan that will satisfy the requirements of internal validity, but the professional educator in you wants to be able to use the results in the classroom.

A Corollary to the Rule

Thus far in this chapter the reason we've talked so much about planning and decision making (with deliberate redundancy) is to drive home the point that they really are crucial issues. A *corollary to the basic rule* for conducting educational research, which is partly implicit, is that all aspects of the research project should be carefully and formally planned out, including the statistical procedures that will be used later for the analysis of data. This should all be done *before* subjects are observed and data are gathered.

At each phase of the planning, the researcher must keep asking whether the project will properly answer the research question or test the hypothesis of interest. There's an old story about the fellow from the city who stops to ask a farmer for directions to town. The farmer considers the question for awhile and starts to give directions three or four times. Each time, however, the farmer decides that the directions aren't correct and changes them. Finally, in exasperation, he looks at the city fellow and says, "You can't get there from here." The most frustrating thing that can happen to a researcher is to find out that "you can't get there from here," or that "you went in the wrong direction." This kind of failure typically occurs because of poor planning at the outset and results in a research nightmare in which the results don't even address the original question.

If you are able to follow this rule and its corollary, you should never come to conclusions that are not supported by the evidence, or fail to state the limitations of the study, or overgeneralize the results. And if you obey the corollary and carefully plan, you should be able to come to conclusions about the question you were interested in at the beginning.

Although we have stressed the difficulty of obtaining high degrees of both internal and external validity in the same study, you should not be left with the impression that it's impossible. Clever researchers with relatively free access to real-life school settings are sometimes afforded the luxury of both the control and subject-selection procedures necessary to achieve high internal validity as well as the natural settings required for high levels of external validity. Such studies are relatively rare, but, fortunately, they do exist.

Decisions, Decisions

Earlier in this chapter we suggested that there are two ways to do research: the "best" way and the "practical" way. In fact, of course, there are many more than just these two ways to conduct a research project designed to test a particular hypothesis or to answer a research question. The reason for this has to do with the decision-making process the researcher goes through in planning the study. This has been referred to several times earlier, but it bears repeating. Each decision influences the amount of control the researcher will eventually have over subjects and settings, as well as both the amount of measurement error and the degree to which the outcome of the study might be limited. At every decision point, therefore, the researcher's choice will influence the internal and external validity of the research.

Courses in research methods usually offer a sequential list of steps in planning and carrying out a research project. We, too, will provide a description of this *planning process* from beginning to end, but it's important to realize that the exact sequence of steps may vary from project to project and that several steps may even be in process at any given time. The list is as follows:

1. Identify the problem.
2. Review the literature.
3. Define the IV and DV operationally.
4. Specify subjects, materials, procedures, design, and data analysis.
5. Write the research proposal.
6. Replan, rewrite the proposal, and obtain cooperation and permissions.
7. Pilot the plan.
8. Do the project and gather data.
9. Do the statistical analysis.
10. Analyze results and draw conclusions.
11. Write the report for publication.

Not every researcher will go through all these steps for every project, but most projects will require at least eight or nine of them. An analysis of each step follows.

Identifying the Problem

This is always the beginning. A person becomes intrigued with a particular problem or question, and sometimes an answer to the question suggests itself in the form of a research hypothesis. Where does the question or hypothesis come from? Several sources are possible. The person may make an observation quite by accident: "I wonder why the moon looks as if it's larger when it's on the horizon than it does when it's directly overhead." The idea could also come from reading other research: "If that researcher had such good results with using a reading workbook with poor readers, I wonder if it would also produce even better results with learning-disabled students." Finally, the idea may be derived (deduced) from a theory: "If Piaget is right, and children aged seven to eleven years of age are in a concrete operations stage of cognitive development, children taught addition and subtraction in a 'concrete' fashion (through counting, sorting, manipulating, and so on) should learn better than children taught number theory or the 'structure' of mathematical knowledge."

Reviewing the Literature

Chapter 8 contains a good deal of information about the literature review, but for the moment, just keep in mind that the literature review is designed to tell us whether or not the study has been done before, and exactly how it or similar research was done. This very important part of the review describes where it was done, who the subjects were, how the IV(s) and DV(s) were operationally defined, and what procedures were used. Of course, it also describes the results and the conclusions of prior researchers. It is at this point that the very first (and perhaps the most critical) decision is to be made. If the information in the literature is sufficient to answer the question proposed by the problem of interest, new research may not need to be done, and the whole idea can be dropped. If the question is not adequately answered, as is most often the case, the planning of the project goes on.

Defining the IV and DV Operationally

At this point the researcher uses the corollary of the basic rule of research (planning) and begins to plan the study using all that information gathered from the review. Each study in the literature will include the operational definitions for the IV(s) and DV(s), including the specific measures, equipment, and procedures that were used. These might include published tests, researcher-constructed tests or questionnaires, and commercially available hardware, software, workbooks, and texts. The strengths and weaknesses associated with each operational definition should be considered, and, ultimately, choices made. Ideally, the IV and DV definitions will be the best available from the standpoint of reliability and validity, but costs of tests and equipment and the complications arising from their use also become a part of the total picture. Various problems associated with testing involve purchasing the tests, training people to administer, score, and interpret them, the availability of the tests, ease of use, the cost of machine scoring, and the amount of time needed for administration.

The problems related to equipment are similar. In fact, the IV and DV decisions made at this point might be primarily influenced by practical considerations and thus might result in the use of definitions that are not optimal. For example, the school system may already have equipment and testing materials that are in use, although perhaps a bit out of date. But the school system *has* these materials, and they don't have to be purchased or relearned. Expediency is often very difficult to ignore. If you're following the rule of research, note the possible limitations imposed by the decisions made when the IV and DV are specified.

Specifying Subjects, Materials, Procedures, Design, and Data Analysis

Once the IV and DV have been specified, the next step is planning the rest of the project. The basic research design has to be chosen if it hasn't already been influenced by the hypothesis and the IV and DV specifications. The method to be used for subject selection and the characteristics of the subjects must be clearly spelled out. It is to be hoped that the subjects can be randomly selected from a population and randomly divided into treatment groups, but the researcher must consider the limitations that will be imposed if less-than-ideal subject selection is necessary. The researcher must also select a site, especially one that the researcher has reason to believe will be available (usually as a result of preliminary discussions with the site administrator). Any materials needed for the project must also be chosen. These might include teaching or curricular materials, computer hardware and software, and electronic equipment. Each of the procedures to be carried out during the project must be carefully specified. Instructions to experimenters and subjects must be written and standardized, and the timing of each step in the research process must be planned. The statistical techniques that will be used to later analyze the data should be considered and chosen. (See Chapter 7 for more information on choosing the correct statistical procedures). Each of these considerations will require one or more decisions. The important issue here is that the project as now planned should allow the researcher to answer the research question or test the given hypothesis.

Finally, ethical and legal restrictions must be considered for each part of the project. It is always wise to discuss any potential ethical problems with colleagues. Most colleges and many large school systems have human-subjects-research committees or institutional review boards that meet to consider any possible ethical problems in a research proposal. The basic principle is that whenever human subjects are to be used for research, they must be safeguarded from any possible harm. Extensive guidelines for proper treatment of human subjects are available (American Psychological Association, 1982) and should be consulted before conducting *any* project. The most basic ethical considerations include the following areas of concern:

1. All information gathered from or about subjects must be kept confidential.
2. Subjects must be willing to participate and should be informed of any features of the study that might influence them in deciding whether or not to participate. In short, subjects should give *informed consent* for taking part in the study.
3. Subjects should be free to stop participating at any point during the research without penalty (such as loss of compensation or loss of extra-credit points).
4. Study participants should not be subjected to mental or physical discomfort. If discomfort is possible during the study, informed consent is again the rule.
5. Subjects should be *debriefed:* they should receive a complete explanation of the purpose of the study and any procedures that were used. If *deception* was used, it would typically be revealed at this time.

At every step in the planning process the basic rule for research should be kept in mind, and the possible limitations imposed by each decision should be logged for future reference. As the final phase of the project comes to a close—drawing conclusions from the data—those limitations should be noted.

Writing the Research Proposal

Now it's time to put all that elaborate planning down on paper. Essentially, the *research proposal* is a summary of the first four steps of the research process, written in the future tense: "The hypothesis *to be* tested will be . . . ." "The subjects *will be* . . . ." "The statistical test *will be* . . . ." The proposal usually consists of several sections, similar in many ways to the sections contained in a research article. (Considerably more about this will be covered in Chapter 8). The first section is the introduction, including the research question or hypothesis to be tested, and the literature review. The second is the method section, including a description of the subjects, procedures, materials, stimuli, equipment, IV and DV specifications, instructions, and ethical considerations. Next is a results section. This section doesn't contain data, of course, because the project hasn't been done yet. It does contain, however, a description of the statistics that will be used to analyze the data when they are collected.

The proposal should also contain a couple of additional sections. The first of these is a limitations section, which describes the problems anticipated when the final conclusions are drawn. If the researcher keeps a log during the planning process, the limitations of the study, from the standpoint of internal and external validity, should be obvious. The final section usually contains a cost analysis. This section is critical if the researcher is attempting to obtain funds from a school system or is applying for grant funding for the project. The list of expenses should be complete and carefully thought out, especially for contingencies in case anything goes wrong (remember, Murphy's law applies to researchers as much as it does to anyone else).

Some researchers don't write proposals, but it's probably a good idea to do it, even if it's not required. The exercise of going through the project from start to finish, including limitations, can be a valuable lesson, since it forces the researcher to "cross all of the *t*'s and dot all of the *i*'s." For students who write a master's thesis or a doctoral dissertation, a high-quality proposal will be required by the student's supervising committee. If a project is to be conducted in schools, the administration and the school board will probably require a proposal so that they can make informed decisions about whether to even allow the project to be done at all.

Note, of course, that the wise researcher does not suddenly appear at the principal's door or the school committee's meeting table with a written proposal that has never been seen before and about which those in authority have no knowledge. In the first place, researchers rarely go through the first four steps in the planning process without consultation with others. This is particularly important when dealing with the administrators of the research site. You may find early in the process that the project is of little or no interest to them and therefore that the project will have no chance of being conducted in that particular setting. The researcher must then decide whether another setting could be used, whether the project should be altered in its basic conception, or even whether the project should be scrapped. During the planning process, it's important to involve all the constituencies that will be involved in the project. It's often important to the success of a project that the teachers, administrators, school board, and others to be involved feel as if they have been part of the planning process. In fact, their suggestions and ideas might be invaluable to the researcher, and obtaining cooperation is often much easier when they are involved *early* in the process. Nobody said that doing research is easy; in addition to the technical skills involved in design and analysis, it requires tact, negotiating ability, and even powers of persuasion.

Replanning, Rewriting the Proposal, and Obtaining Cooperation and Permissions

Chances are that the researcher may have to change some aspects of the planned project after the proposal has been reviewed. For example, changes might be required if funding is not at the level requested, or an administrator or school board might attach conditions to any project approval. For example, the administrator may say to a researcher who requested access to students in three schools: "You can do the project *but* you can only use students in one school." It is those "buts" that can send the researcher back to the drawing board with rapidly graying hair, because what may seem like minor constraints can actually have major effects on the original planning.

Even when the researcher, during the planning process, has been careful to involve all the constituencies that will be involved in the project, decisions have a way of being made that are somehow surprisingly different from those expected. As administrators and school boards discuss and consider the project, they may discover problems that they hadn't anticipated earlier. The problems may be administrative or political, but whether real or imagined, the effect on the project will be the same. It is at this point that many projects lose internal validity and develop unfortunate research errors. The reason this happens is that constraints placed on the research as originally planned are often not carefully considered, and the whole project replanned. This may result in making improper conclusions at the end simply because limitations were added that were not accounted for in the original plan. When this happens, it may become necessary to rewrite the proposal and resubmit it. Sometimes, alas, proposals may have to be rewritten several times before being approved for funding or for permission to gain access to a research site.

If you've done it right, you probably already have the cooperation of those who will be directly involved in the project. Once the project is funded and basically ready to roll, the next step is to get whatever permissions or consent forms are necessary. As indicated earlier, ethical subject treatment requires informed consent. The experimenters need to obtain the consent of the subjects being used for the research, or if the subjects are school children, the consent of their parents. It is always wise to obtain information about willingness to participate in the study by obtaining signed consent forms.

Piloting the Plan

Many times a mini version of the entire study is done before the full-blown version is carried out. Such a *pilot study* allows the researcher to discover any bugs in the research procedure and iron them out so that they will not affect the outcome. It is especially important to pilot new questionnaires, surveys, or other instruments, and to practice complicated procedures or data-gathering techniques before the study is actually done. Pilots don't always have to be done, but if a researcher has *any* doubts about any aspects of the study, it's good practice to pilot the project first.

Implementing the Project and Gathering Data

As the study is being planned, researchers can often be seen shaking their heads and mumbling to themselves "decisions, decisions." But once this planning is done, the funding and site are ready, and all the subjects (or their parents) have agreed to participate, the study must now be implemented and the data gathered. This may seem anticlimactic, since a good deal of the work in research is in the planning stage, but after all, this is what you planned for.

Doing the Statistical Analysis

You should already know what statistical tests are planned for the data (since you included that as a part of the plan). Those analyses were designed to answer, or help answer, your research question or to test your hypothesis. As researchers look at the data, however, sometimes other statistical tests are done to answer questions that are suggested by the data. Unplanned statistical procedures employed to answer questions that are suggested by the data are often called *post-hoc* or *subsequent tests*. These are usually not essential to the original question or hypothesis but are instead, done because they occur to the researcher after the fact. Such "accidental" findings may shed further light on the question at hand or be a source of questions to be answered by future research projects.

Analyzing the Results and Drawing Conclusions

This, in a sense, is where it all comes together. You can get a solid sense of how this process works by reviewing several of the discussion sections in the article that appears later in this chapter and the articles in Chapters 8, 9, and 10. Researchers try to answer the question(s) with which they began in light of the statistical results obtained and the limitations inherent in the study. Also, they often attempt interpretation of the results with respect to other studies or theories that they feel may be relevant. Research is, after all, a creative task. New knowledge about differences, similarities, causes, or associations is created when doing any research project. Whether that new knowledge is equivocal or unequivocal, clear or fuzzy, also depends to a large extent on the creativity of the researcher during the crucial planning phase.

Writing the Report for Publication

Many research studies, alas, are never published but instead languish in dust-covered file-cabinet drawers. This can really be a shame, because the knowledge generated never reaches a wide audience. However, the research findings might still be made available to a small audience, such as the administrators or teachers in a school or district.

There are several reasons for research not being published. First, the researcher may not write the article because of a lack (or perceived lack) of time. Yet, if you think about it, the proposal contains part of the information that would be included in the final article. It contains most of the introduction and the method sections (which may only have to be changed to past tense instead of future tense: "The subjects were . . ." instead of "The subjects will be . . ." for example). Actually, only the results and discussion sections should need to be written for the first time.

Second, the research may not contain significant statistical differences or large enough correlations, and as we indicated in Chapter 5, many journals and other publications do not publish (or are reluctant to publish) research based on chance results. This is unfortunate, because even the failure of research is important information. The inability to replicate the findings of prior research, for example, could be just as important as when the results are substantiated. It may, for example, lead one to question the validity of that earlier study.

From another standpoint, one could ask whether alpha (or Type-1) error is more serious than beta (or Type-2) error. The following argument could readily be made. The researcher who rejects null when in fact there is no real difference (alpha error) may end up publishing a "false" rejection. If the study is important, however, others will replicate it, resulting in a kind of self-correcting process. Important failures to replicate do tend to get published; therefore, these false rejections will sooner or later be uncovered. If the study isn't important, the false rejection may not be important either. (Note, however, that studies not important at one time might become important at some later time.)

The other side of the coin is the situation in which the researcher accepts null when in fact there really is an IV effect (beta error). In this case the researcher may simply place the results in the back of a file drawer and they may never see the light of day. In this case no correction is possible, since no one else will ever see these results. Perhaps what's needed is a new journal, say the *JOF* (*Journal of Failures*), devoted exclusively to "negative" results.

Finally, research may be so limited as to be useful *only* to a small audience. A good deal of action research, survey research, and evaluation research is so specific to a particular school or population that it may hold little or no interest for a wider group of readers. In planning research, every time a decision is made that limits the usefulness of the result, a corresponding limitation is also placed on the breadth of its appeal.

A Final Note on Planning Research

As has been said several times, every real-life setting has a number of constituencies that must be considered and satisfied in conducting research. Schools, in particular, have a number of groups of people who may be critically important to a project. These might include the school board, superintendent, principals, teachers, students, parents, guidance counselors, and even janitors or lunch-room personnel. To the extent that these people have an impact on the project, they must be involved early in the planning process and satisfied that the research is doable (in a practical sense), useful to the school system and its personnel, and of enough importance to be worth doing. The research hypothesis itself might even be considered a "constituent" in the sense that it too needs to be satisfied as to the use of methods with as much internal validity as possible.

It is often relatively easy to involve teachers, administrators, and other school personnel in the research process, especially if they can see the potential usefulness of the results and if the researcher has set that process in motion early in the planning stage. Of all the constituencies, however, school boards are often the most difficult to convince. There are several reasons for this. First, the school board must carefully consider any political consequences the project might have. It may appear that school personnel must also consider any possible political effects, but they often act in terms of how they think the board will react. In fact, school personnel usually don't have to consider politics to the same degree as the elected officials who serve as the schools' "board of directors."

Second, the large majority of school-board members are not educators, though increasing numbers of professionals are becoming involved. The NEA has, for example, encouraged its members to become more active in local politics both as supporters of candidates and as candidates for office themselves. The board may be reluctant to allow researchers to "play around" in the schools or to "tinker" with ongoing programs they may not fully understand. Third, they must almost always be convinced that the project will not require any great financial commitment on the part of the school system, since they may already be having difficulty managing scarce resources. Finally, they will need to be fully convinced that the results will be usable, especially in "their" system. As for theoretical research, they may respond, "Theory shmeory, what's in it for us?" In short, school boards are usually the most difficult to convince, and when they finally do allow a project, they are the ones who are most likely to place restrictions on it.

If these constraints on design, access to subjects, resources, and so on, place severe limits on the usefulness of the project, it may be time for the researcher to ask (after the replanning in step 6) an important question before doing the project. That question is: Will the imposed limitations result in conclusions so equivocal as to render the results virtually useless to the local system or to the wider audience? This is not to say that all school boards are composed of a bunch of crusty, self-serving old fogies. Most often they are hard-working people who serve their communities well, have too little money to work with, and do the work of the board for little or no pay. They will listen, but they will need to be convinced.

All of this may sound rather gloomy and may even make you so depressed and cynical that you won't even want to *consider* doing educational research, especially research in the school setting, but before throwing in the towel consider this more optimistic scenario. More first-rate research is being conducted in the schools today than ever before, research that is well-planned and well-conducted (though not necessarily without some limitations). This is partly a result of increasing numbers of school professionals who have had courses like the one you are now taking. It is also partly because there are now a number of commonly available computer packages for doing the statistical chores, even for complicated designs based on large subject pools. And you no longer have to be a computer whiz to run these programs. Twenty years ago, many of the now commonly used analyses were available only to a relatively small number of technically sophisticated professionals. The researcher of today, of course, does need to know what the statistical procedures are and be able to read the computer outputs correctly, but those skills are far more easily obtained now than they were previously. In addition, schools and school personnel have been under pressure to be accountable for what they do, and research is one very practical way to meet that goal. Because of that, in some cases you may even be surprised to learn that the school welcomes your proposal. Finally, there has been a trend, primarily in higher education, but in public and private schools as well, toward gathering more knowledge about the ways that individual schools and their characteristics influence students. This might be called a search for school self-identity or school self-understanding. It is becoming a case of the school heeding the advice, Know thyself. What the future might bring is, of course, a matter of speculation, but sometimes new trends can be discerned fairly early by the careful observer. A discussion of the possibilities and probable future trends in educational research, as well as the impact of computers on education, is presented in Chapter 11.

A RESEARCH EXAMPLE

By now it should be clear that there is no single right way to do research on any given topic. There are certainly better ways (experiments with random division of subjects, when possible) and, to some extent, not-so-good ways (quasi-experiments or post-facto research, if necessary), but there are always several ways to approach any problem. As has been said over and over again, it's largely a matter of the decisions made in the first six steps of the planning process. Now it's time to take a look at a research question and take a guided tour through the thought processes a researcher might go through in an attempt to find some empirical answers. Following that an example of how two researchers actually examined that same question will be presented.

Will Teachers Alter Their Teaching Behavior Based on Research Results on Good Teaching Practices?

Hundreds of research articles have been published over the past ten years on the basic question of what constitutes good teaching. These articles have examined and described dozens of teaching practices that consistently lead to desirable outcomes in terms of student behavior. This suggests several research questions. For example, one could ask whether all that knowledge has been consistently conveyed to prospective teachers in their college's education courses, so that it can be put into classroom practice. That is, have classroom teachers been made aware of these results, and even more important, are they being used?

One question—an important one—is whether teachers will change their own classroom teaching practices if they are informed of what some of these good teaching practices are. In short, does knowledge of research results lead to better teaching? (This is a particularly appropriate question, because if nobody is listening to and using the knowledge gained through research, one could ask, Why bother?) At this point, step 1 of the process is completed; a research question has been identified that could be stated as a hypothesis, as follows: teachers who are given knowledge of research on good teaching practices will be more effective teachers than those not given such knowledge.

The next step in the process—step 2—is the literature search. We won't take you through an exhaustive search right now, but we urge you to see

Walberg's (1986) summary of research on teaching. Your primary interest would, of course, be to look for information on the effects of providing teachers with research results. You will find several studies in which providing knowledge to teachers from the research literature has had a positive effect on both teacher and student performance. You decide, however, that you still want to do the study in your own school setting, and so go on with the process.

Here are several selected teaching practices that have been shown to lead to desirable student behavior and several behaviors that can be altered by teaching practice.

Research Information on Effective Teaching Practices (Possible IVs)

1. task-oriented approach to teaching
2. use of praise (positive reinforcement)
3. frequent and consistent evaluation of student work
4. clear presentation of material
5. engagement of class in the lesson

Student or Class Behaviors (Possible DVs)

1. attitude toward school
2. classroom climate
3. academic achievement
4. self-concept
5. speed of learning

Assume, for a moment, that these are the only practices and behaviors derived from the literature. The next step, then, (step 3) is to decide *which* teaching practice(s) and student behavior(s) are of the most interest and how they will be used or measured. This is an important step in specifying the IV and DV. Note, incidentally, that a list of desirable *teacher* behaviors could also be created and considered as possible DVs. You have five choices each for IVs and DVs, resulting in five times five or twenty-five possible combinations. For example, IV_1 could be paired with DV_1, or IV_1 with DV_2. Your decision might be to use IV_3 with DV_3. Note that the research hypothesis now states that giving knowledge of research results about the positive effects of frequent and consistent evaluation will increase student achievement. By now you've already made a number of *informed* (based on the search) decisions and also narrowed down the procedural and DV possibilities.

The actual specification of the IV in operational terms requires a clear and complete description of *how* the knowledge will be given to the teachers and what the *content* of that knowledge will be. You decide that your design will include two groups of teachers in a school, randomly divided, with half the teachers receiving information from research on the effectiveness of consistent and frequent evaluation of student work and the other group receiving different unrelated or irrelevant information. The specific content provided to teachers in both groups, the amount of instruction, when the instruction will be given, and by whom, are all a part of the operational definition of the IV (providing research information to teachers).

The operational definition for the DV, achievement, is a wide-open choice. You could choose to use students' final examination grades, achievement test results (such as the Iowa Test of Basic Skills), and so on. Whatever you choose, the specific measure used must be clearly specified.

At step 4 (subject and procedure specification) all the remaining details must be described. In this experiment, the subjects receiving the treatment are the classroom teachers. If the IV influences the teachers in the experimental group (E group) and they put that knowledge to work, those teachers' students should perform at a higher level than the students of the teachers in the control group (C group). If some teachers in the E group put the knowledge into practice, their students should improve, but if the other teachers in the E group do not use the knowledge, their classes should perform at about the same level as the students in the classes of the C group teachers. What we have ended up with in this case is called a *nested design*. The students' performance depends on, or is nested within, the teacher's classroom. Students in teacher A's class do not experience the teaching of teacher B, even though teachers A and B might both be in the E group. Thus, the students' performance depends not only on the overall characteristics of their teacher but also on whatever effect the IV might have had on the teaching practice. Procedural specifications would include the time interval between the treatment and the testing of the students, when during the school year the treatment will be applied, and how the students will be tested.

The statistical analysis could be performed via a *t* test, comparing the performance of the students in the E-group classes with the performance of the students in the C-group classes. However, since the design is nested and student performance may depend both on which teacher they had *and* whether their teacher was in the C or E group, a form of analysis of variance, or ANOVA, might be a more appropriate approach.

Each of the many choices you have made in getting to this point has had a powerful impact on the limitations of the overall study. The IV is manipulated and the subjects are to be randomly divided; therefore, the research is definitely a true experiment. The internal validity should, therefore, be strong, but care must still be taken to control factors that could confound the results. If, for example, teachers find out which group they are in (and they probably will since teachers in the same building are bound to talk with one another), the outcome could be affected. In this instance, there is a good chance that the demand characteristics of the study could easily affect teacher performance. Remember, the study is being done with teachers who were not randomly selected from a defined population, and all of them do teach in the same school. This means that the external validity is limited. Despite this, however, the results might still prove to be useful in that *particular setting*.

Assuming that you decide to do the project after examining the limitations, all the remaining steps will then be done, one by one. As outlined previously, your findings must, of course, be interpreted in light of the limitations imposed by the design and circumstances.

A Real-Life Example

Despite what may seem like exhaustive coverage, we have not been able to include every possibility or every consideration in this research example. You may very well be able to identify other factors that could be considered in the planning, or even other potential limitations or control problems. You might also have decided to use teacher behavior as a DV instead of, or in addition to, student behavior. The article that follows, by Griffin and Barnes (1986), uses an experimental design to test the same general hypothesis as the example. As you read the article, look for the points at which they had to make decisions about the IV and DV, subjects, design, and so on. Note that each paragraph in the article has been numbered. In our discussion of this article we will use these numbers to identify the portion of the article that we are referring to.

Using Research Findings to Change School and Classroom Practices: Results of an Experimental Study

GARY A. GRIFFIN

University of Illinois at Chicago

and

SUSAN BARNES

Texas Education Agency

A quasi-experimental, treatment-control group investigation was designed to test the effects of introducing research findings from effective teaching and school leadership into ongoing school settings. Research findings were translated into observable staff developer and teacher behaviors. Following 5 days of training 3 weeks prior to the beginning of school, treatment staff developers implemented self-designed plans to increase effective teaching behaviors. Both staff developers and teachers recorded journal entries, and teachers were observed. Based on staff developer journal entries, a significant treatment effect was found for the transfer of all staff developer behaviors. Based on classroom observations, a significant

Griffin, G. A. & Barnes, S. (1986). 'Using research findings to change school and classroom practices: results of an experimental study,' *American Educational Research Journal 23*, pp. 572–86. Copyright © by the American Educational Research Association. Reprinted by permission of the publisher.

treatment effect was found for teacher behaviors in 4 of 10 categories of effective teaching behaviors: academic planning and preparation, academic presentation, organizing for class-room management, and presentation of rules and procedures.

Criticism of educational research frequently centers on the perceived lack of impact of research upon classroom and school practice. Often termed the "research into practice gap," this point of view assumes that there should be an immediate and observable influence of research findings upon schooling, and that the research work should assist in making teaching and learning more predictable, economical, and effective. Indeed, this point of view has become pervasive as policymakers, for example, search for the best ways to certify teachers, implement master teacher programs, and develop teacher evaluation schemes. Although the wisdom of widespread application of research findings as regulatory or reward systems is certainly open to serious question, it is reasonable to assume that there should be some improvement-oriented relation of certain of the findings to school change. Indeed, a number of scholars have demonstrated this point of view in studies and syntheses of research that appear to have some potential for influencing practice (Brophy, 1983; Fullan, 1985; Gage, 1984; Purkey & Smith, 1983; Rosenshine, 1983).

The Research in Teacher Education (RITE) program of the Research and Development Center for Teacher Education at the University of Texas at Austin designed a research-into-practice study as a means to test the effects of introducing teacher effectiveness and staff development research findings into an ongoing school system. The research was based upon three assumptions: (a) Research findings can be used to provide a systematic focus to teaching and schooling and thereby serve as a school improvement tool; (b) research findings can be transmitted to school practitioners in forms if the findings are viewed as legitimate and useful guides to practice; and (c) research findings can be interpreted positively by school-based administrators and teachers if careful attention is given to style and manner of delivery, with particular emphasis placed upon situation-specific issues that vary from one school setting to another.

The purpose of the Changing Teacher Practice (CTP) study was to determine the effects upon staff developers (principals and resource teachers), teachers, and students of an intervention that included research findings drawn from studies of teacher effectiveness and school change. The intervention was provided only to the staff developers in an attempt to assess the impact of instructional leadership on teaching practice and student behavior.

The line of inquiry generally termed "teacher effectiveness research" (Medley, 1979) has identified certain teaching behaviors as positively related to high student scores on standardized mathematics and reading tests. Findings from the research on teaching effectiveness emphasize the learning environment, management of behavior, classroom instruction, teaching styles, and how the teacher assumes responsibility for these aspects of the classroom (Brophy & Evertson, 1974; Good & Grouws, 1981; Stallings, Needels, & Stayrook, 1979). In this research the effective teacher is defined as one whose classes regularly score higher on standardized achievement tests than do classes of other teachers after entering differences among classes are statistically controlled. A composite picture of effective teachers drawn from this body of research findings would give attention to the following: the teacher's establishment of a work orientation while maintaining a warm, supportive environment; a high level of organization with emphasis on management of the class to increase the productive use of time; active involvement with students to prevent misbehavior and prompt interventions to stop misbehavior; clear presentation of new material with opportunities for students to practice new skills; monitoring of student behavior; provision of feedback to students; assignment of individual seatwork; and systematic evaluation of student products. These effective teachers generally interact with the whole class during classtime and move students through lessons at a brisk pace with a high level of student success. | 4

The research findings that contribute to this composite picture of the effective teacher were translated into specific statements of teacher behavior as guides to classroom practice and then included in the CTP intervention (Barnes, 1981). | 5

The CTP intervention also included research findings directly related to positive school change (Edwards, 1981). Three frequently cited research efforts provided the knowledge base for teacher and school change: (a) The Institute for Development of Educational Activities (I/D/E/A) 5-year study of change in individual schools (Bentzen, 1974), (b) the Rand Corporation study of federal programs supporting educational change (Berman & McLaughlin, 1978), and (c) the Concerns-Based Adoption Model work on the implementation of innovations (Hall & Loucks, 1978). Additional insights about school change were derived from Sarason's (1971) perspective on school regularities, Goodlad and Klein's (1974) hypotheses regarding why change is blunted in schools, Bentzen's propositions regarding the positive effects of the school-level peer group strategy, and Berman and McLaughlin's propositions about system characteristics that foster and support school change efforts. In addition, and related to the I/D/E/A findings and processes, leadership strategies were drawn from organization development theory and practice. | 6

From studies of school and teacher change it can be inferred that effective leadership will take into account opportunities for teacher interactions that are focused on teaching issues, provision of technical assistance to teachers, adaptation of ideas and programs that are complementary to school and classroom norms and regularities, opportunities for teacher reflection and analysis, and focused and precise (rather than general and diffuse) attention given to important teaching and schooling issues. These broad areas of leader behavior were defined operationally and presented to staff developers as part of the CTP intervention. | 7

RESEARCH QUESTION

The CTP study examined the effects of an intervention that introduced selected findings from teaching effectiveness research and school change research into ongoing school settings. The research question that guided the study was: Did the CTP intervention increase the frequencies of research-derived teaching and staff developer behaviors and, further, was there an effect upon students in terms of on-task behavior? (On-task student behavior was used as a proxy for student achievement. See Anderson, Evertson, & Brophy, 1979; Emmer, Evertson, & Anderson, 1980; Sanford & Evertson, 1981.) | 8

DESIGN

The study was an experimental, nested design with treatment ($N = 5$) and control ($N = 5$) groups of staff developers, two teachers associated with each staff developer, and the students associated with each teacher. | 9

SITE AND PARTICIPANTS

The study was conducted in a large urban school district with multicultural student and educator populations. The district has a demonstrated history of emphasis on school improvement, recently manifested by a locally developed curriculum and instruction program designed to raise scores on standardized achievement tests. Ten staff developers in elementary schools were nominated by district officers for participation in the CTP study. Participants were matched according to role, socioeconomic status of school, prior experience, years in current position, sex, and district reputation for effectiveness. Members of each pair were then randomly assigned to either treatment or control condition. Each staff developer selected two teachers with whom he or she worked for participation in the study. Treatment condition of teachers and of students in classes was determined by the treatment condition of the associated staff developer.

10

THE CTP INTERVENTION

The CTP intervention consisted of 1 week of intensive training for the five treatment-group staff developers conducted 3 weeks prior to the beginning of the 1982–1983 school year. The 5-day training acquainted staff developers with the findings from research on teaching effectiveness and from research on school change. The teaching behaviors were presented in the form of videotapes of natural environments, a videotape designed specifically for the purpose of demonstrating effective teaching (Association for Curriculum Development and Supervision, 1980), typed classroom observation narratives, manuals based on effective teaching research and designed for teacher use (Evertson et al., 1981; Good et al., 1977), discussion, and lecture. Particular attention was paid to developing an understanding of the definitions of teaching effectiveness as exemplified by the body of research, and on skill in recognizing the behaviors in the videotape materials.

11

Likewise, the school change research was presented through a variety of stimuli, including lecture, text, filmstrips, and slides. Throughout the CTP intervention, the RITE staff modeled the effective change strategies in their interactions with the treatment group staff developers, particularly in relation to guiding the staff developers to pertinent and available materials and resources, depending upon the issue under consideration.

12

Finally, the staff developers were asked to prepare a brief profile of their schools in terms of pupil population characteristics, teacher and school strengths and weaknesses, curriculum requirements, available resources, and persistent and anticipated problems. These descriptions were then used as bases for the development of school-specific staff development plans as staff developers selected the research-based teaching behaviors upon which they would focus and the change strategies they would use to provide structure for that focus. The RITE staff emphasized that the research findings provided only one way to look at teaching and school improvement. Participants were encouraged to supplement the research-based information with their own craft knowledge. Thus, the CTP intervention was designed to preserve and capitalize on the ecological validity of the school settings rather than introduce artificial conditions into the schools and classrooms of study participants.

13

The intervention was reinforced modestly on two occasions. The first was a 3-hour workshop, requested by the staff developers, that focused on achieving greater skill in recognizing the research-based effective teaching behaviors and the second was a 45-minute interview with each staff developer that focused on participants' perceptions of

14

their own effectiveness. The workshop provided additional detail to the original intervention but the interview served more as a morale builder than as substance related to the intervention. | 14

INSTRUMENTATION

Both qualitative and quantitative data were collected. Teachers and staff developers in both control and treatment groups recorded in structured journals their recollections, factual and impressionistic, of each staff development activity in which they participated during the study. The activities included both formal (e.g., a staff meeting devoted to direct instruction) and informal (e.g., a hallway conversation about grouping of students for instruction). They were asked to include information about purpose, focus, context, result, and their own evaluation of each activity. Teachers and staff developers also responded to personal history questionnaires. Teachers completed a second questionnaire that focused on their planning for the beginning of school and their perceptions of confidence in teaching their assigned curriculum to their assigned students. | 15

Teachers, control and treatment, were observed in their classrooms. A low inference instrument designed specifically for this study (Barnes, 1983) was used. The Barnes Teacher Observation Instrument (BTOI) was based upon the teaching behaviors suggested by the research as being effective. The BTOI allows for notation of frequencies of specific teaching behaviors in 10 categories: planning and preparation for academics, presentation of content, teacher-student interactions, conducting practice, conducting seatwork, holding students responsible for assignments, organizing the classroom, presenting rules and procedures, holding students responsible for behavior, and reacting to student behavior. Each of these categories, or factors, included specific technical statements of research-based effective teaching. The percentage of agreement among trained observers on the occurrence or nonoccurrence of the specific teaching behaviors was .89. | 16

An estimate of student on-task behavior was obtained using the Student Engagement Rating (SER) whereon were recorded the numbers of students engaged in academic, procedural, or off-task behavior at 10-minute intervals during classroom observations. The percentage agreement among trained observers on the numbers of students exhibiting these behaviors was .83. | 17

PROCEDURES

The CTP intervention, as noted, took place with treatment group staff developers 3 weeks prior to the opening of the school year. After the intervention, treatment group staff developers began implementation of the plans developed during the intervention. These plans were school-specific in that they attended to what the staff developers believed to be of highest priority in their buildings, and were also largely research-based in that they included as content the research findings that were most suited to the priorities. Control group staff developers also began their work with teachers. There was no attempt to obtain control group staff developers' intentions or strategies. That information was collected as part of the entire sample's journal entries. All staff developers and teachers in the study began journal entries upon commencement of any staff development activity and continued until February of the school year. | 18

Although the numbers of staff developers ($N = 10$) and teachers ($N = 20$) were relatively small, the amount of data collected was extensive. Staff developers recorded 8,073 entries in journals and teachers a like number. Also, beginning with the first day of | 19 the school year, both treatment and control group teachers were observed teaching reading and mathematics. Twelve hours of teaching observation were obtained for each teacher: 4 hours during the first 2 weeks of school, 4 hours in October, and 4 hours in January. [19]

ANALYSIS OF DATA

The journal entries were analyzed to determine the self-reported frequency of the research-based leadership strategies. Four coders, trained to a .86 agreement level, worked independently and then in pairs to note the frequency of reports of the leadership strategies. Disagreements between paired coders were resolved through re-examination of the journal entries. Of 8,073 possible instances of coding agreement, only 29 disagreements between coders were not resolved and were then excluded from the analysis of staff developer behavior. For staff developers, treatment, and control, the frequencies of research-based behaviors were divided by the number of journal entries for each staff developer. This procedure was used to obtain a uniform score for the staff developers, whose journals differed in numbers of entries. Thus, a mean frequency of research-based staff developer behaviors was obtained for each participant. Further, the frequency of each discrete behavior was also determined for each staff developer as well as for the total of treatment and control groups. [20]

The frequencies of research-based teaching behaviors, collected through the use of the low inference instrument noted above, were converted to rates per minute for each teaching behavior. Next, the teaching behaviors within each of 10 categories on the instrument were averaged to produce means in each category for each teacher for each of 12 observations. Finally, the two 2-hour observations in each subject area, reading and mathematics, for the September, October, and January observation periods were collapsed to produce mean rates for each observation period. This resulted in 3 mean rates in both reading and mathematics for the 10 observation categories for each teacher. Because the sample size of 20 teachers was small, mean rates were used to provide data that more closely approximated the normal distribution (Hayes, 1973). [21]

Observed teaching data were analyzed using a hierarchically nested, repeated measures analysis of variance with five factors. One factor was the *treatment* factor with two levels, treatment and control. Nested within each treatment condition was the second factor, *staff developers;* nested within each staff developer was the third factor, *teacher.* These factors were crossed with two others, *time* and *content.* Because time was not an interval variate, it was treated as a factor in the analysis of variance. Observations occurred in early September, late October, and late January (Time 1, 2, and 3, respectively) over 2-week time periods. [22]

FINDINGS

The three levels of effects of the CTP intervention were staff developer effects, teacher effects, and student effects. Each is discussed briefly. For a more complete and detailed presentation of findings, see Griffin et al. (1983). [23]

The CTP intervention was directed, in part, toward the adoption of research-based leadership behaviors by treatment group staff developers. The treatment group members demonstrated slightly more than twice as many of the desired staff developer behaviors than did the control group members. The results of a Mann-Whitney test indicate that this difference is statistically significant at the .01 level. The within group mean for the control group was lower than the lowest mean for the treatment group. [24]

The frequencies of each of the desired staff developer behaviors provided the substance of the difference between the group means (Table I). The most dramatic difference between the two groups was in the treatment group's far greater attention to teacher behavior as the focus of staff development work. Obviously, this difference can be attributed to the inclusion in the CTP intervention findings from research on teaching. Also, it can be seen that, in general terms, the treatment group staff developers paid more precise attention to the classroom and school variables in their work with teachers, 25

Table I   Mean Frequencies of 23 Desired Staff Developer Behaviors Per Journal Entry by Group

BEHAVIOR	TREATMENT	CONTROL
1. Diagnose school- and classroom-specific regularities	.49	.27
2. Provide teachers with opportunities to interact with one another about teaching and schooling	.25	.12
3. Provide teachers with opportunities to observe one another and to discuss what was observed	.04	.02
4. Provide teachers with opportunities to plan together	.11	.02
5. Provide teachers with opportunities to implement their plans	.00	.00
6. Provide teachers with feedback that is objective, concrete, and focused	.22	.12
7. Use teacher time to deal with teacher problems, issues, and concerns (rather than with administrative, routine, or procedural matters)	.27	.26
8. Interact with teachers in friendly and positive ways	.03	.02
9. Adapt staff development behavior according to personal and organizational characteristics of "users"	.24	.05
10. Demonstrate knowledge of "effective" teaching as revealed by research	.37	.05
11. Provide in-classroom technical assistance (e.g., coaching) to teachers	.06	.03
12. Provide teachers with specific, concrete resources	.29	.18
13. Engage teachers in problem identification, solution formulation and testing activities	.16	.11
14. Work with teachers on adaptation of teaching strategies according to the characteristics of students, the classroom, and the school	.24	.11
15. Provide teachers with evidence that teachers can make a difference in pupil outcomes	.08	.02
16. Link teachers to technical assistance outside the immediate school environment	.22	.09
17. Communicate expectations clearly and precisely	.18	.12
18. Diagnose individual stages of concern of teachers	.03	.00
19. Formulate interventions based, in part, on teachers' stages of concern	.02	.00
20. Provide consistent, ongoing assistance to teachers	.09	.08
21. Include the building principal or resource teacher in activities	.17	.06
22. Reflect upon the effects of teacher behavior and use that reflection as a basis for decisions about maintenance or modification of that behavior	.14	.06
23. Focus on teacher behavior	.45	.09

dealt more directly with the issues of adaptation of ideas and plans in relation to those variables, linked teachers to sources of technical assistance, and provided more opportunities for teachers to work together on teaching and schooling issues. The smallest differences between treatment and control group staff developers were found in the attention given to teacher-based issues (both groups were high), provision of ongoing and consistent assistance to teachers (both groups were moderate), and the use of teacher concerns data and provision of in-classroom technical assistance (both groups were low).

As revealed by analysis of journal entries, the control group staff developers, although exhibiting some of the research-based leadership behaviors, tended to focus more than treatment group members on managerial issues (e.g., procedures for using the school lunchroom), affective issues (e.g., reducing the student conflicts on the playground), and administrative issues (e.g., using a staff meeting to explain how to comply with record-keeping mandates). There was no evidence suggesting that more time was spent on staff development activities by either treatment or control group staff developers.

Clearly, then, the CTP intervention was effective in causing treatment group staff developers' behavior to reflect what research has shown to be effective practice.

The CTP intervention was also directed toward altered teacher behavior as a consequence of staff developers' work with teachers. In the categories dealing with academics (Table II), the treatment group teachers exhibited greater frequency in planning and preparation, presentation, and holding students responsible for assignments. Planning and preparation for academics was seen nearly twice as often in the classrooms of treatment teachers as in the classrooms of control teachers ($p < .09$). For academic presentation, teachers in the treatment group again exhibited a statistically significant mean rate ($p < .01$). Although the treatment group teachers' rate for holding students responsible for assignments was in the desired direction, it was not statistically significant.

A similar pattern was seen in the four observation categories related to classroom management. In each of these categories, the treatment group teachers demonstrated the research-based behaviors more frequently. For two categories, holding students responsible for behavior and reacting to student behavior, the differences were slight. For the two remaining categories, organizing the classroom and presenting rules and procedures, the differences were statistically significant ($p < .03$ and $p < .06$, respectively).

Table II Mean Rates of Observation Categories for Treatment and Control Teachers from ANOVA Results

OBSERVATION CATEGORIES	GRAND MEAN	TREATMENT MEAN	CONTROL MEAN	p
Academic				
Planning and preparation	.00667	.00865	.00489	.09
Presentation	.04255	.48310	.03739	.01
Interaction	.05041	.04692	.05354	.64
Practice	.00700	.00682	.00716	.94
Seatwork	.01456	.01291	.01640	.60
Holding students responsible for assignments	.01199	.01365	.01050	.32
Classroom management				
Organizes classroom	.01142	.01591	.00740	.03
Presentation of rules and procedures	.00484	.00715	.00276	.06
Holds students responsible for behavior	.00980	.01102	.00905	.33
Reactions to students' behavior	.02671	.02741	.02608	.80

In some observation categories significant differences among teachers were associated with particular staff developers. This was true for planning and preparation for academics ($p < .06$), practice ($p < .04$), and seatwork ($p < .04$). In other words, individual staff developers had significant effects upon the pairs of teachers with whom they worked. In some categories, the mean rates of teaching behaviors increased significantly over time for both treatment and control groups. This was true for interactions ($p < .003$), seatwork ($p < .08$), and holding students responsible for assignments ($p < .08$). Mean rates for presenting rules and procedures decreased significantly over time ($p < .001$) as would be expected. Finally, significant differences in content were usually associated with greater frequency of behaviors demonstrated in the teaching of mathematics as in practice ($p < .01$), seatwork ($p < .04$), and reacting to students' behavior ($p < .005$). Reading produced significant content effects ($p < .003$) only in the category of interactions.

The CTP intervention, then, was effective in causing teachers to demonstrate certain of the research-based teaching behaviors (planning and preparation for academics, academic presentation, organizing the classroom, and presentation of rules and procedures) and not effective for others (interactions, practice, seatwork, holding students responsible for assignments, holding students responsible for behavior, and teacher reactions to students' behavior).

In terms of the CTP intervention's effect upon student behavior, treatment group students were more frequently on-task in academic activities (e.g., completing a seatwork assignment) than were control group students, whereas control group students were more frequently on-task in procedural activities (e.g., preparing to leave the classroom at lunch time). In neither case were these differences statistically significant. Both treatment and control group students exhibited significantly greater frequency of on-task academic behavior over time ($p < .03$) and significantly fewer frequencies of on-task procedural behaviors over time ($p < .04$). However, because of the lack of statistical significance between the percentages of treatment and control group students engaged in on-task behaviors, it cannot be concluded that the CTP intervention was successful in altering this aspect of treatment group student behavior.

DISCUSSION

In terms of staff developer behavior, the self-reports of participants corroborate the observations of the RITE staff in providing strong evidence of the positive impact of the CTP intervention at this level. The treatment group of staff developers reported initiating significantly more inservice activities that research indicates to be effective and that the CTP intervention identified as desirable staff developer behaviors. The significance level ($p < .01$), and the lack of overlap in observed mean frequencies across treatment and control groups militate against attributing these differences to reporting bias. The treatment group staff developers in the CTP study can be described as persons who used research-based knowledge to focus attention on specific teaching behaviors that are desirable within a given school context and who provided appropriate support and resources in helping teachers increase the incidence of these behaviors in their classrooms.

It must be recognized, however, that differences in frequency of certain of the desirable staff developer behaviors did not distinguish the treatment and control groups. For some (e.g., using teacher time to deal with teacher problems), it is probable that this is such a strong convention in schools that there is a ceiling on the number of opportunities for this to occur. For others, (e.g., providing in-classroom technical assistance such as coaching), it is possible that the knowledge and skill necessary to accomplish them depends upon a much greater investment of time and other resources than were allocated to the CTP intervention. In particular, the use of concerns theory requires both conceptual and methodological knowledge of a high order and only a cursory acquaintance with the theory was accomplished during the workshop for treatment group staff developers. | 34

Teacher observation data collected through the use of the BTOI identified areas in which treatment group teachers exhibited desired behavior more frequently than control group teachers. In spite of expected individual effects, there was a treatment "override" sufficient to indicate a significant impact of the CTP intervention on the behaviors of the participating teachers. Differences between teacher group and control group frequencies in certain categories of teaching behaviors were statistically significant. | 35

From these data, the logical conclusion can be drawn that staff developers knowledgeable and skillful in the content of the CTP intervention will more likely facilitate the increased incidence of the specified teaching behaviors by the teachers with whom they work than will staff developers who do not have knowledge and skill. In that the RITE staff did not interact directly with the teachers, except as classroom observers, the CTP intervention proved successful in increasing classroom use of research-based effective teaching through secondary impact. | 36

It is important, however, to speculate on the reasons for the differential impact across categories of teaching behavior. We hypothesize that for the categories for which significant differences were found between treatment and control group teachers (planning and preparation for academics, academic presentation, organizing the classroom, and presentation of rules and procedures), three major factors may account for the difference. First, these areas of teaching behavior have only recently received disciplined research and conceptual attention and, therefore, have not been codified in teacher preparation programs. For example, the notion that teachers use as content of lessons the rules and regulations of life in particular classrooms, much the same way that division of fractions is the content of an arithmetic lesson, is not a widely-demonstrated practice. Second, the participating school district had developed and mandated the use of curricula in reading | 37 and mathematics that included systematic attention to some of the teaching variables included in the observation instrument. An example is seatwork. All teachers using the mandated curricula were expected to observe certain conventions in regard to seatwork. It is unlikely, therefore, that the CTP intervention would replace an already-established set of expectations for teacher behavior. This perspective is reinforced when it is recalled that the CTP intervention was presented as an additional professional resource for staff developers and teachers, not as a prescription for practice. Third, the research procedures may not have been sensitive enough to capture certain of the teaching behaviors. In particular, for the category of interactions the BTOI did not discriminate, in terms of desirability, among certain patterns of teacher and student behavior. This blurring of expectations became a methodological problem as data were analyzed.

Probably the most dramatic expectation of the CTP intervention provided to staff developers was that it would result in greater on-task student behavior, with on-task behavior serving as the proxy for student achievement. This expectation was not realized. The classroom observation data indicate that students in all 20 classrooms were high in on-task behavior, perhaps as a consequence of the mandated curricula noted | 38 above and related attempts by the district to improve student achievement. This may have mitigated against a CTP effect. Also, it is possible that the observation techniques used by the RITE research team were not discriminating enough to discern subtle student behavioral differences. Whatever the reason, the finding of no significant differences between treatment and control group students raises important questions about the adequacy of research procedures used, the appropriateness of on-task behavior as a reliable proxy for achievement, and, crucially, the feasibility of expecting experimentally-induced teaching behavior to be associated with certain pupil behaviors as found in the correlational research upon which much of the CTP intervention was based.

The findings of this experimental study, however, do support the contentions that research findings can be used as content for school improvement efforts, that there is a relation between staff developer and teacher behavior, and that such school improvement efforts can be cost effective. Related to the last point, the participating school district adopted the CTP intervention for all of its school-based staff developers and, with the assistance of RITE staff, adapted it for district development, as opposed to research, purposes. A cost analysis of the district-wide effort revealed that the cost of providing this professional growth opportunity to school professionals was only $204.45 per staff developer, $15.33 per teacher, and $.66 per student (Leighty, 1984).

In times characterized by heightened attention to the quality of schooling, dismay over the quality of the professional development of teachers and administrators, and disappointment in the perceived lack of impact of research upon practice, the CTP intervention is a promising indicator of how research and practice issues can be joined toward the end of accomplishing school change.

REFERENCES

Anderson, L. M., Evertson, C. M., & Brophy, J. E. (1979). An experimental study of effective teaching in first-grade reading groups. *The Elementary School Journal, 79*, 193–223.

Association for Supervision and Curriculum Development. (1980). Effective classroom management for the elementary school (Videotape). Alexandria, VA: Author.

Barnes, S. (1981). *Synthesis of selected research on teaching findings* (Research Rep. No. 9009). Austin: University of Texas.

Barnes, S. (1983). *Observer training manual for the Changing Teacher Practice Study* (Revised Research Rep. No. 9050). Austin: University of Texas, Research and Development Center for Teacher Education.

Bentzen, M. (1974). *Changing schools: The magic feather principle*. New York: McGraw-Hill.

Berman, P., & McLaughlin, M. W. (1978, May). *Federal programs supporting educational change, Vol. VIII: Implementing and sustaining innovations*. Santa Monica, CA: Rand.

Brophy, J. E. (1983). Classroom organization and management. *Elementary School Journal, 83*(4), 265–286.

Brophy, J., & Evertson, C. (1974, June). *Process-product correlations in the Texas teacher effectiveness study: Final Report* (Research Rep. No. 74-4). Austin: University of Texas, Research and Development Center for Teacher Education.

Edwards, S. (1981). *Changing teacher practice: A synthesis of relevant research* (Research Rep. No. 9008). Austin: University of Texas, Research and Development Center for Teacher Education.

Emmer, E. T., Evertson, C. M., & Anderson, L. M. (1980). Effective classroom management at the beginning of the school year. *The Elementary School Journal, 80*, 219–231.

Evertson, C. M., Emmer, E. T., Clements, B. S., Sanford, J. P., Worsham, M. G., & Williams, G. (1981). *Organizing and managing the elementary school classroom*. Austin: University of Texas, Research and Development Center for Teacher Education.

Fullan, M. (1985). Change processes and strategies at the local level. *The Elementary School Journal, 85*(3), 391–423.

Gage, N. (1984). What do we know about teaching effectiveness? *Phi Delta Kappan, 66*(2), 87–93.

Good, T. L., Grouws, D. A., Beckerman, T., Ebmeier, H., Flatt, L., & Schneeburger, S. (1977, September). *Teachers manual: Missouri mathematics effectiveness project* (NIE-G-770003). Columbia: University of Missouri.

Good, T., & Grouws, D. (1981, May). *Experimental research in secondary mathematics classrooms: Working with teachers* (NIE-G-79-0103). Columbia: University of Missouri.

Goodlad, J., & Klein, M. F. (1974). *Looking behind the classroom door* (Rev. Ed.). Worthington, OH: Charles A. Jones.

Griffin, G. A., Barnes, S., O'Neal, S., Edwards, S. E., Defino, M. E., & Hukill, H. (1983). *Changing teacher practice: Final report of an experimental study* (Research Rep. No. 9052). Austin: University of Texas, Research and Development Center for Teacher Education.

Hall, G. E., & Loucks, S. (1978). Teacher concerns as a basis for facilitating and personalizing staff development. *Teachers College Record, 80*(1), 36–53.

Hays, W. L. (1973). *Statistics for the social sciences* (2nd Ed.). New York: Holt, Reinhart, & Winston.

Leighty, C. (1984). *Focus on effective teaching/staff development: District adaption of the changing teacher practice study.* Unpublished manuscript, University of Texas, Research and Development Center for Teacher Education, Austin.

Medley, D. M. (1979). The effectiveness of teachers. In P. Peterson & H. Walberg (Eds.), *Research on teaching: Concepts, findings, and implications* (pp. 11–27). Berkeley, CA: McCutcheon.

Purkey, S. C., & Smith, M. S. (1983). Effective schools: A review. *The Elementary School Journal, 83*(4), 427–452.

Rosenshine, B. (1982). Teaching functions in instructional programs. *The Elementary School Journal, 83*(4), 335–352.

Sanford, J., & Evertson, C. (1981). Classroom management in a low SES junior high: Three case studies. *Journal of Teacher Education, 38*, 34–38.

Sarason, S. B. (1971). *The culture of the school and the problem of change.* Boston: Allyn & Bacon.

Stallings, J., Needels, M., & Stayrook, N. (1979). *How to change the process of teaching basic reading skills in secondary school, phase II and III, final report.* Menlo Park, CA: SRI International.

AUTHORS

GARY A. GRIFFIN, Professor and Dean, College of Education, University of Illinois, Box 4348, Chicago, IL 60611. *Specializations:* Teacher education, staff development, school improvement.

SUSAN BARNES, Director of Programs, Texas Education Agency, 1701 N. Congress Ave., Austin, TX 78701. *Specializations:* Teacher evaluation, classroom research, staff development.

Brief Comments on Griffin and Barnes 1986

The numbers in parentheses in the following text correspond to the paragraph numbers we have added to the article itself.

The nested design used by Griffin and Barnes began with staff developers who were matched on a variety of characteristics (10). The researchers applied the IV (11), which consisted of providing information about effective teaching (4, 5) to staff developers, each of whom worked with two teachers (9). The DVs were based on measures of staff-developer performance (15), teacher performance (15, 16), and a measure of student behavior (17). The effects of the treatment were thus assessed at three different DV levels: on staff developers, on teachers, and on students. Note the apparent deviation from the procedure as originally planned (14). The fact that the staff developers themselves "requested" a workshop altered the original intervention.

The effects of the intervention on staff-developer behaviors were described (Table I) and were statistically significant overall (24–27). Several significant results for teacher behavior (28, 29 and Table II) were also found, with some of those differences associated with particular staff developers (30). The mean rates in Table II are rates per minute, thus the small numbers. Although we would have opted for a p level of at least .05 for significance, one could argue for a liberalization of that typical standard because the IV was not *directly* administered in this case, and any possible IV effect might have been diluted by the fact that the subjects were one step removed from the treatment. Thus, any impact of the IV would in this instance be secondary. No differences were found in student on-task time (32).

In the discussion section the authors do not explicitly state the limitations of the study. It is, of course, limited to the school district in which it was conducted (10), and to the form of intervention used. Because of these limitations, the study does lack some external validity, but a closer look at the discussion reveals a careful interpretation of the results *within that school system* (33–38). In fact, no broad generalizations are ever made. The only speculations about the wider application of the results in other settings (39, 40) are appropriately very cautious.

Why did these authors decide to do this study in this particular way? Perhaps they already had access to a school system with much of the needed personnel. The use of in-place staff developers as the intervention group was clearly cost-effective (39) and reduced the possibility that teachers could be subjected to undue demand characteristics, although, of course, the developers could still have been affected. Depending on the level of funding and the availability of a site and personnel, other researchers might have chosen a different design, sample sizes, instrumentation, and so on. Clearly, however, their approach did follow the basic rule of research.

SUMMARY

Laboratories and schools are, obviously, different in a variety of ways. Laboratories generally offer better opportunities for randomization and control but frequently lack ecological or external validity. Research in schools, on the other hand, may be limited in internal validity by practicalities ranging from inflexible school schedules to political considerations, but it generally offers greater ability to generalize the results to other settings.

The key to resolving the problem is proper planning. As long as the researcher keeps the limitations clearly in mind as the project is planned, the conclusions will be appropriately cautious. Thus, the basic rule of research is that when planning a research study, (1) look for a natural research setting, (2) optimize control by using the strongest method and design that the situation allows, and (3) consider threats to internal validity that may make interpretations equivocal and rival hypotheses reasonable. A corollary to this rule is that all aspects of the research project should be carefully and formally planned out, including the statistical procedures that will be used later for the analysis of data.

As the planning process progresses from identification of a problem, through literature review, IV and DV specification, and specification of subjects, materials, and procedures, to writing a proposal (and rewriting, if necessary), the researcher makes many decisions. Following the basic rule of research, when drawing conclusions from the data analysis, the impact of each decision on internal and external validity should be carefully considered before writing the report for publication.

The wise researcher will be sure to involve all the school constituencies in planning as early in the process as possible. This will give all those involved time to consider any problems or political consequences, as well as an opportunity to make suggestions that might be important. If they feel that they are a part of the project, they will more likely be supportive and cooperative.

KEY TERMS

Basic rule of research
Corollary to the basic rule
Debriefing
Deception
Ethical restrictions in research
Informed consent

Limitations to research conclusions
Nested design
Pilot study
Planning process (research)
Post-hoc test
Research proposal

REFERENCES

AMERICAN PSYCHOLOGICAL ASSOCIATION. (1982). *Ethical principles in the conduct of research with human participants.* Washington, D.C.: Author.

GRIFFIN, G. A., & BARNES, S. (1986). Using research findings to change school and classroom practices: Results of an experimental study. *American Educational Research Journal, 23* (4), 572–586.

WALBERG, H. J. (1986). Syntheses of research on teaching. In M. C. Wittrock (ed.), *Handbook of research on teaching* (3d ed.). New York: MacMillan.

CHAPTER

7

Research Simulations and Errors

GETTING STARTED

John Dewey, the great philosopher and educational theorist, always stressed the concept of active learning, summarized best in his phrase "learn by doing." It is one thing to sit passively in your armchair, reading chapters on how research is most effectively conducted, and quite another to be actually involved in making the critical decisions necessary to evaluate and conduct a good, or even adequate, piece of research. In this chapter, the spotlight falls on you, the reader, and demands will be made on you that will put you squarely in the researcher's driver's seat. Rather than being a passive recipient of research information, like a passenger in a chauffeur-driven limousine, you are now going to take the wheel and, it is hoped, learn how to steer the correct course and avoid all the roadblocks and detours that may seem to lie ahead.

In the first section that follows, a series of research simulations will be provided, in most cases simulations that model actual research studies that can be found in the educational literature. We say here "model", since in some cases the actual procedures have been modified for the sake of clarity, and in other cases they have been simplified (since, after all, this is an introductory course). In all cases, however, the actual results of the study will be provided in a form that you should find understandable. It is therefore a double experience, because while wrestling with the critical research decisions, you'll also be exposed to some of education's most provocative and important studies.

While going through these simulations, a series of guideposts will be presented—a checklist of things to watch for at each fork in the road. Also, a flow chart, a kind of researcher's road map, is provided. As you answer the questions and follow the various routes offered on the chart, the eventual statistical solution should become clear.

In the second section, called Research Errors: Case Studies, a series of actual studies will be presented, all having been published, but each with a possible methodological flaw. Although there is probably an endless list of ways in which a researcher can create ambiguous results when conducting a study, this section will focus only on the most common errors. In fact, these errors are the kind that may even lead to uninterpretable results, regardless of the power or elegance of the statistical analysis. As you go through these studies, you will be using a case-study approach, that is, learning by example. One thing you'll learn is that you can't simply read the author's conclusions. You must bore in and analyze the methodology on which these conclusions were based.

Analysis and Checklist Questions

After reading each simulation the first thing to do is spend a moment reflecting on the overall study and analyzing the methodology. By this we mean you should identify the IVs and DVs and determine first what kind of research is involved, experimental or post-facto. This is crucial, since unless the research is experimental, no direct cause-and-effect conclusion can be made. Remember, this decision, experimental or post-facto, must be made on the basis of having clearly identified the IV. Once the IV has been spotted you may go on to decide whether the IV has been manipulated by the experimenter or is instead a subject variable. If the IV has been manipulated, the research is, of course, experimental, but if the IV is based on a subject variable, the research is post-facto. When the methodology has been analyzed, you should next turn to the following checklist questions.

Question 1: What Scale of Measurement Has Been Used?

The decision of which statistical test to use depends first on which scale of measurement the data represent. When the data are in nominal form, for example, you can't use an ANOVA or a *t* test, but you can use chi square. For ordinal data, you may select from such tests as the *U*, the *H*, the Wilcoxon *T*, or the Spearman r_S. Tests that employ nominal or ordinal data make very few assumptions concerning the shape of the population distribution and are thus called *distribution-free tests*. Also, because these tests are not being used to estimate certain population parameters, such as the mean and standard deviation, they are all nonparametric. When the scores are in interval-ratio form, that is, when the distances between successive scale points are assumed to be equal, the parametric statistical tests, such as the Pearson *r*, the *t* test, and the various forms of ANOVA become appropriate. The only exception to this is when the interval-ratio measures are known not to distribute normally in the population. In this instance, as you have seen, the scores are rank ordered and subjected to ordinal test analysis. Tests that are designed to use interval-ratio data are parametric because they do make assumptions concerning the underlying population distribution—for example, that the distribution approximates normality.

Question 2: Which Hypothesis Has Been Tested?

The second major issue in choosing the correct test is based on determining which hypothesis, difference or association, has been tested. With experimental research, identifying the hypothesis is fairly straightforward: experimental research always, at least somewhere in the analysis, tests the hypothesis of difference. This hypothesis states that although the samples may have been originally selected from a single population, they now represent different populations (presumably because of the action of the IV). With post-facto research, however, the researcher may have tested for differences or may have tested the hypothesis of association. The hypothesis of association states that a correlation exists in the population from which the sample was selected. This correlation may exist between different measures taken on the same group of subjects (for example, when a single group of subjects is measured on both IQ and academic performance) or between the same measure taken on different subjects (for example, comparing IQ scores between pairs of identical twins).

Question 3: If the Hypothesis of Difference Has Been Tested, Are the Samples Independent or Correlated?

This question, as you can see, is only relevant when the hypothesis of difference has been tested. Which test should be applied to the suspected difference, however, depends on whether the samples are independent (the selection of one subject has no effect on the selection of other subjects) or correlated (the selection of a subject for one group determines who will be selected for the other group, or the same subjects are used in different treatment conditions). Typically, when the experiment is based on a between-subjects comparison in an after-only design, the groups should be independent. If, on the other hand, the experiment is based on a repeated-measures, within-subjects design, or on a matched-subjects design, the groups will be correlated.

Question 4: How Many Sets of Measures?

Finally, the choice of which statistical analysis to choose depends on how many measures the researcher has utilized. For example, if only two sets of measures are being compared (and the data are in interval-ratio form), the t test might be appropriate, whereas if three or more measures are being compared, the F ratio becomes the analysis of choice. Similarly, when testing the hypothesis of association (with interval-ratio data), if two measures are being compared the Pearson r should be used, but with three or more measures the multiple R becomes available.

Critical Decision Points

Once the checklist questions have been answered, turn to the flowcharts shown in Figures 7.1 and 7.2. Each flowchart presents a series of critical decision points, going from top to bottom, and is based on the checklist questions just outlined.

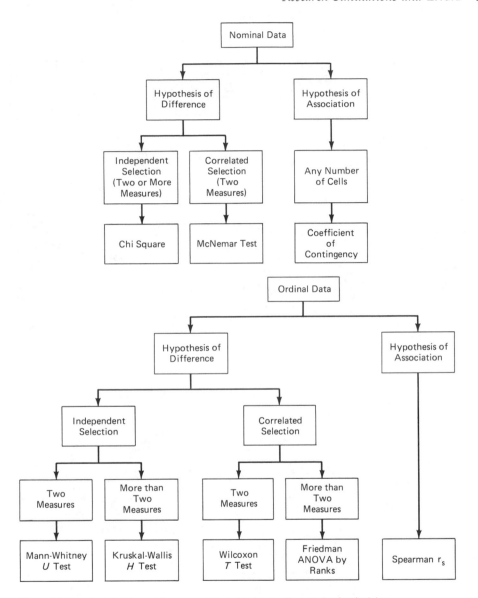

Figure 7.1 Flow charts for determining appropriate statistical test with nominal and ordinal data

At each critical decision point the answer to the next question dictates which route should be followed and, if all goes well, points you directly to the appropriate statistical test.

In the first simulation (1), the analysis will be provided immediately following the presentation of the study. That is, for this first example, you will be given an outline of how the analysis of methodology and checklist questions should be used to direct you to the solution. For simulations 2 through 27, however, the decisions will be left up to you. Space is provided following each of these

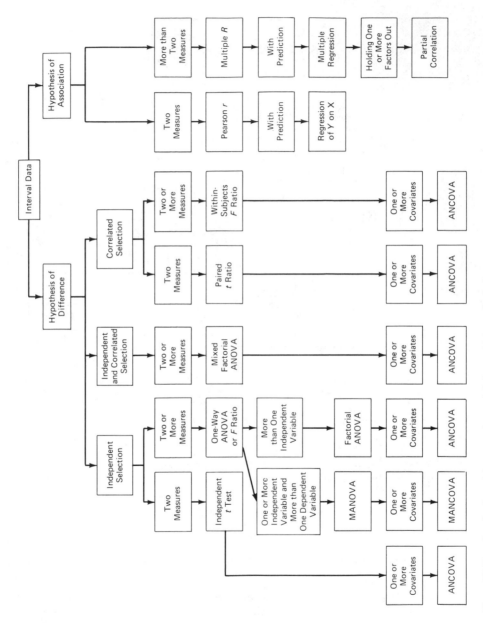

Figure 7.2 Flow chart for determining appropriate statistical test with interval/ratio data

simulations for you to write in your analysis, decisions, and solution. (Solutions appear at the end of the chapter).

SIMULATIONS

Simulation I

A researcher randomly selected a group of four-year-old children from a population of low-income families. Half the children were randomly assigned to a Head Start preschool program for a period of one year. The other half did not attend any preschool program. Years later, when the subjects reached the age of nineteen years, the two groups were compared regarding those who could be identified as being involved in delinquent behavior.

Analyzing the Methodology

This is experimental research: the IV (whether the subjects attended preschool) was clearly manipulated by the experimenter. The DV is the measure of whether the subjects later exhibited delinquent behavior. This is a between-groups, after-only experimental design.

Answering the Checklist Questions: The Critical Decisions

1. *Scale of measurement?* The measures in this study are nominal, the numbers of subjects having been categorized on the basis of whether they had engaged in delinquent behavior.
2. *Hypothesis?* The hypothesis being tested was that of difference: whether there would be a significant difference between the two groups with regard to the number of subjects who had engaged in delinquent behavior.
3. *If the hypothesis of difference has been tested, are the groups independent or correlated samples?* The subjects, at age four, were independently assigned to the two experimental conditions.
4. *How many sets of measures?* There are two sets of measures, one for the Head Start group and one for the group that did not attend preschool.

Solution

Use the chi square, in this case a 2×2 chi square, with the IV (preschool versus no preschool) in the rows, and the DV (delinquent behavior versus no delinquent behavior) in the columns.

	DELINQUENT BEHAVIOR	NO DELINQUENT BEHAVIOR
PRESCHOOL	a	b
NO PRESCHOOL	c	d

Note: This simulation was modeled after a study that showed that those children who had been enrolled in the preschool program were less apt to be later involved in delinquent behavior (Berrueta-Clement, Schweinhart, Barnett, Epstein, & Weikart, 1984).

Simulation 2

A researcher in the area of learning theory wished to test the spacing hypothesis, that is, that increased spacing between practice trials increases the retention of learned material, in this case, meaningful material. Two groups of ten-year-old children were randomly selected from the school population of fifth-grade students. The two groups were then randomly assigned to different treatment conditions. At 9:00 A.M, Group A was given one hour in which to memorize a certain short poem, whereas, also at 9:00 A.M. Group B was given four 15-minute practice sessions in which to memorize the same poem (each practice session was separated by a fifteen-minute play break). Four hours later, both groups were tested on their ability to recite the poem. The scoring was based on the number of errors each child made.

Analyzing the Methodology

1. Scale of measurement?
2. Hypothesis?
3. If hypothesis of difference, sample groups independent or correlated?
4. How many sets of measures?

Solution

Note: This simulation was based on a review by Dempster (1988), in which it was found that spacing produced significantly higher retention scores.

Simulation 3

Attempting to discover whether racial identification is age related, a researcher randomly selected a large group of black children and grouped them according to age. Twenty of the children were age three, twenty-two were age four, eighteen were age five, and twenty were age six. The experimenter then asked each child to show them which doll (a black doll or a white doll) the child would like to play with. Of the three-year olds, seven chose the black doll; of the four-year-olds, ten chose the black doll; of the five-year-olds, seventeen chose the black doll; and of the six-year-olds, sixteen chose the black doll.

Analyzing the Methodology

1. Scale of measurement?
2. Hypothesis?
3. If hypothesis of difference, sample groups independent or correlated?
4. How many sets of measures?

Solution

Note: This simulation was modeled after work by Clark and Clark (1947), who found that racial identification was age related among black children.

Simulation 4

A researcher attempted to establish whether information processing among six-month-old infants could be used to predict WISC-R IQ scores, taken later at age six years. A random sample of twenty-five 6-month-old infants was selected. To assess the infants' processing ability, the researcher measured the amount of time they would spend watching a series of moving stimuli before losing interest and turning away. The assumption was that the more intelligent the infant, the sooner he or she would lose interest in the stimuli (since the more intelligent infants would process the information more quickly in the form of an internal stimulus representation). Each infant's time score was then compared with his or her WISC-R IQ score, taken later when the children reached six years of age.

Analyzing the Methodology

1. Scale of measurement?
2. Hypothesis?
3. If hypothesis of difference, sample groups independent or correlated?
4. How many sets of measures?

Solution

Note: This simulation was modeled after the work of Bornstein (1985), who found that processing time at age six months did predict later IQ scores.

Simulation 5

A researcher wished to find out whether the grades teachers receive on teacher-competency tests predict teacher success in the classroom. A random sample of one hundred working math teachers was selected from the population of public-school math teachers in the state of Texas (where all teachers had to take the competency test). A panel of three experts visited the classrooms of all the selected teachers and evaluated each teacher's classroom performance. The judges then rank ordered all one hundred teachers on the basis of the effectiveness of their teaching.

Analyzing the Methodology

1. Scale of measurement?
2. Hypothesis?
3. If hypothesis of difference, sample groups independent or correlated?
4. How many sets of measures?

Solution

Note: This simulation was based on the work of Pugach and Raths (1983), who found no significant relationship between competency-test scores and level of classroom performance.

Simulation 6

A researcher, interested in the possible link between level of physical maturity and personality factors among teenage boys, selected a random sample of fifty, 14-year-old boys. The boys were each evaluated with regard to their physical-maturity level and then assigned to one of three categories: early maturers (EM), average maturers (AM), and late maturers (LM). Each boy was then given a standardized paper-and-pencil personality test and scored on the introversion-extroversion scale, high scores indicating more extroversion. The three groups were then compared on these introversion-extroversion scores.

Analyzing the Methodology

1. Scale of measurement?
2. Hypothesis?
3. If hypothesis of difference, sample groups independent or correlated?
4. How many sets of measures?

Solution

Note: This simulation was based on a review by Wilson, Robeck, and Michael (1969), who suggested that EM boys were significantly more extroverted than were either the AM or LM boys.

Simulation 7

It has been suggested that among college-prep students, a tenth-grade student's grade-point average, for that year, is a function of (a) the grade average accumulated through grades 7, 8, and 9, (b) scores on the Otis-Lennon IQ test, and (c) sociometric popularity. A large random sample of tenth-grade students was selected from the population of college-prep tenth-graders in a certain eastern state. The records of all the students in the sample were checked, and grade averages for the three previous years were calculated for each student. IQ scores were also obtained, as were sociometric scores (derived from such questions as, Who would you like to sit next to in class? or Who would you like to have lunch with in the cafeteria?).

Analyzing the Methodology

1. Scale of measurement?
2. Hypothesis?
3. If hypothesis of difference, sample groups independent or correlated?
4. How many sets of measures?

Solution

Note: This simulation was based on suggestions by Moreno (1953), who found sociometric popularity to be positively related to current academic performance, although the relationship was not as strong as with IQ and previous grades.

Simulation 8

A researcher suspected that, after mainstreaming, those previously designated special-education students would evaluate themselves less positively than would their regular classroom peers. Random samples of twenty-five main-streamed classes were selected, and the children categorized with respect to whether they were (a) regular children, (b) physically handicapped, (c) learning disabled, or (d) emotionally disturbed. All children were given a standardized "self-regard" test. The scores of the various groups were then compared, high scores indicating a positive self-image.

Analyzing the Methodology

1. Scale of measurement?
2. Hypothesis?
3. If hypothesis of difference, sample groups independent or correlated?
4. How many sets of measures?

Solution

Note: When a study very similar to this was conducted (Parish & Copeland, 1978), the difference was found to be not significant. The children who had previously been in special-education classes rated themselves just as highly as did their regular-classroom counterparts.

Simulation 9

A researcher suspected that learning would increase as a function of the type of positive reinforcement provided by the teacher. A random sample of fifty, 7th-grade students was selected and randomly divided into two groups. Each group was given a two-week course on a certain social-science unit. In group A the teacher used positive reinforcement, which was delivered randomly and for mere participation without consideration of outcomes. In group B, the same teacher taught the same unit, but reinforcement was delivered contingently (on the basis of specified performance criteria). Both groups were given a standardized test on the material in the unit, both before and after taking the course. A comparison was then made between the pre-post change scores for both groups.

Analyzing the Methodology

1. Scale of measurement?
2. Hypothesis?
3. If hypothesis of difference, sample groups independent or correlated?
4. How many sets of measures?

Solution

Note: This study was modeled after the work of Jere Brophy (1981), who found that group B showed a significantly more positive change.

Simulation 10

A researcher wished to test whether different styles of teaching are more effective with some types of students than with others. Two groups of high-school students were selected, one group composed of low-anxiety students, and the other group of high-anxiety students. Each of these groups was then further broken down into two randomly assigned subgroups. Two different teaching-treatment conditions were introduced. Style 1 was student directed and involved open-ended questions and a great deal of student participation and initiative. Style 2 was teacher oriented and highly structured. All groups were taught the same material by the same teacher. Finally, a standardized test on the material covered was presented to each of the four subgroups.

	FACTOR A	
	HIGH ANXIETY	LOW ANXIETY
TEACHING STYLE 1	a	b
TEACHING STYLE 2	c	d

Analyzing the Methodology

1. Scale of measurement?
2. Hypothesis?
3. If hypothesis of difference, sample groups independent or correlated?
4. How many sets of measures?

Solution

Note: This simulation is based on the work of Peterson (1984), who actually went beyond the outline shown in this simulation, in that the groups were further categorized with regard to ability levels. The findings were that high-anxious, low-ability students profited the most from the direct teaching style.

Simulation II

A researcher in the area of child development theorized that there are a number of stages of moral growth, and that these stages are distinctly different. Further, this researcher found that moral development occurs in a specific sequence of stages, regardless of culture or country. The stage of "postconventional morality" was shown to occur typically by age sixteen. Postconventional morality consists of a person's understanding of the universality of such democratic principles as the necessity for free speech, majority will, and minority rights. In attempting to establish whether this level of moral development remains relatively consistent over the years, the researchers conducted a longitudinal study, comparing PC (postconventional) scores taken at age sixteen with PC scores at age thirty (higher scores indicating a higher degree of moral development). The question in short was, Did a person's PC score taken at age sixteen remain stable enough to be a reliable predictor of the score that same person would receive at age thirty? A large random sample of sixteen-year-old students was selected and given the standardized PC test. At age thirty these subjects were retested, and the two sets of scores were compared.

Analyzing the Methodology

1. Scale of measurement?
2. Hypothesis?
3. If hypothesis of difference, sample groups independent or correlated?
4. How many sets of measures?

Solution

Note: This simulation is based on the work of Kohlberg (1984), in which it was found that a significant positive correlation did exist between the two sets of PC scores (indicating that the level of moral development at age sixteen could be used to reliably predict development during adulthood). It was also discovered that moral development continued from age sixteen through age thirty, or that PC scores taken at age thirty were consistently higher than those taken at age sixteen, even though the individuals involved did tend to retain their relative position over the years. In this case, then, although you weren't told this in the simulation, the researchers also tested the hypothesis of difference.

Simulation 12

Erik Erikson, the psychological theorist, has suggested that personality growth occurs on the basis of a series of developmental stages, and that the critical stage for college-age students focuses on the resolution of the identity-versus-diffusion crisis. Personal maturity, Erikson states, may only result when the adolescent can create a strong concept of self-identity. Researchers in the area of teacher education have further suggested that there may be a link between a college student's (majoring in education) degree of self-identity and that same student's level of success during practice teaching. A large random sample of over three hundred education majors was selected and given a standardized personality test designed to measure strength of self-identification (high scores indicating greater maturity). Each student was also scored on the basis of IQ, grade-point average, and college boards (SAT). Expert judges then visited the classrooms of all the student teachers and evaluated them on teaching effectiveness, using the following criteria: responsiveness to student questions, empathy, accuracy of content, and use of positive reinforcement. The judges assigned each student teacher an overall score on teaching effectiveness, ranging from a low of 50 to a high of 96. Score comparisons were then made on all the subjects.

Analyzing the Methodology

1. Scale of measurement?
2. Hypothesis?
3. If hypothesis of difference, sample groups independent or correlated?
4. How many sets of measures?

Solution

Note: This simulation was modeled after the work of Walter and Stivers (1977), in which they found that although all the predictors to some extent correlated positively with the criterion, Erikson's identity score produced the highest of the internal correlations.

Simulation 13

Many learning theorists believe that effective metacognitive (internal learning-strategy) skills aid in the comprehension of learned material. One researcher wondered whether children who were trained in a special technique designed to increase metacognitive functioning would produce higher levels of reading comprehension. The researcher also wanted to see whether children who were diagnosed as dyslexic would also profit from this rehearsal technique to the same extent as the nondyslexic children. Two groups of six-year-old children were randomly selected, one group from the population of dyslexic children and the other from the population of normal children. Both groups were then randomly divided into two subgroups, producing a total of four groups. For each breakdown, dyslexic versus nondyslexic, one group was trained in a rehearsal strategy and the other group received no training. Finally, all groups were given the same passage to read, followed by a standardized comprehension test. The scores in all the groups were compared. At this point the researcher discovered that there were significant IQ differences between the dyslexic and nondyslexic children and thus decided to apply a statistical adjustment to this discrepancy.

Analyzing the Methodology

1. Scale of measurement?
2. Hypothesis?
3. If hypothesis of difference, sample groups independent or correlated?
4. How many sets of measures?

Solution

Note: This simulation was modeled after the work of Sullivan (1988), in which it was found that although both groups profited from the rehearsal training, the dyslexic group gained significantly more than did the nondyslexic group (after prior IQ differences were accounted for).

Simulation 14

A school psychologist was interested in the use of both personality (in this case a measure of possible depression) and academic-aptitude measures in predicting final measures of high-school academic ability. A large random sample of college-prep high-school sophomores was selected. Each student was given the RADS (Reynolds Adolescent Depression Scale) as well as the PSAT (Preliminary Scholastic Aptitude Test). Two years later, a comparison was made between these scores and each student's final high-school grade average.

Analyzing the Methodology

1. Scale of measurement?
2. Hypothesis?
3. If hypothesis of difference, sample groups independent or correlated?
4. How many sets of measures?

Solution

Note: This simulation was based on the research findings of Psychological Assessment Resources, Inc., Odessa, Florida. Analysis of the data indicates that scores on the RADS, used in conjunction with other measures, increased the predictive efficiency of the intellectual measure in forecasting final academic performance.

Simulation 15

A researcher in the area of learning disabilities wished to establish whether the effects of listening to versus reading certain passages would produce differences in students' abilities to correct errors of grammar and syntax. Further, the researcher wished to find out whether learning-disabled and non-learning-disabled students would react differently to this treatment difference. A large random sample of students was selected from the population of fourteen-year-old students, all with similar IQs. The sample was categorized on the basis of whether or not they were learning disabled. The two groups were then randomly divided, one a listening group and the other a reading group. The design was as follows:

                                   FACTOR A
                            LD   Non-LD
              Listening
FACTOR B
              Reading

Subjects in the listening condition had the passage read to them, first listening to the entire passage without pauses, then to the passage with pauses between the sentences. During the pauses the students circled perceived errors on a printed sheet. Subjects in the reading condition were given the same amount of time as was the other group, although in this condition they read the passage themselves before attempting to identify the errors. The "correction" scores were then compared among the four groups.

Analyzing the Methodology

1. Scale of measurement?
2. Hypothesis?
3. If hypothesis of difference, sample groups independent or correlated?
4. How many sets of measures?

Solution

Note: This simulation was modeled after the work of Espin and Sindilar (1988), in which it was found that differences did occur between the listening and reading groups, in favor of the listening groups, and further, that the LD students profited the most from this treatment.

Simulation 16

A school psychologist wanted to examine the relative effectiveness of two approaches to teaching learning-disabled students literal comprehension during content-area instruction. An approach that used a visual, spatial display was compared with an approach in which students were presented content via printed text. Groups of fifth- and sixth-grade LD students were randomly assigned to the two treatment groups. After being taught by one or the other method for a period of two months, the students were rated by their teachers as either being improved or not improved regarding their comprehension of content material.

Analyzing the Methodology

1. Scale of measurement?
2. Hypothesis?
3. If hypothesis of difference, sample groups independent or correlated?
4. How many sets of measures?

Solution

Simulation 17

A school superintendent was interested in the phenomenon of "burn-out" among the teachers in her district. She felt that among teachers who had been teaching for less than ten years, there would be a negative relationship between the number of years of teaching and (1) the teachers' enthusiasm for teaching and (2) their likelihood of teaching five years from now.

Analyzing the Methodology

1. Scale of measurement?
2. Hypothesis?
3. If hypothesis of difference, sample groups independent or correlated?
4. How many sets of measures?

Solution

Simulation 18

The headmaster at a private academy wanted to know if the salaries of the teachers at the academy differed based on the ages of the teachers. Younger teachers were complaining that the older teachers, regardless of experience, were being paid more because they had families to support. To investigate this, teachers from three age groups (less than thirty years old, thirty to thirty-nine years old, forty years or older) were matched on teaching experience. That is, trios made up of one teacher in his or her twenties, one in his or her thirties, and one in his or her forties or older, all with roughly the same experience, were put together. The yearly income of each teacher was ranked from 1 (highest) to 3 (lowest).

Analyzing the Methodology

1. Scale of measurement?
2. Hypothesis?
3. If hypothesis of difference, sample groups independent or correlated?
4. How many sets of measures?

Solution

Simulation 19

An educational researcher was interested in whether a personalized system of instruction would improve high-school juniors' attitudes toward school. A random sample of high-school juniors was selected from an urban school district, and each student was given personalized instruction for the full year. A questionnaire measuring attitudes toward school was administered to each student at the beginning of the school year and at the end of each of the four marking periods. The distribution of attitude scores was normal.

Analyzing the Methodology

1. Scale of measurement?
2. Hypothesis?
3. If hypothesis of difference, sample groups independent or correlated?
4. How many sets of measures?

Solution

Simulation 20

A director of educational research was interested in discovering if competency-test scores for high-school teachers could be increased by the introduction of a three-day in-service workshop in the teachers' own specialty area. A random sample of high-school teachers from the district was selected. They were given a competency test, sent to the workshop, and then given the competency test again. The distribution of test scores was positively skewed.

Analyzing the Methodology

1. Scale of measurement?
2. Hypothesis?
3. If hypothesis of difference, sample groups independent or correlated?
4. How many sets of measures?

Solution

Simulation 21

An academic dean was interested in the relationship between students' ratings of the quality of their instructors and the students' achievement in those instructors' courses. A random sample of second-semester freshmen was selected. For each of these students, one of their courses was then randomly selected. The students' ratings of their instructor for that course were rank ordered by the dean and their final grades for that course were also noted.

Analyzing the Methodology

1. Scale of measurement?
2. Hypothesis?
3. If hypothesis of difference, sample groups independent or correlated?
4. How many sets of measures?

Solution

Simulation 22

An educational researcher wished to investigate differences in students' independence as a function of receiving open versus traditional education and the students' gender. Subjects were all seventh graders in a certain school district. The researcher was able to randomly determine which classes of seventh graders received traditional and which received open education but could not control this on a student-by-student basis. The students were also grouped according to their gender (male versus female). At the end of the school year all were given a personality test that measured independence, among other factors. The independence scores from the personality inventory were normally distributed.

Analyzing the Methodology

1. Scale of measurement?
2. Hypothesis?
3. If hypothesis of difference, sample groups independent or correlated?
4. How many sets of measures?

Solution

Simulation 23

A researcher was interested in establishing whether attendance in a preschool program affects the social-maturity level of children. A random sample of thirty kindergarten children was selected and watched closely by trained observers for one full week. The children were then rank ordered on the basis of perceived social maturity. The children were then divided into two groups on the basis of whether or not they had previously attended a day-care center.

Analyzing the Methodology

1. Scale of measurement?
2. Hypothesis?
3. If hypothesis of difference, sample groups independent or correlated?
4. How many sets of measures?

Solution

Simulation 24

A university researcher wished to find out whether a dependable relationship exists between the amount of financial aid granted to a student and the amount that that student earned during the summer. Furthermore, the researcher wished to exclude grade-point average as a variable. A large random sample of financial-aid recipients was selected, and each student was checked for amount of aid granted, amount of summer earnings, and grade-point average.

Analyzing the Methodology
1. Scale of measurement?
2. Hypothesis?
3. If hypothesis of difference, sample groups independent or correlated?
4. How many sets of measures?

Solution

Simulation 25

A researcher wished to test the hypothesis that male business majors earn more in later life than do either male liberal-arts or education majors. A random sample of alumni was selected from the university files from each of the three subject-major categories. To attempt to control for length of experience on the job, all subjects were selected from the same graduating class, the class that graduated ten years previously. All the selected alumni were contacted and asked to indicate their yearly incomes. The men were promised that the information would be held in strict confidence and would not be given to the chairperson of the upcoming alumni fund drive. Because a few of the subjects reported enormously high incomes, the resulting distribution became so skewed that it was decided to rank order the incomes.

Analyzing the Methodology

1. Scale of measurement?
2. Hypothesis?
3. If hypothesis of difference, sample groups independent or correlated?
4. How many sets of measures?

Solution

Simulation 26

A researcher wanted to find out whether IQ is a function of family size. The speculation was that among families with fewer children, each child receives more parental attention and intellectual stimulation and should, therefore, have a higher IQ than would a child reared in a larger family. A large random sample of two-child families was selected as well as a similar sample of six-child families. The IQs of all the children were measured, and the two sample groups were compared.

Analyzing the Methodology

1. Scale of measurement?
2. Hypothesis?
3. If hypothesis of difference, sample groups independent or correlated?
4. How many sets of measures?

Solution

Simulation 27

An investigator wished to test the hypothesis that reading speed is a function of how extensively a student reads. A random sample of high-school seniors was selected in September, and the subjects were asked how many books they had read during the summer. The subjects were then categorized in the following groups: group 1, no books read; group 2, one to three books; group 3, four to six books; and group 4, more than six books. Reading-speed tests were then administered, the scores being in the form of words per minute.

Analyzing the Methodology

1. Scale of measurement?
2. Hypothesis?
3. If hypothesis of difference, sample groups independent or correlated?
4. How many sets of measures?

Solution

RESEARCH ERRORS: CASE STUDIES

In this next section a series of studies are presented, all of which come from the published literature, and all of which contain the potential for flawed results and conclusions. In experimental research, as you will recall, direct cause-and-effect conclusions are only justified when, all other things being equal, the manipulation of an IV leads to a concomitant change in the DV. The fact that other things should "remain equal" means, among other things, that the experimental and control groups must first be as nearly alike as possible.

When other factors are inadvertently allowed to vary, these factors are called confounding variables and may often produce *secondary variance* (as opposed to primary variance, which is the variability in the DV that is presumably caused by the action of the IV). The experimenter who is attempting to show a causal relationship is, of course, hoping to demonstrate primary variance and *avoid* secondary variance. When an experiment is designed in such a way that the potential for secondary variance is high, the study loses its internal validity, and this, as we have seen, is a definite fact of life, even when the study seems to retain a high degree of external validity. That is, no matter how elegantly representative the sample may be, or how true-to-life the experimental conditions may appear, the results of any study become impossible to evaluate when secondary variance is allowed to seep into the research mix. Be especially alert, then, to take note of the possibility of secondary variance in evaluating those studies that are based on the experimental method.

If, for example, you suspect that in a particular study the researcher has failed to provide an adequate control group, be ready to explain the reason(s) for your suspicions, and perhaps even to provide a suggestion or two about what the researcher might have done to improve the study's overall effectiveness. Although in some cases severe problems of external validity may present themselves, with the experiments to follow pay special attention to the problems of internal validity. Also, be sure to make the distinction between experimental and post-facto research, since problems of internal validity are only of concern in the area of experimental methodology.

When you find a post-facto study, your focus should be on problems of sampling (is the sample representative of the population to which the results are to be extrapolated?), external validity, and that age-old post-facto issue of determining the direction of the relationship (which comes first, the chicken or the egg?)

Case 1

Some time ago, a researcher attempted a study aimed at discovering the possible efficacy of the Rogerian client-centered therapy technique in cases of reading retardation. A sample of thirty-seven first- and second-grade children was selected, all of whom had been diagnosed as retarded in reading, on the basis of a standardized reading test (the Gates Primary Reading Test) *and* teacher evaluations. These children were then placed in a special class, taught by a teacher trained in Rogerian nondirective techniques. The atmosphere in this classroom was described as therapeutic, the children being encouraged to express their feelings openly in the presence of a warm, permissive, and accepting teacher. The Stanford-Binet IQs of the children ranged from 80 to 148. At the end of the school term, the children were again tested on the Gates Primary Reading Test, and in general their reading-age scores improved, in one instance by a phenomenal seventeen months. The gains were seen as so dramatic, in fact, that the researcher indicated that no statistical tests were necessary to prove significance. Furthermore, the gains were interpreted by the researcher as resulting from the nondirective teaching technique, the assumed independent variable.

Case 2

Perhaps one of American psychology's most cherished theories of aggression was formulated many years ago and called the frustration-aggression hypothesis. In its briefest form, this hypothesis stated that frustration (in the form of goal blockage) typically leads to aggression. It was also believed that the aggression produced by frustration could sometimes be displaced onto other things, or other people, especially minority groups. In this form the displaced hostility might then be exhibited in the form of racial prejudice.

To test this, researchers went to a summer camp, situated out in the woods, yet close enough to civilization to allow the boys to get to a nearby town about once a week. Needless to say, the boys eagerly looked forward to these visits to town. On one occasion, the boys were especially eager. The town's movie theater had been holding a series of "bank-night" drawings, and the previous week one of the workers at the camp had won a large sum of money. On the appointed night for the trip to town, the boys were all brought together and given an attitude test toward Japanese and Mexicans. They were told that as soon as they finished filling out the questionnaires, the bus would be ready to take them to town. The boys amiably filled out the questionnaires, and then waited for the bus. It never came! Instead of going to town that night, they were told that they had to stay in camp and take a series of difficult intelligence tests. No question about it, these researchers knew how to manipulate the goal-block-age IV. After a lot of grumbling, the boys settled down, took the tests, and then, to add insult to injury, were told they had to again take the Japanese-Mexican attitude test. Their scores on the posttest declined precipitously, indicating an increase in racial prejudice. This was interpreted by the researchers as resulting from the action of the IV: not going to town led to out-group aggression.

Case 3

In another study in the area of frustration, one researcher hypothesized that frustration, again in the form of goal blockage, would cause psychological regression in young children. In this study the independent variable was manipulated by allowing the children to view, but not reach, a glittering array of brand-new toys. Here's how it went. The children were all placed in a single room and allowed to play with serviceable, but obviously well-used toys. Observers followed the children around and rated each child with respect to the level of maturity displayed by the child's play behavior. Next, a curtain was drawn, revealing the beautiful, shiny new toys; but alas, a wire screen prevented the children from getting at these toys. Then the children were again assessed with respect to the maturity level of their play with the used toys, a level that dropped significantly from the pre measure. The hypothesis therefore seemed to be substantiated, and the conclusion was drawn that among children, frustration indeed causes regression.

Case 4

In a partial test of Albert Bandura's modeling hypothesis—that a large part of learned behavior is acquired through the imitation of the actions of others—the question was raised whether male teenage motorists would stop on the highway to assist a woman who was changing a flat tire. The question being asked in this study was based on whether male drivers would be more apt to stop to help if they had just passed a scene in which another male driver, the model, was helping another woman change a tire. Two groups of high-school senior boys were randomly selected, and all subjects were asked to drive a certain prescribed route as part of their driver-education program. For one group, a scene was staged so that each of the male drivers would see a young man helping a woman change a tire. Farther down the road the subjects would then see a lone woman standing beside a car with an obviously flat tire. The other group drove the same route, but did not witness the helping behavior before coming on the scene of the lone woman with the flat tire. The results showed that those subjects who had first observed the modeling behavior were far more apt to stop to help the lone woman than were those who had not passed the helping scene. The results were interpreted as lending support to the modeling hypothesis.

Case 5

Many years ago a study was done in which the behavior of elementary-school boys was observed as a function of an adult's style of leadership. One of the dependent variables, the quality of production, was measured as a function of the style of adult leadership. There were three conditions of leadership style (the IV): democratic, laissez-faire, and authoritarian. In one phase of the study the subjects were, among other things, learning to build model airplanes, and one of the DVs was a measure of how well these planes had been constructed. It was found that the quality of construction was judged to be highest among the boys who were led in the democratic style. But it was also revealed that when the democratic leader left the room he left the plans with the boys, whereas when the authoritarian leader left he took the plans with him.

Case 6

In a study of college teaching techniques, three different introductory-psychology classes were taught by three different methods, but in each case by the same instructor (who also happened to be the researcher). One class met at 9:00 A.M., the second at noon, and the third at 2:00 P.M. The first class was taught in the traditional lecture format, the second in a student-centered fashion, and in the third class, the two techniques were alternated at each meeting. At the end of the semester the students were given questionnaires and asked to indicate their degrees of enjoyment and interest, their opinion regarding the "social-emotional" value of the course, and their assessment of how much information and knowledge they had gained. Also, the three groups were compared on an objective test that covered the course content.

The results showed that students in groups 2 and 3 indicated higher interest and enjoyment in the course than did students in the traditional class. Students in these groups also felt that the social-emotional value of the course was greater. On the objective test of the course's content, however, there were no significant differences among the three groups (although, interestingly, the students in the traditional class felt that they had gained more information and knowledge).

Case 7

In a study conducted at a large eastern women's college, the hypothesis was tested that feminine women would view themselves and others differently than would women who were identified as androgynous. The sample was chosen by mailing copies of the Bem Sex Role Inventory (BSRI) to the entire freshman class of over six hundred female students immediately after their arrival on campus. Only 211 women mailed back the completed BSRI forms, and of these, twenty-three subjects who scored high in androgyny and twenty-six who scored high in femininity were selected for the study. The independent variable, androgyny versus femininity, was therefore assigned to the subjects on the basis of observed traits they already possessed. The results of this study supported the hypothesis that feminine women view themselves differently than do women identified as androgynous. The feminine subjects used significantly more feminine constructs and feminine terms to describe themselves than did the androgynous subjects.

Case 8

In this study the investigators wished to examine the impact of personality variables on academic achievement among elementary-school children. In this case the students' measurements on one trait were compared with the measures the same observers assigned to the students on other traits. The researchers asked the classroom teacher to assign personality ratings to each student and then compared these ratings with the grades the students received from the same teacher. A series of Pearson r's were calculated, and all the correlations were high and positive; that is, the more favorable the personality ratings, the higher the grade received.

Case 9

In another study from the educational literature, the hypothesis was tested that students would achieve more academically when the classroom teacher spent more time smiling. Observers visited a number of different classrooms and monitored the amount of time each teacher spent smiling. These results were then compared with the grades being received by the students in each of the classrooms. The results were significant and in the predicted direction: the more the teachers smiled, the higher the students' grades.

Case 10

In a study conducted at the Institute for Child Behavior in California, a researcher attempted to show a link between a child's lack of selfishness and that same child's feelings of happiness. A sample of children was taken from those enrolled at the clinic, and the subjects were all asked to rate the ten persons whom they "knew best" on two variables, happiness and selfishness. The analysis of the data showed a strong and significant negative correlation between the two traits; that is, the less the individual was seen as being selfish, the more that same individual was viewed in terms of personal happiness. The conclusion offered by the author implied a causal connection between the two traits, or that being unselfish (helping others) tended to create a state of personal happiness in the helper.

Case 11

This study was designed to test whether nondirective group therapy might influence racial prejudice. The investigators chose to use a before-after experimental design, but with no separate control group. A group of twenty-four subjects was tested on an "ethnic-hostility" scale, then given six weeks of client-centered group therapy, and then tested again for ethnic hostility. The statistical results were clearly significant, the "after" measures revealing less ethnic hostility than had the "before" measures. The investigators concluded that this reduction in hostility was a result of the group therapy.

Case 12

In this study the researchers wanted to test whether nondirective play therapy might improve personality-adjustment scores among institutionalized children. All forty-six residents of a children's home were tested on the Roger's Test of Personality Adjustment, and the seven children with the lowest scores were selected for the special treatment. The other thirty-nine children thus served as the separate control in this before-after design. During the course of the study, however, sixteen members of the control group were lost because of their being allowed to leave the institution and return to living at home. The play-therapy children were treated twice a week at a clinic that was located ten miles from their institutional home. At the end of six weeks, both groups were again tested on the adjustment inventory. An evaluation of the scores showed significant gains in adjustment scores for the play-therapy group, whereas the control group did not show gains. The major conclusion drawn from these data was that nondirective play therapy caused an improvement in the personal adjustment of these institutionalized children.

Conclusions

There they are: twelve case studies (the dirty dozen?) in which the results were either misinterpreted or, more often, were uninterpretable. Three basic themes, it is hoped, will become apparent to you.

1. In experimental research, the best way to prevent confounding of the IV is to be sure to have appropriate control groups or counterbalanced conditions, or both.
2. When an independent variable is not actually manipulated by the experimenter, there is no experiment. The research must then be post-facto, and *prediction,* not causation, becomes the only tenable goal.
3. Sample results may only be extrapolated to the population they represent.

With these caveats clearly in mind, you are now in a far better position to both conduct and evaluate research studies.

SIMULATION SOLUTIONS

Simulation 1 (see Simulation 1 on page 199)

Simulation 2

Analyzing the Methodology

This is experimental research, the IV (massed versus spaced trials) having been manipulated by the experimenter. This is a between-groups, after-only experimental design.

Answering the Checklist Questions: The Critical Decisions

1. *Scale of measurement?* The DV (retention scores) is the measure of the number of errors each child made. These measures are thus in at least interval form.
2. *Hypothesis?* The researcher was testing whether differences in retention scores had occurred between the two groups.
3. *If hypothesis of difference, sample groups independent or correlated?* The groups are clearly independent, both having been randomly selected from a single population.
4. *How many sets of measures?* There are two sets of measures, one for the massed group and one for the spaced group.

Solution

Use the independent *t* to evaluate the difference between the two sets of error scores.

Simulation 3

Analyzing the Methodology

This is a post-facto research, the IV clearly being a subject variable (age) on which the groups were categorized.

Answering the Checklist Questions: The Critical Decisions

1. *Scale of measurement?* This is an example of nominal scaling, the DV being based on the numbers of children within each age group choosing which doll.
2. *Hypothesis?* The researcher was testing for differences between the age-groups in their choice of dolls.
3. *If hypothesis of difference, sample groups independent or correlated?* The groups were randomly and independently selected.
4. *How many sets of measures?* There are four sets of nominal measures, depending on the ages of the children.

Solution

Use chi square, in this case a 4×2 chi square, with the IV in the rows and the DV in the columns.

	CHOSE BLACK DOLL	CHOSE WHITE DOLL
Age 3	7	13
Age 4	10	12
Age 5	17	1
Age 6	16	4

Simulation 4

Analyzing the Methodology

This is a post-facto study, the IV (processing time) clearly being a subject variable, and in this case used as a predictor for the DV, which was the WISC-R IQ score.

Answering the Checklist Questions: The Critical Decisions

1. *Scale of measurement?* For both the IV and DV, the data are in at least interval form (and probably normally distributed).
2. *Hypothesis?* The hypothesis being tested was one of association: that the time scores would correlate with the later IQ scores.
3. *If hypothesis of difference, sample groups independent or correlated?* Not applicable, since in this study the hypothesis of association was tested.
4. *How many sets of measures?* There are two sets of measures, time scores at age six months (IV) and IQ scores taken at age six years (DV).

Solution

Use the Pearson *r* to establish whether a correlation exists (in this example, the correlation should probably be negative, with shorter processing times associating with higher IQs). The researcher may then wish to use the regression equation for predicting specific IQ scores on the basis of various processing-time scores.

Simulation 5

Analyzing the Methodology

This is post-facto research, the IV (scores on the competency test) being a subject variable (not manipulated by the experimenter).

Answering the Checklist Questions: The Critical Decisions

1. *Scale of measurement?* Although the competency-test scores are originally in at least interval form, they must be converted to the ordinal scale to be compared with the ordinal ranks the judges assigned to classroom performance. In this case, then, the comparison will be made between the two sets of ordinal measures.
2. *Hypothesis?* The hypothesis being tested in this example was that of association: whether competency test scores would correlate with classroom effectiveness.
3. *If hypothesis of difference, sample groups independent or correlated?* Not applicable, since the hypothesis of difference was not being tested.
4. *How many sets of measures?* There are two sets of measures, competency scores (IV) and classroom-ability scores (DV).

Solution

Use the Spearman r_S, and if it is found to be significant and, in this case, positive (although no cause-and-effect conclusions are warranted), the researcher could say that competency-test scores could be used to predict classroom effectiveness.

Simulation 6

Analyzing the Methodology

This is an example of post-facto research, the IV (level of maturity) being a subject variable and obviously not under the control of the experimenter as a manipulated variable.

Answering the Checklist Questions: The Critical Decisions

1. *Scale of measurement?* The DV (personality score) was measured at the interval level, and since the test was standardized, the distribution of scores is probably normal.

2. *Hypothesis?* The hypothesis tested here was that of difference: that the maturity-level of the sample groups would differ with respect to the personality measures.

3. *If hypothesis of difference, sample groups independent or correlated?* The groups represent independent samples, since the formation of the groups depended solely on the evaluation of the boys' maturity level, not on whether one boy had already been placed in a certain group.

4. *How many sets of measures?* There are three sets of sample measures, each set representing one of the three maturity groupings.

Solution

Use the one-way ANOVA, and if the *F* ratio is significant, follow it up with one of the multiple comparison tests, such as the Tukey HSD. Even if the *F* ratio is significant, and even if Tukey HSD shows significant differences among all three groups, we still cannot attribute a causal link to this difference. Since it is post-facto, the three groups may possibly differ systematically on a number of traits other than maturity level.

Simulation 7

Analyzing the Methodology

This is post-facto research, the IVs (predictors in this example) all being subject variables. None of the IVs—previous grade average, IQ, and sociometric popularity—were, or could have been, manipulated by the experimenter. The DV (criterion variable) was the student's grade average in the tenth grade.

Answering the Checklist Questions: The Critical Decisions

1. *Scale of measurement?* For all the measures used in this study, the data are in interval form.

2. *Hypothesis?* The hypothesis in this study was one of association. The researcher was attempting to ferret out a correlation between these variables that would allow for better-than-chance predictions of tenth-grade performance.

3. *If hypothesis of difference, sample groups independent or correlated?* Not applicable, since the hypothesis tested was one of association.

4. *How many sets of measures?* There are a total of four sets of measures, three IV measures and one measure of the DV.

Solution

Use the Pearson *r*; in fact, calculate three values for the Pearson *r*, in each case between the DV and each of the three IV measures. Use these correlations in a multiple *R* to determine whether the predictive efficiency of the multiple *R* is higher than any of the internal correlations between the DV (criterion) and the three predictors.

Simulation 8

Analyzing the Methodology

This is post-facto research, the assignment of the children to the various groups being based on a subject IV. The DV is composed of the scores on the self-regard test.

Answering the Checklist Questions: The Critical Decisions

1. *Scale of measurement?* The self-regard test scores provide interval data, and the distribution, as with most nationally standardized tests, most likely approximates normality.
2. *Hypothesis?* The researcher was testing the hypothesis of difference (assuming that the previously mainstreamed children would evaluate themselves less positively).
3. *If hypothesis of difference, sample groups independent or correlated?* The groups are independent of each other.
4. *How many sets of measures?* There are four sets of sample scores to be compared.

Solution

Use the one-way ANOVA, and if the *F* ratio is significant, follow it up with one of the multiple comparison tests, such as the Tukey HSD.

Simulation 9

Analyzing the Methodology

This is experimental research. The IV (type of positive reinforcement) was actively manipulated by the experimenter. The DV (outcome) was measured on the basis of the change scores. The experimental design used for this study was a before-after design with a separate and independent control group.

Answering the Checklist Questions: The Critical Decisions

1. *Scale of measurement?* The change scores provide at least interval data.
2. *Hypothesis?* The hypothesis was based on the suspected difference between the performance changes between the two groups.
3. *If hypothesis of difference, sample groups independent or correlated?* The two groups are independent, having been randomly assigned to the two treatment conditions.
4. *How many sets of measures?* Although there are a total of four sets of measures, two pre and two post, there are only two sets of change scores.

Solution

Use the independent *t* on the change scores, being careful to heed the cautions on change-score reliability covered in Chapter 5.

Simulation 10

Analyzing the Methodology

This is combination research, with factor A clearly a subject IV, and factor B a manipulated IV. Although the possibility exists for determining a cause-and-effect relationship between teaching style and outcome, any differences relating to treatment A must be kept at the level of prediction.

Answering the Checklist Questions: The Critical Decisions

1. *Scale of measurement?* The DV measures (scores on the standardized test) are at the interval level, and the underlying distribution can be assumed to approach normality.
2. *Hypothesis?* The researcher was looking for differences among the four groups.
3. *If hypothesis of difference, sample groups independent or correlated?* The groups are independent of each other.
4. *How many sets of measures?* There are four sets, one for each treatment condition.

Solution

Use the factorial ANOVA, and if there is an interaction, interpret it with great care (see Chapter 5). There is no need for a multiple comparison test in this case, since there are only two levels for each of the IVs.

Simulation 11

Analyzing the Methodology

This is post-facto research, in which the IV (PC scores at age sixteen) was used to predict the DV (PC scores at age thirty).

Answering the Checklist Questions: The Critical Decisions

1. *Scale of measurement?* Both the IV and the DV are at the interval level.
2. *Hypothesis?* This study tested the hypothesis of association (between the IV and the DV).
3. *If hypothesis of difference, sample groups independent or correlated?* Not applicable, since the hypothesis of association was being tested.
4. *How many sets of measures?* There are two sets of interval measures, both taken on the same subjects.

Solution

Use the Pearson r, and then the bivariate regression equation, to predict later PC scores on the basis of those taken at an earlier age.

Simulation 12

Analyzing the Methodology

This is post-facto research. There are four separate subject-variable IVs (identity strength, IQ, GPA, and SAT) and there is one DV (teaching effectiveness).

Answering the Checklist Questions: The Critical Decisions

1. *Scale of measurement?* All variables were measured at the interval level. Even the judges' ratings were transformed into interval scores, not ranks.
2. *Hypothesis?* The hypothesis of association was being tested in this case.
3. *If hypothesis of difference, sample groups independent or correlated?* Not applicable.
4. *How many sets of measures?* There are five sets of measures, four for the IV and one for the DV.

Solution

Run a series of Pearson *r*'s, and then set up a multiple regression.

Simulation 13

Analyzing the Methodology

This is combination research, in which one of the IVs (dyslexic versus nondyslexic) is a subject variable and the other IV (training versus no training) is manipulated by the experimenter. The DV consists of the scores on the reading-comprehension test.

FACTOR A

DYSLEXIC   NONDYSLEXIC

TRAINING

FACTOR B

NO TRAINING

Answering the Checklist Questions: The Critical Decisions

1. *Scale of measurement?* The DV measures (as well as the IQ scores) are all at the interval level.
2. *Hypothesis?* The researcher tested for possible differences.
3. *If hypothesis of difference, sample groups independent or correlated?* The groups are all independent of each other.

4. *How many sets of measures?* There are four sets of DV measures (as well as the four sets of IQ scores).

Solution

Use the ANCOVA for independent samples. In this analysis of covariance, the covariate would be the IQ measures.

Simulation 14

Analyzing the Methodology

This is post-facto research, the two IVs, RADS and PSAT scores (both subject variables), having been used to predict the DV, final high-school grade average.

Answering the Checklist Questions: The Critical Decisions

1. *Scale of measurement?* These measures are all at the interval level.
2. *Hypothesis?* The researcher tested the hypothesis of association.
3. *If hypothesis of difference, sample groups independent or correlated?* Not applicable.
4. *How many sets of measures?* There are three sets of interval measures, two IV measures and one DV measure.

Solution

Use the Pearson *r*, finding correlations between each of the IVs and the DV, and then run a multiple correlation (to assess whether the multiple *R* correlates higher with the criterion than either of the separate predictors).

Simulation 15

Analyzing the Methodology

This is combination research, one of the IVs (LD versus non-LD) clearly being a subject variable, and the listening-versus-reading conditions being a manipulated IV. The DV is composed of their correction scores.

Answering the Checklist Questions: The Critical Decisions

1. *Scale of measurement?* The DV measurements in this study, correction scores, are at least at the interval level.
2. *Hypothesis?* The hypothesis, in this case, is the hypothesis of difference.
3. *If hypothesis of difference, sample groups independent or correlated?* The subjects were randomly assigned to the treatment conditions and were completely independent of each other.
4. *How many sets of measures?* There are four sets of interval measures.

Solution

Use the factorial ANOVA for independent samples. See Chapter 5 for a discussion of the interpretation of a significant interaction in combination research. Notice that because of the sampling technique (random selection from a population of students of similar age and IQ), the analysis of covariance was not needed for these measures (since in this case, both were constants).

Simulation 16

Analyzing the Methodology

This is experimental research in that the IV (teaching approach) was manipulated by the researcher. If the two approaches produced significant differences in comprehension, a cause-and-effect relationship could be claimed.

Answering the Checklist Questions: The Critical Decisions

1. *Scale of measurement?* The dependent variable (teachers' ratings of improvement) is in nominal form, in that the teachers merely indicated improvement or no improvement for each student. These were mutually exclusive categories that did not indicate any *degree* of improvement.
2. *Hypothesis?* The school psychologist attempted to show differences between the visual, spatial-display approach and the traditional text approach.
3. *If hypothesis of difference, sample groups independent or correlated?* The two groups of students are independent of one another because subjects were randomly assigned to the treatment conditions.
4. *How many sets of measures?* There are two sets based on the teaching approaches that were used.

Solution

Use the 2 × 2 chi square.

	IMPROVED	NOT IMPROVED
VISUAL, SPATIAL-DISPLAY GROUP		
TEXT GROUP		

Simulation 17

Analyzing the Methodology

This is post-facto research, in that the IV (number of years teaching) is a subject variable based on a characteristic the subjects already possessed. This is also developmental research, in that it examines how teachers may differ over time. By treating teaching experience as the IV, we have multiple response measures, namely, teachers' enthusiasm and likelihood of teaching five years hence.

Answering the Checklist Questions: The Critical Decisions

1. *Scale of measurement?* Enthusiasm for teaching and likelihood of future teaching were measured by five-point scales with 1 representing both very little enthusiasm and very little likelihood and 5 representing both very high enthusiasm and very high likelihood. These measures then produced at least interval data, along with number of years of teaching.
2. *Hypothesis?* The superintendent attempted to identify an association between number of years teaching and each of the other two measures.
3. *If hypothesis of difference, sample groups independent or correlated?* Not applicable; the hypothesis of association was being tested.
4. *How many sets of measures?* There are three sets: number of years teaching, enthusiasm scores, and likelihood-of-future-teaching scores.

Solution

The Pearson *r* would be calculated twice. One would correlate number of years teaching with enthusiasm and the other would correlate number of years teaching with likelihood of future teaching. Significant negative correlations on each of these calculations would support the superintendent's hypothesis that burn-out increases as teachers continue to teach, at least up to ten years.

Simulation 18

Analyzing the Methodology

This is post-facto research because the headmaster certainly could not manipulate the teachers' ages (IV). Even if the salaries differed according to age, other factors such as level of education might explain the differences in salaries. Teachers were matched on teaching experience but not on every conceivable variable that might be involved.

Answering the Checklist Questions: The Critical Decisions

1. *Scale of measurement?* The dependent variable (salaries) is in ordinal form. Salaries were ranked because the distribution was often skewed.
2. *Hypothesis?* This study tested the hypothesis of difference: that salaries would differ with the ages of the teachers.
3. *If hypothesis of difference, sample groups independent or correlated?* The three groups of teachers in this study are correlated in that they were matched according to their years of teaching experience.
4. *How many sets of measures?* There are three sets, one for each age-group.

Solution

Use the Friedman ANOVA by ranks. Compare the ranked salaries in the three age-groups.

Simulation 19

Analyzing the Methodology

This is experimental research; the independent variable (amount of time receiving a personalized system of instruction) was manipulated by the researcher. Ideally, another group of juniors who did not receive personalized instruction would have served as a control group.

Answering the Checklist Questions: The Critical Decisions

1. *Scale of measurement?* The dependent variable (attitudes toward school) provides interval data. As has been stated, the attitude scores distribute normally.
2. *Hypothesis?* The researcher was testing the hypothesis of difference, as is always the case in experimental research.
3. *If hypothesis of difference, sample groups independent or correlated?* The groups are clearly correlated; the same subjects were used in each treatment condition.
4. *How many sets of measures?* There are five sets of measures of attitudes toward school (at the beginning of the school year and after each of the four marking periods).

Solution

Use the within-subjects F ratio for repeated measures.

Simulation 20

Analyzing the Methodology

This is experimental research because the independent variable (presentation of the workshop) was manipulated by the director. Since the same teachers were tested prior to the workshop and then again after it, the design is before-after. This is not the best design for testing this hypothesis because the competency-test scores may have improved simply because of the teachers' familiarity with the items. They may have discussed them among themselves during the workshop. It would have been better to set up a separate control group of teachers who took the competency test at the same times as the other teachers but who received no in-service workshop in between.

Answering the Checklist Questions: The Critical Decisions

1. *Scale of measurement?* The competency-test scores produced at least interval data, but because they were skewed it was necessary to rank order all the teachers' scores (ordinal data).
2. *Hypothesis?* The researcher was testing the hypothesis of difference: that competency scores would be higher after an in-service workshop.
3. *If hypothesis of difference, sample groups independent or correlated?* These samples are definitely correlated in that the same teachers were tested before and after the workshop. The samples are always correlated in a before-after design.
4. *How many sets of measures?* There are two sets of measures, one taken before the workshop and the other taken after the workshop.

Solution

Use the Wilcoxon T test.

Simulation 21

Analyzing the Methodology

This is post-facto research. The IV (students' ratings of their instructors) was not manipulated by the dean. She simply gathered the information regarding students' ratings and their final grades without trying to manipulate them in any way. Therefore, the issue of causation is not relevant here, although the probability of accurately predicting students' grades based on the ratings of the instructor is very much at issue.

Answering the Checklist Questions: The Critical Decisions

1. *Scale of measurement?* The students' ratings of their instructors were ranked by the dean from best to worst; thus we have ordinal data. Although instructor 1 was rated more positively by his students than instructor 2, we do not know how much more. Although students' grades are at least interval data, they must be converted to ordinal rank before the statistical analysis can be completed.
2. *Hypothesis?* The hypothesis being tested here was that of association: the dean wanted to see if students' ratings of their instructors correlated with their final grades.
3. *If hypothesis of difference, sample groups independent or correlated?* Not applicable; the hypothesis of association was being tested.
4. *How many sets of measures?* There are two sets of measures, students' ratings of their instructors and their final grades in the course.

Solution

Use the Spearman r_S. Even if this correlation is positive and significant it does not necessarily mean that being a highly rated instructor brings out the best in students. It's possible that a third variable, such as an instructor's grading policy, may be responsible for this relationship. Perhaps some instructors were rated very favorably because they were easy graders and so, of course, the grades of the students in these courses were high.

Simulation 22

Analyzing the Methodology

This is an example of combination research involving two independent variables. The first independent variable (open versus traditional education) was controlled by the researcher, but he was not able to create completely equivalent groups because he was dealing with already intact groups (quasi-experimental). The second IV (gender) was a subject variable that could not be manipulated by the researcher (post-facto). If significant main effects, a significant interaction, or both are found, cause-and-effect statements are not warranted because equivalent groups were not created at the outset of the study.

Answering the Checklist Questions: The Critical Decisions

1. *Scale of measurement?* The independence factor of the personality inventory was scored as interval data and we were told that the scores were normally distributed.
2. *Hypothesis?* The researcher attempted to show differences in independence scores as a result of the independent variables.
3. *If hypothesis of difference, sample groups independent or correlated?* The seventh-graders were independently assigned to the type-of-education IV on a class-by-class basis. On the gender IV, the groups were also independent.
4. *How many sets of measures?* There are four sets, one for each of the four treatment conditions.

Solution

Use the factorial ANOVA, with the data set up in four cells.

	OPEN EDUCATION	TRADITIONAL EDUCATION
FEMALES		
MALES		

Test for the main effects, columns and rows, separately, and then test for the interaction. Because each independent variable had only two levels in this study, a Tukey HSD or other post-hoc tests are not needed. The between-columns value of F will indicate if type of education made a difference, and the between-rows value of F will indicate if gender made a difference. The value of F_{rxc} will reveal if an interaction occurred.

Simulation 23

Analyzing the Methodology

This is post-facto research; each child's parents, not the researcher, decided whether or not the child was to attend a day-care center. The independent variable (whether the child attended the day-care center) is thus a subject IV, not manipulated. Perhaps parents were more apt to send a less mature (or more mature, who knows?) child to the day-care center in the first place.

Answering the Checklist Questions: The Critical Decisions

1. *Scale of measurement?* This is an example of ordinal data, since the dependent variable is the ranking of the child's social-maturity level.
2. *Hypothesis?* This is the hypothesis of difference: that maturity levels should differ as a function of day-care attendance.
3. *If hypothesis of difference, sample groups independent or correlated?* The groups are independent of each other. The fact that one child was placed in a given category had no influence on where another child was placed.
4. *How many sets of measures?* There are two sets, those children who had attended the day-care center versus those who had not.

Solution

Use the Mann-Whitney *U* test, which compares the ranks of two independent groups.

Simulation 24

Analyzing the Methodology

This is post-facto research; the independent variables are assigned, not manipulated. If the results prove to be significant, predictions, not cause-and-effect inferences, are possible.

Answering the Checklist Questions: The Critical Decisions

1. *Scale of measurement?* The three sets of measurements (financial aid, amount earned, and grade-point average) are all at least interval measures. Furthermore, all three measures distribute in a fairly normal fashion. (The summer earnings of students, unlike family incomes, are not apt to be badly skewed. Few, if any, students earn so much during the three-month summer period as to cause a dramatic shift from normality.)
2. *Hypothesis?* This is the hypothesis of association: that a correlation exists between the disparate measures of financial aid and summer earnings.
3. *If hypothesis of difference, sample groups independent or correlated?* Not applicable; the hypothesis of association was being tested.

4. *How many sets of measures?* There are three sets: financial aid, summer earnings, and GPA.

Solution

Use the Pearson r. In fact, calculate three values of the Pearson r:

1. between financial aid and summer earnings
2. between financial aid and grade-point average
3. between summer earnings and grade-point average

Then, if the obtained values of r are significant, calculate a partial correlation between financial aid and summer earnings, thereby nullifying (partialing out) the effects of grade-point average.

Simulation 25

Analyzing the Methodology

This is post-facto research. The independent variable, college major, is a subject IV, not manipulated.

Answering the Checklist Questions: The Critical Decisions

1. *Scale of measurement?* Although income is an interval measurement, the skewed distribution forced a rank ordering of the data, thus, creating a series of ordinal measures.
2. *Hypothesis?* The researcher was testing for differences among the income ranks of the three groups.
3. *If hypothesis of difference, sample groups independent or correlated?* The groups are independent. The assignment of alumni into subject-major categories was strictly independent. The selection of one person from the "education" category did not demand or preclude another subject being selected from the "liberal arts" category.
4. *How many sets of measures?* There are three sets, one for each of the subject-major categories.

Solution

Use the Kruskal-Wallis H test for three or more independent groups and ordinal data.

Simulation 26

Analyzing the Methodology

This is post-facto research. The independent variable (family size) was assigned, not manipulated. (Natural forces or their own decision, not the decision of the experimenter, determined which families had small or large numbers of children.) Thus, even if significance is established, the causal factor will remain in the realm of speculation. Could it be, instead, that lower-IQ parents have more children?

Answering the Checklist Questions: The Critical Decisions

1. *Scale of measurement?* IQ scores are considered to be interval measures, and the underlying distribution to be fairly normal.
2. *Hypothesis?* The researcher was looking for IQ differences among children from small and large families.
3. *If hypothesis of difference, sample groups independent or correlated?* The sample groups are independent. The selection of a given family depended on its size, not on whether some other family had been selected.
4. *How many sets of measures?* There are two sets of IQ scores, one taken from large families and one taken from small families.

Solution

Use the independent *t*. If the score for each child is to be used separately, use the equation for unequal values of N (there are three times as many IQ scores in the six-child families). If the children's IQ scores are to be averaged within each family, equal values of N can be maintained.

Simulation 27

Analyzing the Methodology

This is post-facto research; the independent variable (number of books read) was not manipulated. The subjects were assigned to groups on the basis of how many books they themselves had chosen to read. A unidirectional interpretation of this study will therefore be impossible. Does extensive reading increase reading speed, or do fast readers prefer to read more? Or is it a combination of the two? One can never know from this study.

Answering the Checklist Questions: The Critical Decisions

1. *Scale of measurement?* The dependent variable (reading speed in words per minute) provides at least interval data. The distribution is close enough to normality to use interval tests.
2. *Hypothesis?* The researcher was looking for differences in reading speed among the subjects.
3. *If hypothesis of difference, sample groups independent or correlated?* The groups are independent of each other. The placement of a subject in a given group depended on the number of books read and not on the placement of some other subject.
4. *How many sets of measures?* There are three sets of measures of reading speed.

Solution

Use the one-way ANOVA, the *F* ratio. If *F* is significant, proceed with the Tukey HSD.

RESEARCH ERRORS: EVALUATIONS AND COMMENTS

Case 1

The lack of a separate control group leaves this study seriously flawed. We cannot tell if the gains were really the effect of the teaching technique, or of the several confounding variables (teacher personality, the novelty effect of being placed in a special class, and the growth changes that normally take place among children during a school term). Finally, in this particular published study no statistical tests were conducted at all, leaving the reader unable to determine whether the reading gains were in fact simply a result of chance, whether the high-IQ children profited more from the special class than did the low-IQ children, or, really, anything at all.

Case 2

As it stands, the problem with this study is that one cannot really be sure that the increase in prejudice resulted from not being allowed to go to town (the goal blockage). This was a one-group, before-after experimental design where the same group was used as its own control. In fact, a separate control group was desperately needed here, a group not told anything about going to town but still forced to take the attitude test, the intelligence tests, and the attitude test a second time. Without this control, the researcher can't be sure whether the attitude change was the result of not going to town or the result of the boredom generated by being forced to sit still for such a long period of time taking these tests or the anger generated by having to take the attitude test a second time.

Case 3

Here it is again, a before-after experimental design, with the same children serving as their own controls. Remember, by the time the children were measured the second time, they had been cooped up in that room for some time. Could boredom have set in? Could attention spans have begun to diminish? We simply can't tell from this study. Only with a separate control group (another group of children playing with similar toys for the same length of time, but with no view of the unattainable toys) could one hope to eliminate some of the most blatant of the confounding variables found in this study.

Case 4

In this case, the independent variable (whether a scene was staged in which helping behavior was exhibited) was seriously confounded. Not only did the driver-subject witness the helping scene; he also viewed a woman in distress, and perhaps this alone was what prompted his helping behavior. The researchers should have used another scene, in which the male driver would have seen, in succession, two scenes of women alone attempting to change a tire. In this way the researcher could have established whether the helping behavior in scene 1 caused the motorist to stop at scene 2, or whether just seeing a woman in distress in a new scene 1 would produce the same results when the driver arrived at scene 2. The point is that in the experimental method, all variables, other than the independent variable, should be held constant in both control and experimental situations. In this study, the subjects in the experimental group witnessed not only helping behavior but also a scene of someone in trouble. Perhaps passing such a scene, with or without the helping model, generates feelings of guilt and makes drivers more apt to stop the next time they see the opportunity arising.

Case 5

In this study the style of leadership (the presumed IV) was being confounded with whether or not the boys had the plans to follow when the leader was out of the room. Perhaps the study only proved that it's more difficult to build quality models without plans, regardless of leadership style. In this study the plans for building the planes should have been left in the room under all the leadership conditions. Or, if the researchers wanted also to test for creativity, the plans should have been removed under all three conditions.

Case 6

The problem with this study is two-fold. First, although this was obviously a quasi-experimental design, there very well could have been systematic differences among the students in the three classes to begin with. Even when using intact groups, the researcher should make every attempt to keep the groups as much alike as possible. Perhaps students who elect afternoon courses are different from those who opt for morning classes. Perhaps students who have part-time jobs, or students on athletic teams, are forced by their schedules to select morning classes. In this study no attempt was made to ensure group equivalence before the IV, teaching style, was manipulated. More serious, however, is that the instructor, playing the different teaching roles, *was also the researcher*. It could very well be that this researcher's own convictions allowed him to carry out one of the roles more convincingly than the other. Also, the students must have been fully aware of who was in the experimental group and who was in the control group. This was, in short, definitely not a double-blind study, and because of this the possibility of extraneous motivational variables could not have been controlled. The potential for confounding variables was far too great for this to be a definitive test of teaching techniques.

Case 7

The basic problem with this study is in the selection of the sample. The women who returned the questionnaires, a minority of the freshman class, may have been more oriented toward feminine issues, or more interested in pursuing the issue of their own femininity or lack of it. Any number of other factors may also have been involved. In short, the sample may not have been representative of the women at that college, never mind college women in general, or women in general. As stated earlier, distortions in potential extrapolations are bound to occur whenever subjects are allowed to select themselves.

Case 8

In many studies, especially correlational, the research becomes flawed as a result of the various evaluations of subjects being conducted by observers who know how the subjects scored on previous evaluations. This knowledge can be extremely intimate when the same observer rates the subjects on several trait measures. In research, this error is called the halo effect, and it results from the very obvious fact that if an observer assigns a positive evaluation to a subject in one area, consciously or unconsciously, the observer tends to assign another positive evaluation when the subject is being measured in another area. In short, the subjects are having their trait measures generalized into a whole host of seemingly related areas.

The halo effect can be a hazard to both the researcher and the research consumer. The issue is especially acute in post-facto research testing the hypothesis of association. In this study, the halo effect could have been prevented if the personality ratings had been assigned by an independent observer, or someone other than the person doing the grading. Also, this independent observer should not have been made aware of what the students' grades had actually been.

Case 9

This is, of course, post-facto research, since the teacher, not the experimenter, determined the amount of smile time. In fact, this would have been a difficult study to conduct experimentally. To actively manipulate the IV, the researcher would perhaps have had to sit in the back of the room and, at random time intervals, signal the teacher that it was time to smile. This could obviously have led to a rather bizarre scene, in which the teacher, in the middle of a stern reprimand, would suddenly have to break out in a broad grin. In this case, though, the study as conducted is post-facto. Because of this, the results *cannot* tell us the direction of the relationship. It may well be as the authors hypothesized, that smiling teachers produce achieving students. Or, it may just as likely be that high-achieving students produce smiling teachers—teachers luxuriating in the fact that the student-success rate is obvious proof of the teacher's competence. Or it could also be that a third variable, say, the personality of the teacher, may have caused both the smiling and the high grades. Perhaps a smiling teacher is a happy optimist who always sees the best in everyone and is therefore more lenient when assigning grades.

Case 10

In this post-facto study, the researcher tested the hypothesis of association, the association between the variables selfishness and happiness. However, since the evaluations of the person's selfishness and happiness were both made by the same observer, the child, these results might be more parsimoniously explained on the basis of the halo effect. When you like someone, you may easily become convinced that that person abounds in a whole array of positive traits, even in the face of contrary evidence. Finally, we must be careful of extrapolating data collected on children visiting a behavior clinic to the population of children at large.

Case 11

Was the IV (group therapy) really the cause of this change? Without at least one separate control group, we'll never know. One other group was an absolute "must" in this study, a group that would have received the pretest and posttest but would not have been involved in the therapy. Further, since the pretest might have sensitized the subjects to be on the alert for ethnic issues, the study should perhaps have been run again with a different design: an after-only design in which neither the experimental nor control groups would be given any pretesting. Thus, two groups would be randomly selected, and only one of these groups would receive the therapy. Then, after six weeks of therapy, the experimental group would be tested for ethnic hostility, and these scores would be compared with those of the no-therapy control group. In this way, the pure effects of the IV could be evaluated, and there would be no added concern over whether the therapy only works in conjunction with a pretest, sensitizing process. The results of this design, when compared with those of the actual study, could determine whether the pretest was interacting with the therapy to produce the reduction of hostility. If this turned out to be the case, this would be a meaningful finding itself, and would indicate that the therapy process is only effective when used together with some sort of pretest, sensitizing instrument.

Case 12

Two important confounding variables were allowed free rein in this study. First, the experimental group not only received the play therapy but also was treated to a ten-mile bus ride twice a week, and hence, to an opportunity to leave the possible boredom of the institution's confines. Second, the two groups were not equivalent to begin with. Although it may seem especially fair to select only the most maladjusted children for the special-treatment condition, it might very well be that these were the very children who would change the most, regardless of the independent variable, simply because on the measurement scale they had the most upward room in which to change. If you recall our earlier discussion of a phenomenon called regression toward the mean, you might remember that persons who score low on any test are more apt, if they change at all, to change upward than persons who score high. Finally, this study is triply flawed, in that sixteen of the control-group children left the institution during the six weeks the study was in progress and could therefore not be retested. This fact produces the nagging concern that the departure of these children might have resulted from their having been perceived as becoming adjusted enough to go home.

REFERENCES

Berrueta-Clement, J. R., Schweinhart, L. J., Barnett, W. S., Epstein, A. S., & Weikart, D. P. (1984). *Changed lives: The effects of the Perry preschool program on youths through age 19*. Ypsilanti, Mich.: High/Scope Press.

Bornstein, M. (1985). How infant and mother jointly contribute to developing cognitive competence in the child. *Proceedings of the National Academy of Science, 82*, 7470–7473.

Brophy, J. (1981). Teacher praise: A functional analysis. *Review of Educational Research, 51*, 26–28.

Clark, K. B., & Clark, M. (1947). Racial identification and preference. In T. M. Newcomb (ed.), *Readings in Social Psychology*. New York: Holt, Rinehart & Winston.

Dempster, F. N. (1988). The spacing effect: A case study in the failure to apply the results of psychological research. *American Psychologist, 43*, 627–634.

Espin, C. A., & Sindilar, P. T. (1988). Auditory feedback and writing: Learning disabled and nondisabled students. *Exceptional Children, 55*, 45–51.

KOHLBERG, L. (1984). *Essays on moral development.* New York: Harper & Row.

MORENO, J. L. (1953). *Who shall survive?* New York: Beacon.

PARISH, T. S., & COPELAND, T. F. (1978). Teacher's and student's attitudes in mainstreamed classrooms. *Psychological Reports, 43,* 51–54.

PETERSON, P. (1984). Classroom aptitude by treatment interactions: An alternate analysis strategy. *Educational Psychologist, 19,* 43–47.

PUGACH, M. C., & RATHS, J. D. (1983). Testing teachers: Analysis and recommendations. *Journal of Teacher Education, 34,* 37–43.

SULLIVAN, C. (1988). The use of a self-summary strategy to enhance reading comprehension in learning disabled students. Unpublished doctoral dissertation, American International College, Springfield, Mass.

WALTER, S. A., & STIVERS, E. (1977). The relation of student teachers' classroom behavior and Eriksonian ego identity. *Journal of Teacher Education, 38,* 47–55.

WILSON, J. A. R., ROBECK, M. C., & MICHAEL, W. B. (1969). *Psychological foundations of learning.* New York: McGraw-Hill.

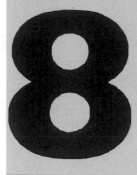

CHAPTER

8

The Anatomy of a Research Report

CAUTION SIGNS

DOCUMENTING YOUR WRITING

THE FORMAT OF THE RESEARCH REPORT

The Title (What Is It?)
The Author(s) (Who Did It?)
The Abstract (Did It Work?)
The Introduction (What's It All About?)
The Method (What Was Done?)
The Results (What Was Found?)
The Discussion (What Does It Mean?)
The References (Who Did Something Like It?)
The Appendix (What Else Do You Want to Know?)

READING REPORTS FIRSTHAND

A Journal Article

SUMMARY

KEY TERMS

REFERENCES

Now that you are beginning to feel somewhat comfortable with the ins and outs of conducting research, we must next consider how to tell the world about the educational breakthroughs you expect to accomplish. It's not enough to simply tell your roommate and your parents about the discoveries that you'll be making. You will also want to share your findings with the educational community. Research may be virtually useless if not properly disseminated, discussed, and evaluated.

Although there have been many different styles and formats used in education for reporting research findings, the majority of the educational journals today have adopted what are called the APA guidelines. Our discussion will therefore focus on the practices developed and endorsed by the American Psychological Association (APA). (For more details, see American Psychological Association, 1983.)

Initially you may feel that the guidelines imposed by the APA are unnecessarily picayune and designed to add to your academic headaches. It is hoped, however, that you will come to appreciate the necessity for such rigor. To communicate effectively and efficiently with others in the field, such standardization has really become essential. And as a bonus, you will find that understanding these guidelines will also help you in reading the research reports of others. Without question, it will make it much easier for you to identify and comprehend the key features of a study.

CAUTION SIGNS

Before delving into the specifics of the APA style of report writing, you should be aware of some more general guidelines to follow and mistakes to avoid. The technical report is designed to interest your readers, inform them of your findings, and convince them that your interpretations are, at the very least, plausible. Technical writing such as this differs from the creative writing you may have been required to do for your English-composition classes. The emphasis here is not on uniqueness of style or dazzling creativity but on that traditional scientific necessity: uniformity. Individualized writing styles must be sacrificed to enhance comprehension and facilitate speed of reading.

First, reports should not sound overly personal and therefore should be written in the past tense and in the passive voice throughout. (The only exception to this rule is during the discussion of the possibilities for future research; see the section on discussion later in this chapter). It is also customary to use the third person in your writing. Using pronouns such as *I, we, you* again tends to personalize the report and detract from its objectivity. Also, be careful to avoid the use of sexist language in your writing. In certain instances, word choices such as *man* or *he* may be inaccurate, misleading, or discriminatory. The following are some examples of the right and wrong ways to write a report:

Wrong	*Right*
In earlier research I found . . .	Previous studies indicated . . .
I selected 40 second-grade subjects . . .	The subjects were 40 second graders . . .
I hypothesize that . . .	It was hypothesized that . . .
Man's search for knowledge . . .	The search for knowledge . . .

Students who are new to the technicalities of report writing sometimes have a tendency to use qualitative statements in their reports that, again, may detract from the tone of scientific objectivity. Statements such as "The results were good because . . ." or "The best finding in the study was that . . ." should really be avoided. Simply present your findings and conclusions and let your readers make their own judgments.

However, the quest for scientific objectivity should not force you into a style that is so cryptic as to be almost incomprehensible. For example, you should avoid using a *telegraphic style* of writing when presenting a series of events, findings, or conclusions. In describing the procedures followed in your study you may be tempted to write, for example,

The following procedures were followed:

> subjects recruited
> assigned to conditions
> read instructions
> exposed to new teaching method
> measured for comprehension
> debriefed

Although it is certainly true that one of the objectives of report writing is to be concise and to the point, this telegraphic style is so abbreviated that the reader really can't know what you did, let alone how to replicate the study. Full sentences, with subject, verb, and so on, should be used and organized into para-graphs.

A grammatical point that you might easily overlook has to do with some of the commonly used terms in our field, such as *data, phenomena, criteria,* and *hypotheses.* All four of these terms are plural and as such must agree with the verb being used. You may be tempted to write "The data in this study is . . ." or "The phenomena observed was . . ." Correctly stated, these should read "The data in this study *are* . . ." and "The phenomena observed *were* . . ."

One more helpful hint bears mentioning in this context. You have no doubt learned from the time you began to write your name that you should proofread your work before submitting it. The present case is no exception. You may find it additionally helpful to read your writing aloud to yourself. (Do this when your roommate is out so that he or she does not think you're losing your mind.) This will enable you to pick out sentences that do not "sound right" and will also enable you to avoid overly lengthy sentences. One hint you might use to avoid the run-on sentence is that if you have to catch your breath several times before completing a sentence aloud, you should probably break it into several shorter ones. It is easy to fall into this trap when describing a lengthy procedure or when unfolding an involved interpretation of your findings.

DOCUMENTING YOUR WRITING

As you have no doubt noticed in reading a journal article or textbook in the field of education, repeated references are made to the works of others. Typically, all the ideas presented are certainly not the author's(s'); it therefore becomes neces-sary in reporting your research to refer to those previous findings or theories that are related to your study. When referring to the works or ideas of others, it is absolutely necessary to differentiate them from your own. Don't try to pretend that your study laid the groundwork for the entire area of, say, behavior modifi-cation, as though B. F. Skinner never existed.

The major purpose of such *documentation* is, of course, to give proper credit to the researchers and theorists who have preceded you. As a bonus, it is also very helpful to the reader who is interested in a more detailed discussion of the topic. Proper referencing directs the reader to the appropriate journal or book where he or she can learn more about the specifics of the work being cited. Virtually any statement that is made in a report that refers to a theory, a research finding, an unusual statistical technique, and so on, that is not the original work of the author needs to be documented. As you will learn when we discuss the specific sections of the report, most of this documentation takes place in the introduction and discussion sections.

Now let's look at the specifics of standardized documentation. The stan-dard documentation procedure established by the APA is used throughout the field of education and, not coincidentally, throughout this text. This style requires that the last name of the author(s) and the year of publication be inserted in the text at an appropriate point. For example, consider the following:

> Erikson (1959) felt that adolescence was a time of . . .
>
>   or
>
> In a discussion of adolescence (Erikson, 1959), it was suggested that . . .

If, however, there happens to be more than one author for a single work, separate the second or last author from the other(s) by *and* if the author's names are not enclosed by parentheses, and by the ampersand (&) if they are so enclosed. Here are a couple of examples:

> Sternberg and Nigro (1980) found . . .
>
> In a developmental study (Sternberg & Nigro, 1980) it was found that . . .

If a work has more than two authors, the names of all the authors only have to be listed the first time that reference is made to them. For example:

> Everston, Emmer, Clements, Sanford, and Worsham (1984) stated that . . .

Subsequent references to the same study should only list the name of the first author, followed by *et al.* and the year of publication. For the previous example, the next time these authors are mentioned you'd only have to write

> Everston et al. (1984) suggested that . . .

When more than one study is involved, the citations are listed in alphabetical order on the basis of the first author's last name, and then the studies themselves are separated by semicolons:

> Recent studies (Anderson, Klossen, & Johnson, 1982; Bowman, 1982; Senter, 1981) have stated that . . .

THE FORMAT OF THE RESEARCH REPORT

The key features of the research report are outlined in the *Publication Manual of the American Psychological Association* (American Psychological Association, 1983), and the organization of the features are as follows:

1. title
2. name and affiliation of author(s)
3. abstract
4. introduction

5. method
6. results
7. discussion
8. references
9. appendix

To aid you in identifying the major sections of a report, we have reprinted an actual journal article and pointed out the key points as they appear (see the section Reading Reports Firsthand, in this chapter). Please do yourself a favor and refer to this as you read through the rest of this chapter.

The Title (What Is It?)

Do not overlook the importance of the *title* of your research report. Overly creative or "cutesy" titles should be avoided in favor of more descriptive ones that will provide the reader with at least some idea of what you're doing. Usually the title conveys to the reader the major independent variable(s) as well as the major dependent variable(s). For instance, in the study by Harrison, Strauss, and Glaubman (1981) entitled, "The Impact of Open and Traditional Classrooms on Achievement and Creativity: The Israeli Case," the independent and dependent variables are readily identified. In this case the type of classroom is the independent variable, and we can easily gather from the title that the researchers attempted to discover whether it might influence the dependent variables, which were measures of achievement and creativity.

The title is also important in that the key words can be used for cataloging your report in the event that it is someday published. (Listen, you never know.) If it is published it will usually find its way into such summary publications as *Educational Resources Information Center (ERIC), Psychological Abstracts,* and *Sociological Abstracts*.

Also, in this, the age of the computer, automated literature searches can now be done by accessing the key words in the title of a journal article or book. As you can well imagine, computerized literature searches can save us a lot of time, which we can use for doing other things—such as more research!

The Author(s) (Who Did It?)

By far, the easiest section of your report to write is the listing of the *Author(s) and their affiliations*. Typically, the author who has made the most significant contribution is listed first, along with his or her personal affiliation (i.e., college, university, school, or other educational institution). In deciding how you would like to have your name appear in print, keep in mind that you should stick to your decision. Using alternate forms of your name such as Ingrid M. Smart, I. M. Smart, or I. Melissa Smart on subsequent publications may add to confusion on the part of the reader. Titles, such as Dr. or Ms., and degrees, such as B.S. or Ed.D., should be omitted.

The Abstract (Did It Work?)

The *abstract* of your paper provides the reader with a brief (100 to 150 words) thumbnail sketch of your entire report. It appears at the beginning of your write-up and, as such, is the first, and alas sometimes only, part of your report that will be read. The abstract should contain statements of the problem, procedures, results, and conclusions of your study. Although the abstract appears at the beginning of the report, it should be the last part to be written (since, of course, it contains the conclusions). It is often difficult to include the key features of your research in such a short summary, but this task is made easier if you wait until the rest of the report is written; you can then simply paraphrase your own words.

The Introduction (What's It All About?)

If you have managed to whet the intellectual curiosity of your reader with your abstract, a difficult task at best, you want to maintain your hold by presenting a clear, cogent *introduction* to your research. This section should first and foremost inform the reader of the problem under study. By citing previous research or theories pertinent to your problem, you are able to set the stage for showing where your particular study fits into the overall scheme of things.

To accomplish this, you will need to spend some time in the library. Familiarize yourself with those reference books that list the abstracts of studies done in the field of education, for example, *ERIC, Psychological Abstracts*, and *Sociological Abstracts*.

ERIC is a national information system that serves as a major source of documents on education. Most libraries have access to the entire *ERIC* file and also subscribe to *Resources in Education (RIE)*, which updates the *ERIC* file every month as new documents become available. This publication includes a document section, which is divided according to sixteen major content areas in education. The areas covered are career education; counseling and personnel services; early childhood education; educational management; handicapped and gifted children; higher education; information resources; junior colleges; languages and linguistics; reading and communication skills; rural education and small schools; science, mathematics, and environmental education; social studies and social-science education; teacher education; tests, measurement and evaluation; and urban education. The content areas in this document section are then broken down into (1) the abstracts of all the *ERIC* documents; (2) "descriptors," which identify the documents' essential subject matter; and (3) the corresponding ED number, which is used to identify each *ERIC* document.

In addition to the document section, *RIE* also has an index section, which catalogs each entry alphabetically into a subject index by major descriptor. The index section also includes an author index, which is arranged alphabetically by the authors' last name, and even an institution index, which is arranged alphabetically by the institution responsible for the document. Each of these three indexes includes the documents' ED number, but not the abstracts themselves (since they have already appeared in the document section).

In addition, there is the *Annual Cumulation Index* for *RIE*. This cumulative index is very similar to the three aforementioned index sections of *RIE* (subject, author, and institution). The difference is, however, that the annual index contains *all* the information that was in each of the twelve monthly editions for that year. This *Annual Cumulation Index* also includes a publication-type index, which catalogs the information according to what type of document it has been published in (for example, book, collected works, dissertation, guide).

A third publication, *Annual Cumulation Abstracts*, is like the document section of the *RIE*. Once again, the difference is that the *Annual Cumulation Abstracts* contains *all* the abstracts that were in each of the twelve monthly editions for that year. These are organized according to the sixteen major content areas mentioned previously and are consecutive by ED number.

In addition to the aforementioned documents, *ERIC* also publishes *Current Index to Journals in Education (CIJE)*. The format for using *CIJE* is very similar to that for using *RIE*. Whereas *RIE* indexes documents contained in the *ERIC* files, *CIJE* indexes articles in nearly eight hundred education and education-related periodical publications. The *CIJE*, which covers from 1969 to the present, is similar to, yet an improvement over, a publication entitled *The Education Index*, in that it also provides the abstracts for the articles if not enough information is provided by the title of the article.

Until you have some firsthand experience with volumes of this kind, it may at first seem somewhat overwhelming. Actually, they are quite simple to use; probably easier to use than to read about. The best thing to do is to get yourself over to the library and have a few trial runs. You can begin by searching the subject-index section of the *Annual Cumulation Index*. First, look under the descriptors that correspond to your area of interest and write down the ED numbers that seem most relevant to your study. Next, go to the *Annual Cumulation Abstracts* and read the abstracts whose ED numbers you've just identified. At this point, you can quickly see if they are as pertinent to your study as you had initially thought. For those that are, note the ED number and look up these documents elsewhere in the library. Many libraries will have the *ERIC* file on microfiche, which is also categorized by ED number.

In some instances it may be to your advantage to conduct a computerized search of the *ERIC* file to avoid having to search through many volumes of the *Annual Cumulation Index* and the *Annual Cumulation Abstracts*. Depending on the particular system in use at your library, the procedure involves searching data bases such as *ERIC* to identify references related to your study. By giving the computer some key words or descriptors related to your research, you will receive, in return, a listing of the references and, very often, the abstracts of studies pertinent to your project. Consult the librarian at your school to determine if this service is available and, if so, how you can make use of it. Above all, don't be intimidated by the thought of using the library's computer. It's simple, fast, and even sort of fun.

Once your literature search is completed, either by looking up the studies directly in the volumes or by having the computer do it for you, in a relatively short time you are likely to be inundated with a great many studies that appear to be pertinent to your topic—perhaps, even, too many studies. As your Xerox bills pile up you may wonder how on earth you will ever organize so much research into a coherent introduction. The obvious solution is to weed out some of the studies—but which ones? A good approach is to find a recent article that seems to be most pertinent to your study. From here it is a matter of working backward by checking the references or studies cited in that article. Find and read the studies cited and then note the references in each of these studies. Repeat the procedure for this group of references and continue on as needed. For instance, let's say that you've found a recent article that appears to be closely allied to the topic you've chosen and that this article contains four references, A, B, C, and D. Each of these references, in turn, also contains its own references. For example, consider the setup in Figure 8.1.

At this point you have now accumulated even more studies than you began with and you are still wondering what to do with them all. About now, however, you will probably begin to notice that the studies are starting to look familiar, since the most important studies are likely to be referenced time and again. For example, in Figure 8.1, references A_1, B_3, and D_3 may all be referring to exactly the same study. If you find that the three studies (A,B,D) are all pertinent to your topic, and they have all cited this same study, it is probably important. By noting those studies that are continually being referenced, you will develop a feel for the important literature in your area. This will also help you to cull those studies that seem to stray too far from your topic.

The Funnel Approach

One way to pull these studies together into some organized fashion is to use a *funnel approach* (Warm, 1973). Begin with broad statements that can then be used to isolate your problem from the vast number of topics covered in your field. Continue this funneling by systematically eliminating irrelevant research, and then summarize those articles that direct the reader's attention to your study. The introduction should unfold like a story in which you tell the reader

Figure 8.1

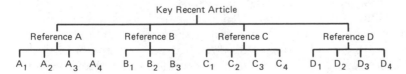

about the important studies and theories (if applicable) that preceded your work. This review should not be so extensive as to attempt to cover every single article or summary that's ever been written in the entire topic area. You can assume that the reader is a professional with some degree of sophistication in the field of education. Therefore, you need not start from square one with each research report by stating, for example, that public education in the United States grew out of the principles and values advocated by the Puritans of Massachusetts during the seventeenth century.

The introduction should conclude with a paragraph that describes, in general terms, what was actually done in your study. This often includes a statement of your major hypothesis. However, don't overdo your explanation of these procedures because they're going to have to be spelled out in detail in the next section, the method section.

Ideally, a well written and clearly organized introduction section may even leave your readers mumbling to themselves, "That makes a lot of sense. Why didn't I think of that?"

The Method (What Was Done?)

In the *method section* you get the opportunity to tell the education community exactly how you conducted your study. Here you can showcase your creativity and all that you have learned about experimental design, confounding variables, and overall precision. The method section should include the operational definitions of your variables, and these should be written in sufficient detail to allow another researcher to replicate your study in all its essential details. In a study designed to measure the effect of computer-assisted instruction on the acquisition of math skills, for example, the color of the walls in the classroom is probably not an essential detail to be included. However, such variables as the sex, grade level, and aptitudes of the students are likely to be important and should be included in your write-up.

When reading an article that does contain flaws or confounding variables, it is usually in this method section that they become most clearly visible. Did the researcher use an appropriate control group to warrant his or her conclusions? Were the influential extraneous variables appropriately kept from clouding the results? Since the information necessary to answer these types of questions must be included in the method section, you should read this section with special care to properly evaluate the study.

The method section is usually divided into labeled subsections for the sake of organization and enhanced readability. The most commonly used subsections are (1) subjects, (2) apparatus or materials, and (3) procedure.

Since some flexibility is allowed here, these subsections should not be regarded as etched in stone. For example, if your only materials consist of a questionnaire that can be simply described, it can perhaps be included along with the procedure, thus eliminating the second category. However, if the procedures employed are quite complex, further subheadings such as "pretesting," "experimental manipulation," and "follow-up" may be warranted. You really have to use your own judgment to determine how many and what types of subsections will best organize your method section.

The Subjects

Obviously, in this section we describe the characteristics of the subjects under study, including relevant demographic information. In almost all studies, it is important to note the age and sex of the subjects. Depending on the particular study, characteristics such as race, aptitudes, and socioeconomic status may also be vital.

In any case, you must always indicate how many subjects were used and how they were selected: were they randomly chosen from the population of sixth-graders in the city, or were they the first forty who happened to show up and who had previously repeated a grade in school? You should also mention any inducements that the subjects received: Were they volunteers? Paid? Given credit toward their course grade?

How were the subjects assigned to the research conditions? How many subjects failed to complete the entire experiment, and why did this attrition occur? What was the final number of subjects that participated in each research condition? All these questions should be answered in the subjects section.

The Apparatus or Materials

In this section you must describe the equipment and materials used in your study. Obvious materials such as furniture, tape recorders, and projection screens need only be mentioned and do not have to be described in minute detail. Commercially acquired equipment, however, should be identified by the firm's name and model number, if available (for example, Industrial Acoustic Chamber, Model 400; Wechsler Adult Intelligence Scale—Revised). Equipment that is custom-made for your particular study should be sufficiently described to allow the reader to understand its general function. If the apparatus is very complex, the reader may have to write to the author for further details. After all, your report need not include blueprints and wiring diagrams. Keep in mind that in conducting educational research your materials may consist simply of a specially designed questionnaire, but even this needs some measure of description. When conducting research for a class assignment, you should include a copy of the actual questionnaire in the appendix (see the Appendix section, this chapter). For a published study, the journal editor will usually decide whether it is appropriate for the appendix.

The Procedure

The procedure subsection should provide a step-by-step account of the happenings in your study. You should account for the subjects' time from the moment they show up for the study until they are dismissed. This will include the instructions the subjects received. These may be summarized or para-phrased, but if in any way important to the understanding of the study, they should be presented verbatim.

Various design specifications such as randomization and counterbalancing should be described here, and in experimental studies the manipulation of the independent variable should be detailed. For instance, how was test anxiety induced in some students and not in others? How was the differential motiva-tion of second graders achieved? How were the different dosages of Ritalin administered to those students identified as having an attention-deficit-hyperac-tivity disorder?

The Results (What Was Found?)

This is what the reader has been waiting for. What did you find? In the *results section* you summarize your data and describe the statistical tests you have conducted to determine the possible significance of your findings. All the perti-nent results should be presented here, regardless of whether or not they support your hypotheses. Even though the results may be contrary to your expectations, they may be important in and of themselves or as groundwork for future re-search.

Your goal in presenting your results is to do so in a clear and objective manner, without attempting to interpret or evaluate them. The general format is to begin by describing your dependent variable, how it was scored, and what unit of measurement was used in your analyses. Examples of opening phrases are

Mean gains on the Attitude Behavior scale were obtained . . .

Reading comprehension was defined by students' total scores on the Houghton Mifflin Pupil Placement Test . . .

Educational aspirations were measured by responses to three questions on the College Student Questionnaire . . .

It is often convenient to present your results according to the hypotheses you made. A brief restatement of a hypothesis is usually helpful here, followed by the type of statistical test that was used to evaluate it. It is customary to describe the finding in words and then follow up this description with the statistical result that substantiates it. For example, in a study by Amabile (1982), dealing with children's artistic creativity, she stated that

although there were no significant differences between the group means for the objective features of the collages, the groups showed significantly different vari-abilities on some of these features. The control group showed more variability in the number of colors used, $F(14,6) = 4.75$, $p < .05$, the number of pieces used, $F(14,6) = 8.02$, $p < .01$, and the percentages of pieces altered, $F(14,6) = 4.09$, $p < .05$.

The statistical information presented in the foregoing excerpt represents the standard format for the presentation of the results of an analysis of variance. The *F* represents the name of the test, followed by the degrees of freedom in parentheses, the actual calculated value for the statistic, and the alpha or significance level used. The *p* is an abbreviation for probability. (If necessary, review your statistics notes or see Chapter 5).

You may want to present some of your data in the form of a *table* or *graph* to depict them more clearly and economically. Although tables and graphs should be used sparingly, they are most beneficial when presenting a substantial quantity of data that cannot be as clearly described using words alone (a picture is worth a thousand words). These media should be used to supplement the text rather than replace it; they should not stand alone without references to them in the text.

You should be aware of some general format considerations to follow in the use of tables and graphs (for more detail see American Psychological Association, 1983). Tables should be numbered consecutively as they appear in your report, and the same applies to graphs (which are always referred to as figures). Titles that are descriptive and unambiguous must be provided for each. When presenting data in a graphic format, place the independent variable on the x-axis (abscissa) along with a label and, if there is more than one IV, it should be presented in the body of the graph. The dependent variable belongs on the y-axis (ordinate) along with an appropriate label.

Remember, the purpose of the results section is to inform in as objective a manner as possible, not to present fancy interpretations. Above all, be organized, and concise.

The Discussion (What Does It Mean?)

Now it's time to pull it all together. You have stated your problem, explained what you did to address it, presented what you have found, and now you must put it into perspective and explain what it all means. The *discussion section*

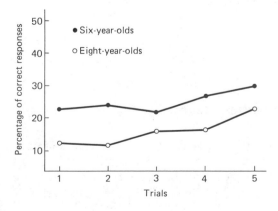

Figure 8.2 Percentage of correct responses as a function of number of trials and age of subjects

contains your interpretation of your findings. Your results are discussed in light of any recent literature that can be shown to be specifically related to the problem presented in your introduction. Any theoretical consequences of your results should be presented here as well.

In the discussion section you will have the opportunity to discuss any important flaws or weaknesses that may have existed in your study. Be careful, however, not to overdo this. Some novice report writers have a tendency to list, *ad infinitum*, trivial fluctuations or inconsistencies in their methodology. Minor changes in the temperature of the experimental room or a brief interruption in the presentation of stimuli for one subject, and so on, are the types of flaws that are probably not always necessary to mention. Try to identify the limitations that most likely affected your study.

Another mistake is to provide elegant reasons for why your results did not occur as expected and then go on to draw the same conclusions that you had hoped to draw in the first place (Warm, 1973). Explaining, or overexplaining, your flaws does not, alas, make them disappear. It is quite possible that your data reflect the true state of the world, and that your original expectations were wrong.

You may find it helpful to keep the following major points in mind when organizing your discussion section. All these points may not apply for every study that you conduct, but they should serve you well as a general framework.

1. Restate your research question so that the reader is reminded of your major purpose.
2. Briefly review your *major* findings in a sentence or two without reference to statistics.
3. Indicate specifically whether your findings confirmed or disconfirmed your hypotheses.
4. Indicate whether your study is in agreement or disagreement with previous related research.
5. If there is disagreement with previous work, try to account for this discrepancy.
6. Explain your results. Tie them in with any existing theories that may apply to your study.
7. Briefly summarize your study and suggest, in a few sentences, some possibilities for further research.

Your discussion should leave the reader with a clear indication of what your study has contributed and what conclusions and theoretical implications you have drawn.

The References (Who Did Something Like It?)

The most difficult and also most interesting part of the report is now behind you, but an important section still remains. The *references* section is a listing of every study that was cited in your report. However, don't overdo it by confusing the references section with a general bibliography. Whereas a bibliography contains a reference to all background material read, the references section lists only those works that have been directly referred to elsewhere in the paper. The purpose is to enable the reader to find any study or book you have referred to and then, if needed, read it firsthand.

Although this section is quite mundane, it is nonetheless important. Here is where you will feel that the specific format guidelines set forth by the American Psychological Association were purposely designed to ruin your day. The details are necessary, however, to ensure that all the important information is included and presented in a consistently uniform way. References are listed alphabetically by the last name of the first author of each study. For a journal article, the general format is as follows:

> Author's(s') Last Name(s), Initials. (Year). Title of article. *Name of Journal, Volume Number,* pages.
>
> Perfetti, C. A., & Hogaboam, T. (1975). The relationship between single word decoding and reading comprehension skill. *Journal of Educational Psychology, 67,* 461–469.

For a book, it looks like this:

> Author's(s') Last Name(s), Initials. (Year). *Title of book.* City where published: Publisher.
>
> Dewey, J. (1956). *The child and the curriculum: The school and society.* Chicago: University of Chicago Press.

There are several important points to be especially noted in the foregoing examples:

> author's last name first, followed by a comma and his or her initials, followed by periods
>
> year of publication in parentheses, followed by a period
>
> title of article with first letter of first word capitalized, followed by a period
>
> title of journal underlined with first letter of each major word capitalized, followed by a comma
>
> volume number underlined, followed by a comma
>
> inclusive page numbers separated by a dash and followed by a period

The Appendix (What Else Do You Want to Know?)

An *appendix* is an optional supplement to your report. In most instances it is omitted altogether. If there are lengthy details of your study that you feel are essential for understanding, evaluation, or replication, they probably should be included in an appendix—for example, complicated mathematical proofs, customized questionnaires, and innovative computer programs. When writing research reports for class assignments, theses, or dissertations, you should probably include summary tables of statistical tests, copies of printed materials given to the subjects, instructions, debriefings, and so on.

READING REPORTS FIRSTHAND

One of the best ways to become more comfortable with writing research reports is to *read* research reports. Once you've gotten more experience with the writing you will also find that the reverse is true. Do not hesitate to use a published report as a guide for your own writing. Remember, the aim here is not to be creative but to follow a uniform style that is readily recognized and understood by those in your field.

A Journal Article

What follows is an actual journal article in which the report format described in this chapter was followed. Comments have been included in the margins to point out specific features of the report.

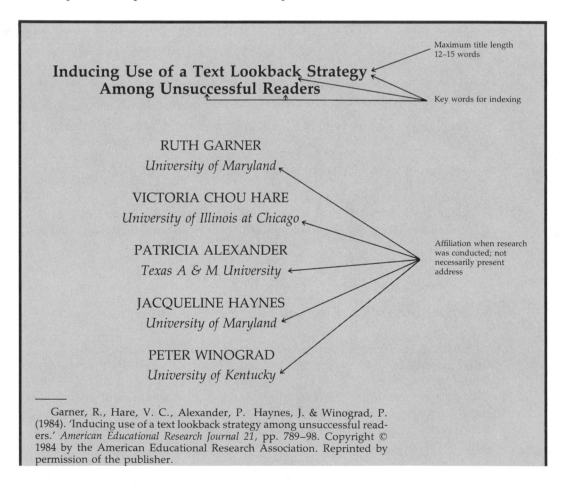

Inducing Use of a Text Lookback Strategy Among Unsuccessful Readers

Maximum title length 12–15 words

Key words for indexing

RUTH GARNER
University of Maryland

VICTORIA CHOU HARE
University of Illinois at Chicago

PATRICIA ALEXANDER
Texas A & M University

JACQUELINE HAYNES
University of Maryland

PETER WINOGRAD
University of Kentucky

Affiliation when research was conducted; not necessarily present address

Garner, R., Hare, V. C., Alexander, P. Haynes, J. & Winograd, P. (1984). 'Inducing use of a text lookback strategy among unsuccessful readers.' *American Educational Research Journal 21,* pp. 789–98. Copyright © 1984 by the American Educational Research Association. Reprinted by permission of the publisher.

A text lookback strategy was taught to 12 remedial readers in three sessions. Readers were taught why to use lookbacks, when to use them, and where to use them with expository texts and accompanying questions. Five days after training was completed, the 12 subjects and 12 students in a control group were assessed for use of lookbacks and question-answering accuracy. Significant differences between training and control groups emerged both for percentage of correct answers with lookbacks (for questions not answered correctly from memory) and for percentage of lookbacks used (sometimes leading to an accurate answer, sometimes not) when needed. Classroom instruction in the use of text lookbacks is suggested.

Summary of 100–150 words

What do we do when we teach strategies? We provide organized, purposeful actions to learners that should change processing and performance (Belmont & Butterfield, 1977). We hope, that is, to improve *how* the learners process and *how well* they process. After strategy instruction, we hope the learners will perform much like proficient, spontaneous users of the strategies (Brown, Palincsar, & Armbruster, 1984).

Source of idea cited

All authors listed for first citation

Usually we are concerned that the benefits of strategy instruction will be durable. Unfortunately, there are few demonstrations of durability of gains in the psychological and educational literatures (see, for instance, Brown & Campione, 1978; Paris & Cross, 1983). It appears that "children can be trained to use effective strategies, but once trained, they frequently revert to their immature strategies when no longer explicitly constrained to play the instructor's programs" (Belmont & Butterfield, 1977, p. 465).

Statement of basic problem

Reading is a complex cognitive task that learners engage in with varied processing repertoires and with varying degrees of success. Recently, reading theorists and researchers have begun to examine useful reading strategies that differentiate successful and unsuccessful readers (i.e., successful readers use them, and unsuccessful readers do not). One such strategy is the use of text lookbacks to retrieve unrecalled information needed to answer questions (Garner, Macready, & Wagoner, 1984; Garner & Reis, 1981; Garner, Wagoner, & Smith, 1983). Proficient users of this strategy recognize that when a comprehension-memory obstacle arises (e.g., an answer to a question is not remembered), the text is available for reexamination.

The present intervention study was designed to test the results of lookback strategy instruction for unsuccessful readers.

Brief description of what was done

The research reported here was completed while the first author received support as a Division Research Scholar from the Division of Human and Community Resources at the University of Maryland, College Park, and the third author received small grant support from the Office of University Research, Texas A & M University.

By employing a workable instructional routine we hoped to modify the "learning to learn" (Brown, Bransford, Ferrara, & Campione, 1982) activities of readers enrolled in a summer remedial clinic and to improve their question-answering success. We hoped that the predicted instructional benefits would be maintained over time.

Ampersand used when citing reference inside parentheses

Several factors demonstrated to facilitate training success in the literature were incorporated in the study. Those factors were (a) a detailed analysis of the sequence of activities to be trained (Case, 1978; Kail & Bisanz, 1982; Meichenbaum & Asarnow, 1979); (b) movement from simple to complex tasks (Brown, Campione, & Day, 1981); (c) explicit instruction, including modeling and feedback (Brown, Campione, & Murphy, 1977); (d) active participation (Kestner & Borkowski, 1979) and self-checking (Pearson, 1982) by learners; (e) use of school materials (Baumann, 1982); and (f) some measurement during and after instruction to assess *how* learners are meeting task demands.

Important prior research

METHOD

Major heading is usually centered in middle of page

Subjects and Design

From 45 upper elementary and middle school students attending a remedial clinic (M age = 11 years, 2 months; range = 9 years, 6 months to 13 years, 4 months), 24 were selected who were decoding-proficient (i.e., they scored at least 3-1 level on the Botel, 1978, word recognition instrument) but were at least one grade level below assigned level on the clinic comprehension screening instrument. None of the 24 students had repeated a grade, and all were native English speakers. All 24 attended school in one of two rural Maryland counties.

Appropriate abbreviation for mean

Description of subjects and selection procedures

An experimental design was employed. Subjects were randomly assigned to training or control groups, with 12 students in each group. Regular clinic instructors were directed to refrain from providing any direct lookback strategy instruction to any of the 24 subjects. (Although training was deferred for control group subjects, it was not wholly withheld; after data collection was complete, untrained students were given lookback instruction for remediation, not research, purposes.)

Materials

The *Reading for Concepts* series (Liddle, 1977) is used as supplementary material in the target counties. From the series, six expository passages of about 200 words each were selected for their topical variety and informational density. No text modifications were made other than pagination (i.e., all articles were presented, with titles intact, on two pages for easier documentation of page-flipping accompanying lookbacks).

For each passage, three questions were written. Two of the three (*text-based* questions) cued text recall or reaccess, as the answers were stated explicitly either within a single sentence or within two contiguous sentences. The third question (a *reader-based* question) cued use of reader knowledge base, as the answer was not stated explicitly in text. Naturally, it is for text-based questions that lookbacks are most useful. Cueing of the information source was quite blatant; text-based questions included the wording "in the article" or "what did the author write," and reader-based questions began with "do you think." Three possible orders of questions were used twice across the six texts.

Validation of text and question appropriateness was accomplished in two steps. First, three active reading researchers were asked to read the six texts and to label the accompanying questions by information source, given the definitional distinction above. Agreement with the investigators was 100%. Next, 12 third grade students scoring at the 3-1 level on a recently administered standardized reading test were asked to read two of the articles orally and to answer the text-based questions in both text-unavailable and text-available conditions. Two pilot subjects read each text. The average number of word recognition errors per 200-word text was only 3.6, and decodability of the materials was judged adequate. Only two of the students were able to remember any information required to answer the questions, but 9 of the 10 remaining students located appropriate text information; comprehensibility and nonmemorability of information were judged acceptable as well. Four of the six texts were randomly assigned to training slots, and two were assigned to testing slots.

Numbers less than 10 are spelled out and numbers 10 and above are expressed as figures, with some exceptions

Procedure

Task analysis, including reexamination of data from earlier strategy studies, produced a list of three things successful readers know about text lookbacks: *why* to use them (one cannot remember everything one reads), *when* to use them (when a question directs attention to text), and *where* to use them (sampling or skimming the entire text to locate a key segment to be reread carefully). Three hints about why, when, and where to use text lookbacks were presented in 3 days of training. Each subject was seen individually for all strategy instruction.

Training, day 1. The child was first told he or she would be asked to answer three questions after reading the initial 200-word text silently. No time limit was given. Unknown words were pronounced in the instances where assistance was requested (a total of 12 requests from 7 subjects over 3 days was recorded). After a filler activity, the three questions were asked, and the subject was told, "As I ask you each of the questions, you can look back at part one (displayed) or part two (displayed) or both parts of the article to answer the questions." The subject was

Simple instructions do not require reprinting them verbatim

asked to restate the task, and directions were repeated in instances of even slight confusion. At this point, evidence of relatively spontaneous use of the strategy was sought. While the child answered each question, the investigator recorded accuracy, lookback frequency, and sampling (skimming) instances on a structured response form used for all training sessions.

Still on day 1, the *why* script was provided after a second text was read and a filler activity was completed, but before questioning. The subject repeated the *why* hint to criterion, the questions were asked, and process and outcome behaviors were again noted. The entire first session took about 20 minutes.

Training, day 2. On the following day, the first hint was reverbalized by the subject. Then, the third text was read, the filler activity was completed, the *when* script was delivered, the hint was repeated, and the questions were asked, with behaviors recorded as on the day before. During presentation of the *when* hint, the investigator modeled differentiation of reader-based and text-based questions, using the second text from the previous day's work. As subjects demonstrated lookback behaviors, positive feedback was given. The second session averaged 15 minutes per subject.

Training, day 3. Two days later, the standardized *where* script was presented after reverbalization of the first two hints and the usual silent reading and filler activity. The investigator modeled use of the skimming-rereading tactic for two already read texts.

After this work on the fourth text was complete, some attempt was made to summarize the hints in the following scripted fashion:

> One of the good things about the hints I gave you that you used (well) is that they work well with most things you have to read—especially books and articles for school. What you need to remember about looking back to articles for answers to questions is:
>
> *Why* do it? You can't remember everything you read.
>
> *When* should you look back? When questions ask about what articles or authors said, not about what you think.
>
> *Where* should you look? Skim the whole article to find the part that might have the answer.
>
> I think if you keep practicing looking back for answers to questions that you'll get better at getting correct answers in your school reading. What information you can't remember, you'll find. I'd like you to tell me one last time what the hints are.

The third training session lasted about 20 minutes.

During the same days that training group subjects received lookback instruction, control group students worked either individually or in pairs with the investigator on text-processing strategies other than lookbacks (e.g., summarizing) for 15–20 minutes per day. The same 200-word texts were used. In this manner, engaged time and short text familiarity were controlled to some degree within the study.

Testing. After a 5-day interval following training, the last two texts were used to measure posttraining processing behaviors and outcomes in the absence of the trainer. An investigator who had not yet worked with the students provided directions and supervised video/audio recording of these episodes, assisted by two adolescent clinic helpers. A full videotaped record of the testing was generated so that "fine-grained analysis" (Wilkinson, Clevenger, & Dollaghan, 1981, p. 211) would be possible without task interference.

For each of two testing episodes, the child was seen individually. The subject sat at a small table to which a microphone had been attached unobtrusively. The camera, positioned to pick up subjects' facial expressions as well as page-flipping behaviors, was left in a stationary position about 30 feet away, and was activated by the helpers. Article pages were color-coded for ease of differentiation later. To diminish the novelty of the apparatus, the investigator taped a few nonresearch segments with the students. The investigator was "blind" to the group classifications of the students.

All trained and untrained control subjects ($N = 24$) were given ←——— Appropriate abbreviation for number of subjects
the two texts and were told only, "I am going to ask you to read a short article. You will read it slowly. I will ask you three questions about the article when you're done reading." The pages of the first text were left print side down, whereas the pages of the second were left print side up. In this latter condition, if a subject did *not* use any lookbacks, he or she was prompted with the cue, "You can look back at any part of the article to answer the questions."

Coding

The videotaped record was reviewed by three of the authors. Each sat apart from the others facing the video screen, using answer keys and coding sheets to log the following: accuracy of response, use of lookbacks or memory, use of sampling, presence of investigator cueing, and presence of a subject's "can I look back?" query. Whenever one coder requested that a tape segment be replayed, it was done without comment.

Simultaneous, independent coding was performed for 48 observations (i.e., two texts each for 12 trained and 12 untrained students). Although the coders who had trained and tested the students were by now familiar with them, the third coder performed this data reduction task "blind" to the group classifications of the students. Agreement levels among the three coders (proportion of agreements to agreements plus disagreements) were .97 and .95 for the two texts.

RESULTS

Both *how* the trained and control subjects processed (lookback strategy execution) and *how well* they processed (question-answering accuracy) were of interest in the study. Though trained subject-untrained subject comparisons were the central focus in analysis of data, it can be mentioned that a relatively low level of lookback performance was observed in the day 1 check on spontaneous lookback behaviors for text 1. Across the 12 to-be-trained subjects, 6 of the 24 text-based questions were answered accurately by recall alone, 8 were answered accurately with text lookback use, and 10 were answered inaccurately with no lookbacks. Only one instance of sampling occurred in this session.

To compare trained and untrained students' performances on the four text-based questions of the two test texts, three calculations were performed: (a) percentage of correct answers provided by recall alone (i.e., no lookbacks were necessary); (b) percentage of correct answers with lookbacks (cued or uncued) for questions not answered correctly from memory; and (c) percentage of lookbacks (leading to either a correct or incorrect response) used when needed, that is, used for questions not answered correctly from memory. Mean percentages appear in Table 1.

A series of one-way ANOVAs showed no significant differences between groups on percentage of correct answers, recall alone, $F(1,22) = .05$, $p > .05$, but showed significant differences on percentage correct with lookbacks, $F(1,22) = 8.53$, $p < .01$, and on percentage of lookbacks used when needed, $F(1,22) = 5.37$, $p < .05$. In both cases of significant differences, trained students' performance was superior to that of untrained students. ← Statistic, degrees of freedom, calculated value, and probability level

A few other behaviors of interest can be noted. No students in either group used lookbacks inappropriately for the reader-based questions. Text sampling occurred in every instance of lookback use by trained subjects and in half the instances of use by untrained subjects. Of all the instances of lookback use by trained subjects, 13% were cued by the investigator, whereas 100% of the instances among untrained subjects were similarly cued. In addition, whereas 33% of the lookback instances for trained students occurred in the print side up condition, 100% of the instances for

Table 1 Mean Percentages for Two Groups' Performance on Four Text-Based Questions ← Each table or figure is consecutively numbered. Number is not spelled out even if less than 10.

Title of table placed at top

	TRAINING GROUP	CONTROL GROUP
Correct, recall alone	31.3	33.3
Correct, with lookbacks	69.5	22.3
Lookbacks used when needed	72.3	31.3

untrained students appeared in this condition. Finally, no untrained students did so, but six trained students asked the tester,
"Is it okay to look back?"

DISCUSSION

Within the study there is evidence that text lookback instruction was needed, that it worked, and that the effects were maintained, at least over a 5-day interval. The training group outper-
formed control group peers both in lookback strategy execution
and in accuracy of question answering. That is to say, both *how*
the trained students processed text and questions and *how well* ←——— Review of major findings
they processed them seem to have been improved by direct
lookback strategy instruction. Performance differences are particularly noteworthy because the alternative strategic instruction
given the control group was neither vacuous in content nor hap-
hazard in delivery, and because improvement was shown for
learners with deficient comprehension skills.

One question that arises at this point is, *Why* is text lookback
instruction needed? Why, that is, is it not the case that learners,
even unsuccessful learners, just note working memory limits and
access information in text? This particular strategy is not terribly
costly in time or effort. Our answer to that question is that upper
elementary and middle school students view lookbacks as "ille-
gal" (Hewitt, 1980). Evidence of this perception was abundant
within the study. During training, and even in testing after much
prodding to reaccess text, subjects reacted with surprise to the
idea of using lookbacks; they asked repeatedly for verification of
the possibility. During testing of untrained students, many complained they "couldn't remember" answers, but employed no
strategic remedy, some even after cueing from the adult present.
Differences in print side down performance and print side up
performance further suggest a concern with lookback legitimacy.
Obviously, changing read-and-remember-only routines to read-
remember-reread routines can be accomplished only if this "ille-
gal" notion is disconfirmed.

Just as school is a likely candidate for the place where this
conception originated, it is an excellent candidate for the spot
where it can be dismantled. Learners early in academic careers
can be informed about the purposes and benefits (Paris & Lin-
dauer, 1982) of lookbacks, so that hasty compliance and just as ←——— Implications and potential
hasty scrapping of the strategy will be less likely to occur. Teach-   application
ers can model flexible use of the strategy, not by rereading text
from start to finish in all cases where a question response is
elusive, but by looking quickly for information cued by text-based
questions and rereading in some detail the key segment located
(Garner, Wagoner, & Smith, 1983). Teachers can distinguish between ideal lookback settings (nearly all reading and studying

contexts) and inappropriate lookback settings (testing situations, where use of in-head, not at-hand, information is required).

As lookbacks seem to work with a variety of texts and tasks that appear in educational settings, we suggest that withholding the strategy from learners makes no sense whatsoever. The present study indicates that the strategy can be taught, and that the results of instruction are favorable. We submit that even while further research is conducted to sort out what specific factors contributed most to training efficacy and to begin to sequence most effective delivery of the components of the strategy, some of this instruction can begin.

Tentative conclusions

REFERENCES

Baumann, J. F. (1982). Research on children's main idea comprehension: A problem of ecological validity. *Reading Psychology, 3*, 167–177.

Belmont, J. M., & Butterfield, E. C. (1977). The instructional approach to developmental cognitive research. In R. V. Kail, Jr., & J. W. Hagen (Eds.), *Perspectives on the development of memory and cognition* (pp. 437–481). Hillsdale, NJ: Erlbaum.

Botel, M. (1978). *Botel reading inventory: Administration manual.* Chicago: Follett.

Brown, A. L., Bransford, J. D., Ferrara, K. A., & Campione, J. C. (1982). *Learning, remembering, and understanding* (Tech. Rep. No. 244). Urbana: University of Illinois, Center for the Study of Reading.

Brown, A. L., & Campione, J. C. (1978). Memory strategies in learning: Training children to study strategically. In H. L. Pick, Jr., H. W. Leibowitz, J. E. Singer, A. Steinschneider, & H. W. Stevenson (Eds.), *Psychology: From research to practice* (pp. 47–73). New York: Plenum.

Brown, A. L., Campione, J. C., & Day, J. D. (1981). Learning to learn: On training students to learn from texts. *Educational Researcher, 10*, 14–21.

Brown, A. L., Campione, J. C., & Murphy, M. D. (1977). Maintenance and generalization of trained metamnemonic awareness of educable retarded children. *Journal of Experimental Child Psychology, 24*, 191–211.

Brown, A. L., Palincsar, A. S., & Armbruster, B. B. (1984). Instructing comprehension-fostering activities in interactive learning-situations. In H. Mandl, N. E. Stein, & T. Trabasso (Eds.), *Learning and comprehension of texts* (pp. 255–286). Hillsdale, NJ: Erlbaum.

Case, R. (1978). A developmentally based theory and technology of instruction. *Review of Educational Research, 48*, 439–463.

Garner, R., Macready, G. B., & Wagoner, S. (1984). Readers' acquisition of the components of the text-lookback strategy. *Journal of Educational Psychology, 76*, 300–309.

Garner, R., & Reis, R. (1981). Monitoring and resolving comprehension obstacles: An investigation of spontaneous text lookbacks among upper grade good and poor comprehenders. *Reading Research Quarterly, 16*, 569–582.

Garner, R., Wagoner, S., & Smith, T. (1983). Externalizing question-answering strategies of good and poor comprehenders. *Reading Research Quarterly, 18*, 439–447.

Hewitt, G. (1980). A preliminary study of pupils' reading difficulties. *Educational Review, 32*, 231–244.

Kail, R. V., Jr., & Bisanz, J. (1982). Cognitive strategies. In C. R. Puff (Ed.), *Handbook of research methods in human memory and cognition* (pp. 229–255). New York: Academic Press.

Capitalize first letter of major words in journal title

When typing reports, italics indicated by underscoring

For technical reports list university or agency affiliation

Ampersand before last author's name

Capitalize first letter of the title of the article

After first line of reference, usually indent three spaces

Note space between initials

Kesiner, J., & Borkowski, J. G. (1979). Children's maintenance and generalization of an interrogative learning strategy. *Child Development, 50,* 485–494.

Liddle, W. (Ed.). (1977). *Reading for concepts, book E* (2nd ed.). New York: McGraw-Hill.

Meichenbaum, D., & Asarnow, J. (1979). Cognitive-behavioral modification and metacognitive development: Implications for the classroom. In P. Kendall & S. Hollon (Eds.), *Cognitive-behavioral interventions: Theory, research, and procedures* (pp. 11–35). New York: Academic Press.

Paris, S. G., & Cross, D. R. (1983). Ordinary learning: Pragmatic connections among children's beliefs, motives, and actions. In J. Bisanz, G. L. Bisanz, & R. Kail (Eds.), *Learning in children: Progress in cognitive development research* (pp. 137–169). New York: Springer-Verlag.

Paris, S. G., & Lindauer, B. K. (1982). The development of cognitive skills during childhood. In B. W. Wolman (Ed.), *Handbook of developmental psychology* (pp. 333–349). Englewood Cliffs, NJ: Prentice-Hall.

Pearson, P. D. (1982). *A context for instructional research on reading comprehension* (Tech. Rep. No. 230). Urbana: University of Illinois, Center for the Study of Reading.

Wilkinson, L. C., Clevenger, M., & Dollaghan, C. (1981). Communication in small instructional groups: A sociolinguistic approach. In W. P. Dickson (Ed.), *Children's oral communication skills* (pp. 207–240). New York: Academic Press.

←── First word following a colon in title is capitalized

←── Editors' initials precede last name

AUTHORS

RUTH GARNER, Associate Professor, University of Maryland, College of Education, Reading Center, College Park, MD 20742. *Specializations:* Reading, educational psychology.

VICTORIA CHOU HARE, Associate Professor, University of Illinois at Chicago, College of Education, Box 4348, Chicago, IL 60680. *Specialization:* Comprehension instruction.

PATRICIA ALEXANDER, Assistant Professor, Texas A & M University, Department of EDCI, College of Education, College Station, TX 77843. *Specializations:* Reading comprehension, learning and study strategies.

JACQUELINE HAYNES, Faculty Research Associate, University of Maryland, Institute for the Study of Exceptional Children and Youth, College of Education, College Park, MD 20742. *Specializations:* Comprehension of text, computer applications in education.

PETER WINOGRAD, Assistant Professor, University of Kentucky, Department of Curriculum and Instruction, College of Education, Lexington, KY 40506. *Specializations:* Reading difficulties, text comprehension.

Comments regarding the author's(s') research interests are optional

So, there you have it. You know now what the basic elements of a research report consist of and you have seen them as they actually appear in a journal article. Certainly there will be some variation from one report to another, but the basic outline and format presented in this chapter reflect the style that is characteristic of most research reports in education. With this guide in hand, you have the foundation for communicating effectively and efficiently with others in the field of education.

SUMMARY

To communicate our research findings effectively and efficiently, we need to adhere to a format and writing style that is widely used in education. Our needs are met by the guidelines endorsed by the American Psychological Association, which are commonly followed in education, as well as in psychology.

From the standpoint of writing style, we should always use the past tense, the passive voice, the third person, and nonsexist language. Pronouns such as *I*, *we*, and *you* are inappropriate.

Great care must be taken when writing a research report to properly document the ideas you've presented. Any time that you refer to the works of others you must differentiate them from your own by citing them properly. The most common way to do this is by including the author's(s') name(s) and the year of publication right in the paragraph where the work is being discussed. More detail regarding the title of the report, where it was published, and so on, will be provided at the end of the paper in the references section. This practice of properly documenting our writing enables us to give credit to those who deserve it and makes it easier for the reader to get a more detailed discussion of the topic by reading the original references.

The research report is divided into the following sections:

title
name and affiliation of author(s)
abstract
introduction
method
results
discussion
references
appendix

The title should be descriptive and contain key words such as the independent and dependent variable(s). Next comes the name(s) of the author(s) in the order of their contribution to the research, and their university or agency affiliation.

A very useful and widely read section of the report is the abstract. This is simply a brief summary of your entire report, which outlines the problem, describes the procedures, and presents the major results and conclusions.

The introduction of your report informs the reader of what your study is all about. What is the point of the study? What previous research is related to your topic? What did you do? What did you expect to find?

To write a good introduction you need to become familiar with reference works such as *ERIC* in the library, which will allow you to find out what pertinent research has been done previously. Once you have accumulated a pile of relevant studies, your task is to organize them cohesively. The studies should be summarized and presented in such a way that you "walk" the reader through the past research smoothly. The well-written introduction unfolds like a predictable story, with the reader able to anticipate how it will end. The "end" is the study that you've carried out. Your research follows directly from the previous studies that you've cited.

The method section of your report contains the nuts and bolts of what has been done in your study. The key features of the method section include a description of the subjects under study, the materials or apparatus used, and an outline of the procedures that were followed.

In the results portion of the paper you get an opportunity to showcase your statistical expertise: What statistical tests were performed? Were the results statistically significant? Statistical information should be presented numerically *and* in plain English. A carefully written results section would be understandable to the reader even if all the numerical information was removed. Graphs and tables are also often used in this section of the report to further clarify your findings.

The last major component of your report is the all-important discussion section. Here, you briefly rehash your results and explain what they mean. How do your findings tie in to the relevant recent literature? Are there theoretical consequences to consider? Were there flaws in the study that forced you to temper your conclusions? Finally, what are the bottom-line conclusions? Where do we go from here with future research?

The final two pieces of the report are rather mundane yet informative. In the references section you must list every study that you have cited previously in your report. Precise formats are provided by the American Psychological Association for listing the author(s), the year of publication, the title of the work, where it was published, the page numbers, and so on. These guidelines vary somewhat, depending on whether the study was published as a journal article, book, book chapter, or dissertation.

The appendix contains any additional information that you feel is necessary for a clear understanding of your study. Materials such as complicated mathematical proofs, customized questionnaires, and innovative computer programs would be included here. If your study did not involve any materials such as these, the appendix can be omitted.

The details presented in this chapter are essential for effectively communicating with others in the field of education. It takes practice to learn the ins and outs of writing an abstract, of properly citing references, and of logically substantiating your conclusions, but the hard work will pay off in a well-written and clearly understandable account of the important research you have conducted.

KEY TERMS

Abstract	Introduction section
Appendix	Method section
Discussion section	References
Documentation	Results section
ERIC	Table
Funnel approach	Telegraphic style
Graph	Title

REFERENCES

AMABILE, T. M. (1982). Children's artistic creativity: Detrimental effects of competition in a field setting. *Personality and Social Psychology Bulletin, 8,* 573–578.

AMERICAN PSYCHOLOGICAL ASSOCIATION. (1983). *Publication manual of the American Psychological Association* (3d ed.). Washington, D.C.: Author.

ANDERSON, R., KLOSSEN, D., & JOHNSON, D. (1982). Why we need to view computer literacy comprehensively. *Education Digest, March,* 19–21.

BOWMAN, R. F. (1982). A Pac-Man theory of motivation. *Educational Technology, September,* 14–16.

DEWEY, J. (1956). *The child and the curriculum: The school and society.* Chicago: University of Chicago Press.

ERIKSON, E. H. (1959). Identity and the life cycle. *Psychological Issues, 1,* 1–165.

EVERSTON, C. M., EMMER, E. T., CLEMENTS, B. S., SANFORD, J. P., & WORSHAM, M. E. (1984). *Class-room management for elementary teachers.* Englewood Cliffs, N.J.: Simon & Schuster Prentice-Hall.

HARRISON, J. A., STRAUSS, H., & GLAUBMAN, R. (1981). The impact of open and traditional classrooms on achievement and creativity: The Israeli case. *The Elementary School Journal, 82,* 27–35.

PERFETTI, C. A., & HOGABOAM, T. (1975). The relationship between single word decoding and reading comprehension skill. *Journal of Educational Psychology, 67,* 461–469.

SENTER, J. (1981). Computer technology and education. *Educational Forum, Fall,* 55–64.

STERNBERG, R. J., & NIGRO, G. (1980). Developmental patterns in the solution of verbal analogies. *Child Development, 551,* 27–38.

WARM, J. S. (1973). Laboratory manual for experimental psychology. Unpublished manuscript, University of Cincinnati, Department of Psychology.

CHAPTER

9

Case Studies I: Experimental Research

CASE 1: THE TRUE EXPERIMENT WITH INDEPENDENTLY SELECTED SAMPLES (BETWEEN-GROUPS)

A Research Example (reprinted journal article)
Research Keys
Case Comments

CASE 2: THE QUASI EXPERIMENT

A Research Example (reprinted journal article)
Research Keys
Case Comments

SUMMARY

KEY TERMS

REFERENCES

"People don't usually do research the way people who write books about research say that people do research" (Bachrach, 1981, p. 2). It's not enough for us to discuss the fundamentals of research methodology; we need to actually "dig in" to the real thing. It's important to see these basic fundamentals applied as they actually appear in the educational literature. We can talk about the basics in an abstract sense but at some point you have to "get your hands dirty" by handling the actual journals.

Whether you are conducting your own research or are trying to become a more critical consumer of the research of others, it is crucial to refer to examples of previously published works. From these you can observe the correct way to carry out and write up a research project and, in many instances (we wish we could say only a few), identify misapplications of research fundamentals, as well. Yes, the "experts" make mistakes too, as we saw in Chapter 7.

In this and the following chapter we present actual research studies that illustrate selected issues pertaining to research in education. You will see how researchers develop the idea for their study as an outgrowth of previous research. You will see how subjects are recruited, compensated, placed into treatment groups, and measured with respect to certain characteristics. Probably one of the most important tasks confronting the researcher in designing a clearly interpretable study is to choose the statistical test that is best suited for the type of research being done. You will see the steps taken to arrive at this critical decision. Finally, you will see how the educational researcher ties it all together in the discussion section of the report.

The examples of research presented in these two chapters are organized according to the basic method of research employed (experimental, post-facto, or "other"). In this chapter we look at experimental research, including the true experiment and the quasi experiment.

CASE I: THE TRUE EXPERIMENT WITH INDEPENDENTLY SELECTED SAMPLES (BETWEEN-GROUPS)

As you learned in the earlier chapters, when conducting experimental research the researcher actively manipulates the independent variable and then waits to see if there is a resulting change in the dependent variable. This is in contrast to the post-facto method, in which the IV is not directly manipulated by the researcher. In post-facto research subjects are measured for a trait or characteristic that they already possess and are assigned to a research category on the basis of that trait.

For instance, consider the study in which the researchers were interested in the relative effectiveness of two approaches to teaching learning-disabled students factual information in their coursework (Darch & Carnine, 1986). The independent variable that was manipulated by the researchers was the type of instructional approach used with the students. The LD students were exposed to either (1) an approach that utilized a visual display of content using an overhead projector or (2) the commonly used approach of presenting content via textbook. The researchers controlled (flipped a coin, perhaps) which students received which instructional approach. It was *not* determined by some characteristic that the students already possessed. For example, it would have been post-facto research if something like the eye color of the students had been used to determine who received each instructional approach (brown, visual display; blue, text). That the researchers had direct control over the IV in this study made this experimental research. After assigning the students to the instructional groups, the effectiveness of the two approaches was assessed by a series of tests (the dependent variable).

Experimental research may be of one of two varieties. We refer to the experimental research as a true experiment if the researcher is able to create equivalent groups of subjects at the outset of the study. If the researcher is not able to create equivalent groups yet is still able to manipulate the IV (experimental research), we refer to this as a quasi experiment. (Refer to Chapter 3 for a review of true versus quasi experiments.)

When the true experiment is carried out with independently selected samples, it means that the choice of one sample of subjects has no bearing whatsoever on the choice of the other sample(s). To achieve this, each subject could be independently selected from all possible subjects in the population. That is to say, we could put the names of all the potential subjects in our population of interest into a large hat and pull out however many we wanted to include in our sample. Another approach would be to gather all the subjects who were willing and able to participate in our research (clearly not a random sample) and randomly assign them to one of the research groups (to one level of the IV) so that each subject would have an equal probability of being assigned to any one group. In rare instances, researchers are lucky enough to do both—randomly select their subjects *and* randomly assign them to research groups. (See Chapter 3 for a review of independently selected samples.)

In the aforementioned study involving learning-disabled students, the researchers created equivalent groups (true experiment) by randomly assigning the subjects to either the "visual display" group or the "text" group. The assignment of one student to the "text" group in no way affected to which group the next subject would be assigned. The subjects were independent of one another. The students in the two groups were not matched on some relevant variable, such as IQ, nor were any of the students measured more than once on a given dependent variable. Instances such as these would have involved correlated (paired) samples.

A Research Example (reprinted journal article)

What follows is an example of experimental research (more specifically, of a true experiment with independently selected samples), conducted by Benware and Deci (1984). As we did in Chapter 6, we have added numbers in the margins of the research report that correspond to numbered comments that you will find following each report in this and the following chapter. This will make it easier for you to relate our comments directly to the original research report.

Quality of Learning With an Active Versus Passive Motivational Set

CARL A. BENWARE
New York State Division for Youth

and
EDWARD L. DECI
University of Rochester

This study tested whether students who learned with an active orientation would be more intrinsically motivated to learn and would learn more than students who learned with a

---

Benware, C. A. & Deci, E. L. (1984). Quality of learning with an active versus passive motivational set. *American Educational Research Journal* 21, pp. 755-65. Copyright © 1984 by the American Educational Research Association. Reprinted by permission of the publisher.

This research was supported by a grant (MH 28600) from the National Institute of Mental Health to the second author. We would like to thank David Elkind and Gerry Gladstein for their inputs to the design and interpretations; John Nezlek, Donald Ash, and Lynne Carlson for assisting with the experiment; and Allan J. Schwartz for helping with the data analyses.

passive orientation. The active orientation was created by having subjects learn material with the expectation of teaching it to another student; the passive orientation was created by having subjects learn the same material with the expectation of being tested on it. The results indicate that subjects who learned in order to teach were more intrinsically motivated, had higher conceptual learning scores, and perceived themselves to be more actively engaged with the environment than subjects who learned in order to be examined. The two groups were equal, however, in their rote learning scores. The effects of exposure to the material were ruled out as an explanation because the two groups reported spending equal time with the material. The results are discussed in terms of intrinsic motivation theory.

Tutoring has long been used to facilitate students' learning; when given individual help, students seem to respond with more interest and improved learning. Tutoring has also been shown to have a positive effect on the teacher. For example, Cloward (1967) found that when high school volunteers tutored fourth and fifth graders in reading, the reading of the tutors improved even more than the reading of their pupils. Allen and Feldman (1973) reported similar results. A subsequent study (National Commission on Resources for Youth, 1972) indicated that the gains for teachers may be even more extensive than just improved learning. In this study teenage tutors also gained in self-esteem and perceived competence. Further, Goldschmid (1970) found that students who were tutors as part of a college course reported being more motivated to learn the course material than other students in the course who used different types of learning models. Taken together, these studies suggest that tutoring can enhance learning, motivation, perceived competence, and self-esteem of the tutors.

One obvious explanation for these findings is that the tutoring exposes persons to the material, which facilitates their learning and leaves them feeling better about the material and themselves. However, there may also be other psychological processes involved, such that the process of learning itself is different when one learns material to teach it rather than for some other reason. If this were the case, some of the positive effects of teaching or tutoring could be achieved even before the teaching or tutoring occurred. The study reported in this paper explores this question. It contrasts learning material in order to teach it with learning material in order to be tested on it. We hypothesize that learning material to teach it will lead to enhanced learning and to a more positive emotional tone than learning material to be tested on it, even when the amount of exposure to the material being learned is the same.

The hypothesis is derived from the motivational theory of Deci (1980) and Deci and Ryan (in press), which distinguishes between intrinsic and extrinsic motivational processes. In short, we suggest that learning in order to teach facilitates greater intrinsic motivation than learning in order to be tested, that intrinsically motivated learning is more "active," and that this results in greater learning and in more positive self-related affects and cognitions. Let us consider this in more detail.

First, consider the issue of why expecting to teach might facilitate intrinsic motivation and active learning. According to White (1959) and Deci (1975), intrinsic motivation is based in the need to be effectively self-determining and to have a meaningful impact on one's environment. Being a teacher or tutor can provide the means through which one can have such an impact and could therefore facilitate one's intrinsic motivation. As Bruner (1966) and Rogers (1969) suggested, when one learns things that are useful to a task that one is undertaking, learning will be more active; in other words, there will be a fuller engagement with the material. One approaches the material with the anticipation of using it, so one becomes more fully involved.

On the other hand, if one is assigned material in order to be tested on it, the learning may be more passive. People may absorb the facts, but they will be less active in interpreting and integrating them. Tests are widely used as instruments of evaluation and control, and many research studies have confirmed that controlling, evaluative events tend to undermine intrinsic motivation and leave people feeling passive (Deci & Ryan, 1980).

Garbarino (1975), for example, studied tutoring where one group of sixth grade girls was rewarded for tutoring second grade children and one group was not. He reported that the tutors who were not rewarded were less critical and demanding and made more efficient use of their time than the tutors who were rewarded. This suggests that tutoring is intrinsically interesting and that the addition of extrinsic incentives may interfere with the intrinsic motivation.

If the expectation of teaching facilitates intrinsic motivation and active engagement with the material to be taught, it is not surprising that learning would improve and feelings would be more positive. In fact, several studies have provided evidence, albeit indirect, to support this assertion. For example, Harter (1981) found that children's intrinsic motivation in the classroom was positively related to their perceived competence in the cognitive domain. Similarly, Deci, Nezlek, and Sheinman (1981) found that children in autonomy-oriented classrooms were more intrinsically motivated and displayed higher self-esteem and perceived cognitive competence than children in control-oriented classrooms. Further, deCharms (1976) reported that children in autonomy-oriented classrooms learned more as measured by standardized achievement tests than children in control-oriented classrooms. From this set of studies, we suggest that autonomy-oriented classrooms tend to promote to a greater degree intrinsic (relative to extrinsic) motivational processes and that intrinsic processes involve higher self-esteem, greater perceived competence, and enhanced learning.

McGraw (1978) reviewed a variety of studies that have shown that learning and the performance of other activities that require attention, creativity, and resourcefulness tend to be worse when people are rewarded extrinsically than when they are not. Because rewards tend to promote extrinsic rather than intrinsic motivation, this evidence suggests that intrinsic motivation tends to result in better performance of complex activities, such as conceptual learning.

There is other, more direct, evidence that learning material with the expectation of teaching it may improve learning, relative to learning it with the expectation of being tested, although the two studies providing this evidence did not consider motivational variables. Zajonc (1960) suggested that the receipt of information instigates a different cognitive set from that required for transmitting information. He found that when subjects were instructed to transmit information, their organization of the material tended to be more differentiated and complex, and tended to show greater unity and organization, than when subjects were instructed to receive the information.

Bargh and Schul (1980) designed a similar experiment. They suggested that when people learn in order to teach they use different cognitive structures that allow greater content-specific learning as well as greater process learning (they learn how to learn) than when they learn without expecting to teach the information. In their experiment one group of subjects studied material with the expectation of teaching it, and another group studied it simply to learn it. The design called for 5 minutes of learning, 3 minutes of being tested with short-answer, recognition and recall questions, then 15 minutes for learning a second passage, and 8 minutes for being tested on it. Their results revealed that the subjects who learned with the expectation of teaching did better on the short-answer exams than subjects who were instructed simply to learn the material. | 7

There are several things to be noted about these two studies. First, both were done for short periods in the psychological laboratory, raising questions about generalizability. Second, although Bargh and Schul suggested that learning in order to teach may affect a person's learning how to learn, their dependent measure considered only content-specific, rote learning. And although Zajonc did use conceptual variables as dependent measures, he employed very simple material, which subjects were asked to organize | 8 after they had learned it in a 2-minute reading period. One wonders whether these results would be applicable to situations in which students were, say, reading a week's assignment in physics or history. Finally, although it is certainly important to understand the impact of one's expectations about teaching on one's rote and conceptual learning, the real problem is more general. Learning in order to teach is, we suggest, an instance of the more general case of *active learning*—learning that is done with the expectation of using the material.

The present study explored rote and conceptual learning under conditions of active versus passive learning. This was operationalized by learning done with the expectation of teaching the material versus learning done with the expectation of being tested on | 9 it. Because we used a motivational derivation, linking more active learning to intrinsic motivation and more passive learning to extrinsic motivation, we collected data to test the difference in subjects' reported intrinsic motivation when given an active motivational set versus a more passive motivational set.

The structure of the experiment is conceptually similar to that of Bargh and Schul, although in our experiment the procedure was longer (subjects spent about 2 hours and 40 minutes studying, rather than 20 minutes), the studying was not done in the labora- | 10 tory, conceptual as well as rote learning was measured, and motivational variables were assessed.

METHOD

Overview

College student subjects were given an article on brain functioning ("The Other Side of the Brain"—Bogen, 1969), which they were asked to take home and learn. The control subjects were told that they would be examined on the material, and the experimental subjects were told that they would teach the contents of the article to another student. When subjects returned to the laboratory 2 weeks later, they completed a questionnaire that assessed their motivation and attitudes, and then they were examined on the material.

Subjects

Forty-three first year students from the University of Rochester's introductory Psychology course responded to a request for subjects to participate in a "Study on Learn- | 11 ing." These students were randomly assigned to two groups: 21 in the experimental | 12 group and 22 in the control group. One control subject and two experimental subjects failed to appear for the first session, so the experimental group (learning in order to | 13

teach) consisted of 19 subjects, and the control group (learning in order to take an exam)
consisted of 21 subjects.   13

Procedure

Subjects reported individually to the laboratory where the learning task was explained
to them. Subjects took the article with them to read and study at their leisure during the
following week, which was an academic vacation. Subjects were asked to spend about 3
hours studying the article. It was explained that it was not necessary to spend exactly 3
hours, that that was merely a guideline, and that they should spend as long as they
wanted or needed. Each subject was asked to keep track of how much time he or she
spent studying the article. The article, which was 25 pages long, was a moderately
difficult article about brain functioning.   14

Subjects in the control and experimental conditions were presented with the following
instructions:

> Please read the article in the same manner that you would read any article assigned in one of
> your college courses. Read and study it so that you have learned it as well as you can in a
> period of about 3 hours. If you are the type of person who learns best by underlining the
> material, do that. If you prefer to take notes, do that. Use whatever methods are most natural
> and most beneficial to you for learning the material.

Control subjects were then given the following instructions:

> The purpose of studying and learning the article is so that when you return to the laboratory
> you will score as high as possible on an examination based on the article. The examination will
> be like a typical examination based on a reading assignment. Again, use whatever study
> methods seem most appropriate for you.

15

Experimental subjects, instead, got the following instructions:

> The purpose of studying and learning the article is so that when you return to the laboratory
> you will be able to teach the contents to another student. The student to whom you teach the
> contents will then be given an examination based on the article. The examination will be like a
> typical examination based on a reading assignment. Again, use whatever study methods
> seem most appropriate for you.

When a control subject returned to the laboratory, he or she was asked to respond to a
short questionnaire that assessed intrinsic interest, and then the subject was given a
written, 24-item examination on the article. Following the examination, the subject was
debriefed.

When an experimental subject returned to the laboratory, he or she was given the
same short questionnaire and the same exam. It was explained to these subjects, before
they took the exam, that some participants were being selected at random to take the
same examination that would eventually be administered to their students. The purpose
of this unexpected exam, they were told, was to enable the investigators to understand   16
the learning process better by first looking at how well the teacher understands the
material and, in comparison, how well his or her student comes to understand the same
material. The experimental subjects never actually taught the material. Following the
exam, the subjects were debriefed.

Dependent Measures

The three dependent measures for assessing intrinsic motivation asked (a) how interesting subjects found the contents of the learning material, (b) how enjoyable they found the experiment, and (c) how much additional time they were willing to volunteer for the experiment. The answer to the questions in interest and enjoyment were given by circling a number on a 10-point, Likert-type scale. The answer to the third question was given on a 6-point scale ranging from 0 hours to 5 or more hours. | 17

The active/passive dimension, which served as a manipulation check, was measured on two 10-point scales that were given on a separate sheet, after the intrinsic motivation questions. The scales ranged from 1 (extremely passive) to 10 (extremely active) in response to the following two questions: (a) When a teacher assigns a particular reading to you such that he or she might examine you on it, how active or passive do you perceive yourself to be in dealing with your environment? (b) When a teacher assigns a particular reading to you such that you might teach the material to another student, how active or passive do you perceive yourself to be in dealing with your environment? | 18

The dependent measure to assess learning was a 24-item examination that included the following question types: true/false, fill in the blanks, definitions, multiple choice, identifications, and explanations. Each question was designed primarily to measure either rote memory or conceptual understanding of the material. Fifty percent of the point value of the examination was allotted to each of these two types of learning. | 19

Questions were categorized as "rote" or "conceptual" in the following manner. Two of our colleagues studied the article and then took a longer version of the exam, rating each question on the rote/conceptual dimension. Only those items that received an identical rote/conceptual classification by the two independent raters were used in the study. Subsequently, another colleague, who was blind to the conditions and hypotheses of the experiment, scored the subjects' answers. | 20

RESULTS

The differences that were predicted for the two groups were based on the assumption that learning in order to teach would promote a more active engagement with the material than learning in order to be tested. This was verified by having subjects rate the activity/passivity of the two types of learning.

Subjects who learned in order to teach rated the activity dimension "learning in order to teach" quite high ($\bar{X} = 8.47$). These same subjects rated "learning in order to be examined" as significantly less active ($\bar{X} = 4.63$). On the other hand, subjects who had learned in order to be examined did not perceive the two types of learning as differentially active. Learning in order to teach had a mean rating of 7.72, and learning in order to be examined had a mean rating of 7.09. When the data for all subjects were combined the differences were significant at the .001 level. Still, the different responses of the two groups are quite striking and will be discussed. The actual manipulation check for this experiment compares the perceived activity of "learning in order to teach" by those subjects who learned in order to teach ($\bar{X} = 8.47$) with the perceived activity of "learning in order to be examined" by those who learned in order to be examined ($\bar{X} = 7.09$). This difference is significant ($t = 2.53$; $df = 38$; $p < .02$). Thus, the manipulation was successful. | 21

Data relevant to subjects' intrinsic motivation appear in Table I. Subjects who learned in order to teach expressed more interest in the material ($t = 3.52$; $p < .001$), more | 22

Table I Means and Standard Deviations on Levels of Interest in the Learned Material, Enjoyment of Participation in the Experiment, and Willingness to Participate Further

	EXPERIMENTAL ($n = 19$)	CONTROL ($n = 21$)
Interest	7.13	4.43
	(2.41)	(2.30)
Enjoyment	7.00	4.67
	(2.27)	(2.50)
Participation	2.11	.76
	(2.34)	(.68)

Table II Means and Standard Deviations of Rote and Conceptual Learning Scores

	EXPERIMENTAL ($n = 19$)	CONTROL ($n = 21$)
Rote learning score	18.21	16.24
	(4.58)	(4.13)
Conceptual learning score	18.84	10.76
	(4.89)	(4.23)

enjoyment of the experiment ($t = 3.01$; $p < .01$), and more willingness to return ($t = 2.36$; $p < .05$). Thus, the data confirm that subjects who learned with the expectation of teaching were more intrinsically motivated than subjects who learned with the expectation of being examined.[1]   22

Table II presents the mean learning scores, rote and conceptual, for the experimental and control groups (maximum scores on each part were 24). Subjects who learned in order to teach evidenced significantly greater conceptual learning than subjects who learned in order to be tested ($t = 5.42$; $df = 38$; $p < .001$), although the two groups did not differ on rote learning ($t = 1.39$).   23

As indicated earlier, subjects were asked to keep track of how long they spent learning the material, after it was suggested that they spend approximately 3 hours. Results revealed no difference in the amount of time spent ($t = .69$); the experimental group reported spending an average of 2.55 hours working on the material, and the control group reported spending an average of 2.71 hours.   24

DISCUSSION

This study tested the hypothesis that having subjects learn material in order to teach it would create a more active orientation, facilitating intrinsic motivation and resulting in greater learning, than having them learn material in order to be tested on it. Results strongly supported this hypothesis. Subjects who learned material to teach it expressed greater evidence of intrinsic motivation and reported feeling more active in their learning than subjects who learned the material to be tested on it. Further, the experimental   25
    26

---

[1] Correlations among these three measures of intrinsic motivation indicated that there is considerable shared variance. The three correlations among the three pairs of questions were .73, .60, and .63.

subjects demonstrated greater conceptual understanding of the material than the control subjects. 26

The learning results complement those of Zajonc (1960). In our study, subjects took the material home to study as they typically do, thereby adding to the external validity of our results at the expense of internal validity, since their learning could not be monitored. On the other hand, in the Zajonc study, subjects' learning was monitored in the laboratory over a short period, adding to the internal validity at the expense of external validity. The combination of results, both showing that active learning—learning in order to use the material—led to greater conceptual learning, represents a rather convincing case. 27

A related question has to do with subjects' rote learning. Bargh and Schul (1980) found that learning in order to teach improved subjects' rote learning relative to learning in order to be tested. We found no significant difference between the two groups on rote learning. It is probable that our failure to find the difference is a reflection of the high external validity of our study for our subject population. Undergraduates in a competitive setting have become adept at learning material in order to pass exams. Even though the exams may interfere with their conceptual integration of the material, they have become quite proficient at memorizing the material that is necessary for exams. With the external validity of this study being so high, the students were probably behaving just as they usually do. 28

An interesting finding with respect to perceived activity/passivity was that subjects who learned in order to teach perceived themselves to be very active in the teaching paradigm and very passive in the examination paradigm. In sharp contrast, subjects functioning in the traditional learning-in-order-to-be-examined paradigm perceived no significant activity/passivity differences between their paradigm and one in which they would learn material in order to teach it to others. In making these contrasting perceptions, the experimental subjects were operating from personal knowledge unique to subjects in their group. They were able to compare their subjective impressions relating to the learning-in-order-to-teach paradigm in which they had just functioned, with the traditional learning-in-order-to-be-examined paradigm in which they frequently function. The control subjects, however, were asked to discriminate between activity/passivity levels in the traditional examination paradigm and a teaching paradigm about which they probably had no personal knowledge. This is an interesting finding because it indicates that students need to have had a recent experience with a more active type of learning paradigm to recognize the passivity of the traditional examination paradigm.

In summary, we argue that the opportunity to use information to act on one's environment facilitates intrinsic motivation for learning that information and results in improved conceptual learning, relative to learning that is aimed merely at passing an examination. Given that the aim of most educators is to promote conceptual learning, educational climates and procedures that facilitate intrinsically motivated learning would seem to be of central importance. 29

REFERENCES

Allen, V. L., & Feldman, R. S. (1973). Learning through tutoring: Low achieving children as tutors. *Journal of Experimental Education, 42,* 1–5.

Bargh, J. A., & Schul, Y. (1980). On the cognitive benefits of teaching. *Journal of Educational Psychology, 72,* 593–604.

Bogen, J. E. (1969). The other side of the brain: An appositional mind. *Bulletin of the Los Angeles Neurological Societies, 34*(3), 135–162.

Bruner, J. (1966). *Toward a theory of instruction*. Cambridge, MA: Harvard University Press.
Cloward, R. D. (1967). Studies in tutoring. *Journal of Experimental Education, 36*, 14–25.
deCharms, R. (1976). *Enhancing motivation: Change in the classroom*. New York: Irvington.
Deci, E. L. (1975). *Intrinsic motivation*. New York: Plenum.
Deci, E. L. (1980). *The psychology of self-determination*. Lexington, MA: D. C. Heath (Lexington Books).
Deci, E. L., Nezlek, J., & Sheinman, L. (1981). Characteristics of the rewarder and intrinsic motivation of the rewardee. *Journal of Personality and Social Psychology, 40*, 1–10.
Deci, E. L., & Ryan, R. M. (1980). The empirical exploration of intrinsic motivational processes. In L. Berkowitz (Ed.), *Advances in experimental social psychology* (Vol. 13, pp. 39–80). New York: Academic Press.
Deci, E. L., & Ryan, R. M. (in press). *Intrinsic motivation and self-determination in human behavior*. New York: Plenum.
Garbarino, J. (1975). The impact of anticipated reward upon cross-aged tutoring. *Journal of Personality and Social Psychology, 32*, 421–428.
Goldschmid, M. L. (1970, February). Instructional options: Adapting the large university course to individual differences. *Learning and Development*, no. 5. Toronto: Center for Learning and Development, McGill University.
Harter, S. (1981). A new self-report scale of intrinsic versus extrinsic orientation in the classroom: Motivational and informational components. *Developmental Psychology, 17*, 300–312.
McGraw, K. (1978). The detrimental effects of reward on performance. In M. R. Lepper & D. Greene (Eds.), *The hidden costs of reward* (pp. 33–60). Hillsdale, NJ: Erlbaum.
National Commission on Resources for Youth. (1972, December). *Youth tutoring youth model for inschool neighborhood youth corps: An evaluation* (Grant #42-0-005-034). Washington, DC: U.S. Department of Labor.
Rogers, C. (1969). *Freedom to learn*. Columbus, OH: Merrill.
White, R. W. (1959). Motivation reconsidered: The concept of competence. *Psychological Review, 66*, 297–333.
Zajonc, R. B. (1960). The process of cognitive tuning in communication. *Journal of Abnormal and Social Psychology, 61*, 159–167.

AUTHORS

CARL A. BENWARE, Psychologist, New York State Division for Youth, State School at Industry, NY 14474. *Specialization:* Human motivation.
EDWARD L. DECI, Professor of Psychology, University of Rochester, Rochester, NY 14627. *Specializations:* Intrinsic motivation and self-determination in human behavior.

Now that you have read an actual research report, perhaps you could use some assistance in identifying the major features of the article, to better comprehend and evaluate the study. The following "research keys" should enable you to unlock the mysteries of analyzing and understanding educational research. The case comments will provide you with more detail regarding the various sections and contents of a research report.

Research Keys

 Sample
Independent selection—random assignment of introductory psychology students to treatment groups

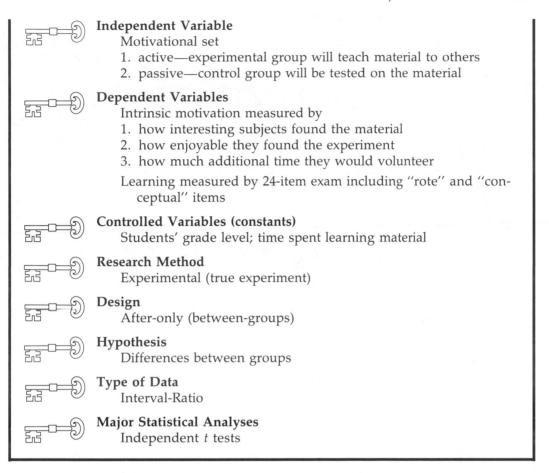

Independent Variable
Motivational set
1. active—experimental group will teach material to others
2. passive—control group will be tested on the material

Dependent Variables
Intrinsic motivation measured by
1. how interesting subjects found the material
2. how enjoyable they found the experiment
3. how much additional time they would volunteer

Learning measured by 24-item exam including "rote" and "conceptual" items

Controlled Variables (constants)
Students' grade level; time spent learning material

Research Method
Experimental (true experiment)

Design
After-only (between-groups)

Hypothesis
Differences between groups

Type of Data
Interval-Ratio

Major Statistical Analyses
Independent *t* tests

Case Comments

The field of education has long recognized the value of tutoring for facilitating students' learning. Tutoring has also been demonstrated to be of value in enhancing the learning and motivation of the tutor, as well (1). Carl Benware and Edward Deci felt that some of these positive benefits of tutoring could be achieved without the tutoring actually taking place. That is, the enhanced learning and more positive emotional tone toward the material that many tutors experience may be achieved by having students *believe* that they will be teaching the material to others without actually requiring them to do so (2). Therefore, they hypothesized (3) that students who learned material to teach it to others would learn it better and feel better about it than would students who simply studied the material to be tested on it.

A general overview of the theory from which this hypothesis was derived was presented (4) along with a more detailed elaboration of the theory (5). The theory basically contends that students who learn in order to teach the material to others are more intrinsically motivated and thus more active in the learning process. This should enhance learning and make the students feel better about themselves and the learning process.

Benware and Deci provided support for their theory by presenting the research of others that suggests that tutoring is intrinsically interesting (6) and that expecting to teach enhances intrinsic motivation and active involvement with the material, thus improving learning and creating more positive feelings (7). Although the research support for this theory was somewhat indirect, the authors wisely pointed out some needed improvements in the previous studies that would allow a more general application of the findings and provide even better support for their theory (8). By taking these steps the authors have increased both the external validity and the internal validity of their study.

The introduction of the report is concluded by presenting the operational definition for the independent variable (9) and an explanation of how the study was designed to be an improvement over previous studies (10). Thus, their research is neatly tucked into the existing literature.

Method

The method section of the report, along with the results section, is critical when examining the research from the standpoint of research methodology and statistical analyses. We must focus our attention on these two sections to determine the type of research being conducted and whether it was designed and executed properly. This is where you really need to roll up your sleeves and dig in.

Although Benware and Deci were not able to recruit a truly random sample of the population (11) (few researchers ever achieve this), independent selection was achieved by randomly assigning (12) the volunteer subjects to the two groups (experimental and control). Each subject had an equal chance of being assigned to the experimental or the control group. Perhaps a flip of a coin or some other random process was used to make the determination for each subject. This independent selection assured us that this would be a true experiment. By randomly assigning subjects to the groups the researchers did in fact create truly equivalent groups. At this point, before introducing the IV, *the experimental group should not differ from the control group in any systematic way.*

Notice that all the subjects who volunteered to participate did not actually show up for the experiment (13). As you may recall from our discussion of the threats to internal validity in Chapter 2, such experimental mortality can result in problems if too many subjects fail to complete the entire experiment or if the attrition from one of the research groups differs substantially from the other group. Fortunately, in this case the number of subjects who failed to complete the experiment was small, and they were rather evenly split between the two groups.

Next we look to the procedure section to determine which basic type of research is being used in this study (experimental or post-facto). We see that this was experimental research because the researchers directly manipulated the IV (15) and, of course, the subjects were randomly assigned. The subjects' motivational set was manipulated by the researchers to be active or passive as a result of being read the instructions for the experimental-group subjects (active) or the instructions for the control-group subjects (passive). These subjects did not necessarily differ with respect to having active or passive motivational sets before the experiment (if they had this would have been post-facto research). Instead, the researchers shaped their motivation by telling them either that after learning the material themselves they would be teaching it to others (active) or that they would simply be tested on it (passive).

We also see in the procedure (14) that the all-important principle of *constancy* was achieved in this study. *All* subjects were told to spend about three hours studying the material to be learned and *all* were given the same verbatim instructions prior to the introduction of the IV. It is essential that the IV be the only factor that is allowed to vary.

To get subjects to respond as they would in the real world, it is necessary to conduct research in a context that is realistic and sensible. The authors achieved such *realism* by explaining to the experimental subjects why they too were being tested on the material that they had prepared to teach to others (16).

To derive any meaning at all from a research report and assess the effects of the IV, we must obviously know exactly what is being measured or tested. What is it about these subjects that we want to know? Here is where the dependent variables enter the scene. In this study the subjects were measured after the introduction of the IV, and only then, making this an after-only research design. Multiple response measures were obtained, in that intrinsic motivation was assessed by asking the subjects three simple questions (17), and the other DV, amount of material learned, was measured by an exam containing twenty-four items that tapped either the students' rote memory or their conceptual understanding of the material (19).

Many studies often include what is called a *manipulation check* to see if the manipulation of the IV really worked as intended. In this case the manipulation check consisted of two questions regarding the subjects' perceived activity or passivity when "learning in order to teach" versus "learning in order to be examined" (18). The authors wanted to determine if the control subjects truly differed from the experimental subjects on this dimension.

Finally, the method section ends with the mention of a very successful technique used to avoid experimenter bias. As we discussed in Chapter 2, it's called double-blind: neither the experimenter nor the subjects are aware of the conditions and hypotheses of the study (20). In this case a variation of the double-blind technique was used. Although the researcher reading the instructions to the subjects was probably aware of the research hypothesis (not blind), a colleague of the researchers scored the subjects' responses on the "learning exam" in order to eliminate the possibility of the researchers themselves "helping out" the students in the experimental group in order to support their hypothesis.

Results

The results section of the report is where you get to test your statistical expertise. Many students (and professional educators, as well) have a tendency to skim over this section of a report thinking, "The author must have done the proper statistical analysis or it wouldn't have been published." Unfortunately, this isn't always true, and it's important for you to see for yourself how strongly (or weakly) the statistical results support the author's conclusions even if the correct statistical test was performed.

When reading a report such as this you should put yourself into the shoes of the researcher: "What statistical test would I do if this were my study?" The first question to be answered to make this determination is, "What type of data do I have?" Looking back to the DVs (17,19), we see that the numbers that we had to work with came from two *Likert-type scales** (scores range from 1 to 10), a question dealing with time (0 to 5 hours), a rote learning score (0 to 24), and a conceptual learning score (0 to 24). All these DVs involve data of the interval-ratio variety. They are not ranks (ordinal) and they are not categorical (nominal) (see Chapter 2 for a review of measurement scales).

Our next question focuses on the type of hypothesis involved in the study: the hypothesis of difference or the hypothesis of association? In this study Benware and Deci hypothesized that there would be a *difference* between the experimental group and the control group in regard to intrinsic motivation and the amount of learning that occurred. Therefore, we're dealing with the hypothesis of difference.

Next we check to determine whether the scores that we are comparing (experimental versus control) are the result of independent selection or correlated (dependent) selection. You'll recall that the subjects in this study were randomly assigned to the two groups (12), thus resulting in independent selection.

The last question focuses on the number of measures, or sets of scores, that are being compared. Here we have just two: scores from the experimental group and scores from the control group.

Where does this leave us? We have

1. interval-ratio data
2. hypothesis of difference

---

* Likert scales are typically used for measuring attitudes. They consist of a series of statements about the attitude object, and the respondent has to indicate his or her degree of agreement with each statement. Degree of agreement is usually indicated by simply marking strongly agree, agree, neither agree nor disagree, disagree, or strongly disagree. A number is assigned to each degree of agreement (such as 1 to 5), which facilitates the calculation of a summary attitude score for each subject.

3. independent selection
4. two measures (sets of scores)

The most appropriate test is the independent *t* test. In this study a *t* test was performed for each of the DVs and for the manipulation check. The manipulation of the IV was successful in that the experimental subjects rated "learning in order to teach" to be a more active process than the control subjects rated "learning in order to be examined" (21).

The major statistical analysis revealed that the experimental group was more interested in the material, enjoyed the experiment more, and was more willing to spend additional time than was the control group, thus confirming the major hypothesis regarding intrinsic motivation (22). Further, the experimental group had higher conceptual learning scores than did the control group but they did not differ significantly in terms of their rote learning scores (23).

The final *t* test compared the two groups in terms of how much time they had spent studying the material (24). Both groups of subjects were asked to spend approximately three hours studying, and as hoped, the subjects did this and did not differ significantly from each other.

Discussion

In the discussion section, Benware and Deci got an opportunity to pull it all together: What did they find? What does it mean? As is the case with most studies, they began by restating their hypothesis (25) and briefly reviewing their major findings (26). They clearly indicated how their findings fit in with previous research (27) and explained why one of their findings was not consistent with an earlier study (28). The discussion is wrapped up with a succinct summary and some implications for education (29).

The authors concluded that learning material with the intention of teaching it to others enhances intrinsic motivation for learning and this, in turn, enhances conceptual learning. What a valuable asset this could be to you as a teacher! When studying for your own courses you may learn the material better and be more motivated if you approach the material as if you'll be teaching it to others. What great practice for future teachers!

CASE 2: THE QUASI EXPERIMENT

Quite often in the field of education a researcher wants to measure the impact of a new teaching method, or the effectiveness of a new type of discipline on unruly students, but is unable to randomly assign the students to the various treatment groups. More often, he or she has to work with existing groups of students (intact classrooms, perhaps). Although the researcher may be able to manipulate the IV (determine which class gets the new teaching method and which class gets the existing one), this cannot always be done on a student-by-student basis. For instance, everyone in Ms. Smart's class is taught with the new techniques and everyone in Mr. Learner's class will learn via the existing methods. In cases like this we must rely on the type of experimental research called the quasi experiment. We can control the IV, but we cannot create equivalent groups. There may be any number of factors that might differentiate the students in Ms. Smart's class from those in Mr. Learner's class—in addition to the fact that they are being taught by different techniques.

A Research Example (reprinted journal article)

What follows is an example of experimental research of the quasi-experimental variety that was conducted by Georgea Mohlman Sparks and published in 1986.

The Effectiveness of Alternative Training Activities in Changing Teaching Practices

GEORGEA MOHLMAN SPARKS

Eastern Michigan University

The relationships between types of inservice training activities and changes in teaching behavior were investigated. Three groups of junior high teachers (N = 19) attended five workshops on effective teaching. Group I received no extra activities, Group II participated in peer observations, and Group III was coached by the trainer. Pre- and posttraining observations, questionnaires, and interviews were used to assess behavior change and attitudes. Profiles of day-to-day variations in teaching practices were examined for stability of teaching behavior. Of the teachers needing to improve, three Group I teachers, six Group II teachers, and two Group III teachers approached or exceeded the criterion level of performance on academic interactions. Peer observation appeared to be more effective than trainer-provided coaching in boosting workshop effectiveness. Further study of the context features related to the effectiveness of peer observations in district-based programs is required.

Sparks, G. M. (1986). The effectiveness of alternative training activities in changing teaching practices. *American Educational Research Journal 23*, pp. 217–25. Copyright © 1986 by the American Educational Research Association.

This research was funded in part by a grant from the California State Department of Education. An earlier version of this article was presented at the annual meeting of the American Educational Research Association in Montreal, April, 1983.

I thank Jane Stallings and Ellen Stevens for their assistance in conducting this research, and gratefully acknowledge N. L. Gage for his comments on an earlier draft of this article.

In the past 10 years great strides have been made in identifying teaching practices that positively influence student learning of basic skills. Teachers' management practices, instructional techniques, and expectancies have been found to be associated with (and, in some cases, to cause) significant gains in pupil learning (Gage, 1985). Yet teachers, administrators, and parents still complain about the inadequate acquisition of basic skills by our nation's children. How can these relatively recent findings be used to improve student learning? | 1

Assuming that change in teaching practices is critical to the improvement of teaching, one finds surprisingly little systematic inquiry into the process of inservice teacher training and its effects on everyday teaching practices. Joyce and Showers (1981) reviewed the training literature and offered the following hypotheses: (a) four components of training—presentation, demonstration, practice, and feedback—are sufficient to induce many teachers to transfer recommended practices to the classroom; and (b) coaching may | 2 be a necessary fifth component for many other teachers.

The study reported here was designed to improve understanding of the relationships between types of inservice training activities and changes in teaching behavior. The training content and organizational context were held constant to focus on the effects of three types of training. The two objectives of the study were as follows (a) to detail | 3 changes in individual teachers' practices before and after inservice training; and (b) to determine whether the changes in the three groups of teachers resulted from differences in their inservice training activities.

METHOD

Sample

Junior high school teachers ($N = 19$) of English, social studies, and math for low-achieving students participated in the study. Two to five teachers were recruited from | 4 each of seven schools in the San Francisco Bay Area. The schools were roughly equivalent in terms of the students' socioeconomic status (SES) and in organizational climate as indicated by teachers' responses to questionnaires. The teachers' training experience | 5 ranged from 7 to 25 years.

Measures

The Stallings Secondary Observation Instrument (SSOI) was used to measure teaching behavior. The validity of measures obtained with this instrument in relation to student achievement and attitude has been established in previous studies (e.g., Stallings, Needels, & Stayrook, 1979). Higher interrater reliability (85% agreement or better) was established for the observers in this study.

The Five-Minute Interaction (FMI) section of the SSOI required that for 5 min, at five | 6 equally spaced intervals throughout the class period, the observer code every interaction between the teacher and students. Over the three 50-min observation periods, approximately 900 interactions were recorded for each teacher. Each interaction frame contained the following information: Who said it (teacher, student, group, etc.), to whom it was said, what form it took (question, lecture, correction, etc.), and what it was about (academic subject matter, organizing, misbehavior, or socializing). Giving directions for an activity was not considered an academic interaction.

Teachers also were interviewed to obtain their views on whether the training activities were helpful, what was hard or easy to change, and what their reactions were to the training. These interviews were conducted and audiotaped by graduate students. Open-ended questions, field notes, and observer logs were other sources of qualitative data. |7

Procedure

In early October, two trained observers observed all teachers during the same class period on 3 consecutive days using the SSOI. The observational data were converted into teacher-behavior profiles that were given to the teachers at workshop 1 in late October. At that time, the teachers also responded to a short questionnaire designed to assess selected teacher characteristics (e.g., teaching experience and attitudes toward the recommended practices), school level organizational factors, and certain characteristics of their students. |8

Next, teachers from geographically close schools were combined into three groups of six or seven teachers each. Proximity was the basis for forming the training groups to minimize the cost of assembling the teachers. These groups then received three variations of Stalling's Effective-Use-of-Time Training (Stallings et al., 1979) during late October and November. In January and February, all teachers again were observed on 3 consecutive days and filled out teacher questionnaires. Interviews were conducted in March, and a final meeting of each group was held to inform them of the results of the class observations. |9

|8

Training Activities

The primary purposes of the Effective-Use-of-Time Training were to help teachers increase student time on task and to improve their interactive instruction. Teaching practices in both of these areas had been found to correlate significantly with secondary students' gains on achievement test scores and with student attendance in previous studies (Stallings et al., 1979). Four weekly workshops of 2.5 hrs each were conducted after school. Each group attended the workshops on a different day of the week. The workshop activities included examination of observation profiles, presentation of research findings concerning relevant teaching practices, demonstration and practice of recommended practices, and discussion of the practices. |10

The three groups participated in different sets of training activities. Group I participated only in the workshops, Group II participated in the workshops and received the results of two classroom observations by a peer, and Group III participated in the workshops and received two in-classroom coaching sessions from the trainer. The peer-observation forms were simple seating charts on which the peer observer recorded either student off-task behavior or student-teacher interactions. The coaching included the use of the seating chart observation forms and a postobservation conference during which suggestions for changes in teaching practices or classroom organization were made by the trainer. |11

RESULTS AND DISCUSSION

The main question addressed in this research was, Which of the three training groups improved the most, the workshops-only group (Group I), the workshops-plus-peer-observation group (Group II), or the workshops-plus-coaching group (Group III)? A prior |12 and ancillary question was, How stable was the measured teaching behavior from day to day? | 12

The Stability of Teaching Behavior

The stability of teaching behavior has been important in the research on teaching effects. Such stability bears upon the reliability and validity of measures of teaching practices. It is essential to establish how accurately the measures based on the average of a set of observation occasions represent the teacher's typical classroom behavior.

Since one purpose of Stalling's Effective-Use-of-Time Training was to increase the amount of academic interaction between teachers and students, Academic Interactions was selected as the major variable on which to measure implementation. To compute the | 13 values for this variable, the number of interactions that dealt with academic matters was divided by the total number of interactions observed during the class period.

In considering the stability of this teaching behavior measure, it is important to note that these data are considered "Bernoulli trial data" (Rogosa, Floden, & Willett, 1982). That is, the scores for this variable were represented by proportions. Rogosa and his colleagues suggested that such data may reflect teacher behavior more accurately than do | 14 the commonly used behavior count data. If there is little interaction one day and much interaction another day, the count of academic interactions would vary greatly, but the proportion of academic interactions to all interactions could remain relatively constant.

To examine the day-to-day stability of Academic Interactions, individual teacher profiles were created for both the pre- and posttraining observation data. When this measure varied considerably over the three occasions, observer logs and interview data were examined for explanations. In five of the cases, the one day with an extremely low score was an all-seatwork, catch-up day that typically occurred one or more days a week. Because these all-seatwork days were a regular part of the class routine, they were included in these teachers' average scores for Academic Interactions. | 15

Clearly, such close examination of observation data in the light of qualitative data yields insights into the measurement and interpretation of teaching behavior. It may help the researcher identify data that should not be included in the overall averages, and it can aid understanding of the day-to-day variance typical of teaching behavior. Merely examining averages of the three observation occasions may hide rich information about teachers' daily activities. These results are especially important when one considers that the SSOI is widely used in studies of teacher behavior (see, e.g., Goodlad, 1983).

Effects of Training Activities

The implementation of the recommended training practices in the three training groups was compared to determine which set of training activities seemed most effective | 16 in producing the desired changes in teaching behavior.

Table I presents descriptive statistics and *t*-tests (for correlated means) of the differences between pre- and posttraining means for each training group. The sample as a | 17 whole ($N = 19$) improved significantly on Academic Interactions ($t = 3.01$, $p < .01$). However, repeated measured analyses of variance (ANOVA) revealed no significant between-group differences, presumably because of the small group sizes and the large | 18 within-group variances. A problem with using ANOVA to assess implementation was that it took into account only the amount of change, not the pre-training level of teaching | 19 behavior or the amount of change needed.

Table I Group Means, Standard Deviations, and t-tests for Academic Interactions

	N	PRE-TRAINING		POSTTRAINING		t	p
		MEAN	SD	MEAN	SD		
Training group							
I (workshops only)	6	55.7	7.1	65.1	16.5	1.54	.19
II (workshops plus peer observation)	7	59.2	14.4	73.1	8.8	4.38	.005
III (workshops plus coaching)	6	58.9	11.0	62.5	20.4	.54	.61
All teachers	19	58.0	10.9	67.2	15.5	3.01	.008

To analyze implementation from a different perspective, a criterion level of 70% was set for Academic Interactions. This standard was derived from previous studies that indicated that teachers with at least this average level tended to have students who gained most in achievement (Stallings et al., 1979; Stallings & Mohlman, 1981). Scatterplots (Figure 1) then were examined to see how teachers related to the criterion before and after training.

Figure 1 shows that two teachers (one in Group II and one in Group III) were to the right of the vertical line, indicating that they were above the criterion (70% on the abscissa) and showed no need for change before training. Those teachers below the horizontal line (70% on the ordinate) did not reach the criterion after the training. Table II

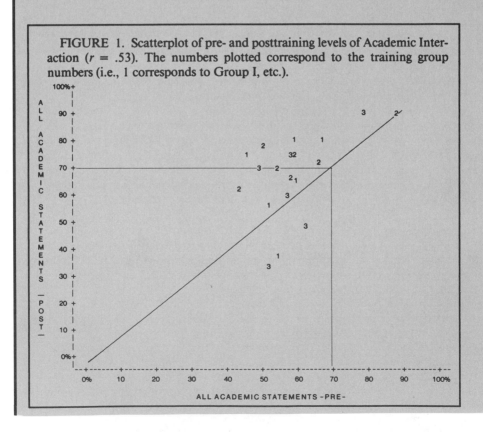

FIGURE 1. Scatterplot of pre- and posttraining levels of Academic Interaction (r = .53). The numbers plotted correspond to the training group numbers (i.e., 1 corresponds to Group I, etc.).

Table II Number and Percent of Teachers in Each Training Group Improving on Academic
Interactions

CATEGORY	GROUP					
	I (N = 6)	%	II (N = 7)	%	III (N = 6)	%
Did not improve	3	50	0	0	3	50
Improved, but not to criterion	0	0	2	29	0	0
Improved to criterion or above	3	50	4	57	2	33
No need to change	0	0	1	14	1	17
Total	6	100	7	100	6	100

shows the number and percent of teachers who needed to change but did not, who
needed to change and did, and so on for each category.

After the training, three of the six teachers in Group I (workshops only) reached the
criterion level and three showed no improvement. In Group II (peer observation), four of
the six teachers needing to change reached the criterion, and two improved to slightly
below the criterion. Before training, five teachers in Group III (trainer coaching) needed
to improve; of these, only two reached the criterion level, and three did not improve at
all.[1]

On the basis of this analysis, the peer observation training activities appeared to be
more powerful than the coaching or workshops-only activities. However, because this
was not a true experiment, with random assignment of subjects to treatments, one must
consider alternative explanations for this finding. Possibly these results occurred not
because of the training treatments, but because of other differences between groups.
Group III differed from the other groups in two possibly important ways: The participants were somewhat older and were predominantly male. These factors may have
accounted for the smaller improvements in Group III.

There are several plausible reasons, however, for inferring the superiority of the peer-
observation treatment. First, secondary school teachers rarely get to see other teachers in
action. Just watching a colleague teach may have been a powerful learning experience,
and one that the teachers in the other groups did not receive. Several teachers mentioned
picking up new ideas from teachers they watched. Second, the peer observers were
involved in the analysis and coding of teacher and student behavior. This experience may
have helped them analyze their own behavior more accurately and enabled them to make
more significant changes in their own teaching.

Another benefit of the peer-observation process may have been a heightened sense of
trust and esteem among group members. Being observed may have seemed slightly
threatening at first, but once the teachers realized that their peer was not there to judge
them, a team spirit began to develop. The morale in Group II seemed exceptionally high
compared to that of the other groups. The cause of this esprit is unclear, but its existence
was unmistakable. Breaking down the psychological walls between the teachers' classrooms through peer observation may have contributed to this group's high morale. As
one teacher put it, "It made everyone feel more comfortable with each other." Alterna-

---

[1] For an investigation of reasons some teachers changed more than others, see the case studies
contrasting improving and nonimproving teachers in Sparks (1983).

tively, these teachers may have had higher morale initially that accounted for their dramatic improvement.

The coaching group (Group III) received only feedback and suggestions from the trainer, and Group I merely filled out the observation forms themselves or had an aide do it. Although these two groups received some form of feedback, they did not have the opportunity to analyze others' teaching. Nor did they have the opportunity to discuss the observation results with their colleagues, as did the teachers in Group II. This difference in experiences is likely to account for the differences between groups in implementation of training recommendations.

IMPLICATIONS FOR RESEARCH AND PRACTICE

These findings suggest several directions for future research. First, the peer-observation activity needs to be tried in a local district. The same results may not obtain in districts that implement inservice training as a mandated program, or where the political setting threatens the teachers. Carefully designed evaluations of district-organized staff development programs are needed to identify the context features that enhance the teacher improvement process.

Second, the long-term effect of such brief training interventions needs to be investigated. How long do the improvements in teaching behavior last? What is required to maintain teachers' levels of growth and competence? Do teachers continue to discuss instructional issues with their peers as they did in the workshops?

This study indicates that teachers can, under certain conditions, and in a relatively short period, make desirable changes in their teaching—a significant finding for inservice education. The effectiveness of the workshops may be accounted for by at least two characteristics: scheduling and format. The four workshops were spaced over 2 months, so the teachers had time to digest the content in small chunks and to try out a few things at a time. This schedule allowed teachers to experiment with and reflect on their teaching behavior in a supportive setting.

The small-group, problem-solving format also contributed to the success of the inservice training. In groups of six or seven, the teachers had ample opportunity to discuss what they had tried, how it had worked, and special concerns or problems. As the group set about finding solutions, they shared their favorite techniques. The role of the workshop leader was to describe the related research and to keep the group focused on seeking solutions to their problems.

This research suggests that the provision of objective, nonthreatening peer-observation activities boosts the effectiveness of normal, workshop-based inservice training. The objectivity of the observations was assured through the use of seating charts for marking student or teacher behaviors. Encouraging teachers to choose their own goals for change assured a lack of threat. And the teachers' principals assured them that the peer-observation information was confidential and unrelated to evaluation. It appears that peer observation is a beneficial training activity when these conditions are met.

Although tentative, the results of this study indicate that peer observation may be a more powerful training activity than trainer-provided coaching. Although Joyce and Showers (1981, 1982) long have supported the idea of coaching as a powerful inservice activity, they have not provided any data indicating which types of coaching are most helpful to teachers. The present findings indicate that trainer-provided coaching may not be worth the cost and time required, and that peer observation may be especially cost-effective.

REFERENCES

Gage, N. L. (1985). *Hard gains in the soft sciences.* New York: Phi Delta Kappa.

Goodlad, J. (1983). *A place called school.* New York: McGraw Hill.

Joyce, B., & Showers, B. (1981, April). *Teacher training research: Working hypotheses for program design and directions for further study.* Paper presented at the annual meeting of the American Educational Research Association, Los Angeles.

Joyce, B., & Showers, B. (1982). The coaching of teaching. *Educational Leadership, 40*(1), 4–10.

Rogosa, D., Floden, R., & Willett, J. (1982). *Assessing the stability of teacher behaviors.* Unpublished manuscript, Stanford University, Stanford, CA.

Sparks, G. (1983). Inservice education: Training activities, teacher attitude, and behavior change. (Doctoral dissertation, Stanford University. Stanford, CA). *Dissertation Abstracts International, 83,* 20778.

Stallings, J., & Mohlman, G. (1981). *School policy, leadership style, teacher change, and student behavior in eight schools.* Final Report, National Institute of Education, Washington, D.C.

Stallings, J., Needels, M., & Stayrook, N. (1979). *How to change the process of teaching basic reading skills in secondary schools.* Menlo Park, CA: SRI International.

AUTHOR

GEORGEA MOHLMAN SPARKS, Assistant Professor, Department of Teacher Education, Eastern Michigan University, Ypsilanti, MI 48197. *Specialization:* Research on teacher change and staff development.

Research Keys

 Sample
Dependent selection—nonrandom sample of junior-high-school teachers grouped according to geographical proximity and measured pre and post

 Independent Variable
Training activities
1. workshops only
2. workshops plus peer observation
3. workshops plus coaching from trainer

 Dependent Variables
Academic interactions between teachers and students measured by
1. Five-Minute Interaction (FMI) section of the Stallings Secondary Observation Instrument (SSOI)

Teachers' attitudes toward training measured by
1. interviews
2. open-ended questions

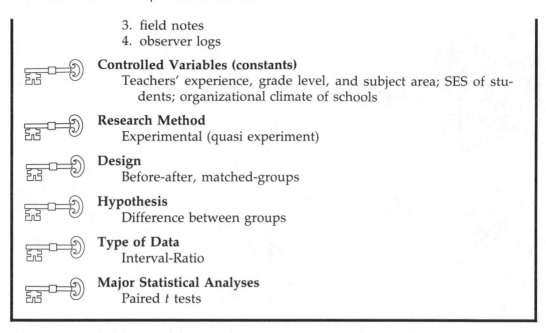

3. field notes
4. observer logs

Controlled Variables (constants)
Teachers' experience, grade level, and subject area; SES of students; organizational climate of schools

Research Method
Experimental (quasi experiment)

Design
Before-after, matched-groups

Hypothesis
Difference between groups

Type of Data
Interval-Ratio

Major Statistical Analyses
Paired *t* tests

Case Comments

As a student of education you are obviously interested in techniques that can be used to enhance the basic skills of students. The educational literature is, of course, replete with examples of teaching methods that have been demonstrated to be successful in improving pupil learning. Despite these successes, many in society feel that children educated in the U.S. are not adequately prepared in the basic skill areas. Georgea Mohlman Sparks was concerned with how these recent findings in the literature could be applied to actually enhance teacher effectiveness in the classroom (1). She reviewed some of the previous literature (2) that pointed out the essential components of training workshops for teachers, that is, those components necessary for teachers to successfully apply new practices in the classroom.

The relatively short introduction to this report is concluded with a general overview of her study and a listing of the basic objectives of the study. Primarily, she was interested in comparing three different types of in-service training procedures with regard to their effect on the teaching behavior of the teachers involved in the research (3).

Method

As is the case with most educational research, Sparks was not able to recruit a random sample of teachers for the study. Typically, you have to settle for the subjects who are willing and able to participate (4). Obviously, this will limit us in generalizing the findings from this study to other teachers and school districts. Do you remember what this is called? (See page 42.)

In analyzing this research we have to determine which basic type of research is being conducted: Does the researcher have control over the IV? We see in the procedure section of the report (9) that the researcher divided the teachers into three groups according to the geographical proximity of the schools that they taught in. The decision to divide the groups according to proximity was made on the basis of a very practical consideration: money. After grouping the subjects, the researcher then determined (perhaps randomly; we're not told) which of the three training activities each group would receive. Thus we have experimental research: the researcher manipulated the IV (training activities).

Next question: Is this a true experiment or a quasi experiment? Were equivalent groups created before the introduction of the IV? No. Teachers were not randomly assigned to the three groups. It was determined by the proximity of the schools to one another (9). Are the teachers from one area of the city different in any way from the teachers in another area of the city? We just don't know. But it does allow for the possibility that differences between the groups of teachers did exist even *before* the IV was introduced. So, our groups are not equivalent, but an IV is manipulated; therefore, this is a quasi experiment. We should point out that Sparks did what she could to make the groups as similar as possible by choosing experienced teachers from schools that were roughly equivalent with respect to SES and the organizational climate within the schools (5).

The specific type of quasi experiment that was carried out in this study most closely resembles the before-after, matched-groups design. The teachers were measured both before and after (8) the training activities in which they participated. As mentioned, the groups were at least somewhat matched in that all the subjects were experienced junior-high-school teachers for low-achieving students from the San Francisco area (4), and the schools that they taught in were similar in some ways (5). Although matching did not occur on a teacher-by-teacher basis (matched-subjects), the *groups* were matched on the previously mentioned criteria. As we noted in Chapter 3, matching groups does not allow for cause-and-effect statements, but some of the threats to internal validity are minimized.

The basic training workshops that all the teachers participated in were clearly described by the author (10). Since the workshops (Effective-Use-of-Time Training) have been standardized and described in detail elsewhere (Stallings, Needels, & Staybrook, 1979), it was not necessary for Sparks to elaborate on them any more than she did. It is important, however, to provide enough detail or indicate where such detail can be found (as was the case in this study) to enable another researcher to replicate the study if he or she so desires. This is an important component of the scientific method; it is therefore vital that enough information be available in the report to allow for *replication*.

Following the description of the basic training workshops, the author presented the operational definition for the independent variable, training activities

(11). Three levels of this IV were used, with each group of teachers receiving one of the levels. These consisted of the basic workshops only (Group I), the workshops plus peer observation (Group II), and the workshops plus coaching from the workshop trainer (Group III).

The operational definition for the major dependent variable in this study was a bit complicated, so you need to read it carefully (6). A standardized measure, the Stallings Secondary Observation Instrument (SSOI), was used to measure teaching behavior, in general. One portion of this instrument, the Five-Minute Interaction (FMI), was used to measure the interactions between the teachers and the students throughout the class periods. But wait—we still haven't gotten to the major DV. Sparks was primarily interested in the *academic* interactions between the teachers and students (13); therefore, these were calculated as a proportion of the entire number of interactions (academic interactions divided by total number of interactions).

In addition, *qualitative data* were collected (7) regarding teachers' attitudes toward the training. These were measured by interviews, open-ended questions, field notes, and observer logs. Qualitative data of this type can be very helpful in clarifying quantitative data (15). The numbers alone don't always tell the full story. The richness and quality of the quantitative data can often be enhanced in this way.

As usual, a lot of information has been included in the method section of the report. The sample of subjects has been described, the basic method of research and the design of the study have been outlined, the IV and DV have been operationally defined, and the factors that were held constant have been enumerated.

Results and Discussion

In this report the results and discussion have been combined into one section. Although this is not the usual format advocated by the American Psychological Association for report writing, it is not uncommon. In cases in which either the results or the discussion section is brief, or where the author wishes to integrate the results and discussion of one aspect of the study before proceeding to the next, this combination of sections may be useful. Again, it is often helpful to begin this section with a quick recap of the research questions under study (12), as was done in this case.

To evaluate the appropriateness of the statistical analysis, we need to determine the type of data available. Here, the measure of academic interactions was based on proportions (14); thus, we have interval-ratio data. The major hypotheses in this study dealt with *differences* in academic interactions prior to the training activities versus after the training activities, and *differences* between the three groups of teachers as a result of the training activities that they received (16). Obviously, in both instances we're dealing with hypotheses of difference as opposed to hypotheses of association.

The next decision focuses on whether the sets of scores obtained in the study were independent of one another or dependent (correlated). The primary data in this study dealt with the academic interactions of the teachers in each group prior to the training activities versus after the training activities. For these analyses (17), the pre and post scores were clearly dependent on one another (correlated). It also becomes clear that for each of these analyses (one for each of the three groups and one for all of the subjects combined) there are just two sets of scores for each: a pre score and a post score. Therefore, with

1. interval-ratio data
2. hypothesis of difference
3. dependent selection
4. two measures (sets of scores)

the appropriate statistical test is the paired *t* test (17). This series of paired *t* tests revealed that, in general, the teachers increased their academic interactions after the training, but that only one group (Group II, workshops plus peer observation) increased significantly after training.

As Sparks pointed out (18), it is often more appropriate to use a fairly sophisticated analysis of variance (repeated-measures ANOVA or MANOVA) to compare the three groups pre and post, but in this case, with so few subjects in each group and so much variability among the subjects in their own groups, it was very difficult to get a statistically significant result. She goes on further to explain that in this study the ANOVA is even less appropriate because it only measures the amount of change that occurred among the teachers without taking into account the level of academic interactions the teachers were exhibiting prior to the training (19). Perhaps there were some that didn't need to increase very much because their academic interactions were already at the upper end of the continuum prior to the workshops.

This example highlights a statistical obstacle referred to as the *ceiling effect*. If the subjects in your study are already performing at a very high level (near the ceiling), it is very difficult for your treatment or intervention to reveal a positive effect. There isn't enough room left on the continuum or scale for your subjects to go any higher. Thus, it appears that your intervention was not successful when in fact, it may just be a shortcoming of your measurement system, in that your subjects couldn't really improve much more, owing to their preexisting high scores.

In her study, Sparks handled this problem quite nicely by using a previously agreed-upon criterion level (70 percent) as an indication of "needed" improvement. Those teachers whose academic interactions represented less than 70 percent of their total interactions were considered to be in need of improvement. Less formal descriptive statistics were used (20) to determine which subjects had surpassed this criterion even prior to the training and which had surpassed it after the training. (If the number of subjects in this study had been higher, a χ^2 analysis could have been used here.) Because they represented only those who needed to change (that is, who were below the criterion prior to the training), the subjects in Group II (workshops plus peer observation) exhibited more improvement than did the other two groups.

Now that we've dissected the results, we need to be very cautious in our interpretation of these findings. It is tempting to think that the workshops plus peer observation caused more academic interactions than the other two strategies (21). However, we need to recall that pesky issue of nonequivalent groups. This was a quasi experiment in which our three groups of teachers were not necessarily equivalent prior to the workshops. Other factors could explain why Group II was superior to the others (22). In situations like this it is up to the author to provide plausible explanations of why the *apparent* cause may be the real thing. In this study, Sparks has offered numerous reasons (23) why the peer observation may indeed have been superior to the other training activities. Cautious conclusions (21,22) and reasonable explanations (23), like those provided in this report, though not conclusive, often spur further research, so that they are subsequently tested further. Sparks has even taken the next step by suggesting exactly what type of future research needs to be done to more conclusively test the effectiveness of the peer-observation training (24).

The implications of this study are that teachers apparently can improve their teaching through in-service training (25). Sparks has even suggested what it is about the workshops in general that likely contributes to successful outcomes (26). The article is concluded with the author's explanation of the value of peer-observation activities from a cost-effectiveness standpoint (27). She contends that, especially compared with the trainer-provided coaching that has been advocated by others in the field, peer observation is more effective, less expensive, and less time-consuming.

Although the findings of this research are meant to be applied to teachers already in the profession, they certainly have applicability to students as well. Students may find it beneficial to receive feedback from their peers on student-teaching activities or on activities or lessons that they may be required to present in their own college classes. Certainly, supervisors or teachers provide valuable feedback, but peers can often provide an additional and helpful perspective as well.

SUMMARY

In this chapter journal articles were taken directly from the educational literature to illustrate some of the most common types of research conducted, and to highlight selected issues pertaining to research in education. The first case was an example of the true experiment with independently selected samples. Benware and Deci wanted to see if the quality of learning was affected by the learner having an active versus a passive motivational set. The IV (motivational set) was manipulated by the researchers, and subjects were randomly assigned to either the passive or the active emotional-set group. Within the context of this study several factors were discussed that relate to the internal validity of a study, such as experimental mortality, the use of the double-blind technique, and constancy. The importance of realism in the research environment as it relates to external validity was also mentioned. This study also provided a look at a common measurement device, the Likert scale, and the manipulation check, which allows the researcher to determine if the IV was properly manipulated, as intended.

The second case presented in this chapter was also an example of experimental research, but in this instance it dealt with a quasi experiment. In her attempt to measure the effectiveness of teacher-training workshops, Sparks was able to manipulate the IV but was not able to create completely equivalent groups at the outset of the study; hence, this was a quasi experiment. With this study there was a reemphasis of the importance of providing enough detail in the method section to allow for replication. Also explained was the benefit of qualitative data for enriching the flavor of the results, and the potential problems involved in the interpretation of the results when confronted with the ceiling effect.

KEY TERMS

Ceiling effect

Constancy

Likert scale

Manipulation check

Qualitative data

Realism

Replication

REFERENCES

BACHRACH, A. J. (1981). *Psychological research* (4th ed.). New York: Random House.

BENWARE, C. A., & DECI, E. L. (1984). Quality of learning with an active versus passive motivational set. *American Educational Research Journal, 21,* 755–765.

DARCH, C., & CARNINE, D. (1986). Teaching content area material to learning disabled students. *Exceptional Children, 53,* 240–246.

SPARKS, G. M. (1986). The effectiveness of alternative training activities in changing teaching practices. *American Educational Research Journal, 23,* 217–225.

STALLINGS, J., NEEDELS, M., & STAYBROOK, N. (1979). *How to change the process of teaching basic reading skills in secondary schools.* Menlo Park, Calif.: SRI International.

CHAPTER

10

Case Studies II: Post-Facto Research and Others

CASE 3: POST-FACTO RESEARCH

The Hypotheses of Difference and
   Association
A Research Example (reprinted journal
   article)
Research Keys
Case Comments

CASE 4: SINGLE-SUBJECT RESEARCH

A Research Example (reprinted journal
   article)
Research Keys
Case Comments

SUMMARY

KEY TERMS

REFERENCES

By now you should be feeling more comfortable at picking apart research reports to get at the choice morsels that make the information easier to digest. You are learning to identify the key ingredients that differentiate the various types of research and the smorgasbord of statistical procedures that may be selected from.

In this chapter we will explore an extremely common form of research in education: post-facto research. In addition, we will delve into a research article that falls into the classification of "other." As we outlined in Chapter 4, this catch-all category includes the forms of research that cannot properly be classified as experimental or post-facto. These include single-subject research, historical research, case studies, and evaluation research. From this grouping we have chosen an example of single-subject research to focus on.

CASE 3: POST-FACTO RESEARCH

Imagine yourself setting out to study alcoholism-induced brain damage in humans. Would you subject a random sample of fifteen individuals to a heavy diet of vodka for six months and then compare their EEG patterns to those of a different random sample of fifteen people who were denied any alcohol for a comparable period of time? Of course not. Consider being interested in determining whether men talk more than women when in a group discussion involving both sexes. Would you randomly assign subjects to the male and female groups and then manipulate their gender (send them to Sweden for sex change operations!) before counting the number of words spoken per minute by each during group discussion? Again, the answer is obviously no. The ethical and practical restraints in both these examples clearly demonstrate the need for an alternative to the experimental method of research.

You will remember from the preceding chapters that when using the experimental method, an independent variable is manipulated by the experimenter in an attempt to note its effect upon a behavior of interest (the DV). For instance, in Case 1 in Chapter 9 the motivational set of the subjects (active or passive) was induced by the experimenter to measure its effect on the quality of learning experienced by the students. Research of this nature, when properly executed, allows the investigator to make cause-and-effect statements about the relationships between variables. The active motivational set of the subjects in the experimental group (they intended to teach the material to others) *caused* their conceptual learning scores and their attitudes toward learning to be enhanced. Only experimental research allows us to directly pinpoint the specific cause of an observed effect.

Since experimental research represents, in many ways, an ideal that often cannot be achieved, alternative methods have been developed. Many research questions in education simply do not lend themselves to a situation in which the researcher is able to "call all the shots." Some variables cannot be manipulated.

Here is where the post-facto method of research enters the picture. Subjects are *assigned* to research conditions on the basis of some characteristic or trait that they already possess. It's not under the control of the researcher to determine this. For example, in a study of the relationship between a father's occupation and his child's SAT scores, students were assigned to research categories based on their father's occupation (Belz & Geary, 1984). Certainly, the occupation of the fathers could not be manipulated by the researchers. Once the students were divided on this basis, their SAT scores were compared to test for differences between the various occupations.

In the foregoing alcoholic-brain-damage example, subjects would be assigned to one of the two levels of the IV (alcoholic versus nonalcoholic) on the basis of already possessing one of these two characteristics rather than having the experimenter manipulate this condition. Thus, people who were alcoholics before having any involvement in the study would be designated as part of the alcoholic group, and those with no past history of alcoholism would make up the nonalcoholic group. Similarly, in the sex differences study you would simply assign subjects to conditions on the basis of a preexisting condition, namely, their gender. Other variables that cannot be manipulated and may only be assigned include age, intelligence, race, educational level, and socioeconomic status.

Although post-facto research allows you to investigate phenomena that cannot be tested by the experimental method, you must remember that cause-and-effect statements cannot be made. If alcoholics do indeed exhibit more brain damage than teatotalers one cannot infer that it was the alcohol that *caused* the brain damage. Nor can one assume that the brain damage *caused* the alcoholism. It would be possible to make a better-than-chance prediction, based on the findings, that the alcoholics were subjecting themselves to brain damage more so than the nonalcoholics, but it would be no more than that. You must be careful not to be like the naive consumer of research who falls into the trap of assuming that a cause-and-effect relationship exists based on post-facto research.

Consider the possibility that a post-facto study revealed a negative correlation between body weight and frequency of sex. Those who weighed a lot were engaging in very little sex, whereas those with lower weights were engaging in sex quite frequently. Is there a cause-and-effect relationship here? Does being very sexually active *cause* you to weigh less? Maybe; it's good exercise. Does being overweight *cause* you to be less sexually active? Maybe; the obese person perhaps isn't perceived as an attractive sexual partner. The point is that *both* these explanations are plausible, as well as others. Post-facto studies don't allow for making accurate cause-and-effect statements because rival hypotheses or explanations are always possible. The subjects in the study may differ on many dimensions—not just on the one or two that the researcher is aware of and has chosen for study. Remember, no attempt has been made to equate the subjects before introducing the IV; indeed, the groups of subjects are known *not* to be equivalent at the outset of the study. The IV is a characteristic that the subjects already possess; thus, they are called subject variables.

You should not get the impression that post-facto research is worthless because a causal factor cannot be isolated. Being able to make better-than-chance predictions is certainly superior to being a "street-corner psychologist" relying on folklore and hearsay to predict human behavior. A good deal of preliminary research in a new area of study is often post-facto. It may be useful in identifying important variables that may later be systematically varied in an experimental study.

The Hypotheses of Difference and Association

Post-facto studies may be of two basic varieties: those that test the hypothesis of difference and those that test the hypothesis of association. In the first instance, subjects are assigned to research groups on the basis of a particular trait and are then measured on some other dimension (DV) to see if a difference between the groups exists. For example, an educator who is interested in the aspiration levels of students in private versus public high schools might ask students at both types of schools if they intend to attend college. The appropriate statistical test (namely, χ^2) would then be performed to evaluate any differences in responses that may exist between the two groups of students.

Post-facto studies that test the hypothesis of association attempt to identify relationships that exist between variables, rather than differences. For instance, in the fictitious study relating body weight with the frequency of sexual activity, a continuum was established for each variable (weight and frequency of sexual activity), then subjects were measured on each variable and the responses were correlated. If this study had been testing the hypothesis of difference, the subjects would have been divided into discrete categories, such as overweight and underweight, and then measured on sexual activity to see if a difference existed. As you can see, the study could be done either way. The important consideration focuses on the statistical analysis of the data. Different statistical tests are warranted depending on whether the hypothesis of difference or association has been proposed. (If necessary, review these statistical issues in Chapter 5).

A Research Example (reprinted journal article)

The following research article exemplifies the post-facto method of research and the hypothesis of difference.

What Do Primary School Children Think about Testing?

Norman E. Gleadow
University of Victoria

A course taught at our university in classroom testing and measurement is approached by many student teachers with a mixture of trepidation and skepticism. The trepidation derives from the reputation of the course as a rigorous and comprehensive treatment of testing. The skepticism originates from a perception of the elementary school child as a person in the school who should *not* be tested—a kind of "achievement test untouchable." One frequently mentioned criticism of testing the elementary (and especially primary) school child is based on the premise that testing will cause some kind of psychological damage. Ebel (1979) mentioned that one of the commonly held—but not necessarily substantiated—criticisms of testing was that "testing places students under harmful stress, and exposes them to unnecessary experiences of failure, destroying their self-confidence and killing the job of learning" (p. 5). [1]

A good source of evidence about how testing is perceived by elementary school children is the children themselves. This article describes the results of structured interviews with more than 200 primary school children. Children were asked about their perceptions of testing. Results of the interviews are discussed, and suggestions are made that will help teachers reduce or eliminate some of the concerns mentioned by children. [2]

METHOD

Subjects

The subjects were from three school districts close to the University of Victoria. There were 126 Grade 2 children selected from forty-two classrooms and ninety-nine Grade 3 [3]

Gleadow, N. E. (1982). What do primary school children think about testing? *The Elementary School Journal 83*, pp. 35–39. Reprinted by permission of the University of Chicago Press.

children selected from thirty-three classrooms. The children came from a broad range of economic backgrounds and from urban, suburban, or rural areas. In each classroom the regular teacher selected three children for the study on the basis of ability—one low, one average, and one high. They identified 120 males and 105 females.

Procedure

Seventy-five professional-year elementary student teachers interviewed three children each. They asked the children the following questions: "(1) Do you like having tests? (2) Why do you like [not like] having tests? (3) Do tests make you feel afraid? If yes, why do they make you feel afraid? (4) Why does your teacher give you tests? (5) Do you think your teacher *should* give you tests? Why or why not?"

The student teachers recorded the responses verbatim. Twelve children did not know what a test was. They were eliminated from the study. Data analyses were performed on 213 interviews.

RESULTS

The results for the questions eliciting yes or no answers are summarized by sex and teacher-judged ability in Table 1. The table shows no significant difference in answers on the basis of sex but some large differences in answers on the basis of ability.

As indicated in Table 1, there was a significant relationship ($\chi^2 = 11.1$, $p < .05$) between ability and whether the children liked tests. A much greater percentage of the high-ability children (76.1 percent) liked tests than the low-ability children (54.4 percent).

The 138 children (64.8 percent) who said that they liked tests were asked why they liked tests. The reasons they gave can be placed in five categories. Tests were liked because: (1) they were enjoyable times or fun (34 percent); (2) they provided an opportunity to demonstrate skills (21 percent); (3) they provided an opportunity to get good marks (19 percent); (4) they were easy to do (15 percent); (5) other (11 percent).

Examples of comments classified as "other" were: "The classroom is quiet"; "You don't have to work after [the test]"; and "You learn things."

The 24 percent of the children who did not like tests were asked why that was the case. Their responses can be placed in four categories. Tests were not liked because: (1) they were difficult (53 percent); (2) they were boring or too easy (24 percent); (3) the student was afraid of getting the wrong answer (15 percent); (4) they were not fun (5 percent).

Of these children, 18 percent were in the high-ability group and 41 percent each in the average and low-ability groups.

Thirteen percent of the children said they were afraid of tests. The reasons they gave were classified as: (1) the fear of not knowing the right answers (54 percent); (2) bad feelings inside, nervousness, and so forth (23 percent); (3) the fear of a negative reaction from the teacher (14 percent); (4) the fear of a poor report card (9 percent).

The children suggested that teachers gave tests for: (1) motivation (36 percent)—"To make you study," "To help you learn"; (2) performance assessment (26 percent)—"To find out how you're doing"; (3) ability assessment (16 percent)—"To see how smart you are," "To see if you have any brains"; (4) readiness (7 percent)—"Get you ready for harder work," "So you can do the work in the next grade"; (5) report cards (1 percent). Thirteen percent of the children did not know why the teacher gave tests.

Table I.   Contingency Tables for Children's Responses to Questions on Testing (Percentages)

		SEX		ABILITY		
	TOTAL (213)	MALE (115)	FEMALE (98)	LOW (68)	AVERAGE (74)	HIGH (71)
Question 1: Do you like having tests?						
Yes	64.8	62.6	67.3	54.4	63.5	76.1
No	24.4	25.2	23.5	36.8	21.6	15.5
Undecided	10.8	12.2	9.2	8.8	14.9	8.5
		$\chi^2 = .69^*$			$\chi^2 = 11.1^{**}$	
Question 3: Do tests make you feel afraid?						
Yes	12.7	14.0	11.2	16.4	14.9	7.0
No	82.1	82.5	81.6	79.1	79.7	87.3
Undecided	5.2	3.5	7.1	4.5	5.4	5.6
		$\chi^2 = 1.68^*$			$\chi^2 = 3.24^*$	
Question 4: Do you think your teacher should give you tests?						
Yes	95.2	95.5	94.8	97.0	94.4	94.2
No	1.9	2.7	1.0	1.5	2.8	1.4
Undecided	2.9	1.8	4.2	1.5	2.8	4.3
		$\chi^2 = 1.73^*$			$\chi^2 = 1.38^*$	

$^*p > .05.$
$^{**}p < .05.$

When asked "Why should teachers give you tests?" the children gave the same responses as above, plus "It is the teacher's job." | 12

DISCUSSION

Questions 1 and 2: "Do you like having tests?" and "Why [or why not]?"

Almost two-thirds of the children reported they liked tests. The reasons they gave suggested that tests provide pleasurable results, such as happy occasions, a chance to demonstrate knowledge, or a chance to obtain good marks. However, these results accrue only to those who can succeed to some extent on the test. As reported in the | 13 results section, 76.1 percent of the high-ability children liked testing, whereas only 54.4 percent of the low-ability children did—a difference of about 22 percent. Higher-ability pupils usually achieve more success on tests than lower-ability pupils. Whether or not | 14 they like tests appears to be related to the success they achieve.

What should the elementary teacher do? Hedges (1969) suggests giving different tests to children of various levels of ability. One method of adapting tests to lower ability levels has been to ask easier questions of the materials being tested. However, doing this neither tells the teacher how the child is doing relative to his peers nor how he or she is | 15 doing relative to the material being tested. It guarantees success for the child but at the expense of providing useful information for the teacher.

A more realistic approach is to construct a balanced classroom test. Such a test would have questions of varying degrees of difficulty at different levels of cognitive functioning on materials designed for children at different levels. A set of materials and administrative procedures for monitoring the continuous progress of the child through elementary school would probably need to be developed.

Twenty-four percent of the children who did not like tests gave as their reason that tests were too easy or boring. In some elementary school classrooms, many tests consist of a large number of questions that present identical tasks at the same cognitive level. (Arithmetic is a particular example.) If a pupil understands the task, he will answer most of the related questions correctly. The likely cause for the few incorrect answers is boredom resulting from a dull, repetitive task. To avoid monotony, teachers should carefully plan tests so that they adequately sample a range of cognitive abilities in the hierarchy of educational objectives. | 15

Question 3: "Do tests make you feel afraid? [If yes, why?]"

Teachers need to ask themselves how they present tests. Are tests serious, infrequent, and arduous affairs? Does a teacher's personality change from that of a helpful, smiling person to that of a stern, task-oriented, test administrator? Is there a countdown to the test? ("You will have a test in three days . . . two days . . . tomorrow.") Is it used as a threat or punishment? ("If you don't stop playing around, then I'll give you a test," or "Since you were uncooperative today, I will test you on what you were supposed to listen to, tomorrow.") Is the importance of the test overemphasized? ("You have to do well on this test, because it will be used to determine your report card mark.") If a testing program has some of these characteristics, then pupils probably will have twinges of fear and nervousness—and quite justifiably.

It is encouraging to note that 82 percent of the pupils reported they were not afraid of tests. That is a credit to their teachers. Tests should not be fear-generating devices. They should be normal, expected, and fairly frequent aspects of the classroom routine. They should not necessarily be lengthy. There should be somewhat more emphasis on the formative (instruction and diagnostic decision making) than on the summative (grading and reporting) function of tests. They should be free of threat, coercion, and punitiveness. | 16

Questions 4 and 5: "Why does your teacher give you tests?" and "Should he or she?"

The most frequently mentioned reason that teachers gave tests was related to the motivational value of tests. "They make you study" was often reported. Yet this is an indirect result of a test. Though a test may make a child study or pay attention in class, that ought not to be the primary use of the test. Less than half of the children (42 percent) gave the same major reasons for testing as are outlined in most books and articles on testing—performance, ability, or achievement assessment. | 18 18

Thirteen percent of the children did not know why they were given tests. Their comments suggested that a test was a somewhat mysterious, and always serious, break in the classroom routine. | 19

What is apparent from the information discussed above is that many teachers are not clearly explaining the purpose of testing programs to their pupils. Motivation should not be the primary purpose of classroom testing. Pupils should be taught how to study as a means of preparing for a test, not motivated to study by the *threat* of a test. | 20

SUGGESTIONS FOR TEACHERS

The results of this survey of primary school children's ideas about testing lead to the following suggestions for elementary school teachers.

1. Balance tests so that there are questions at different levels of cognitive processing.
2. Make tests a regular and expected part of the classroom routine.
3. Use more tests formatively—that is, for making instructional and diagnostic decisions.
4. Tell pupils why they are being tested and how the test results will be used.
5. Do not make test questions so simple that the test is boring and the results become meaningless.
6. Do not give long tests that repetitively measure pupils' ability to answer only one kind of question.
7. Do not use the test as a threat, coercion, or punishment.
8. Do not identify the test as primarily a means to motivate pupils to study or to encourage them to pay attention.

21

REFERENCES

Ebel, R. L. *Essentials of Educational Measurement*. 3d ed. Englewood Cliffs, N.J.: Prentice-Hall, Inc., 1979.

Hedges, W. E. *Evaluation in the Elementary School*. New York: Holt, Rinehart & Winston, 1969.

Research Keys

Sample
Independent selection—stratified sample of second & third graders grouped by ability level and gender

Independent Variables
Ability level
1. low
2. average
3. high
Gender
1. male
2. female

Dependent Variables
Children's perceptions of testing measured by five questions
1. Do you like having tests?
2. Why or why not?
3. Do tests make you afraid? If yes, why?

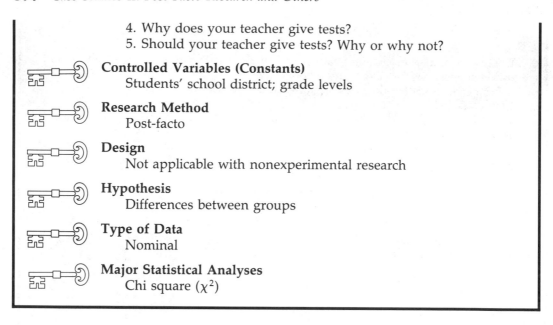

4. Why does your teacher give tests?

5. Should your teacher give tests? Why or why not?

Controlled Variables (Constants)
Students' school district; grade levels

Research Method
Post-facto

Design
Not applicable with nonexperimental research

Hypothesis
Differences between groups

Type of Data
Nominal

Major Statistical Analyses
Chi square (χ^2)

Case Comments

When reading the above article you undoubtedly noticed that there was no abstract leading the way. Although this article by Gleadow (1982) generally conforms to the American Psychological Association's publication format, it does not adhere to it in all details. You will encounter a good number of journals like this one, *The Elementary School Journal,* that develop their own publication formats, which are often based on the APA style without copying it exactly. They are typically similar enough to allow you to identify the major sections of the report quite readily.

The abstract of a report is a short summary of the research that is presented at the very beginning of the article following the name(s) and affiliation(s) of the author(s) (see Chapter 8 for more details). Since an abstract was not provided with this study, we will include one for you as it may have appeared in an APA-style publication.

Educators have long been concerned with the effects that testing may have on primary-school children. To investigate this, 225 children were interviewed regarding their views on testing, and their responses were categorized according to ability level and gender. Generally, the children liked tests, did not fear them, and felt that they should be given. No sex differences were revealed, but liking for tests appeared related to the students' ability level. Reasons for their responses are provided along with suggestions to aid teachers in addressing the students' concerns.

The introduction to this research report is extremely brief. A short statement of the problem is presented (1) along with a general overview of the procedures followed in this study (2). Very little background research is cited to place this study in the context of earlier work.

Method

This section begins with a description of the population from which the subjects were selected (3). After identifying the schools and classrooms to be included in the research, the regular classroom teachers selected three of their students (4) based on their ability (low, average, high). Unfortunately, we don't know exactly how the student was selected (randomly?) from each of the three ability levels. Typically, sampling of this type is referred to as stratified sampling if the three ability levels are equally represented in the population of school children. The students were not randomly selected from all ability levels, in that it was specified that in each classroom one would be selected from the low-ability students, one from the average students, and one from the high-ability students.

This is how *stratified sampling* works. The researcher identifies one or more characteristics that he or she wants to be distributed in the sample in the same proportions as in the population, and subjects are divided according to this factor. Subjects are then randomly selected from each subgroup.

In this study, ability level was the characteristic in question. Once the students were classified according to low, average, or high ability, one student from each category, in each classroom, was selected. This insured that the sample was equally represented by the three ability levels. Unfortunately, we are not provided with Gleadow's operational definition of low, average, and high ability. This was probably left to the discretion of each teacher, but this makes it difficult for future researchers to replicate this study. Finally, the subjects in this study were independently selected, in that they were not matched in any way nor were their scores compared pre and post.

As always, we must scour the method section to identify the basic type of research being employed. Our attention should be immediately focused on the independent variable. Was it manipulated by the investigator? In this study, two IVs were under investigation: the gender of the students and their ability levels in school (4). Obviously these cannot be manipulated by the researcher; therefore, we are dealing with post-facto research. Both gender and ability level are characteristics that the students possessed before being involved with this research at all.

After classifying the students according to ability level and gender, Gleadow needed to measure the students' attitudes and feelings regarding tests. Here's where the DV gets into the act. In this study the DV consisted of the students' responses to five questions related to testing (5). The 225 children were interviewed by 75 student teachers (three children each) (6). Normally, we might be concerned about so many different persons being involved in the data collection process. Do the student teachers possess their own biases about testing or research of this type that might prejudice their reports of the children's responses? It is very unlikely that this was a problem with this research because there was very little room for the student teachers to misinterpret the responses. The responses were recorded verbatim (7) and many of them required simple yes, no, or "undecided" answers.

In studies where biases of this type are more likely to be a problem, the researcher will establish *interrater reliability* (see Chapter 2). This involves having the researchers interview some of the same students to see how much they agree with one another in evaluating the subjects' responses. If there is a good deal of agreement between the researchers, the reliability of the findings is enhanced.

Notice that there was some experimental mortality in this study (8). Unlike the experimental mortality that we discussed in Case 1, in this instance the "drop-out" was not evenly distributed over the three groups. Twelve students were dropped from the study because they didn't know what a test was. These twelve students represented 9 percent (7 out of 75) of the low-ability students, 1 percent (1 out of 75) of the average-ability students, and 5 percent (4 out of 75) of the high-ability students. We need to be aware that this may have somewhat diluted the differences between the ability levels of the three groups. It is reasonable to assume that the 9 percent of the low-ability students who didn't know what a test was were probably the lowest of the low-ability students. With these students dropped from the study, the low-ability group was not quite so low any longer.

Results

This section is begun with an overall summary of the major findings as presented in a table (9). It is often convenient to present data in this manner so that the reader can get the overall picture easily and clearly. As always, before digesting the data, we should determine if the appropriate statistical analyses have been performed.

The data from this study that readily lend themselves to statistical analyses are nominal in form. On three of the questions, the students merely had to indicate yes, no, or undecided. Since the students were required to give one and only one response, these constituted mutually exclusive categories. The actual data, then, represented the number of times each response was given (frequencies).

Our next concern focuses on the type of hypothesis under study (difference or association). Here, Gleadow was interested in whether boys differed from girls regarding test perceptions and whether low-, average-, and high-ability students also differed on the DV; thus, the hypothesis of difference was being investigated in both cases. As mentioned in our discussion of the method section, subjects were independently selected.

How many sets of scores were being compared? In comparing the males to females there were obviously two sets of scores. In comparing the low-, average-, and high-ability students there were three sets of scores. The tally looks like this:

1. nominal data
2. hypothesis of difference
3. independent selection
4. two or more measures (sets of scores)

The chi square is the appropriate statistical test.

For each of the objective questions, "Do you like having tests?" "Do tests make you feel afraid?" and "Do you think your teacher should give you tests?" two chi squares were performed. One assessed the differences between boys and girls, and the other compared the students according to ability levels. As we see from the data in Table 1 and from the narrative in the text (10), no significant sex differences were found, but ability level did appear related to the students' liking for tests. High-ability children were more likely to like tests than were low-ability children.

Even though a difference in test perceptions was revealed as a function of ability level, we must remember that this was a post-facto study. We cannot infer that ability level *caused* this difference. We know that these students may have differed systematically on several other dimensions—in addition to ability level. Any one of these could be responsible for the difference revealed.

In addition to the data derived from the objective questions, valuable information was also obtained from several *open-ended questions* (11). These questions required the students to explain why they liked tests, why they didn't like tests, why they were afraid of tests, why teachers gave tests, and why teachers should give tests.

Open-ended questions of this type pose new problems for investigators. With open-ended questions, subjects can respond in any way that they like—there are no restrictions on their answers—whereas with objective questions (that is, multiple-choice questions) only particular answers are acceptable. By asking the students their reasons for liking tests, fearing them, and so on, Gleadow was running the risk of finding it difficult to summarize his data in a sensible manner. What can you do with hundreds of unique responses? Multiple-choice questions can be easily summarized according to how many subjects responded a, b, c, or d. From there, statistical means can be easily calculated. The advantage of the former approach is that the subjects are not confined to the responses that the *researcher* feels best answer the question. You have probably had the experience in filling out a questionnaire, in which you felt that none of the alternatives on a multiple-choice question really described your feeling or opinion and that you could answer the question better in a sentence or two rather than by circling a, b, c, or d. By opting for the open-ended questions here, Gleadow enabled the students to clearly express their views, but he was left with a pile of answers that couldn't be easily shoveled into the computer for analysis. Fortunately, he was able to categorize the students' unique responses as one of four or five basic reasons for their opinions regarding tests. In this way he was able to summarize the data by reporting the percentage of students who gave each of the various reasons.

Gleadow further enhanced the value of these open-ended responses by including some actual quotes of the students' answers (12). This adds a richness or flavor to the data that cannot be matched by simply reporting frequencies or percentages.

Discussion

The discussion was clearly organized around the five questions that constituted the dependent variables. Gleadow began with a review of the major finding that most of the children liked tests but that this was most true of students who are likely to succeed on tests (13). After accounting for this result (14) the author provided a very thorough explanation of how it could be applied in the classroom (15).

In response to the question, "Do tests make you feel afraid?" the vast majority of students reported no (16). Despite this finding, the author goes on to make recommendations to teachers regarding fear that are not really tied to the data (17). Although these seem to be very sound recommendations, they seem a bit misplaced in that the students in this study generally did not fear tests.

The responses to questions 4 and 5 were succinctly reviewed (18) and followed by a very reasonable interpretation (19). The implication of these findings was that many teachers were not clearly explaining the purpose of testing to their students (20).

The article concludes with a number of suggestions that might help teachers implement more successful testing in their classroom (21). Most of these suggestions are derived directly from the data in this study, but some are not. The discussion is the proper section of the report for being a bit more expansive and speculative, but care should be taken to not stray too far from the data. Remember that a research report is not the proper vehicle for expressing your philosophies or espousing your personal views regarding major issues in education. Although these factors will certainly influence the type of studies that you conduct, the research report should be an objective presentation of the findings and the implications and applications that they suggest.

CASE 4: SINGLE-SUBJECT RESEARCH

Are you overflowing with experimental versus post-facto? IV versus DV? Hypothesis of difference versus hypothesis of association? *t* test versus chi square? Hang in there; we have one more example of research to present. We mentioned in Chapter 4 that there are several types of research that cannot be neatly classified as experimental *or* post-facto. Although they may have some of the

features of one or the other, they don't meet all the criteria and are thus swing-
ing in the breeze looking for a branch of research to grab onto. One such
research variation is single-subject research.

It is fairly common in education for a researcher, teacher, guidance counselor, or school psychologist to want to test out a new strategy for behavior
management, or perhaps to measure the effectiveness of using reinforcement to
increase attending behavior in a certain student. Sometimes examples such as
these are best researched using only one subject as opposed to many.

Despite the fact that you have been learning that more is better when it
comes to the number of subjects to include in a research project, sometimes it is
simply more practical, and even preferable, to use a single subject. Why might
this be so? First of all, in an educational setting, the demand for research often
stems from a practical problem centered around a single pupil. Strategies for
dealing with this student need to be researched to measure their possible effectiveness. It may be impossible to find many readily available students with the
same unique problem, so it becomes much more practical to design a study
based on the single subject. Further, this single-subject approach may be preferable because studies of large groups of subjects can often obscure the effect of
the treatment on individuals. This is because by reporting averages (means) the
identity of any single case is lost in the shuffle. If half the students showed
improvement after receiving the treatment (whatever it may be) and the other
half actually worsened, the apparent effect on the group as a whole would be no
effect at all. Obviously, in a case like this these findings would be very misleading. For these reasons, single-subject research is often appropriate.

Don't get the impression, though, that single-subject research is the best
thing for research since the silicon chip. For one thing, this type of research has
been around much longer than silicon chips and it does have its disadvantages.
Depending on the particular type of research design used in the single-subject
study, threats to internal validity (history, instrument decay) may make it difficult to explain the findings unequivocally. Furthermore, these studies are extremely limited regarding external validity. Can we generalize from this one
subject to other similar subjects in the population who were not tested by the
research? Obviously this is a major problem, but when studies of this type are
replicated and the findings tend to be consistent with earlier studies, our confidence in the generalizability of the research is greatly enhanced.

Before we go any further, perhaps we should briefly review what we mean
by single-subject research, beyond the obvious fact that there is only one subject
involved (see Chapter 4). We mustn't confuse single-subject research with case
studies, which also tend to have only one subject. In the case study, an in-depth
description of the subject being scrutinized is provided. Single-subject research
is much more like an experiment, in that the researcher compares the behavior
in question when the IV is present to that same behavior when the IV is not
present. In this way the single subject serves as his or her own control, in much
the same way that a group of subjects serves as its own control in a repeated-
measures, within-subjects design.

A Research Example (Reprinted Journal Article)

What follows is an interesting example of single-subject research designed to measure the effect of using a computer to aid a learning-disabled student in acquiring multiplication facts.

The Effects of Computer Use on the Acquisition of Multiplication Facts by a Student with Learning Disabilities

RICHARD HOWELL

ELIZABETH SIDORENKO

JAMES JURICA

Two investigations of a single student having a specific mathematics disability were conducted in order to determine the effectiveness of software use alone, or in combination with teacher intervention, on the acquisition of multiplication facts. The types of software were drill-and-practice and tutorial based, with the drill program being used as the sole intervention in the first study and the tutorial program being used in conjunction with teacher intervention during the second study. The teacher intervention involved (1) determination of the student's present problem solution strategy, (2) the teaching of an alternative solution strategy called "The Rule of Nines," and (3) the presentation and use of computer software with the student. Results indicated an initial increase in correct responding and a corresponding decrease in the amount of time to respond for both drill-and-practice and tutorial software, but this effect proved to be transitory with both errors and times increasing when the student was returned to baseline conditions. However, when the software use was combined with directed teacher interventions, the student was able to unlearn the ineffective strategy, learn a new solution strategy, and use the software to practice and incorporate new knowledge and skills. The discussion focuses on implications for developing instructional environments as well as implications for future research.

Although there are a number of articles concerning the use of microcomputers with special populations, there is relatively little research being done on the effectiveness or impact of such use (Blashke, 1982; Hoffmeister, 1982). This is especially true in relation to students who are diagnosed as having learning disabilities (Hasselbring & Crossland,

1

Howell, R., Sidorenko, E., & Jurica, J., The effects of computer use on the acquisition of multiplication facts by a student with learning disabilities. *Journal of Learning Disabilities 20*, pp. 336–41. Used by permission of the publisher.

1981; Shiffman, Tobin, & Buchanan, 1982). It may be that the use of computers and educational software can facilitate the remediation of specific learning problems associated with students having learning disabilities. This study was designed to investigate the effects of the use of a computer, two types of mathematical software, and teacher intervention on the acquisition of multiplication facts by a student with learning disabilities in a special educational setting.

The demand for integrating computers into special education programs for students with handicaps is presently oriented primarily to the use of computer assisted instructional (CAI) software. The primary models, or vehicles, for the delivery of instruction have been drill-and-practice programs, which still constitute approximately 60% of the high priority instructional courseware needs according to special education administrators. The other 40% of the courseware reflects an expressed need for more tutorial, or tutorial-based, programs (Blashke, 1982).

In attempting to explain a significant shift in teachers' priorities for CAI software from mathematics to language arts, Blashke (1982) has asserted that "the large numbers of math courseware packages are meeting priority special educational needs, with and without adaptation" (p. 74). Generally, programs that have been designed for special education teachers in the last 3 years have approached the need for specific adaptations by allowing teachers to exert control over two primary dimensions of the stimulus: (1) the rate of presentation of the stimulus items, and (2) the degree of difficulty of the problems presented. However, several concerns remain regarding the type and focus of the software currently being used by special educators:

1. The programs are primarily educational games incorporating drill-and-practice strategies; very few incorporate tutorial, problem-solving, or simulation strategies.
2. The focus of instruction is not upon *altering the strategies* which the special learner uses to approach the tasks in the software. Rather, it is upon the manipulation of content-related items, in terms of user access and difficulty levels.

Research on the usefulness of drill-and-practice that is specifically focused on the use of mathematical concepts with learning disabled students has shown that drill-and-practice programs do not affect students' performance if they are using a reconstructive strategy for determining a solution to an addition problem (Hasselbring, 1985). However, Hasselbring also found that (1) almost all of the students increased their rate of correct responding as a result of exposure to the drill-and-practice program and (2) few students moved from the use of reconstructive processes (a more primitive strategy) to the use of more sophisticated reproductive processes for solving mathematical computing problems.

Two studies are presented in this article, a pilot study (Study #1) involving the use of drill-and-practice software, and a continuation study (Study #2) involving the use of tutorial-based software under varying conditions of teacher intervention. Study #1 used a single subject, multiple baseline ABAB design (Cooper, 1981), while Study #2 used the same single subject with a multiple baseline withdrawal design (Tawney & Gast, 1984) in order to determine if:

1. The use of drill-and-practice software is an effective intervention strategy for a student with a specific mathematics disability involving multiplication facts.
2. The use of tutorial-based software employing a "gradual recall" method (Skinner, 1974) is an effective intervention in the acquisition of multiplication facts.
3. The combination of teacher intervention and tutorial software is an effective intervention in the acquisition of multiplication facts.

PROCEDURES

Subject

The student selected for this study was a 16-year-old male sophomore in an urban high school. He had been in special classes since entry into the public schools at the first-grade level. Tests performed by school psychologists indicated severe discrepancies between achievement and ability due to a psychological processing disorder, qualifying him for special education services in the school district. Testing showed normal hearing, vision, and motor skills, while evidencing a specific learning disability in the psychological processing of both auditory and visual information. On the Wechsler Intelligence Scale for Children-Revised (Wechsler, 1974), he obtained a Full Scale Intelligence Quotient of 112 (Verbal, 103; Performance, 120; Math Subtest Scaled Score, 8). The student was functioning at the fifth-grade level in mathematics according to the Woodcock-Johnson Battery (Woodcock & Johnson, 1984) evidencing specific difficulties in the reproduction and recall of multiplication facts. | 7

The student was tested by the resource room math teacher previous to intervention using a criterion-referenced test of multiplication skills that revealed a specific difficulty in the student's ability to work with factors from 6 to 9. The student was also questioned during this testing as to the particular type of compensating strategy that he employed to solve the problems. This discussion revealed that the student first established a reference point based on the factor 5, and then added the specified numbers to this referent until the answer was reached. However, this compensating strategy was inefficient since it broke down as problems moved further away from the base 5 starting point, requiring the student to perform successive operations and hold a sequence of numbers in memory. The student exhibited no inappropriate behaviors and was highly motivated to learn the multiplication tables, but had experienced years of failure in attempting to learn them.

Setting

The setting for the study was a resource room for learning disabled students that had a single Apple IIe microcomputer; the school also had a microcomputer laboratory with 15 Apple IIe computers with selected software for this study. Students were allowed access to the classroom microcomputer for either specified activities or upon completion of assigned tasks if the microcomputer was free at that time; laboratory access was limited to scheduled 45-minute blocks of time throughout the semester. Computers had been used in the instructional program for approximately 2 years, but they were being given more emphasis during the period in which this study took place. | 8

The mathematics instruction in the classroom primarily involved reteaching basic mathematics skills, using a combination of traditional textbook and worksheet activities and integrating some educational mathematics software. The software consisted primarily of drill-based activities with some tutorial-based software. Students in the class received both individualized and group instruction in the specific areas in which they were experiencing problems.

Design

The effectiveness of drill-and-practice programs in the acquisition of the multiplication series 7 through 9 was investigated during a pilot study (Study #1). The baseline period (A1) lasted three sessions and was followed by 3 days of intervention (B1). A return-to- | 9 baseline condition (A2) followed session 6 of the experiment with the second baseline lasting three sessions. The final intervention period (B2) lasted four sessions, for a total of 13 sessions. ⁹

After the probe indicated that the student had not maintained the gains established from the drill-and-practice program, a second study was developed with a multiple baseline withdrawal design. Study #2 integrated tutorial-based educational software and a specific teacher intervention strategy on timed and untimed tests of the same multiplication problems. In this study, the baseline period (A1) lasted four sessions, followed by 14 days of intervention (B1). A return-to-baseline condition (A2) followed session 18 with the second baseline period (A2) lasting for five sessions. The final intervention (B2) required seven sessions, for a total of 30 sessions. A probe schedule was initiated as part of an ongoing follow-up that took seven samples of the behavior over a 1-month period. ¹⁰

Method

Study #1. The experimental procedure in Study #1 involved a commercial drill-and-practice mathematics program called "Galaxy Math" (Random House, Inc., 1984). Basically, this package allows the student to play an educational game in which the student races against time to answer randomly generated multiplication problems. ¹²

The number of errors per 20 multiplication problems and the average amount of time to complete the problems were recorded during each observational session. Data points thus represent an average of both errors and the time required for each testing session. The baseline data were gathered from a random sample of 20 multiplication problems presented to the student using pencil and paper. The intervention data were gathered by observing and recording the student's performance as he answered 20 randomly generated multiplication problems on the computer. ¹³

Study #2. The experimental intervention in Study #2 employed a tutorial-based software package called "MemorEase" (Mind Nautilus Software, 1985). This program is designed to stimulate the memorization of information by using "gradual recall" techniques derived from operant theory (Skinner, 1974). In this environment, the student is presented with a stimulus item (a complete multiplication problem) and asked to either say it aloud or to himself; the student is then allowed to vary the number of stimulus elements ("fading") visible at any one time on the screen. Although the student is in control of the number of "fades" that occur, the type, number, and difficulty of problems are under the control of the teacher, who designs the total stimulus package. The student was presented with 20 multiplication problems dealing with the six-to-nine times tables. Once the student accessed the package, he was allowed to work at his own pace as he progressed through the 20 problems. ¹⁴

The second condition of this study involved teacher intervention, during which the student was taught an alternative strategy, called "The Rule of Nines," and used the original drill-and-practice software as a reinforcement and maintenance for any gains made. The Rule of Nines is an algorithmic approach to problem solution in multiplication in which the product of nine with any single digit number (n) is such that the tens digit is one less than (n) and the sum of the digits is nine. An example would be the problem: $n \times 9 = \_$, if (n) is equal to 6, then the tens digit will be one less than 6, or 5. The sum of the digits for the product of $6 \times 9 = 54$, is $5 + 4 = 9$. This algorithm was first taught to the student, and then he was reinforced for demonstrating the use of it to solve problems. ¹⁵

The number of errors per 20 multiplication problems under timed and untimed conditions was recorded during each baseline and intervention session. Data points thus ¹⁶

represent the number of errors for timed and untimed testing for each session. For 16
baseline data, a random sample of 24 multiplication problems from the six-to-nine times 17
tables was presented to the student with pencil and paper. The intervention data were
gathered by observing and recording the student's performance as he answered 20
randomly generated multiplication problems on the computer for the drill-and-practice 16
software and written answers for the tutorial-based software.

The student was exposed to each of the conditions successively and, upon stabilization (a minimum of three trials of criterion responding, Tawney & Gast, 1984), was returned to a baseline condition for at least three sessions. The return-to-baseline condition consisted of no computer intervention and evaluation of daily performance through a standard set of 24 multiplication problems involving the six, seven, eight, and nine 17
times tables.

RESULTS

Study #1

Figure 1 displays the number of errors across the sessions. In the first baseline conditions, errors increased from zero during session 1 to four errors during session 3. The drill-and-practice software was introduced to the student during the first intervention period. The subject used the software for about 20 minutes per session, and errors 18 decreased to one by session 6. After the baseline condition was reintroduced, the error rate climbed to three errors per 20 problems by session 9. The second intervention period started with an increase in errors, but the subject's errors decreased from three during session 10 to 0 during session 11. The error rate then began to climb from one during session 12 to two during the final session.

Figure 2 illustrates the average amount of time the subject required to answer each of the 20 problems. The student's time went from a low of 14.6 seconds to a high of 26.9 19 seconds during the first baseline period. The first intervention period started on session 4

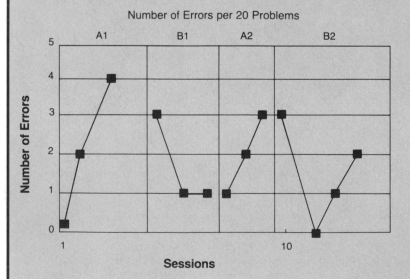

Number of Errors per 20 Problems

Figure 1. Number of errors per 20 problems.

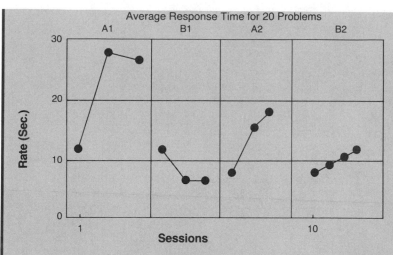

Figure 2. Average response time for 20 problems.

and the student's times for the intervention were 10.1, 6.6, and 6.1 seconds. The average time in the second baseline went from a low of 7.2 seconds during session 7, to a high of 17 during session 9. The subject's response time increased during the first four sessions of the second intervention. The subject's time increased from 7.3 seconds in session 10 to 10.3 seconds during this last session.

Study #2

Figure 3 illustrates the results of the second study on the timed tests, which involved (1) an initial baseline period (A1); (2) the tutorial package (B1); (3) a second baseline period (A2); (4) the teacher intervention strategy (B2); and (5) a probe schedule. After the

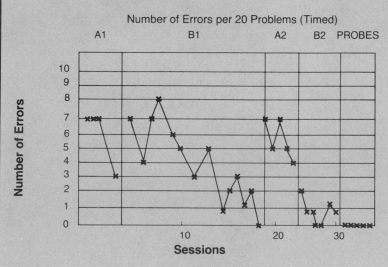

Figure 3. Number of errors per 20 problems (timed).

baseline responding stabilized (4 days) on the timed tests, the student was exposed to the tutorial software with the number of errors slowly decreasing to one error per 20 problems by the ninth intervention session. The error rate then stabilized for five sessions, at which point the second baseline period was initiated. The error rate climbed to an average of five errors per 20 problems and the teacher intervention strategy (B2) was initiated. The error rate dropped to an average of less than one error per 20 problems during this phase. The training sessions were terminated at this point and the student was tested on a probe schedule that ranged from 3 to 7 days between probes, with the student having zero errors per 20 problems throughout this follow-up period.

Figure 4 illustrates the student's responding under untimed testing conditions, when the student had as much time as he wanted for responding. Baseline responding was generally more erratic, with a median response error rate of approximately six errors per 20 problems. However, the first intervention phase with the tutorial software showed a similar pattern of responses with the timed conditions, with the error rate falling to an average of less than one error per 20 problems over the last six sessions. The second baseline period (A2), ended with a moderate increase in error rate at two per 20 problems. The teacher intervention phase (B2) showed a rapid drop in error rate to less than one error per 20 problems, which then dropped to zero errors during the probe phase, which at the time of this writing has lasted slightly over a month.

DISCUSSION

These findings indicate that contemporary drill-and-practice and tutorial software may have an initial, but transitory, effect upon the number of errors and the amount of time required to successfully complete multiplication problems. It appears that without a specific teacher intervention like the one that was introduced in the second study, which was designed to foster more adequate strategies for solving problems, any gains made during the computer interactions will not hold over time. The successful combination of directed teacher intervention and software use has been shown to be effective in reme-

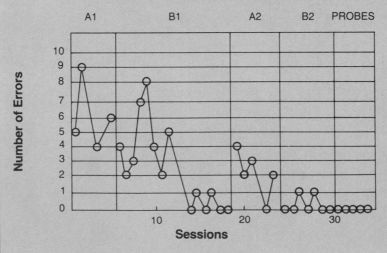

Figure 4. Number of errors per 20 problems (untimed).

diating this student's specific mathematical disability, with the student retaining both knowledge and the new strategy 1 month after the final intervention period. <u>One of the primary limitations of the pilot study was that the baseline and intervention periods were of insufficient duration and may have introduced more variation in response patterns than if 5 to 10 days had been allowed for each period.</u> In addition, it was found that the measure of rate of problems solved was not as sensitive a measure of behavioral change as having both timed and untimed tests of problem solution. This mode of testing is more realistic in that it allows the student the opportunity to respond under low-stress and high-stress situations that more closely resemble normal learning situations. |22 |23 |24

The initial gains evidenced with the drill-and-practice and tutorial software are similar <u>to Hasselbring's (1985) findings; it should be noted that these gains may have been due to novelty effects associated with the computer.</u> The importance of the findings relates to the fact that since these gains did not hold over time, use of this type of software is probably of little or no benefit to the learning disabled student without specific teacher interventions aimed at changing the strategy by which the student approaches the mathematics problem. The rapid improvement in error rate evidenced as a result of the combination of teacher intervention and software indicates that this combination may be a highly beneficial treatment for students with learning disabilities experiencing difficulties in certain areas of mathematics. In addition, the teacher reported that when she *worked with* the student at the computer, she was better able to identify the strategies the student was using to solve problems, and which strategies were missing from his repertoire. The teacher's observations made it much easier to determine the targets for remediation that were needed for the student to succeed at problem solution. |25 |26

The essential differences between the two types of mathematical software programs used in the studies appear to lie more in the functions assigned to the programs, rather than in differences intrinsic to the programs themselves. In the first study, the software was the focus of the intervention and played a primary instructional function. However, in the second study, the software was used to reinforce a previously taught strategy and played an important, but secondary, function in the instructional intervention. Intrinsic differences between the drill-and-practice software and the tutorial software were not investigated in this study, but certainly warrant future attention, since there are obvious questions regarding quality, technical and instructional integrity, and interactional variables. Whatever differences might exist between the two programs used in this study apparently did not significantly influence student performance, since the student's response patterns were similar with each program. The findings of this study indicate that the software can positively influence student performance. But software, used in isolation, is inadequate in effecting lasting achievement changes in mathematics, and must be used with directed teacher intervention in order to be effective. |27

The directions for future research appear to be twofold. A replication of this study with two students experiencing similar problems in multiplication is presently underway to verify that the approach reported in this study is viable. In addition, a new study has been initiated which will investigate the instructional efficiency of the approach by teaching the intervention strategy in a small group setting with eight learning disabled students. |28

Given the widespread use of software in classes for students with learning disabilities, it is important for teachers to recognize that simply using drill-and-practice or tutorial software may not be an optimal application of the computer, because such programs, by themselves, do not seem to evidence lasting benefits. Teachers should also note the role played by the teacher in the present study; her presence seems to have been a vital part of |29 the instructional setting—perhaps a key motivational variable in the maintenance of any gains attributed to the use of the computer and software. It may be that a strategy which combines a specific teacher intervention and selected software could become one of the more powerful remediation tools available to special education at this time.

29

ABOUT THE AUTHORS

RICHARD D. HOWELL is an assistant professor of instructional design and technology at The Ohio State University. He received his PhD in special education from the University of New Mexico.

ELIZABETH SIDORENKO is a special education teacher in a classroom for students with learning disabilities for the Columbus City Schools, Columbus, Ohio, and master's degree candidate in instructional design and technology at The Ohio State University.

JAMES JURICA is a special education teacher for students with learning disabilities in Austin, Texas, and a doctoral student in special education at The Ohio State University. Address: Dr. Richard Howell, The Ohio State University, 225 Ramseyer, 29 W. Woodruff, Columbus, OH 43210.

REFERENCES

Blashke, C. L. (1982, May/June). Microcomputer applications in special education. *Counterpoint*, p. 20.

Cooper, J. (1981). *Measuring behavior* (2nd ed.). Columbus, OH: Charles E. Merrill.

Hasselbring, T. (1985, June). A chronometric analysis of the effects of computer-based drill and practice in addition and subtraction. Paper presented at the First Invitational Research Symposium on Special Education Technology, Washington, DC.

Hasselbring, T. S., & Crossland, C. L. (1981, April). Using microcomputers for diagnosing spelling problems in learning-handicapped children. *Educational Technology, 21(4)*, 37–39.

Hoffmeister, A. M. (1982). Microcomputers in perspective. *Exceptional Children, 49(2)*, 106–113.

Mind Nautilus Software. (1985). *MemorEase* [Computer program]. Pleasanton, CA: Author.

Random House, Inc. (1984). *Galaxy math* [Computer program]. New York: Author.

Shiffman, G., Tobin, D., & Buchanan, B. (1982). Microcomputer instruction for the learning disabled. *Journal of Learning Disabilities, 15*, 557–559.

Skinner, B. F. (1974). *About behaviorism*. New York: Vintage Books.

Tawney, J. W., & Gast, D. L. (1984). *Single subject research in special education*. Columbus, OH: Bell & Howell.

Wechsler, D. (1974). *Wechsler intelligence scale for children-Revised*. New York: Psychological Corp.

Woodcock, R. W., & Johnson, M. B. (1984). *Woodcock-Johnson psychoeducational battery*. Allen, TX: DLM Teaching Resources.

Research Keys

Sample
One subject—16-year-old, learning-disabled male

Independent Variables
Study 1
1. drill-and-practice software strategy

Study 2
1. tutorial-based software strategy
2. teacher intervention

Dependent Variables
Study 1
1. number of errors per 20 multiplication problems
2. average amount of time (seconds) to complete multiplication problems
Study 2
1. number of errors per 20 multiplication problems when timed
2. number of errors per 20 multiplication problems when untimed

Controlled Variables (Constants)
Learning material consisted of multiplication problems from the six-to-nine times tables

Research Method
Single-subject

Design
ABAB

Hypothesis
Differences between performance when IV is present versus when IV is not present

Type of Data
Interval-ratio

Major Statistical Analysis
None used

Case Comments

The microcomputer is touching so many aspects of our lives today that it certainly is of no surprise that it has found its way into our classrooms as well. Although the potential educational uses of the computer are numerous, we must proceed somewhat cautiously by carefully measuring the effectiveness of these uses. Software manufacturers may spend a lot of money writing the programs, but many educators feel that too little is spent evaluating them before they are sold (Cozby, 1984).

In the article that you have just read, Howell, Sidorenko, and Jurica (1987) address this problem, especially as it relates to the learning-disabled student (1). Following their statement of the problem, the authors provided a very brief overview of the purpose of the study (2), which was to measure the impact of two computer software packages, and the intervention of the teacher, on the acquisition of multiplication facts by a student with learning disabilities. To put their study into perspective, Howell et al. presented a general description of the current software packages being used for computer-assisted instruction (CAI) with special needs students (3), and they outlined the problems that still remain regarding the type and focus of this software as it is being used in special education (4).

The authors discussed one example of prior research that was particularly relevant to their study (5). In reading this paragraph you may have experienced some confusion (as we did) over an apparent contradiction. Howell et al. reported that research "has shown that drill-and-practice programs do not affect students' performance if they are using a reconstructive strategy" and later indicated that the same study (Hasselbring, 1985) found that "almost all of the students increased their rate of correct responding as a result of exposure to the drill-and-practice program." This apparent contradiction was cleared up by a telephone call to the author, who indicated that, indeed, something that would have clarified the matter had been inadvertently left out by the journal publisher. The second statement should have been prefaced by mentioning that students who used a *reproductive* process (a more sophisticated means of solving math problems), as opposed to a *reconstructive* process, increased their rate of correct responses. You see, you should question what you read if it doesn't make sense to you. The printed word is not necessarily sacred.

The introduction was concluded with a more specific outline of what was done in the study and why (6). They wanted to determine if a drill-and-practice software package, a tutorial-based package, and the combination of teacher intervention and tutorial-based software effectively improved a learning-disabled student's acquisition of multiplication facts.

Method

You may have noticed that the headings used in this section differ somewhat from those conventionally used in an APA-style report. Rather than having "Procedures" as the major heading, "Method" would be the major heading in an APA report (check with your instructor regarding his or her desire for a strict adherence to APA guidelines). The other subheadings (subject, setting, design, and so on) are compatible with APA recommendations and are especially useful in a research report such as this, which actually consists of two studies. The various sections are clearly partitioned, which aids the organization and understanding of the proceedings.

The authors began the method section with a very thorough description of the one subject used in this study (7). This description is more detailed than it would be in a large-N study because of the issue of *generalizability*. We've mentioned that single-subject research is weak in terms of being able to generalize the findings from the one subject to some larger population of interest. For this reason it is very helpful to have a detailed description of the one subject. This detail allows the reader to determine if the findings of the study might be applicable to other students who resemble the research subject in terms of pertinent characteristics. Without a sufficient description of the subject, such comparisons to other students would be impossible.

In describing the setting for this study (8), Howell et al. provided the context in which the student had been functioning in regard to his math instruction prior to the research project. This information, along with the description of the subject, is valuable to other teachers who might want to apply these research findings to a student or students in their own classroom. It is also helpful to the researcher who may want to attempt to replicate the study.

Before we get too carried away with this issue of redoing (replicating) the study, let's take a closer look at our "research keys" to see what was done. It is fairly easy to identify the basic type of research conducted here, since only one subject was used. We need only to decide between the case-study approach and single-subject research. Since an IV was present at certain times and removed at other times, *and this was determined by the researcher* (12, 14, 15), this was single-subject research rather than a case study, which would have simply provided a detailed description of the student.

Two variations of a single research design were used in the two studies presented in this report. In the first (pilot) study, the *ABAB design* was used (9). The conditions of the study consisted of the following:

A   baseline testing of multiplication facts
B   intervention with drill-and-practice software
A   baseline testing of multiplication facts
B   intervention with drill-and-practice software

Note that the two intervention conditions (B) consisted of exactly the same treatment (use of drill-and-practice software).

In the second study, a modification of the ABAB design was used (11). The ABAB sequence consisted of

A   baseline testing of multiplication facts
B   intervention with tutorial-based software
A   baseline testing of multiplication facts
B   intervention with tutorial-based software *and* teacher intervention

Here, the intervention conditions (B) consisted of *different* treatments, in that the second intervention included input from the teacher, in addition to the tutorial software. In both study 1 and study 2, the final interventions were followed by "probe schedules" (10) that tested the student periodically as a follow-up to determine if the improvement with multiplication facts was maintained.

Although the authors referred to these designs as multiple-baseline designs (6) this term is more commonly reserved for single-subject designs in which baseline rates are measured for several behaviors and then an intervention is successively introduced for each behavior while continuing to measure the other behaviors (see Chapter 4). This design is advantageous when it isn't feasible or ethical to withdraw (reverse) the treatment once it has been introduced. In this study the treatment was withdrawn during the second baseline phase.

The descriptions of the interventions and the DVs used to measure their impact were presented separately for each study in order to facilitate organization. In study 1, the intervention (IV) consisted of allowing the student to interact with a commercially available drill-and-practice software package dealing with multiplication problems (12). The effectiveness of this approach was assessed with two dependent variables. The first consisted of the number of errors made per twenty multiplication problems, and the second was the average time it took to complete the twenty problems during each session (13).

In study 2, two different interventions were employed. The software package used in this study was tutorial based (14) rather than drill and practice. The second intervention combined this tutorial software with input from the teacher regarding an alternate strategy for solving multiplication problems (15). The DVs for study 2 were the number of errors made per twenty multiplication problems when being timed and also when untimed (16). One point of confusion arose in this article regarding the number of multiplication problems that were done during the baseline sessions. In the description of the method for study 2, it was reported that there were *twenty-four* problems (17), yet in the figures depicting the results (Figure 3 and Figure 4) and in the description of the results (21), reference was made to "errors per *twenty* problems." This has no great impact on the significance of the study, but it is somewhat confusing.

Results

The results of this research are very straightforward and readily open to analysis. The hypothesis dealt with differences between the student's performance when the IV(s) were present as compared with when they were absent (baseline). The data (number of errors, time) were of the interval-ratio variety. Although we have all the information that we would need to determine the appropriate statistical test, no statistical analysis was performed. As is often the case with single-subject research, the data are simply presented in graphic form and a visual analysis is performed. To determine if "eyeballing" the data is sufficient, we need to focus on the baseline scores. If the baseline scores are stable, with limited variability, complex statistics probably won't add much to the analysis, but when these conditions aren't met, statistics should be used in addition to visual analysis (Christensen, 1988).

If the authors had chosen to analyze their data statistically, four repeated-measures (within-subjects) analyses of variance would have been carried out, one for each of the DVs (errors per twenty problems and average response time in study 1, and errors per twenty problems when timed and untimed in study 2). Both studies involved interval-ratio data, the hypothesis of difference, correlated selection (scores from the same subject), and four sets of scores (baseline, intervention, baseline, intervention). If statistically significant differences emerged, post-hoc tests such as the Tukey HSD or the Newman-Keuls would have been appropriate to determine exactly which sets of scores differed from the others.

Since no statistical analyses were performed on the data collected in this study, the presentation of the results simply consisted of graphs and a description of each graph that was used to depict the findings from each of the DVs. In study 1, the number of errors committed by the student per twenty math problems seemed to decrease when the interventions were introduced, but the trends were not stable (18). A similar pattern emerged for the average amount of time that it took the student to complete the problems in Study 1 (19).

For study 2, Figures 3 and 4 depicted the number of errors per twenty problems when the student was timed and when he was untimed, respectively. The results of the timed condition (20) were quite similar to those in the untimed condition (21) in that, during the second intervention B2, the number of errors being committed was minimal and quite stable.

Discussion

After describing the data presented in the four figures, the authors began the discussion section with a basic overview of the findings (22). They pointed out that the initial gains observed after the use of the two types of software seemed to dissipate unless they were enhanced by the teacher's intervention, as shown in the second phase of study 2.

Howell and the other authors provided a convincing explanation of why study 1, the pilot study, did not produce more useful information (23). In single-subject research such as this, the observation periods (baseline and intervention) need to be sufficiently long to allow some stability of the responses being observed. As the authors themselves note, the number of sessions (only three) was not sufficient for establishing a consistent pattern. In addition, the authors wisely observed that the DV of average response time was not as sensitive and applicable to real learning situations as it might be, so they used an improved measure for study 2 (24).

To place their study in the context of earlier literature, the authors pointed out how some of their findings were consistent with a similar study (25). They went on, however, to indicate why the combination of computer software and the intervention of the teacher was superior to the use of the software alone (26). They further explained the impact of the two types of software by highlighting the different ways in which they were used in the two studies (27).

Of special interest to other researchers (and students like yourselves) is the authors' suggestions for future research (28). This is a very useful section of the discussion in that it often spawns ideas for one's own research and provides a glimpse into the future of the field.

The article is concluded by presenting the implications that this study holds for special-education teachers (29). There is often the tendency in special education (and in other fields, as well) to enthusiastically embrace a new technology or intervention that shows promise in improving effective learning with special-needs children. This study by Howell, Sidorenko, and Jurica reinforces the need to evaluate new technologies objectively and to develop a means for successfully incorporating them into existing curricula. They feel that computer software and specific teacher intervention could prove to be a very powerful combination for remediating some of the deficiencies of special-education children.

SUMMARY

In this, the second of the "case studies" chapters, an illustration of post-facto research, and from the "other" category, an example of single-subject research, were scrutinized. The post-facto study done by Gleadow was designed to measure young school children's perceptions of testing in school. Children of varying ability levels and gender were compared. Both IVs here were subject IVs—not ones that could be manipulated by the researcher. Although post-facto research may test either the hypothesis of difference or that of association, in this case Gleadow was looking for a difference between ability levels and between the sexes. Within this study there were presentations of stratified sampling in action, the value of open-ended questions, and the importance of obtaining interrater reliability.

The second study presented in this chapter showcased single-subject research as carried out by Howell, Sidorenko, and Jurica. They tested the effectiveness of using a microcomputer to teach multiplication facts to one learning disabled student. A critical issue with research of this type is the ability (or lack of ability) to generalize the findings to other students. In addition to exploring this issue the chapter also included a firsthand look at two research designs that are relatively unique to single-subject and small-N research, namely, the ABAB design and the multiple-baseline design.

KEY TERMS

ABAB design

Generalizability

Interrater reliability

Open-ended question

Stratified sampling

REFERENCES

BELZ, H. F., & GEARY, D. C. (1984). Father's occupation and social background: Relation to SAT scores. *American Educational Research Journal, 21,* 473–478.

CHPISTENSEN, L. B. (1988). *Experimental methodology* (4th ed.). Newton, Mass.: Allyn & Bacon.

COZBY, P. C. (1984). *Using computers in the behavioral sciences.* Palo Alto, Calif.: Mayfield.

GLEADOW, N. E. (1982). What do primary school children think about testing? *The Elementary School Journal, 83,* 35–39.

HOWELL, R. D., SIDORENKO, E., & JURICA, J. (1987). The effects of computer use on the acquisition of multiplication facts by a student with learning disabilities. *Journal of Learning Disabilities, 20,* 336–341.

CHAPTER

Computers, Educational Research, and the 1990s

EDUCATIONAL APPLICATIONS OF COMPUTERS

Data Analysis
Common Procedures
SPSS
Minitab
SAS
Literature Searches
Word Processing
Presentation of Experimental Stimuli
Computer-Assisted Instruction
Simulations
Programming
Some Concerns

A LOOK INTO THE 1990s

Computer Statistical Packages and Research Design
Meta-analysis

CAUSAL MODELING: THE DEBATE OF THE 1990s

Correlation and Causation
The New Look

PATH ANALYSIS

The Critics Speak
A Fallacy Revisited

WHERE DO WE GO FROM HERE?

Computer Overkill
KISS

SUMMARY

KEY TERMS

REFERENCES

During the 1980s we witnessed the dramatic intrusion of computers into our daily lives. It is becoming increasingly difficult to have a casual conversation with a group of people without someone asking how many "K" you have or whether your disk is floppy or hard. It is certainly safe to predict that computers will continue to influence our existence into the 1990s, undoubtedly with increasing force. Surely, the field of education, and more specifically, educational research, will continue to be affected by this technology.

EDUCATIONAL APPLICATIONS OF COMPUTERS

The applications of the computer in education and educational research are numerous. The greatest impact in the research area has centered around the statistical analysis of the data that have been collected. Large and complex data sets can now be analyzed with truly amazing speed and ease, whereas in the past, because of the overwhelming task of managing and synthesizing so much information, studies of equal magnitude would not even have been attempted. In the field of education, computers have also been used (1) to search extensive bodies of research literature, (2) as word processors and writing analyzers to aid in the teaching of writing, (3) for the controlled presentation of auditory and visual stimuli in experiments, (4) for computer-assisted instruction, (5) for creating simulations of real-life and laboratory situations, and (6) for teaching students to program computers. In this chapter, each of these educational applications of the computer will be discussed, and then we will look into the future of educational research.

Data Analysis

The great bulk of the data collected in educational research is now routinely analyzed using the power of computers. Although computers (and the software packages that drive them) are extremely efficient for "crunching numbers," they are, of course, limited by the accuracy of the data and processing instructions entered into them by the operator. As the operator, you have to determine which numbers to enter, and you have to "tell" the computer which statistical procedures to perform. That's where the knowledge that you've acquired throughout this book should serve you well. The best-executed statistical analysis performed by a computer is useless if it is not appropriate to the research methodology being carried out. As we and others have stated repeatedly, watch out for "GIGO," which translates as "garbage in, garbage out." The information retrieved by the computer is helpful only if the information entered into it is meaningful.

There are several commercially available software packages used to perform statistical analyses with computers. The most widely used packages in education are the *Statistical Package for the Social Sciences (SPSS)* (Klecka, Nie, & Hull, 1975), *Minitab* (Ryan, Joiner, & Ryan, 1976), and the *Statistical Analysis System (SAS)* (SAS Institute, Inc., 1982). In all likelihood, one or more of these software packages is readily available to you on your campus.

The software packages described in this chapter are similar to all software packages in that they have to be called into service to be used by your computer. Specific instructions have to be followed with extreme care to use the software on a particular computer system. The details involved in your computing system will be available from the software manual, or perhaps from the staff at your computer center. Once you've entered the software package, you must enter specific commands to instruct the computer as to which statistical analyses to perform on your particular data set. Part of this process will include procedures for properly entering the data to be analyzed.

Information fed into a computer is usually organized according to columns. Consider a sheet of paper with data on it that is divided vertically into columns with only one piece of information or one digit in each column. This is how most computer data files are organized. Typically, if several pieces of information (for example, sex, age, grade in school, or reading achievement scores) are to be entered for each subject in a study, the information would be placed in a common column(s) for every subject. That is, sex may be designated in column 1, age in columns 2 and 3 (remember, one digit per column), grade in columns 4 and 5, and reading achievement scores in columns 6 and 7. This pattern would be repeated for every subject by starting a new row (horizontally) after the previous subject's data has been entered.

Common Procedures

The statistical packages described in this chapter are alike in that the most commonly used data-handling and statistical procedures are included with each package. They do differ, however, in terms of extra features and in terms of the commands used to call these procedures into play. SPSS, Minitab, and SAS all calculate descriptive statistics on the data of your choice, such as the mean, standard deviation, and the minimum and maximum values for a particular variable. Each also provides a procedure for establishing cross-tabulations, which show frequencies as a function of any two variables. See Table 11.1 for an example of the type of information that can be obtained from a cross-tabulation procedure. The numbers in the cells (intersections of the rows and columns) represent the frequencies with which the phenomenon in question occurred. For instance, the numbers in the cells in Table 11.1 represent the number of students retained in their grade in a given school district as a function of gender and grade in school.

The statistical packages discussed here also include correlation coefficients, such as the Pearson product-moment correlation coefficient (r) as well as various statistical significance tests, such as the t test, the one-way ANOVA, the factorial ANOVA, or the chi square. SPSS, Minitab, and SAS also share certain data-handling features. Once the data file has been established, these programs can create new variables by combining two or more existing variables (by adding, subtracting, and so on) or by transforming existing variables (for example, taking the square root) into new values. These statistical packages also have the capacity to perform analyses on selected subjects in the data file, rather than always looking at the entire file. For instance, the program could select only subjects designated as female on the gender variable and analyze these data separately from all the rest.

Finally, the values of selected variables can be recoded to reflect the needs of the researcher. For example, consider a study designed to measure the effectiveness of two new methods for teaching phonics as compared with a traditional approach. Comparing the three approaches (the traditional one and the two new ones) may have yielded nonsignificant findings. In a case like this the researcher may now want to compare the two new approaches (in combination) with the traditional method. To do this, he or she might recode the value for one of the new approaches (let's say it had a designation of 3) so that it now had the

Table 11.1 Cross-tabulation of Retention in Grade by Gender and Grade Level

	MALE	FEMALE	
1st Grade	32	25	57
6th Grade	18	12	30
	50	37	

same designation as the other new approach (say, 2). In this way, subsequent analyses would deal with the subjects who received either of the new approaches as if they had been one large group.

SPSS

The Statistical Package for the Social Sciences (SPSS) is widely used for statistical analyses, not only by educators but by psychologists, sociologists, and economists. It is currently available in a number of different formats. SPSSx is the new, enhanced and more user-friendly version of the original SPSS system and is used on a mainframe or minicomputer system. SPSS/PC+ performs the same basic procedures as SPSSx (and in general does this in the same fashion), but it is designed for use with personal computers. In addition, there is a student version of SPSS/PC+, called SPSS/PC+ Studentware, that is limited to analyzing a maximum of twenty variables and contains fewer statistical commands than does the full version of SPSS/PC+. The manual provided for SPSSx (SPSS, Inc., 1988) is rather difficult to wade through, but the manual for both the SPSS/PC+ and the SPSS/PC+ Studentware (Norusis, 1988) is easier to use yet is quite complete. We strongly recommend the use of one of the PC versions, particularly for the relatively inexperienced user of statistical software. (The remainder of the information presented in this chapter regarding SPSS applies equally to the mainframe and PC versions.)

The use of the SPSS system requires two basic steps for performing statistical analyses. The first involves creating a data file that will contain the raw data collected from the study. As was mentioned earlier, the data in this file are basically arranged in columns. The second step involves writing SPSS instructions that contain the necessary commands for carrying out the desired statistical analysis. To execute the analysis properly, this part of the procedure requires careful attention to the operator's manual. The details of these procedures are beyond the scope of this book, but we will list the names of some of the more basic statistical analyses performed by SPSS so that you'll become somewhat familiar with its capabilities.

Basic SPSS Statistics

1. CONDESCRIPTIVE (for SPSSx): descriptive statistics (mean, standard deviation, variance, and so on) for continuous variables (DESCRIPTIVES in SPSS/PC+)
2. FREQUENCIES: frequency distribution for one or more variables (also does condescriptive functions in SPSS/PC+)
3. CROSSTABS: cross-tabulated frequency table for two or more variables (also calculates chi square)
4. PEARSON CORR (for SPSSx): Pearson correlation (CORRELATION for PC versions) between variables
5. SCATTERGRAM: graph that plots data used in a Pearson correlation
6. T-TEST: test for significant difference between the means of two groups (either independent or paired)

7. ONEWAY: one-way analysis of variance. Only appropriate with independent groups (not repeated measures)
8. ANOVA: factorial analysis of variance
9. NPAR TESTS: many nonparametric statistics, including chi square, runs test, sign test, Wilcoxon T, and Mann-Whitney U test

Minitab

Minitab was developed as a user-friendly statistical package at Penn State University by T. A. Ryan and his colleagues in 1972. It is really an easy-to-use package designed for use with both mainframe and personal computers. Minitab offers simple commands, a useful HELP command, and an interactive approach to data analysis. The interactive feature of this program is a definite asset, especially to the student with limited computer experience. This feature literally walks you through the procedures by continually asking questions that are typically fairly easy even for the beginner. This is in contrast to systems that require the user to supply all the necessary information and commands at the very outset, before the computer takes over in executing the commands. The names and functions of some of the more basic Minitab commands are as follows:

Basic Minitab Statistics

1. SUM: sum of variables
2. AVER: mean of variables
3. STAN: standard deviation of variables
4. MEDI: median of variables
5. DESC: mean, standard deviation, and number of subjects
6. CORR: Pearson r correlation between variables
7. PLOT: graph plotting two variables
8. TWOS: t test for significant difference between the means of two independent groups
9. ONEW: one-way analysis of variance. Only appropriate with independent groups (not repeated measures)
10. TWOW: factorial analysis of variance for two independent variables
11. CONT: cross-tabulated frequency table for two variables (also calculates chi square)

SAS

As with the two previously mentioned software packages, the Statistical Analysis System (SAS) is available for both mainframe and personal computers. SAS is especially strong in its treatment of data, the clarity of its graphics, and in certain business applications (Cozby, 1984). Since it is often necessary to manipulate several data sets for a given analysis, SAS may at times be somewhat more difficult to use than the other two packages, at least in terms of input procedures (Klieger, 1984). SAS is similar to SPSS and Minitab in its ability to define data, modify data, and perform statistical procedures. The various statistical procedures carried out by SAS are always preceded by the word PROC, which stands for procedure. The most commonly used SAS statistical procedures are as follows:

Basic SAS Statistics

1. PROC MEANS: descriptive statistics (mean, standard deviation, maximum and minimum values, and so on)
2. PROC CORR: Pearson *r* correlation between two or more variables
3. PROC TTEST: *t* test for significant difference between the means of two groups
4. PROC ANOVA: analysis of variance for all types of designs (one-way, two-way, and others)
5. PROC FREQ: frequency distribution for one or more variables

Literature Searches

One of the most tedious tasks facing any researcher is the painstaking search through the literature in the library to see what has already been done in a given area of interest. Many researchers may actually enjoy reading all this related literature, but few relish actually digging it out of the library. By expediting this chore, the computer has fast become one of the researcher's best friends.

As was mentioned in Chapter 8, most libraries today have computerized data bases for the various academic disciplines. For instance, your library may have a computerized system for searching the *ERIC* or other files. Although the specific instructions for the use of such a system will vary from library to library, we can provide you with an overview of what to expect.

The basic procedure requires that you provide the computer with some key terms or descriptors for your research topic. The computer then searches through its data base for these key terms in the titles of the articles listed, or in the abstracts if they happen to be included. You may then receive a printout of these references, and in some instances, even the abstract as well.

For example, if you were researching the topic of self-esteem and locus of control among learning-disabled junior-high-school students, key terms would include "self-esteem," "locus of control," "learning disability," and "junior high school." You have the option of entering as many or as few of these terms as you choose. By choosing only a few (for example, self-esteem and locus of control), you might receive a printout that includes a great many articles, so many in fact that quite a few of these will probably not turn out to be relevant to your study. However, if you demand that all your key terms be present in an article before you have it included in your printout, you may be left with a very small, yet narrowly defined, group of studies. You may have to go through some trial-and-error searches before hitting on the one that gives you the most desirable list.

Bear in mind however, that your wallet may suffer accordingly. Some libraries will charge you for the amount of computer processing time used, whereas others may charge you on the basis of how many references or abstracts you eventually receive. If you're very lucky, you might be conducting your research at a well-endowed institution that can afford to provide this service free of charge. In any event, you are likely to find the computerized literature search much more comprehensive, and certainly less time-consuming, than doing the search manually. Of course, after conducting the computerized search, you will still need to find the actual articles or documents in the library.

Word Processing

Certainly one of the most widespread uses of computers today is as sophisticated typewriters. While they definitely serve this function, the *word-processing* capabilities of computers also provide a marvelous opportunity to teach people how to write more effectively.

Word-processing programs such as Apple Writer, PC Write, and Leading Edge are primarily designed to make it easy to correct mistakes in one's writing and to produce neat and attractive final products (reports, papers, and so on). By using word-processing programs, many students improve their writing on their own. Because it is so easy to make changes, insertions, deletions, and so on, students are more likely to experiment with different ways of expressing their thoughts, and discover for themselves better writing techniques. These programs also allow students to electronically "cut-and-paste," so that they can readily move sections of their texts around to better organize their papers. Probably the most important benefit of the word processor is in its motivating influence. Many students begin to find that writing can actually be fun, and obviously if students write more their skills are bound to improve.

When conducting research in education we clearly benefit from word processing. The writing and rewriting of research reports and proposals are made much easier with word processing. Comments from colleagues, coauthors, and journal editors can readily be incorporated into an existing manuscript. People in general are just more willing to do it the "right way" if making corrections is made easier for them. Word processing with computers brings us a giant step closer to the "right way."

Presentation of Experimental Stimuli

Experimental research, in particular, often requires the controlled presentation of stimuli to the subjects. In a word-recognition study, for example, this might involve visually presenting words to second-grade students using a tachisto-scope. Or it might entail presenting auditory tones of varying intensities to subjects in a vigilance study, or even delivering behavior-contingent electric shock to a rat in a laboratory learning experiment. In these instances, and in many others, computers can be extremely helpful.

Computers can be linked to other equipment, such as a tachistoscope, a tape recorder, a shock generator, a slide projector, and then programmed to present stimuli of various types. The computer can control the intensity of the stimulus, the duration of the stimulus, the length of the intervals between stimuli, and so on. This can aid the researcher in trying to maintain those all-important controls that are so necessary for ensuring internal validity. The computer can be an invaluable aid in helping researchers to be consistent and precise in their interaction with research subjects.

Computer-Assisted Instruction

Perhaps the most widely publicized use of computers in education revolves about their use in instruction. The explosive entry of microcomputers into the classroom, and the development of hundreds of commercially available instructional software packages designed to teach everything from the alphabet to complex concepts in physics, was predicted to produce a revolution in education. In the early 1970s, some "experts" even thought that microcomputers would, at least partially, replace teachers in much the same way that computers and automation have greatly reduced personnel needs in many other industries. That hasn't happened, and it probably won't, primarily because it is the classroom teacher who must, ultimately, weave together *computer-assisted instruction (CAI)* and classroom instruction to develop higher-level concepts and more global abstractions. Nevertheless, CAI has become an important instructional alternative in many settings, and this includes computer-based instruction, computer-augmented instruction, and computerized teaching games.

The typical CAI program is interactive, and therefore consistently involves the student in the process. As students progress *at their own pace* through the program, many choices must be made and answers elected on the keyboard. Errors in responding produce a review of the material, and correct responses are consistently reinforced with messages such as "Right on, Mary!" flashed on the screen. Although some (especially earlier) programs were designed as "drill-and-practice" approaches, many good CAI packages are now available that can definitely help develop the mastery of conceptual material.

There has, of course, been a good deal of skepticism about the effectiveness of CAI. When we consider the possible effects of CAI, we usually think first about the direct effects on achievement, retention, and speed of learning. The first question, then, is whether students learn more, faster, or better. Aside from those obvious issues, however, are concerns about the possibly "dehumanizing" effects of CAI in such areas as affect, motivation, and social relationships. In the view of many educators, even if CAI results in more, better, and faster learning, if it is at the expense of these other important areas, CAI shouldn't be used at all.

As you might expect, many research studies have been done on the effects of CAI on a variety of educational outcomes (DVs), in a number of subject areas (mathematics, reading, and so on), and at virtually all levels of education (including primary, secondary, and postsecondary). The typical IV comparison is between CAI and "traditional" teaching methods, but IV comparisons between different CAI programs have also been done.

Since this is a book about research methods, we'll hold off for a moment before telling you what the research says, and point out some of the problems involved in conducting CAI research. In general, internally and externally valid research in the area of teaching is always difficult (though obviously not impossible) to do. There are several confounding factors that typically intrude, including the representativeness of the students' backgrounds in a given setting, the quality of the CAI programs used for comparison purposes, and the training and competence of the teachers whose instruction is being used as a comparison to CAI. If, for example, the CAI program is not especially well conceived or constructed, it may fail to produce superior results when compared with traditional teaching. Similarly, even a good CAI software package may fail against instruction by an unusually talented teacher. Keep in mind, in this regard, that *no* study represents a general comparison of CAI with traditional teaching. A study can only compare one or two specific CAI *programs* with instruction by one or a small number of teachers. If you apply the general statement made at the end of Chapter 4 about the difficulty of obtaining, in one study, high levels of both internal and external validity, you will probably now conclude that internally valid studies may only demonstrate the effectiveness of one CAI program compared with one teacher, an external-validity nightmare when it comes to drawing broad conclusions about the effectiveness of CAI.

Nevertheless, by examining the literature one can examine the effects of a variety of CAI programs (IVs) on a number of educational outcomes (DVs), rather than focusing on just one or even a few studies. Several large-scale studies and reviews (and meta-analyses) of the effects of CAI are currently available. For the advocates of CAI, the results of these studies and reviews have certainly been encouraging. Several literature reviews have shown CAI to be consistently effective (with only a few exceptions) at virtually every level of education. Kulik and his co-workers (1983) found, for example, that sixth through twelfth graders in CAI groups consistently scored better on measures of achievement, retention, and speed in a variety of subject areas. They concluded, in addition, that although CAI is effective for college students, it is even more effective for pupils in the sixth through twelfth grades. In addition, Bracey (1982; 1988) reported that the effects of CAI on affective and motivational, as well as social, outcomes are equally impressive. Finally, a study by ETS (Ragosta, 1983) using thousands of elementary school children further confirmed the effectiveness of CAI.

Several later reviews of the CAI literature have also had largely positive results (Bracey, 1987), but the effects have not held up for all grades, or for all students. In fact, Bracey suggests that the question of whether CAI is effective may even be the wrong question. More appropriately, the questions should be about the conditions under which CAI is effective and the characteristics of good software. Nathan (1985), for example, cites as a "myth" the idea that CAI is effective for all students at all levels.

One review (Becker, 1988)—a *best-evidence synthesis* (which is similar to a meta-analysis in that an effect size is calculated but is done separately for each study)—focused on microcomputer uses of CAI as they affect achievement, but only in research of the highest quality and only for research conducted after 1984. By so defining the review, Becker attempted to limit the analysis to only high-quality studies that relate most closely to current (time-valid) in-school conditions. His conclusion was that the evidence for the overall effectiveness of CAI as a general method was scanty. Nevertheless, as research continues, much of the evidence continues to support the use of CAI, especially at the elementary levels and for use by special-needs children.

One variation of CAI involves devising games as learning tools. This technique is mentioned here only because it represents an approach that uses reinforcement of correct responses in a way that is likely to be most interesting and, perhaps, motivating to students. Programs of this type typically use the graphics capabilities of the computer to create interesting and visually stimulating learning situations. An example might involve a computerized game designed to teach third graders the parts of speech. For instance, a sentence would be presented on the computer monitor with an arrow pointing to one of the words. Below this there would be listed several parts of speech, such as

a. noun
b. verb
c. preposition
d. adjective

The student would simply be required to press the letter on the keyboard that corresponds to what was understood to be the correct answer. The monitor would then depict a graphics display of a soccer player kicking a ball toward the goal. If the response was correct the ball would go into the net and if not, the shot, alas, would be wide of the goal. A scoreboard might even be depicted that would tally the number of "goals" for the student during a session. In this manner the student would receive immediate feedback regarding performance, and would also have some of the same fun enjoyed by playing an electronic game.

We should warn you that there are some CAI programs on the market that are simply not well conceived or constructed. Many for-profit (and, for that matter, nonprofit) corporations and publishers have marketed programs that are not effective, nor are they very interesting to the student. At the same time, many good products are available for classroom microcomputer use (most often for Apple-series and IBM/PC-type machines). Administrators and teachers who are responsible for selecting, purchasing, and using CAI materials should try to be knowledgeable about the characteristics of good—and bad—programs, and thus be able to evaluate the potential effectiveness of CAI packages for their students. Although, in general, CAI is effective for some purposes, that does not mean that *all* CAI programs are effective for all children.

Simulations

In addition to CAI, computers can be programmed to simulate real-life or laboratory circumstances and put the student through even complex problems that might be encountered in these circumstances. Such *simulations* are available for many subjects, mostly at the secondary and college levels. As an example of one simulation, we'll briefly describe the Lake Study developed by Whisnant (1983). In the Lake Study, the student in high-school chemistry (or biology) is presumed to be an ecologist working for the Fish and Wildlife Service whose task is to discover why immature bass in a hatchery are dying. The program requires some knowledge of chemistry, but not much, since the simulation provides much of the information the student will need (and in that sense, overlaps with CAI). To solve the dying-fish problem, the student can "sample" the lake water, "go to" the lab to analyze the samples, "talk" to a colleague for advice, "go to" the library for information about the problem, "check" the condition of the fish, or "check" experimental results. The samples can be analyzed for dissolved oxygen, and the presence of metals and pesticides. In about an hour, the student can go through the process and, using an accompanying worksheet, come up with a solution with respect to the cause of the problem. If the student tries to leave the program before enough information has been gathered to reach the *correct* solution, the program makes it difficult to quit, which is intended to ensure that most students will solve the problem correctly.

As with CAI packages, not all simulations are effective or, for that matter, even interesting to the student. Therefore, be reminded of the same warning about selecting simulation materials as was previously mentioned regarding CAI.

Programming

Yes, computers can even be used to teach people how to use computers. This may seem a bit like the tail wagging the dog, but it is very possible. What better way to learn about programming than by being seated in front of the computer, where you can immediately try out what is being learned.

Actually, teaching how to program a computer by using a computer is no different from using the machine to teach other skills. The basic approach is to present the material to be learned on the screen in relatively small segments and follow it up with exercises and quizzes that are executed via the monitor and keyboard. In this manner the student is getting increasingly familiar with the system, getting practice using it, and receiving immediate feedback on effectiveness. Many variations on this basic theme can be successfully introduced to teach students programming, or at the very least, to provide them with tutorial support.

Some Concerns

Although there are clearly many beneficial educational applications for the computer, there are still some valid concerns. The major consideration focuses on the available software. Although large amounts of educational software have been produced, the quality of all these products cannot be taken for granted. Programs often don't do what they claim, and many even contain critical errors that then become immediate "turn-offs" to struggling students. Finally, in some cases the necessary documentation is totally missing, or so limited as to be virtually useless (Cozby, 1984). Although this situation is admittedly getting better, it needs to be continually improved.

Another concern centers around training teachers to properly utilize the computers for the benefit of their students. As anyone knows who has ever been seated in front of a computer, there are times that no matter what you try, it seems that the gremlins inside the machine won't cooperate with you. It is times like these that you need to turn to an expert. Students are certainly subject to the same frustrations as the rest of us (if not more so), and they too need to be able to turn to someone for help: the teacher. Since teachers are usually perceived as having all the other answers, why not this one as well? Unfortunately, new computer systems or software are often purchased for a school without budgeting the time or money for adequately training the teachers in the critical area of usage. Thus, the new programs become underutilized. Furthermore, courses in "computer literacy" are often worth very little to most students. Such introductory courses often cover little more than programming in BASIC (a fairly simple computer language). That may be useful for those who will become programmers, but these courses sometimes forget to contain information about how to turn the machine on, how to put the floppy disk in the drive, or even how to access existing programs. What teachers need to know are the basics, not BASIC. As computer expertise becomes woven into education, and especially teacher-education programs, this problem will diminish (Ellis, 1986). Until that time, however, many students are left looking for the "expert."

A LOOK INTO THE 1990s

The future of educational research methodology is, in several ways, likely to continue much as it has developed since the late 1960s, 1970s, and 1980s. We have already referred to the impact of microcomputers on education in general, and on research in particular. We believe that methodological developments (and the discussion about their use) will almost certainly revolve around three major areas, of which two involve the use of microcomputers. The first issue, mentioned earlier in this chapter, stresses the broad availability of relatively inexpensive computer packages that are now capable of doing highly complex statistical analyses rarely found in the literature of even the 1960s. The second issue is in the area of the review of research literature, and in particular, meta-analysis, or the statistical integration of diverse research findings. The final issue focuses on the currently raging debate about correlation and causation, or what is sometimes called causal modeling. This debate is related to the first issue, in that the availability of computer statistical packages has suddenly made causal modeling far more accessible than was the case just a few short years ago.

Computer Statistical Packages and Research Design

As we've seen, most colleges and universities, and even many businesses, have access to statistical packages that will perform procedures virtually unavailable only a generation ago. Why is that important to educational researchers (or to researchers in any of the behavioral sciences, for that matter)? The primary reason is that complex factorial designs (using more than one IV), and especially those using a number of DVs or repeated measures of one or more DVs during the course of an experiment, can now be conducted and analyzed as a matter of routine. As was stated before, the frequency of the usage of such techniques as ANCOVA, MANOVA, MANCOVA, and other multivariate approaches to data analysis has increased dramatically. This has greatly expanded the researchers' ability to properly analyze the results of even the most complex designs, which is certainly to researchers' advantage. Knowledge about what works in education is, therefore, increasing at a pace never envisioned in the past. Surely, this is a desirable situation, but a major problem is also inherent in these powerful and seemingly useful techniques.

As an example of a design that would have been difficult to correctly (or inexpensively and conveniently) analyze earlier, consider a research project aimed at examining the effects of a study-skills course. The research might now be conducted at a single high school and at low cost. The design might call for two randomly divided groups of freshman science students. At the beginning of the school year, achievement measures are obtained for the students, and several measures of study effectiveness, note-taking skills and early achievement in freshman science are also gathered. One of the two groups is then given the study-skills instruction during the first semester, and at the end of that semester, achievement and other variables are measured for a second time. The second group is given the study-skills instruction during the second semester, and all the DVs are again measured at the end of the school year. Presumably, the students who received the instruction during the first semester will have higher DV levels than those who did not, but at the end of the second semester those who had the study-skills program during the second semester should have caught up to the first group.

In a study similar to this (Bates, Ahlquist, O'Connor, & Sirois, 1988), the students in the first-semester instruction group gained in a variety of measures by the end of the first semester and, for the most part, held these gains right through to the end of the second semester. The second semester instructional group, however, gained little between the beginning and the end of the second semester. We would certainly not imply that such research could not have been done a generation ago, but we would argue that proper analysis of research using, as in this case, a number of DVs, each measured several times, would have been expensive, time-consuming, and difficult to obtain.

So, what's the problem? The ability to examine complex designs should be a welcome result of the advent of the microcomputer, and it really is. But one must not forget about GIGO—garbage in, garbage out. Fancy statistics are not a substitute for a good, solid, unconfounded, internally valid design. There is a clear and present danger that researchers who are careless regarding the limitations of statistical analyses will come to unwarranted conclusions. This is especially true of the researcher who uses a blizzard of computer output from complex statistical procedures that may, to compound the felony, have been drawn from poorly conducted or poorly designed research.

Placing a computer on a desk does not make a statistician out of the person who happens to be sitting in front of it. Even the person familiar with basic statistics might have difficulty interpreting a MANOVA output. Bray and Maxwell (1982), for example, make the important point that there are a number of different approaches to the analysis of data using MANOVA. They go on to say that there is little consensus about the "proper" way to analyze multivariate data with MANOVA, but rather, that there are "better" as well as "not-so-good" ones. Those unfamiliar with the technicalities of complex procedures will often fail to use or interpret their studies correctly.

Throughout this book, the stress has constantly been on issues of design because that is, as they say, where it's at. That is why the first steps in looking at each of the simulations in Chapter 7 have to do with the examination of the methodology, or the most important basics: the IV(s), the DV(s), and the design. Conclusions about the value or worth of a research project should be based primarily on an examination of methodology and the procedures used, not on any dazzling array of statistical results. This is not to say that statistical procedures can be ignored. Proper analysis is important, but design and proper procedure speak most directly to the twin issues of the internal and external validity of research.

Meta-analysis

In Chapter 4 meta-analysis was discussed as it related to experimental reliability and the ability to generalize results from a number of research studies. It was indicated, without elaboration, that the statistical integration of research findings was not without its critics. The process of meta-analysis is relatively new, its name not having been coined until 1976 (Glass, 1976). In fact, the methods now used were virtually unknown before the 1970s.

A quick review is in order before briefly describing the issues regarding meta-analysis. Most earlier, and even many current, reviews do indeed suffer from a variety of problems. These involve biases on the part of the reviewer, inappropriate selection of the studies to be reviewed, "cognitive overload" on the part of the reviewer of too many studies, and other problems (see, for example, Jackson, 1978). Although there are a number of approaches that could be called meta-analytic, the basic method involves the calculation of an effect size, or in other words, an indicator of the strength of the IV in producing DV changes. The effect size statistic, often symbolized as d, is essentially equivalent to the Z or standard score on a normal distribution curve. Thus, a d of $+1$ would indicate that the average experimental group's performance for any given IV is one standard deviation above the average for the control group, which is, incidentally, a tremendous gain! This d of $+1$ would place the experimental group's performance at the eighty-fourth percentile, compared with the average control group performance at only the fiftieth percentile. Don't hold your breath waiting to see an effect size of $+1$, since most are considerably smaller than that.

The majority, perhaps even the vast majority, of researchers generally agree that well-done meta-analytic studies are useful, at least for most areas of research. In that sense, there isn't a lot of debate about the overall use of meta-analysis, but there is a good deal of discussion about how the process should be carried out. Some of the arguments are extremely technical in nature, suggesting, for example, that there is an inadequate basis in statistical theory for the accumulation of "averages" across studies or for understanding variation in such statistics. There are, furthermore, disagreements about which test statistic is most appropriate for determining statistical significance across such a large number of studies.

Another discussion revolves around comparing different DVs in the same study. How, ask these critics, can one possibly compare the effects of CAI on reading, mathematics, science, and other subject achievement, all in the same set of comparisons? This, they say, is just like comparing apples and oranges, and they therefore question the validity of the conclusions on that basis alone. It should be pointed out that if this is a legitimate argument, it is one that applies to traditional reviews, as well. And, if correct, it tends to limit *all* reviews, and, therefore, the whole concept of generalizing IV effects across studies.

Again, most of this discussion revolves not around whether meta-analysis is useful but, instead, around *how* the analysis should be done. Should, for example, *all* the studies in an area be used in the analysis, regardless of the quality of the research, or should some poorly conducted research be thrown out? There are arguments that go both ways. Kulik and his co-workers' analysis of CAI mentioned previously (Kulik et al., 1983), eliminated from consideration all but about fifty studies on the basis of methodological weakness. Becker (1988) was even more stringent in his best-evidence synthesis on CAI, eliminating all but seventeen studies. Should they have included all the studies? There may be ways to resolve this problem, one of which is to do two meta-analyses, one for all the studies, and another only for the "good" studies. There is some evidence that the results of such an approach might not be very different. For example, using a large body of literature, Smith and Glass (1977) found that psychotherapy led to a variety of desirable outcomes. Landman and Dawes (1982), using only the strongest designs culled from the Smith and Glass analysis, essentially confirmed the original conclusions. Note, however, that Eysenck (1978) called the Smith and Glass meta-analysis an exercise in "mega-silliness" because, as Eysenck sees it, there is a total lack of rigor in the *entire* literature examining psychotherapy outcome. Thus, Eysenck's view is that summarizing a lot of bad research necessarily leads to a bad conclusion (there's that GIGO again). His position rests on the fact that true control groups (those groups receiving a placebo in place of psychotherapy) are in effect impossible to construct, since the equivalent of a "sugar pill" for psychotherapy simply does not exist.

There are a number of other areas of discussion in the use of statistical integration and the methods used in these analyses. Two things, however, are certain: the use of meta-analytic techniques is on the rise, and there is no shortage of topics on which these analyses can be conducted. As the debate continues, more, and better, meta-analyses will be conducted, and most important of all, the methods themselves will most certainly continue to be developed and refined (see, for example, Cooper, 1982).

CAUSAL MODELING: THE DEBATE OF THE 1990s

In these, the last few years of the twentieth century, the house of educational research has become increasingly divided on yet another issue, and it seems likely that this division will become ever more pronounced in the years to come. The issue that seems destined to provoke continued debate among current researcher-practitioners is that of causality. This, of course, is not a new epistemological concern. The empiricist David Hume, back in the 1700s, threw down the gauntlet when he said that the objective concept of cause and effect could not be derived from experience, or that what appears to be a physical, cause-and-effect relationship is merely that the experienced event called the cause is invariably followed by the experienced event called the effect (Hume, 1748). These thoughts, in retrospect, produced a severe attack on what we now call the scientific method, a method, which as we have seen, is anchored at both ends in observation. If the empirical technique cannot demonstrate something as fundamental to science as cause and effect, of what use is continued scientific research? Is it all just an illusion? Can the views of an old empiricist be used to destroy its most valued treasure, the scientific method? Later, Immanuel Kant expressed the belief that although cause and effect could not be derived from experience, neither could it be denied (Kant, 1781). In short, the great cause-and-effect debate didn't just start last week.

The scientific method, as we saw in Chapter 1, assumes a deterministic philosophy, or that events in the universe are not simply random and unconnected. Implicit in every view of science is the belief that we live in an ordered world, that there really are uniformities in nature, and that it is up to us as scientists to discover what these sequences are, and how various lawful relationships might be related. The underlying assumption in science, then, is that there are indeed causal agents that produce predictable effects.

Correlation and Causation

One of the most insistent themes expressed in these pages, a theme that has been as hauntingly relentless as the cadence of a marching drum beat, is that direct inferences of causality may only be expressed through the use of experimental methodology. Notice that we have been careful to say direct inference, but what about the possibility of *indirect* inferences? As any first-year statistics student has been taught to echo, correlation does not imply causation. This was set forth as early as Chapter 3, when we warned of the post-hoc fallacy. However, we have also stated that although correlation does not imply causation, neither does it rule it out. Just because two variables are correlated, it certainly does not follow that variable X did not cause a change in variable Y. Think about the experimental method for a moment, in which there has been active manipulation of the IV. If this is followed by a concomitant change in the DV, there must certainly be a correlation between the IV and the DV. For example, if we were to randomly divide a group of Olympic sprinters, and give one group (the experimental group) anabolic steroids and not give any steroids to the other group (control group), and if the experimental group then ran significantly faster than the control group, we would, of course, have produced evidence for an experimental validation of the causal nature of the steroids. However, as a by-product, we would also have obtained a *correlation* between steroid consumption and running speed.

During the past few decades, slowly at first, but with increasing frequency, researchers in the social sciences have taken another look at the correlational model and have loudly wondered, "why not?" There are, after all, some major advantages to using *causal modeling*, advantages that may outweigh the concerns of the "nagging nitpickers." For example, important studies, studies that truly examine the big picture, often lend themselves to causal modeling, even though they cannot be carried out in any other way. Many studies that examine real-world issues cannot be recreated in the artificial confines of the laboratory. Such issues as whether schools make a difference on the adult lives of students, or whether the use of cocaine has a deleterious effect on academic achievement, are simply not possible using the strict ethical guidelines of the experimental method. Sometimes natural circumstances become the ultimate manipulator of the IV, and the researcher has the opportunity to evaluate those data that nature has already fortuitously provided. Causative models also give the educational researcher a stronger basis for applying theory to the solving of social problems. If the data backfit the model, that is, are consistent with the model, the theory may possibly be translated into public policy and social action.

Finally, the advent of the computer has allowed every researcher to have the power of the old mainframes right on top of his or her desk. Researchers who now use causative models on a regular basis feel that one of the reasons for the current popularity of these models is that complicated correlational analyses were just not available to most researchers even a few short years ago. As we have seen, with a desktop computer, and a statistical program like SPSS/PC+, the researcher can now apply sophisticated multivariate regression techniques that were literally out of the question just a few short years ago. Either the researcher tried to analyze the data on a calculator, or waited in line to turn the data over to the mainframe computer center. With more than, say, three or four variables, doing the regressions out on the calculator was anything but a happy chore. And in the 1950s and 1960s waiting to get time on the mainframe was neither easy nor cheap and often resulted, when the results finally did come back, in the researcher wondering whether any reanalysis was worth that much time and trouble. The causative modelers have definitely discovered the mini- and microcomputers, and since programs are now available to run extremely complex analyses, the modelers now say, "Why not run them"?

The New Look

The new look in educational research can be seen in what seems like an explosion of articles using correlational data to create causative models. The essential logic behind this approach depends on three fundamental criteria (Kenny, 1979): (1) *time precedence,* (2) *relationships,* and (3) *nonspuriousness.*

Time Precedence

If two variables X and Y are to be causally related, such that X is to be viewed as causing Y, X must obviously precede Y in time. For example, if it has been found that X, whether or not a school has been desegregated, correlated with Y, a minority student's scholastic achievement, it must be shown that the desegregation came before the minority student's measured gain in achievement.

Relationships

Before any attempt is made to infer the possibility of a causal factor, the variables in question, X and Y, must be found to be significantly correlated. That is, the correlation coefficient between X and Y must be strong enough to have led to a rejection of the null hypothesis. Only then can it be assumed that information about Y, the effect variable, is being contained in X, the causal variable.

Nonspuriousness

If a significant correlation is found, it must not be spurious. A spurious correlation occurs when it is found that although X correlates significantly with Y, some third variable, say Z, may be causing changes in both X and Y. In causal modeling this is known as the infamous third-variable problem. The most frequently used example of spuriousness is the obviously positive correlation that exists between shoe size and verbal ability among elementary school children: the larger the feet, the higher the verbal test scores. From the point of view of causality, the correlation is certainly spurious, since age (the third variable) is almost certainly producing increases in both foot size and verbal ability.

PATH ANALYSIS

Although educational researchers have been turning to a number of structural models, the most popular of these currently seems to be *path analysis* (Keith & Page, 1984). This isn't to say that path analysis is a recent creation. Its use can actually be traced as far back as 1921, when a biologist, Sewell Wright, suggested a correlational analysis for ferreting out causal factors in genetic studies (Wright, 1921). Briefly, path analysis is a sophisticated correlational technique designed to test a set of hypothesized cause-and-effect relationships between a series of variables that are logically ordered on a time basis. Thus, the researcher begins with an explanatory model that hypothesizes the ordering of the assumed cause-and-effect relationships. Since, as stated earlier, a causal variable must precede the variable it is presumed to influence, the analysis is done on a set of variables, each hypothesized to show a causal ordering. The analysis is focused on determining whether a given variable is being influenced by the variable(s) that precede it and then, in turn, is influencing the variables that follow. A multiple regression is calculated from the various internal correlations, and a path diagram is then drawn that portrays the assumed direction of the various relationships.

Since much of this may sound like word salad to you, let's clarify this issue by looking at an example. Ever since the now famous (and educationally pessimistic) Coleman and Jencks reports (Coleman et al., 1966; Jencks et al., 1972), the world of education has been attempting to establish a scientific proof that schools do indeed make a difference in the lives of students. Needless to say, it would be virtually impossible to test this hypothesis directly on an experimental basis. Imagine a scene in which five-year-old children are being randomly divided into an experimental group, those children who must go to school for twelve years, or a control group, those children who will not be allowed to ever go to school. This is hardly a realistic scenario, even for the most extreme educational provocateur. (Would Coleman or Jencks allow their children to be chosen as members of the control group?) The hypothesis might be tested indirectly, however, by using a causal-modeling approach. This approach is built on an as-if-by-experiment assumption; that the results will be analyzed as if nature has randomly assigned subjects to the different treatment conditions.

In attempting to determine the impact of education on the later lives of U.S. students, Hope developed a causal model, using education (in this case, secondary education) as a predictor, and adult occupation (the presumed measure of success) as the criterion (Hope, 1984). To factor out other possible causative variables, Hope also included the subject's IQ as well as the occupation of the subject's father. Notice that the inclusion of these latter two variables was crucial in this study if the criterion of nonspuriousness was to be addressed. For example, if IQ had been left uncontrolled, even if there had been a correlation between secondary education and occupational success, it might easily be concluded that both these variables were effects of IQ. Brighter children may be more apt to stay in school and also more likely to achieve occupational success in later life. Also, occupation of the father is important, since a student whose father is, say, president of General Motors may have more career alternatives than a student whose father is on welfare. A path diagram, adapted from Hope's study, is shown in Figure 11.1.

Notice that in the figure the two variables, IQ and father's occupation, are both used as predictors and may or may not be correlated (in this case they are correlated, as is shown by the curved line with arrows at both ends). This correlation between the predictors should not be interpreted causally, nor is the researcher bound to offer any model or reason for specifying any structural relationship as a reason for this particular correlation. The unidirectional lines, however, with arrows at only one end, are viewed as cause-and-effect relationships. The values listed for each line represent what are called path coefficients. These path coefficients are based on either ordinary correlation coefficients or on partial correlations, in which the correlation between two of the variables is found after the influence of a third variable has been statistically ruled out. (For a further discussion of path coefficients, see Cohen & Cohen, 1983.)

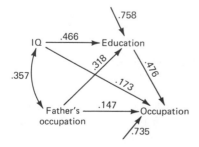

Figure 11.1 Path diagram adapted from Hope (1984) for predicting occupational success

Although the stress here has been on path analysis as a statistical technique, it should again be pointed out that the statistical analysis should be *preceded by the formulation of a theoretical model.* The researcher should carefully hypothesize an explanatory model and then analyze the path coefficients in an attempt to backfit the model.

The Critics Speak

Despite what may seem like the statistical and theoretical elegance of such modeling procedures as path analysis, causal modeling is not without its critics. One of the major arguments presented by those opposed to causal modeling is aimed at the three basic criteria listed previously, and thus goes right to the heart of the modelers assumptions.

Time Precedence

Just because two variables, X and Y, may be arranged so that X precedes Y in no way justifies the conclusion that X caused Y. This argument speaks to the post-hoc fallacy mentioned in Chapter 3, the fallacy that "because it came after this, therefore it was caused by this." In other words, just because you washed your car before the rainstorm does not justify the conclusion that washing the car caused it to rain.

Significant Correlations

Because two variables may yield significant correlations does not, in and of itself, prove a causal connection. This is because, as stated previously, the correlation alone cannot specify the direction of the relationship. This issue was also addressed in Chapter 3, under the heading The Cause-and-Effect Trap.

Nonspuriousness

Of all the criteria used in causal modeling, this is the most difficult to prove. Defining a time precedence and establishing a significant correlation are both straightforward and relatively unambiguous. But ruling out spuriousness is sometimes a tall order. Although it may be obvious that the correlation among elementary school children between foot size and verbal ability is spurious, both being enormously influenced by the third variable, age, other spurious correlations are not always so obvious. In Hope's path analysis, for example, it may seem as though the "third variable" problem has been addressed, since the correlation between secondary education and later occupation was determined only after the effects of the father's occupation had been nullified. But there may have been other variables that were not accounted for in this model. The father's friendship patterns may be important (the father may have a job that rates at the low end of Hope's status hierarchy but still have influential friends who could lend a helping hand when the subject reaches the job market). Or perhaps the father's age should be included (since an older man has had more opportunity to increase both his wealth and his occupational status).

A Fallacy Revisited

In Chapter 1 we discussed the fallacy of affirming the consequent, and this argument has been used in attacking the very foundation of the causal modeler's structure (Games, 1988). Let's turn again to the syllogism presented in Chapter 1:

(Premise A) All dogs bark.
(Premise B) Fido is a dog.
(Conclusion C) Fido barks.

This is a legitimate argument. If x (all dogs), then y (bark), and if Fido is an x (dog), then Fido can y (bark). The syllogism should not, however, be magically reversed to prove that y also implies x, as in the following invalid argument:

(Premise A) All dogs bark.
(Premise B) Fido barks.
(Conclusion C) Fido is a dog.

As we saw in Chapter 1, Fido might be the name of a trained seal. Thus, the conclusion that Fido is a dog commits the fallacy of affirming the consequent. With path analysis, the concern that Games has expressed is that the causal model is created (x), which then predicts a certain correlational pattern (y). The correlational data are then examined to see if they backfit, or are consistent with, the original model, and if they do fit, the model is judged to be valid. This, says Games, is a prime example of the fallacy of affirming the consequent, since if x is presumed to cause y, it cannot then be used to show that y also affirms x. Says Games,

> There may be many other models that would also yield a correlational pattern that would be consistent with the data. The most that can be said of these correlational studies is that the data do not contradict the model. (Games, 1988, p. 9)

Because of these problems, some research methodologists are returning to the age-old dictum:

"NO CAUSATION WITHOUT MANIPULATION" (Holland, 1986)

Holland's reaffirmation of this dictum is based on the view that the effect of a cause can only be interpreted when it is related to another cause: treatment (one cause) versus control (another cause). Further, every subject must be *poten-*

tially exposable to either cause (a subject's appearance in either condition must have the same likelihood). This, as can readily be seen, rules out the possibility of subject variables ever enjoying the status of being considered causal variables. Says Holland,

> As an example, the schooling a student receives can be a cause, in our sense, of the student's performance on a test, whereas the student's race or gender cannot. (Holland, 1986, p. 946)

This would mean that studies in which subject variables are used as IVs, clearly post-facto studies, should be viewed with extreme caution when the researcher claims to have identified a causal relationship. For example, in one study the suggestion was clearly made that scores on tests and performance in primary school can cause (that is, affect) a student's choice of a secondary school (Saris & Stronkhorst, 1984). In Holland's view, since a subject variable, such as scholastic achievement, could never be a manipulated treatment variable, such an IV cannot be construed as a causal factor. Kempthorne made the same point:

> It is epistemological nonsense to talk about one trait of an individual causing or determining another trait of an individual. (Kempthorne, 1978, p. 15)

WHERE DO WE GO FROM HERE?

Although the criticisms of Games and Holland may seem harsh, they serve as clear and compelling warnings to the educational researcher of the 1990s. And these warnings should at least be heard. Certainly the sophistication of the path-analysis approach is a far cry from the naive extrapolations of causation found among many of the correlational studies of thirty years ago. Before cavalierly jumping to the conclusion that causal modeling offers a direct test of causality, however, it is well to be reminded that all is not total harmony in the research patch.

Some indicators, however, are more positive than others. For example, Holland admits that there are occasional natural experiments in which, for example, preventative actions have impinged on the population at large and may offer strong, although indirect, causal evidence. An observational study may rightly ask if the actions work. Does the person wearing a seatbelt lower his or her risk of fatality in an auto accident? Does the student who is enrolled in a study-skills course become less apt to later become a high-school dropout? Holland believes that the underlying notion of cause operating in an experiment may actually be the same as in an observational study.

> The difference is in the degree of control an experimenter has over the phenomena under investigation compared with that which an observer has. (Holland, 1986, p. 954)

Nor should it be assumed that causal inferences from correlational analyses are forever impossible. For now, however, that alluring prospect should be viewed with a critical eye of uncertainty. Says Freedman,

> There are some such techniques on the horizon, which do not depend on prior specification the way path models do: see Asimov (1985), Huber (1985), or Mc-Donald (1984). It remains to be seen whether these innovations can be used to make improvements over path analysis. (Freedman, 1987, p. 125)

Computer Overkill

As was mentioned earlier, another reason for the current popularity of causal modeling is the easy access researchers now have to extremely complex statistical computer programs. For most researchers, sophisticated multivariate analyses are now only a few keystrokes away. Researchers of the 1990s might easily be seduced by such statistical power and then, flushed with the excitement of having so many techniques on the menu, simply enter the data and try them all, regardless of assumptions. Many programs, for example, can easily handle ANOVA designs with a half-dozen or more independent variables, but making any real sense out of the many interactions, especially those involving four or five variables, is virtually impossible.

KISS

In designing the studies of the future it is well to be reminded of the acronym KISS; Keep It Simple, Stupid. The research design should always be kept simple enough to generate results that can indeed answer the research question. The computer, alas, can often perform far more number-crunching calculations than are logically possible to interpret.

SUMMARY

Computers are here, and their present and future impact cannot be ignored. A major computer use for researchers is in the area of the analysis of data from studies. SPSS, Minitab, and SAS are available for microcomputers, which puts a variety of fast and powerful analytic techniques on top of the researcher's desk, just a keyboard away.

Microcomputers may also be used by researchers to present experimental stimuli to subjects. The educational and related literatures may also be searched, using computers, for studies similar or related to one being planned. This saves hundreds of hours of time in scanning library resources. In addition, researchers, like millions of others, use word processing when writing research proposals, or in preparing a manuscript for publication.

The impact of microcomputers, more than two million of them, has been, and will continue to be, felt in elementary and secondary schools, too. Computer-assisted instruction, although not quite living up to the expectations of its early advocates, is increasingly being used in classrooms, especially for special populations. Similarly, computer simulations have also found their way into many curricula, and most high-school students will take a computer literacy or programming course before they graduate and then enter college, the work force, or the military. There is concern about the quality of some of the educational material available, and computer-literacy courses vary tremendously from school to school. Progress, however, is being made in both areas.

There are several issues of concern to researchers in the 1990s. One of the concerns involves the availability of powerful statistical analyses to people untrained in the proper interpretation of the results. Secondly, the methods used in integrative research analyses such as meta-analyses have been a topic of discussion, and will continue to be of concern.

The real debate of the 1990s, however, is predicted to revolve around the issue of correlation and causation. The often-repeated warning that correlation does not imply causation is being challenged by researchers who argue that correlational support for previously developed causal models (via path analysis and other techniques) represents a substantiation of the model and thus implies causation. Critics of the approach argue that nothing in these approaches avoids the necessity for showing causation by means of the manipulation of an IV. For them, correlation still does not imply causation because the necessary conditions for establishing such relationships cannot be demonstrated in correlational research.

KEY TERMS

Best-evidence synthesis	Relationship(s)
Causal modeling	SAS
Computer-assisted instruction (CAI)	Simulation
Minitab	SPSS
Nonspuriousness	Time precedence
Path analysis	Word processing

REFERENCES

ASIMOV, D. (1985). The grand tour. *SIAM Journal of Scientific and Statistical Computing, 6,* 128–143.

BATES, S., AHLQUIST, C., O'CONNOR, D., & SIROIS, L. (1988). The effects of study-skill training on high school science students' achievement. Unpublished manuscript, American International College.

BECKER, H. J. (1988). *The impact of computer use on*

children's learning: What the research has shown and what it has not. Baltimore: Johns Hopkins.

BRACEY, G. W. (1982). Computers in education: What the research shows. *Electronic Learning,* November/December, 51–54.

BRACEY, G. W. (1987). Computer-assisted instruction: What the research shows. *Electronic Learning,* 7 (3), November/December, 22–23.

BRACEY, G. W. (1988). Computers in class: Some social and psychological consequences. *Electronic Learning,* 7 (8), May/June, 28.

BRAY, J. H., & MAXWELL, S. E. (1982). Analyzing and interpreting significant MANOVAs. *Review of Educational Research, 52* (3), 340–367.

COHEN, J., & COHEN, P. (1983). *Applied multiple regression analysis for the behavioral sciences* (2d. ed.). Hillside, N.J.: Lawrence Erlbaum.

COLEMAN, J. S., CAMPBELL, E. Q., HOBSON, C. J., McPARTLAND, J., MOOD, A. M., WEINFIELD, F. D., & YORK, R. L. (1966). *Equality of educational opportunity.* Washington, D.C.: U.S. Government Printing Office.

COOPER, H. M. (1982). Scientific guidelines for conducting integrative research reviews. *Review of Educational Research, 52* (2), 291–302.

COZBY, P. C. (1984). *Using computers in the behavioral sciences.* Palo Alto: Mayfield.

ELLIS, J. (1986). Point and counterpoint: Computers in the classrooms. *NASSP Bulletin, 70* (489), 10–14.

EYSENCK, H. J. (1978). An exercise in mega-silliness. *American Psychologist, 33,* 517.

FREEDMAN, D. A. (1987). As others see us: A case study in path analysis. *Journal of Educational Statistics, 12,* 101–128.

GAMES, P. A. (1988). Correlation and causation: An alternate view. *The Score, 11,* 9–11.

GLASS, G. V. (1976). Primary, secondary and meta-analysis of research. *Educational Researcher, 5,* 3–8.

HOLLAND, P. W. (1986). Statistics and causal inference. *Journal of the American Statistical Association, 81,* 945–960.

HOPE, K. (1984). *As others see us: Schooling and social mobility in Scotland and the United States.* New York: Cambridge University Press.

HUBER, P. (1985). Projection pursuit. *Annals of Statistics, 13,* 435–475.

HUME, D. (1748). *An inquiry concerning human understanding.*

JACKSON, G. B. (1978). *Methods for reviewing and integrating research in the social sciences.* Final report to the National Science Foundation for Grant No. DIS 76-20309. Washington, DC: Social Research Group, George Washington University, April.

JENCKS, C., SMITH, M., ACLAND, H., BANE, M. J.,

COHEN, D., GINTIS, H., HEYNS, B., & MICHELSON, S. (1972). *Inequality: A reassessment of the effect of family and schooling in America.* New York: Basic Books.

KANT, I. (1781). *The critique of pure reason.*

KEITH, T. Z., PAGE, E. B., & ROBERTSON, S. D. (1984). Aspiration and causal research. *Educational Researcher, 13,* 22–23.

KEMPTHORNE, O. (1978). Logical epistemological and statistical aspects of nature-nurture data interpretation. *Biometrics, 34,* 1–24.

KENNY, D. A. (1979). *Correlation and causation.* New York: John Wiley.

KLECKA, W. R., NIE, N. H., & HULL, C. H. (1975). *SPSS Primer.* New York: McGraw-Hill.

KLIEGER, D. M. (1984). *Computer usage for social scientists.* Newton, Mass.: Allyn & Bacon.

KULIK, J., BANGER, R., & WILLIAMS, G. (1983). Effects of computer-based teaching on secondary school students. *Journal of Educational Psychology,* 75(1), 19–26.

LANDMAN, J. T., & DAWES, R. M. (1982). Psychotherapy outcome: Smith and Glass' conclusions stand up under scrutiny. *American Psychologist* 37(5), 504–516.

McDONALD, J. A. (1984). *Interactive graphics for data analysis (Report ORION 11).* Stanford, Calif.: Stanford University Press, Department of Statistics.

NATHAN, J. (1985). *Micro-myths: Exploring the limits of learning with computers.* Minneapolis: Winston.

NORUSIS, M. J. (1988). *SPSS/PC+ studentware.* Chicago: SPSS, Inc.

RAGOSTA, M. (1983). Computer-assisted instruction and compensatory education: A longitudinal analysis. *Machine Mediated Learning, 1* (1).

RYAN, T. A., JOINER, B. L., & RYAN, B. F. (1976). *Minitab student handbook.* North Scituate, Mass.: Duxbury.

SARIS, W., & STRONKHORST, H. (1984). *Causal modeling in non-experimental research.* Amsterdam: Sociometric Research Foundation.

SAS INSTITUTE, INC. (1982). *SAS introductory guide.* Cary, N.C.: SAS Institute.

SMITH, M. L., & GLASS, G. V. (1977). Meta-analysis of psychotherapy outcome studies. *American Psychologist, 32,* 752–760.

SPSS, INC. (1988). *SPSSx user's guide* (3d ed.). New York: McGraw-Hill.

WHISNANT, D. M. (1983). *Lake study* [computer program]. Ypsilanti, Mich.: Project Seraphim, NSF Developments in Science Education, John W. Moore, Project Director.

WRIGHT, S. (1921). Correlation and causation. *Journal of Agricultural Research, 20,* 557–585.

Glossary

ABA Design A reversal design typically used in single-subject and small-N research. The initial IV condition (A) is followed by a second IV condition (B), which in turn is reversed back to the original condition (A).

ABAB Design A reversal design typically used in single-subject and small-N research. The initial IV condition (A) is followed by a second IV condition (B), which is then reversed back to the first (A) condition and, finally, reversed a second time back to the second (B) condition.

Abstract A brief (100–150 word) summary of the research report that appears at the beginning of the write-up. It contains statements of the problem, procedures, results, and conclusions of the study.

Action Research Research planned and conducted primarily for direct application within the setting in which the research is conducted. There is usually no concern about generalizability of results to other settings, only about the usefulness of the results to the researcher.

Active IV An independent variable that is completely controlled by, and is actively manipulated by, the experimenter. An active IV is required if cause-and-effect conclusions are to be directly drawn from an experiment.

After-Only Design An experimental design in which the subjects are measured on the DV only after being subjected to the possible influence of the IV. The control and experimental groups are assumed to be equivalent at the outset on the basis of random selection and assignment.

Alpha Error The probability of falsely rejecting the null hypothesis when the null hypothesis is, in fact, true, or in other words, the probability of error when rejecting the null hypothesis.

Alternate-Form Reliability When two different, but equivalent, forms of a test are constructed, alternate-form reliability is established by giving both tests to the same group of test takers and obtaining a reliability coefficient by correlating the results of the two tests.

Alternative Hypothesis The alternative (sometimes called the research) hypothesis states that chance has probably been ruled out: that there are population differences or that there are population correlations that can be extrapolated from sample results. The alternative hypothesis is the opposite of the null hypothesis.

ANCOVA ANalysis of COVAriance is a statistical procedure that allows the researcher to statistically equate groups that might differ because of the existence of an uncontrolled variable in the research. Ideally, ANCOVA requires that groups be randomly assigned at the outset of the research, but in practice ANCOVA is used to equate nonrandomly assigned (intact) groups. ANCOVA should probably not be used by the statistical novice as the basis for design, since interpretations can be tricky.

ANOVA ANalysis Of VAriance is a statistical procedure used primarily for the examination of differences between two or more group means. The ANOVA indicates the presence or absence of significant differences but does not indicate which means are significantly different. Subsequent tests may be used to investigate specific group differences predicted by research hypotheses or to determine specific patterns of significance on a post-hoc basis.

ANOVA between Groups An analysis of variance done to examine differences between groups that have been independently selected and given different levels of the IV treatment. The DV measures of groups containing different subjects that have received different IV levels are compared.

ANOVA within Groups An analysis of variance done to examine differences between treatments or IV levels that have been administered to the same group(s) at different times. Often called a repeated-measures ANOVA, the comparison is of DV measures on the same subjects under different treatments.

Appendix An optional supplement to the research report that contains any lengthy details of the study that are essential for the understanding, evaluation, or replication of the study. It may involve complicated mathematical proofs, customized questionnaires, or innovative computer programs.

Archival Research Often called historical research, this descriptive, and often qualitative, approach involves examination of historical or other archival documents found in libraries, city halls, churches, and so on. The result of the research is a description of the information contained in the records examined.

Aristotle (384–322 B.C.) The early Greek philosopher who believed that knowledge could be acquired both through one's powers of reason (deductively) and through direct sensory observation (inductively). Also created method of syllogistic logic.

Baseline In reversal and nonreversal designs such as ABA, the baseline is the phase indicated by the first "A". Establishing a typical or ongoing DV behavioral level before manipulating the IV.

Basic Rule of Research When planning a research study, try to (1) use a natural research setting, to increase external validity, (2) optimize control by using the strongest possible design, and (3) consider all threats to internal validity so that the results will be clear and unequivocal.

Before-After Design An experimental design in which subjects are measured both before and after the introduction of the manipulated IV. Unless there are adequate control groups, the before-after design is virtually certain to produce threats to the experiment's internal validity.

Berkeley, Bishop George (1685–1753) Irish theologian who stressed the empirical method of epistemology. Berkeley believed that sensory experience was the basis for obtaining knowledge, a position summarized in his famous statement, "esse est percipi," or "to be is to be perceived."

Best-Evidence Synthesis A form of meta-analysis in which only research studies of the highest methodological quality are included in the statistical integration of results.

Beta Error The probability of being wrong when accepting the null hypothesis, or the probability of accepting the null hypothesis when, in fact null should have been rejected.

Between-Groups Comparison Analysis based on comparing the DV measures that occur between independently selected groups of subjects (experimental and control), rather than on comparing measures of change taken within subjects, as in a repeated-measures design.

Bias A consistent distortion in one direction. A biased sample, for example, is unrepresentative of the population because some segments of the population are overrepresented and other parts of the population are underrepresented.

Bimodal Any distribution of scores that has two modes, or two separate scores that each have the greatest frequency of occurrence.

Carryover Effects A type of sequencing effect that results when a subject's performance under one treatment condition is influenced by the previous treatment(s) that he or she received. This makes it difficult to assess the true impact of the treatment currently being received.

Case Study An exhaustive study, usually of a single individual, that describes the past history, contains a description of the present circumstances (and symptoms), and may examine possible future trends. Some case studies may be descriptions of institutions (such as schools) or communities.

Causal IV An independent variable that has been actively manipulated by the experimenter and can thus be viewed as the potential cause of any DV differences between the subjects' DV measures.

Causal Modeling A theory-based approach to research that attempts to identify causal relationships between variables by using sophisticated nonexperimental techniques such as correlation and regression, as opposed to experimental procedures. (See Path Analysis as an example of causal modeling.)

Cause-and-Effect Trap In post-facto research, coming to the conclusion that the IV has caused the DV to change, when, in fact, the only appropriate conclusion (since the IV has not been manipulated) is that the IV and DV are correlated.

Ceiling Effect A condition that exists in a study when subjects' scores on the dependent variable are as high or nearly as high as they can be (near the ceiling). This may make it difficult to identify the effect of a manipulation if the scores are already as high as they can go.

Central Tendency (measures of) The term applied to those measures that describe the typical, midmost, or most centrally located scores in any distribution. The most commonly used measures of central tendency are the mean, the median, and the mode.

Chi Square A statistical test applied to nominal data, in which the frequencies observed are compared with frequencies expected on the basis of chance (or, in some cases, on the basis of an a priori hypothesis). Chi square is a nonparametric test, since it requires no assumptions regarding any of the population parameters.

Classification IV This is the same as a subject, or assigned, IV. An IV which is not manipulated by the researcher, but which is, instead, a variable that can be used to divide subjects into groups. These are characteristics, such as gender, that the subjects already possess.

Coefficient of Contingency A statistical test of correlation based on the chi square and used when the data are in nominal form.

Combination Research A factorial design in which at least one of the IVs is manipulated and at least one other IV is post facto.

Computer Assisted Instruction (CAI) The use of computers and computer programs for teaching. The information covered may range from facts taught by drill and practice methods to broader concepts. The effectiveness of CAI is largely dependent on the type of material taught and the quality of the instructional computer program.

Concurrent Validity A form of criterion-related validity in which test scores are correlated with an independently derived measure of current subject behavior that is related to the purpose of the test. This is usually used for diagnostic instruments.

Confounding A research error that occurs when two or more variables could have contributed to an experimental result in an unknown manner. When confounding occurs, the researcher does not know the relative contribution of each variable, nor can the pure effects of the IV be isolated.

Constancy A critical feature of all good research. Requires that all the conditions in the study, such as the characteristics of the research room, the demeanor of the researcher, and the instructions to the subjects, be the same for all subjects. The independent variable(s) is the only thing left to vary.

Constant A factor that does not vary, or that is not allowed to vary, in the context of a research project.

Construct A factor that, although not directly observable, hypothetically exists and gives rise to measurable differences in behavior. Such characteristics as intelligence and anxiety are considered constructs.

Construct Validity A type of test validity for tests designed to measure the degree to which subjects possess differing amounts of a construct (such as intelligence). The validation typically consists of comparisons of subjects' test scores in terms of the degree to which those subjects are hypothesized to differ in amount of the construct based on the definition of the construct.

Content Validity The validation of a test based on the procedures used to construct the test. The validation is accomplished by doing a close examination of the areas to be tested, developing a set of test specifications, and carefully constructing a test that meets the specifications that have been drawn up. Content validity is usually established for achievement tests.

Corollary to the Basic Rule of Research All aspects of the research project should be carefully and formally planned out, including the statistical procedures that will be used later for the analysis of data, and this should be done before subjects are observed and data are gathered.

Correlation A statistic that indicates the degree to which two or more variables are related, and that can be used to predict unknown values on one variable from known values on the other(s). The degree of relationship is indicated by a number that ranges from 0 (no correlation) to 1.00 (the highest possible correlation) and a sign (plus or minus) that indicates either a negative or a positive correlation.

Counterbalancing Any technique applied to counter the possibility of the sequencing effects produced by repeated-measures designs. Counterbalancing is used to reduce the threats to internal validity (or prevent confounding of the IV).

Criterion The behavior measured in criterion-related validity to establish the concurrent or predictive validity of a test. Test performance is correlated with the criterion.

Criterion Contamination This may occur in establishing criterion-related validity if the measurement of the criterion is influenced by knowledge of the test scores. Criterion measures should be obtained independently of test scores.

Criterion-Related Validity Concurrent and predictive validity. These are established by correlating subjects' scores with an independently measured behavior that the test is supposed to predict or diagnose.

Cross Sectional Approach Developmental research in which independent groups of subjects in different developmental stages are examined at the same time.

Debriefing Providing research participants with information about the nature of the study after the data are collected, and removing any misconception that may have arisen, or that may have been deliberately created by deception.

Deception An ethical consideration when conducting research. Deliberately misleading the participants with respect to certain aspects of the research because of the methodological requirements of the study.

Deciles Points which divide a distribution into tenths. Each decile represents 10 percentiles, such that the fifth decile is equal to the fiftieth percentile.

Deduction A logical proof based on arguing from a general premise, or premises, to a specific conclusion. If the premises are true, and the argument is valid, the conclusion must also be true. (Also see Induction.)

Demand Characteristics A threat to the internal validity of a study that exists when clues or tips allow the subjects to figure out the research hypothesis or purpose of the study. This may cause the subjects to behave differently because of their expectations of the study rather than as they would more naturally behave.

Dependent Variable (DV) The outcome variable that may be effected by the IV in experimental research. The DV may also be the predicted variable in correlational research or the behavior measured and correlated with a subject variable in post-facto research.

Descartes, René (1596–1650) The French philosopher famous for his use of the deductive method for establishing proof. Descartes stressed the importance of reasoning in establishing his proofs and is therefore known as an epistemological rationalist.

Descriptive Research Research in which the purpose is the description of a person, a group of persons, an institution, or a community. Descriptive-research approaches include qualitative research, case studies, developmental studies, and archival or historical research.

Descriptive Statistics Techniques used to describe data in meaningful ways. Among the measures and procedures used to describe data are the following: central tendency, variability, skewness, kurtosis, and transformed scores (such as z and T scores). Descriptive statistics also include the presentation of tables and graphs.

Developmental Research A type of descriptive research that is used to examine differences that occur over time. Cross-sectional or longitudinal studies are conducted to understand changes that occur purely as a result of the passage of time.

Discussion Section A major section of a research report that explains the results, interprets them, and ties the study into previous research and theory. It also may point out the limitations of the study and offer suggestions for future research.

Documentation The process of giving credit for the ideas and work of other researchers or theorists in a research report. The name of the author(s) and the year in which the work was published must be included in the body of the paper where the work is mentioned.

Double-Blind Procedure An ideal research situation in which neither the experimenter nor the subjects are aware of the treatment being received or the hypotheses of the study. In this way the subject is not likely to act unnaturally and the researcher is not likely to allow his or her biases or expectations to influence the findings. Of course, the principal investigator would know the hypothesis and which subjects received which treatments.

Duration A measure of the length of time that a subject engages in a specified behavior. Time on task is a duration measure.

Ecological Validity A term used to indicate that a research study has been conducted in a setting the same as, or similar to the one in which the results will be applied.

Effect Size In meta-analysis, the indicator of the amount of influence that an IV has on a DV. It is often presented in the form of d, a statistic that indicates control and experimental group differences in terms equivalent to that of a Z score. A d of $+.5$, for example, indicates that the experimental group's performance was one-half of a standard deviation above that of the control group.

Empiricism The epistemology that is based on the belief that observation, or direct sensory experience, is the root source of all knowledge.

Epistemology The study of how knowledge is acquired. The two main epistemological positions are rationalism and empiricism.

Equivalent Groups Groups of subjects that are equivalent to one another by means of random assignment or matching. A group that is used again under different experimental conditions is also equivalent, since their scores are being compared with their own scores under different conditions.

ERIC *Educational Resources Information Center.* A national information system that serves as a major source of documents on education. Available on microfiche in the libraries of most colleges and universities.

Ethical Restrictions in Research Researchers must insure that subjects will not be harmed, embarrassed, or have their privacy invaded. The rights of subjects are often protected by having research proposals carefully reviewed by a group of peer researchers.

Ethnography A form of qualitative research in which a true-to-life description of observations is presented without interpretation on the part of the researcher. It includes as accurate a representation as possible of the things that people say, write, and do in their own environments.

Evaluation Study Research that may use any or all of a number of research approaches but is designed to provide information about whether a program or service is meeting its objectives.

Expectancy A form of experimenter bias in which the experimenter's expectations about the outcome of research actually influence the outcome of the research project. This is one of the threats to internal validity.

Experimental Mortality A threat to internal validity in which groups of subjects lose differing numbers of subjects, thus destroying the equivalency of the groups.

Experimental Research Research in which the IV is manipulated. True experiments also require random assignment of subjects.

External Validity Refers to the degree to which subject-selection procedures and the design of research allow generalization of the results to other settings, subjects, IV and DV definitions, and times.

F Ratio Statistical test that is based on the ratio between two estimates of population variance. In its most basic form the F ratio is equal to the variance estimated to be occurring between the groups divided by the estimated variance occurring within the groups. The larger the F ratio, the higher the likelihood of establishing a significant difference.

Face Validity Not a true form of test validity, but refers to the degree to which a test appears to measure what it purports to measure.

Factorial ANOVA Statistical test based on the F ratio where the effects of two or more IVs are being compared. The factorial ANOVA allows for the evaluation of the effect of each IV taken separately, as well as all possible IV interactions.

Factorial Design A design in which two or more independent variables (or factors) are used in such a way that their analysis allows for conclusions based on each of the IVs taken separately (main effects) as well as on their possible interactions.

Field Study A case study conducted on a group, institution, or community, but the term is also used to refer to any approach to descriptive research that is conducted in a natural setting.

Formative Evaluation Process evaluation involving an examination of program delivery and the degree to which the implementation of the program matches the original program plan.

Frequency A measure of the number of times that a subject performs a specified behavior during a given time unit. The number of worksheets completed per hour is a frequency measure.

Frequency Histogram Graphic representation of frequency distribution data where vertical bars are placed over the scores, the height of each bar representing the frequency of occurrence for the given score (or interval of scores). Used when the data are continuous.

Frequency Polygon Graphic representation of frequency distribution data where a single point is used to designate frequency of occurrence. Adjacent points are then connected by a series of straight lines.

Friedman ANOVA by Ranks A statistical test of the hypothesis of difference on ordinal data when samples have either been repeatedly measured, or the subjects within the sample groups have been matched.

Fully Repeated Measures Design A factorial design in which each subject is observed in every possible experimental condition. The research contains only a single group of subjects which is tested or observed in all of the IV combinations.

Funnel Approach A preferred method for presenting previous research in the introduction section of the research report. Involves beginning with generally related research and subsequently presenting studies that are more closely related to the current study. Thus the prior studies are "funneled" into the current one.

Generalizability The extent to which the results of one study may be applied to other subjects and other settings. This is important when evaluating the external validity of a research project.

Graph A type of figure used in a research report to show a relationship in a set of data such as a comparison or distribution. Most common are line graphs showing continuous change by plotting the IV on the horizontal (x) axis, and the DV on the vertical (y) axis. A graph is more time-consuming and more expensive than text or tables to prepare and reproduce. (Also see Table.)

Hawthorne Effect A threat to internal validity in which what appear to be IV effects are actually due to the attention or flattery that subjects are given during the research process.

Historical Research Also called archival research, this descriptive approach involves the examination of documents contained in archives, libraries, churches, and so on.

History as a threat to internal validity Specific events that occur during the research differentially affect the performance of subjects in different treatment groups.

Hypotheses Educated guesses induced from direct observation concerning an assumed relationship between measured variables.

Independent *t* An inferential statistical test for comparing the means of two independently selected sets of sample scores. Measures of the DV must be in at least interval-data form.

Independent Variable (IV) The variable(s) manipulated by the experimenter in experimental research. Also refers to the variables used to predict dependent-variable values in correlational research or to the classification variable (subject variable) in post-facto research.

Induction The logical technique of arguing from a specific case to a general conclusion. Induction is based on a probabilistic model, such that only the likelihood of its validity can be claimed. Statistical analysis utilizes this technique when attempting to extrapolate the specific measures found in the sample to the general measures assumed for the population.

Inferential Statistics Techniques used in which samples are measured (producing statistics), and on the basis of these observations, population measures (parameters) are estimated.

Informed Consent An ethical consideration when conducting research. The researcher must inform the participants of all aspects of the research that might reasonably be expected to influence their willingness to participate and explain all other aspects of the research about which the participants inquire.

Instrumentation A threat to internal validity in which measuring instruments may change, thus resulting in a bias in measuring values for different treatment groups.

This also refers to the possible measurement bias that may occur if raters or observers change during the research process.

Intact Groups The use of groups of subjects in quasi-experimental research that are not randomly assigned by the experimenter. Groups as already composed (such as groups of students assigned to different classes) are given different treatments and are compared on the DV (sometimes using ANCOVA).

Interaction The combined effects of two or more IVs acting together in factorial designs. These effects are often called nonadditive because when an interaction occurs, the effect of the combined IVs is different from the added effects of each of the IVs when they are manipulated singly.

Interaction of Selection and Experimental Variable A threat to external validity that occurs when experimental treatments (IVs) may affect the performance (DV values) of some groups of subjects differently than other groups. The generalizability of the results of the research is thus compromised.

Internal Consistency Reliability A form of test reliability in which the internal characteristics of the test are examined for consistency. Split-half reliability is usually considered an internal consistency method, and several statistical procedures, such as the Kuder-Richardson formulas or coefficient alpha, are also used.

Internal Validity A characteristic of well-conducted and well-designed experimental research in which conclusions from the research are clear, unequivocal, and unconfounded.

Interrater Reliability The extent of agreement between research observers when witnessing or rating the same event(s). There must be a good deal of agreement between raters for their observations to be considered reliable.

Interval Scale An equal-interval scale of measurement that does not have a true zero point. Most parametric statistics, such as ANOVA and the independent t, require that measures be interval or ratio.

Introduction Section The first major section of the research report, which introduces the topic, presents related research, and briefly outlines the study.

Kruskal-Wallis *H* Test A nonparametric statistical test of the hypothesis of difference among three or more independently selected samples when the DV is measured as ordinal data.

Kuhn, Thomas The philosopher of science who authored *The Structure of Scientific Revolutions*, a book in which he traces how scientific theories and paradigms may change on the basis of an abrupt revolution rather than a continuous evolution. (See Scientific Revolution.)

Kurtosis A measure of the peakedness or flatness of the curvature of a unimodal frequency distribution. A relatively small amount of variability results in a positive value (leptokurtic distribution), whereas a large amount of variability produces a negative value (platykurtic distribution). An intermediate amount of variability (in which the value of the range equals six times the value of the standard deviation) produces a mesokurtic distribution.

Leptokurtic A unimodal distribution in which the curve is peaked, rather than flat. It indicates that most of the scores are occurring around the middle of the distribution and that the standard deviation is relatively small (less than one-sixth of the range). A leptokurtic distribution reflects homogeneity among the scores.

Likert Scale A series of statements about a topic whereby the respondent has to indicate his or her degree of agreement with each statement (strongly agree, agree, neither agree nor disagree, disagree, strongly disagree). Typically used to measure a person's attitudes toward a particular topic.

Limitations in Research Conclusions Whenever threats to internal or external validity exist in any research, the conclusions drawn from the research should reflect the limitations inherent in the design and other research procedures used.

Longitudinal Approach Developmental research which tracks the progress of a single group of subjects over a long period of time.

Main Effects A statistical term referring to the impact of an independent variable on a dependent variable. A main effect exists when there is a statistically significant difference in performance between the subjects receiving the various levels of an independent variable. In other words, the subjects who received one level of the IV behaved differently than those who received the other level(s) of the IV.

MANCOVA Multiple ANalysis of COVAriance is a form of ANOVA used when there are multiple DV measures as well as one or more variables on which groups are to be statistically equated.

Manipulated IV A variable changed by an experimenter in a planned and controlled way in order to see its effect on a DV.

Manipulation Check A feature of many research studies in which the researcher wishes to determine if the treatment IV was really manipulated as intended.

Mann-Whitney *U* Test A nonparametric statistical test of the hypothesis of difference between two independently selected samples when the DV is being measured as ordinal data.

MANOVA Multiple ANalysis Of VAriance is a form of ANOVA used when there are multiple DV measures.

Maturation as a threat to internal validity Occurs when subjects in an experiment change as a result of the passage of time during the research process. Subjects may physically mature, or grow more tired or practiced as the research progresses.

McNemar Test A statistical adjustment to the chi square test, used for the analysis of nominal data that has been taken on correlated (dependent) samples.

Mean A descriptive statistic indicating central tendency. Calculated by adding a group of scores and then dividing by the number of scores.

Measurement A method of quantifying observations by assigning numbers to them on the basis of specific rules. The rules chosen determine which scale of measurement is being used: nominal, ordinal, interval, or ratio.

Measurement Error The proportion of a measure (score) that is due to chance or uncontrolled factors instead of due to the phenomenon being measured. A certain degree of measurement error is always expected.

Measurement Scales Four general levels of measurement: nominal, ordinal, interval, and ratio. See specific definitions of each.

Median A descriptive statistic indicating central tendency that specifies the middlemost point in an ordered set of scores. The median always represents the fiftieth percentile.

Mesokurtic A unimodal distribution that conforms exactly to the criteria established for the normal curve. (See the normal curve.)

Meta-analysis A method for reviewing research that consists of the statistical integration of the results of all the research related to a particular IV and DV. The result is an estimate of effect size, or the degree to which the IV affects the DV in terms of the amount of difference in standard deviation units between typical experimental and control groups.

Method Section A major section of the research report that follows the introduction. Includes a description of the subjects, the materials or apparatus used, and the procedures followed in the study.

Minitab A computer software system that performs statistical analyses of data.

Mixed Design A factorial design in which at least one of the IVs is between groups and at least one of the IVs is within groups. Also called split-plot design.

Mode A descriptive statistic indicating central tendency that specifies the most frequently occurring score in a distribution of scores.

Multimodal Any distribution that has more than two points of greatest frequency (or more than two modes).

Multiple-Baseline Design A research design typically reserved for small-N or single-subject research. Baseline rates are established for several behaviors and then an intervention is successively introduced for each behavior while continuing to measure the other behaviors. Ideally, changes in the respective behaviors will coincide with the presentation of the appropriate intervention.

Multiple Comparison Test A statistical test used after the F ratio, to determine where the significant differences between the group means are occurring. Should be computed whenever there are more than two treatment conditions, and the F ratio is significant. An example of a multiple comparison test would be Tukey's HSD.

Multiple Correlation See Multiple R.

Multiple R An overall correlation that describes the degree of relationship between a single dependent variable and several predictor (or independent) variables. The multiple R is typically used to increase the accuracy of the DV prediction by combining the input of several independent variables.

Multivariate Study Usually refers to studies in which the researcher is interested in one or more IVs on at least two (but often more) DVs. Univariate research has only one DV of interest.

Naturalistic Observation An approach to descriptive research in which observations are made in a completely natural setting.

Nested Design Research designs in which different groups of subjects receive the same or similar treatment. When, for example, several teachers receive the experimental or control treatment (IV) and the behavior of their students is the DV of interest, several groups of students are indirectly influenced by the IV. The student groups are nested within the treatment conditions.

Nominal Scale Measurements or data in which numbers are used to label discrete, mutually exclusive categories. Nose-counting data that indicate the frequencies of occurrence within independent categories.

Nonparametric Tests Statistical tests that neither predict a population parameter such as the population mean, nor make any assumptions regarding the distribution of values in the underlying population. These tests are typically run on ordinal or nominal data and have less power than parametric tests.

Nonreversal Design (AB design) A small-N or single-subject design that, unlike the ABA or ABAB design does not contain a switch or reversal to the original condition. This is typically done when removal of a treatment may be unethical or impossible, and represents a single-subject version of the before-after design.

Nonspuriousness One of the three fundamental criteria (along with time precedence and relationships) underlying the logic of causal modeling. A significant correlation between X and Y should not be reasonably explainable by some third variable, say Z, causing changes in both X and Y consistently.

Normal Curve A unimodal frequency distribution curve resulting when scores are plotted on the abscissa and frequency of occurrence on the ordinate. It is a theoretical curve, shaped like a bell and fulfills the following criteria: (1) most of the scores cluster around the center, with the frequency of the scores falling off as they approach either tail of the curve; (2) the scores fall into a symmetrical shape—each half of the curve being a mirror image of the other; (3) the mean, median and mode all fall at precisely the same point, the center; (4) there are constant area characteristics regarding the standard deviation, with the standard deviation approximating one-sixth of the range; and the curve is asymptotic to the abscissa.

Null Hypothesis The hypothesis of no difference or no correlation, also called the chance hypothesis. The null hypothesis states that the differences or correlations obtained from measuring the sample are strictly due to chance, and its acceptance casts strong doubt on the validity of the alternative or research hypothesis.

Open-Ended Questions Items on a questionnaire or test that allow respondents complete freedom in how they respond. The respondent is not limited to certain responses, as is the case with multiple-choice questions or true-false items.

Operational Definitions Definitions of concepts or constructs in experimental terms. These definitions consist of specific descriptions of the methods that will be used to measure concepts such as achievement, aptitude, or intelligence.

Order Effect A type of sequencing effect that results when a subject's performance under a treatment condition is influenced by that treatment's ordinal position in the sequence (first, second, third, and so on). This makes it difficult to assess the true effect of the treatment if its place in the sequence of treatments is also contributing to its effect.

Ordinal Scale Data that indicate only relative position, but not how far above or below values are from one another. Rank ordered data derived only from the order of values and indicating nothing about differences between successive points on the scale.

Outcome Evaluation The same as summative or product evaluation. Refers to evaluation studies in which the primary focus is on the question of whether the objectives of a program have been met.

Paired t An inferential test of the hypothesis of difference between two sample means when the two sets of sample scores are not independent, as in the analysis of interval data taken from a before-after design.

Parameter Any measure that has been achieved by having measured the entire population. Most parameters are estimated, rather than known for certain.

Parametric Test Inferential tests of significance that assume parameter characteristics of the population, such as the population mean, standard deviation and shape (normality). Such tests utilize at least interval data.

Parsimony, Law of The principle that researchers should use the least abstract explanation of their results. It is based on the premise that the best explanations are those that have shaved away any excess meaning.

Participant Observer The researcher in a qualitative study is a participant observer if he or she actually has a role in the situation being examined. A researcher who takes part in a brainstorming session while doing qualitative observation of the roles of the other participants would be a participant observer.

Path Analysis A popular type of causal modeling that uses sophisticated correlational techniques to test hypothesized causal relationships between several variables that are logically ordered on a time basis.

Pearson r A statistical test designed to indicate the degree of linear relationship between two variables. Pearson r values range from +1.00, a perfect positive correlation, to −1.00, a perfect negative correlation. The Pearson r is sometimes called the product-moment coefficient.

Percentile A raw score transformation that is set up so that each score point indicates the percentage of scores that fall below it. Thus, a percentile score of 75 indicates that 75 percent of the scores in the distribution are below that point.

Pilot Study A miniature version of a planned full-scale study that is carried out to work any "bugs" or problems out of the proposed measurement and research procedures to be used in the actual research.

Planning Process (Research) Before a researcher selects subjects, manipulates variables, or measures behavior, a great deal of planning has to be done. One of the surest ways to go wrong in the research process is to improperly plan the project. Such planning should be complete and attempt to cover even small details. At the completion of the project, conclusions should be drawn in light of decisions made in the planning process.

Plato (427–347 b.c.) The early Greek philosopher and rationalist who argued that knowledge could be obtained through the use of meditation and reasoning powers, rather than through direct, sensory experience.

Platykurtic A unimodal distribution in which the curve is relatively flat, rather than peaked. It indicates that many scores are occurring away from the middle of the distribution and that the standard deviation is relatively large (greater than one-sixth of the range). A platykurtic distribution reflects heterogeneity among the scores.

Population The entire number of persons, things, or events that have at least one trait in common.

Post-facto Factorial Design A factorial design in which all the IVs are subject or classification IVs and therefore allow for no direct cause-and-effect statements.

Post-facto Research Research that does not involve a manipulated IV. Subjects are assigned to groups on the basis of characteristics that they already possess, and cause-and-effect relationships cannot be directly established. (See Cause-and-Effect Trap.)

Post-hoc Fallacy A fallacy that is based on the mistaken assumption that because a certain event followed another event, therefore it was caused by that previous event. This fallacy is especially evident in post-facto research.

Post-hoc Tests After-the-fact statistical comparisons that were not originally planned as a part of the research design. Such subsequent tests provide information in addition to that sought in the research proposal, and several statistical techniques may be used for such comparisons.

Power The ability of a statistical test to detect a significant difference or correlation. Power is equal to 1 − beta error. Any methods the researcher might use to reduce the likelihood of beta error will therefore increase the power of the statistical test. The higher the power of the test, the greater the likelihood of rejecting the null hypothesis.

Predictive IV An IV which can be used to predict DV values but which is not considered as a causal variable.

Predictive Validity A form of criterion-related validity in which test scores are correlated with a criterion, or behavior that is measured after the test has been given. The validity coefficient indicates how successful the test is as a predictor of the criterion. Often used for aptitude tests.

Process Evaluation Formative evaluation used to examine the delivery of program services and to assess the degree to which the program plan is being carried out.

Product Evaluation Summative evaluation carried out after a program has been completed, designed to assess the degree to which the objectives of a program have been met.

Product Measure A measure of the quality or accuracy of a subject's performance on a task. Number of words read per minute is a product measure.

Qualitative Data Nonnumerical data derived from interviews, direct observations, and examinations of written documents, used descriptively in qualitative research.

Qualitative Research Descriptive research including many forms of developmental and archival research, naturalistic observation, and case-study and field-study research. The descriptive data are not numerical, consisting instead of written descriptions of interviews, direct observations, and examinations of written documents.

Quantitative Research Research projects in which numerical data are gathered and statistically described or examined.

Quartile Points which divide a distribution into quarters. Each quartile represents 25 percentiles, such that the 2nd quartile is equal to the 50th percentile.

Quasi Experiments Research approaches that usually involve manipulated IVs but non-random assignment of subjects to groups, or IVs that are not completely and systematically manipulated by the researcher.

Random Assignment A technique used to obtain equivalent groups. Subjects in the research each have an equal probability of being placed in any of the treatment groups.

Random Sample A technique used to obtain groups that are representative of a population. All members of the population have an equal chance of being selected for the sample. Equivalent groups that are also representative of a population may be obtained by randomly selecting two or more samples and randomly assigning groups to experimental treatments.

Range A measure of variability that is based on the entire width of the distribution of scores. The range is equal to the highest score minus the lowest score.

Ratio Scale An equal-interval measurement scale that also contains a true or absolute zero point. Differences between scores are equivalent as in interval measures, but in addition, ratios of scores are also equivalent. This allows comparisons such as A being twice as large as B or one-half of B.

Rationalism An epistemology that is based on the premise that the acquisition of knowledge is best obtained by the use of the reasoning powers of the mind, rather than on direct, sensory observation.

Reactive Effect of Testing A threat to external validity that occurs when a pretest sensitizes subjects to a treatment. Because of the content of the test, the subject may pay attention to some aspects of the treatment in ways that would be different from nontested groups.

Reactive Effect of Experimental Arrangements A threat to external validity that results from doing research in settings that are different from the setting in which the results would ordinarily be applied. Also called ecological validity, since results obtained in laboratories might not apply to school settings.

Realism A criterion for good research. Involves creating a research context that is realistic and sensible to the subjects. Without this realism it is difficult to generalize the findings of the study to the "real world".

References One of the last sections of the research report. Contains an alphabetized list, by author, of all the research studies referred to throughout the report. Each study is listed in accordance with a very precise format as defined by the American Psychological Association.

Relationship(s) As used in correlational research, this term is used to express the degree to which two or more variables occur together, or are related. In this context, the term is used synonymously with correlation. That is, the stronger the correlation between (among) variables, the stronger the assumed *relationship* and the more accurate the resulting predictions.

Reliability of Measurement The consistency with which an instrument measures. A test that is reliable tends to give generally the same results every time it is taken by a subject. The index of reliability is the coefficient of reliability, which, in its simplest form, is a correlation between test scores taken on two different occasions.

Replication Doing an experiment over again, exactly as it was done originally. Replications are done to check the reliability of IV effects on a DV. Systematic replications involve conducting essentially the same research project but using different operational definitions or treatment levels for the IV and DV, thus enhancing the generalizability of effects.

Representative Sample A sample drawn using procedures (such as random sampling or stratified sampling) that should result in a sample that is as much like the population as possible.

Research Error Not a mistake made by a researcher. Refers to the possibility of inconsistent findings in different studies using the same IV and DV, limited ability to draw cause-and-effect conclusions, or a limited ability to generalize results to other subjects, settings, or times.

Research Proposal An overview of a proposed research study. Usually submitted to a granting agency in an attempt to secure funding to carry out the project. Typically contains a statement of the problem, a literature review of related research, a methodology that would be involved, and a budget outlining the anticipated expenses.

Research Reliability Consistency in the effect of an IV on a DV. Research consistency is established by doing replications of original research.

Research Review An examination of the research in the literature related to the effect of an IV on a DV. The reviewer critically examines the research with the purpose of drawing general conclusions.

Results Section A major section of the research report that follows the method section. Includes the results of all the statistical analyses, expressed both numerically and in words. Often includes figures (graphs) and tables, as well.

Reversal Design A single-subject research design in which the experimenter returns to an original control condition after manipulating the IV. (See ABA and ABAB designs.)

Rival Hypothesis Researchers hypothesize that the IV is responsible for changes in the DV in an experiment. If the experiment is confounded, other explanations (rival hypotheses) may account for DV change, since factors other than the IV may have caused the observed results.

Sample A group of any number of observations drawn from a population, so long as the number is smaller than the population.

SAS The Statistical Analysis System is a computer software system that peforms statistical analyses of data.

Science A body of organized knowledge and the techniques used in acquiring that knowledge. (See Scientific Method.)

Scientific Method (Hypothetico-Deductive) A method of producing an organized and systematic body of knowledge that is based on the following steps: observation, induction, creation of an hypothesis, deduction, and observation. The scientific method is thus grounded at both ends in observation.

Scientific Revolution The position taken by Thomas Kuhn, which portrays science as changing on the basis of abrupt revolutions. Scientific revolutions go through three stages of development: (1) normal, when theories and paradigms are largely accepted by the scientific community, and any anomalies (inconsistencies) are explained away as being insignificant; (2) crisis, when the anomalies become so persistent as to cast doubt on the underlying theory; and (3) the new theory, when an alternative theory is put forth that accounts for the previous anomalies, predicts more accurately, and uses fewer assumptions.

Selection as a threat to internal validity May occur if research begins with nonequivalent groups. Research with intact groups may result in an inability to distinguish IV effects from group differences that may have existed at the outset.

Selection Bias Any sampling or assignment procedure which results in a consistent distortion of the groups' characteristics in a particular direction. Random sampling or assignment eliminates selection bias.

Sequencing Effects Potential confounding factors in a repeated-measures (within-subjects) type of research design. These may result when the subjects' behavior under one treatment condition is influenced by other treatments that they receive in addition to the effect of the treatment itself. (See Carryover Effects and Order Effects.)

Significance A statistical term used to indicate that the results of the study are probably not just due to chance. Researchers talk about significant differences or correlations, the assumption being that chance has been ruled out (on a probability basis) as the explanation for these results.

Simulation An educational use of the computer that depicts real-life situations (such as in business, science, and psychology) and allows the student to solve problems that might arise in these situations.

Single-Blind Procedure An experimental procedure in which the subject is uninformed of which level(s) of the IV(s) he is receiving. Thus subjects are more likely to respond naturally as opposed to behaving consistently with their expectations regarding the IV.

Single-Subject Design Any research approach that has only one research subject. (See ABA and ABAB Designs, Reversal Designs, and Nonreversal Designs.)

Skewness A descriptive measure of the shape of any distribution of scores that may lack symmetry. Skewed distributions result when there are a few extreme scores in one direction.

Small-*N* Research Any research approach in which the number of subjects studied is small. Such research is usually experimental and involves rigorous control of all potentially confounding factors.

Solomon Four-Group Design A between-groups factorial design that is especially well suited to control for the possible confounding effects of pretesting. Pretesting is treated as one IV (pretest versus no pretest), and the treatment is the second IV (treatment versus no treatment).

Spearman r_s A statistical test of correlation, derived from the Pearson r, that handles data from the ordinal scale of measurement.

Split-Half Reliability A form of internal consistency reliability usually involving the calculation of a correlation between even-numbered and odd-numbered test items.

Split-Plot Design A term used synonymously with mixed design. In studies with more than one IV in which one is a within-subjects IV and the other is a between-groups IV.

SPSS The Statistical Package for the Social Sciences is a very widely used computer software system that performs statistical analyses of data.

Standard Deviation A descriptive measure of the amount of variability present in any distribution of scores. The standard deviation is calculated to produce a measure of how far all the scores in the distribution vary from the mean.

Standard Normal Curve Normal (mesokurtic) curve, plotted in z score units, with a mean of zero and a standard deviation of 1.00. (See Normal Curve.)

Stanine A transformation based on the normal curve, in which the distribution is divided into units of nine intervals. The mean of the stanine distribution equals 5.00 and the standard deviation approximates 2.00.

Statistic Any measurement that has been taken on a sample, rather than on the entire population. An example of an important statistic would be the sample mean.

Statistical Decision The decision, following the statistical test, as to whether the null hypothesis should be rejected or accepted. In either case, the decision is a probability statement, not a statement of absolute certainty.

Statistical Regression A threat to internal validity that may occur when subjects are placed in experimental groups on the basis of having either very high or very low scores. Subsequent measurements will often demonstrate regression toward the mean of all the observations. This results in high scores that tend to drop (down toward the average) and low scores that tend to rise (up toward the average).

Stem-and-Leaf Display A technique used for graphing data, in which the first digit is displayed in the first column (the stem) and the trailing digits in the second column (the leaf).

Steps in Planning and Doing Research The planning of research involves several steps. These include identification of the problem, review of the literature, defining the IV and DV, specification of subjects, materials and procedure, writing the research proposal, obtaining cooperation and permissions, pilot study, carrying the project out, statistically analyzing the results, drawing conclusions, and writing the report for publication.

Stratified Sampling A method used for obtaining a representative sample. The researcher identifies one or more characteristics that he or she wants to be distributed in the sample in the same proportion as they are distributed in the population, and subjects are divided according to this characteristic. Subjects are then randomly selected from each of these subgroups.

Subject IV An independent variable that is based on the inherent characteristics of the subjects, rather than on any manipulated stimuli. Such variables as gender, race, or any measures based on the subjects' previous history are considered to be subject variables. Any research that attempts to relate subject independent variables with the dependent variables is called post-facto research.

Summative Evaluation Product evaluation carried out after a program has been completed, designed to assess the degree to which the objectives of a program have been met.

Survey Research Research in which information is gathered using a survey or questionnaire, and sometimes from interviews. The data provide information about respondents' attitudes, beliefs, or opinions, or other psychological or sociological variables.

Systematic Replication A replication which uses different operational definitions for an IV and DV, or which uses different subjects or settings. If the results of a systematic replication are similar, the external validity of IV effects on the DV is enhanced.

***T* Score** A score transformation of normal distribution in which the mean is set at 50 and the standard deviation at 10. Typically the *T*-score range is thus from 80 to 20 (from three standard deviations above the mean to three standard deviations below the mean).

Table A means of comparing and classifying related items in a research report. A table usually presents quantitative data but occasionally consists of words that present qualitative comparisons. A table should be used only when necessary, for presenting important data more clearly than can be done in the text alone. (Also see Graph.)

Telegraphic Style A style of writing that omits nonessential words, as in a telegraph. Although it is sometimes tempting to write certain portions of a research report, such as the procedure, in this style, it should be avoided in lieu of full sentences organized into paragraphs.

Test-Retest Reliability A form of reliability in which the scores on a test are correlated with the same subjects' scores from a retest using the same test items.

Testing as a threat to internal validity May occur whenever a pretest is used in research. Changes in a DV may occur as a result of the manipulation of an IV, but they could also be a result of a practice effect from having seen the test before. The results are therefore confounded.

Theory A series of statements that attempt to explain why certain relationships between variables exist. Typically derived from hypotheses.

Time Precedence One of the three fundamental criteria (along with relationships and nonspuriousness) underlying the logic of causal modeling. If two variables, X and Y, are causally related, so that X is causing Y, X must precede Y in time.

Time Sampling A behavioral measure in which observations are made at specific time intervals in order to discover when a subject performs a specific task. Examining a baby's diaper every 15 minutes would provide information about when the baby wets.

Time Validity Research conducted at one time may not apply to other times. Research done in the late 1960s may not be valid in the 1990s, and may thus lack time validity.

Title The very first portion of the research report conveying the key characteristics of the study, usually by mentioning the major IV(s) and DV(s). Typically, twelve to fifteen words long.

Transformed Scores Any new set of scores that result from having changed all the raw scores in a given distribution by the same function. Typical transformed scores are z scores, T scores and stanines. Transformed scores allow for a direct comparison of an individual score with the entire distribution of scores.

Treatment IV An independent variable that has been actively manipulated by the experimenter (see Active IV). The levels of the IV are determined by the experimenter, not the subjects, and the subjects are exposed to these different levels of environmental or treatment conditions.

True Experiment Research situation in which the IV is manipulated by the experimenter and the subjects are randomly assigned to the various treatment conditions.

Unimodal A distribution of scores in which there is only one mode, or score with the greatest frequency.

Validity of Measurement An indication of the degree to which a test measures what it purports to measure. Established by content, criterion-relation, or construct validation.

Variability The extent to which subject measures differ from each other. The three most popular measures of variability are standard deviation, range, and variance.

Variable Anything that varies and can be measured. Opposite of constant. If one were measuring IQ scores among a group of males, IQ would be a variable and gender would be a constant.

Variance A measure of variability that indicates how far scores deviate from the mean. Variance is equal to the square of the standard deviation.

Wilcoxon *T* A nonparametric test of the hypothesis of difference between two sets of ordinal measures when the two sets of measures are correlated (not independent). For example, this test would be used on ordinal data collected from a pre-post experimental design.

Within-Subjects Comparison Comparison of DV measures taken on the same subjects across different treatment conditions.

Word Processing Flexible and powerful computer programs used for the writing, storage, editing, organization, and printing of written material.

***z* Score** A score that is based on the standard normal distribution, in which the mean is equal to zero and the standard deviation equals 1.00. All z scores above the mean are thus positive in value, and all scores below are negative. More than 99 percent of the z distribution distributes between z scores of +3 and −3. A raw score may be transformed into a z score by subtracting the raw-score mean from the raw score and dividing by the raw-score standard deviation.

Index

A

ABA design, 89
ABAB design, 331
Abstract, in research report, 251
Action research, 99–100
  procedure in, 99–100
  uses of, 100
Active independent variables, 25–26, 54
  manipulated independent variables, 25–26
After-only experimental design, 60–61
  procedure in, 60–61
Age of Reason, 8
Alpha error:
  increasing power with, 135
  type 1 error, 130–31
Alternate-form method, in reliability of measurement, 35
Alternative hypothesis, 130
American Psychological Association (APA):
  ethical guidelines, 168–69
  research report guidelines, 246, 249–50
Analysis of covariance (ANCOVA), 64
  procedure in, 145–46
Analysis of variance (ANOVA):
  factorial ANOVA, 140–43
  Friedman ANOVA by ranks, 151–52
  mixed designs, 144–45
  one-way ANOVA, 139–40
  procedure in, 139–45
  within-subjects ANOVA, 144
Annual Cumulative Abstracts, 252
Annual Cumulative Index, 252
Anomalies, 17
Appendix, research report, 259
Archival research, procedure in, 96–97
Aristotle, 5
Assigned independent variables, 27
Authors, research report, 250

B

Baseline:
  meaning of, 89
  multiple-baseline design, 90–91
Before-after experimental design, 61–65
  Hawthorn effect, 63–64
  procedure in, 61–62
  with separate control groups, 64–65
  threats to, 62–63
Berkeley, George, 8–9
Beta error, type 2 error, 131
Between-group comparisons, 55
Bias:
  effect on internal validity, 44
  in sampling, 29–30
Blinding subjects:
  double-blind procedure, 44
  single-blind procedure, 44
Bridgeman, Percy, 14

C

Carryover effects, 66, 67
Case studies:
  procedure in, 91–92
  research errors:
    analysis of, 218–23
    evaluation/comments, 239–43
  uses of, 92
Causal modeling:
  advantages of, 354–55
  criticisms of, 358–59
  nonspuriousness in, 356, 358–59
  relationships in, 355–56, 358
  time precedence in, 355, 358
Cause and effect trap, 27
  example of, 54

Ceiling effect, 301
Chi square, 153–54
Classification independent variables, 27
Coefficient of contingency, 155–56
Combination research, 74–75
  design of, 74–75
  factorial designs, 85–86
Computers:
  common procedures, 340–41
  computer-assisted instruction (CAI), 345–48
  concerns related to, 349
  data analysis, 339
  literature searches, 343–44
  Minitabs, 342
  presentation of experimental stimuli, 344–45
  programming, 348–49
  simulations, 348
  Statistical Analysis System (SAS), 342–43
  statistical packages, 350–51
  Statistical Package for Social Sciences (SPSS), 341–42
  word processing, 344
Concurrent validity, 39
Confounding, 24
  Hawthorn effect, 63–64
  internal validity and, 42
Constants, 23–24
Construct, meaning of, 39–40
Construct validity, 39–40
Content validity, 37–38, 40
Control groups:
  in matched-group design, 67–70
  separate, use of, 64–65
Correlation:
  hypothesis of association, 133–34
  positive and negative, 118
  tests for, 147–49
Counterbalancing, 67–68
Cramer's *V*, 156
Criterion, meaning of, 38
Criterion-related validity, 38, 40
Cross-sectional research, procedure in, 96, 97
Current Index to Journals in Education, 252

D

Data gathering, research in schools, 171
Deciles, 124
Deduction:
  examples of, 5–7
  in scientific method, 11
Demand characteristics, of study, 44
Dependent group selection, in experimental research, 59
Dependent variables, 25, 54
  analysis of:
    between-group comparisons, 55
    within-subject comparisons, 55

in experimental research, 58
in post-facto research, 71–72
Descartes, René, 8, 12
Descriptive research, 98–99
  procedure in, 98–99
  types of, 99
Descriptive statistics, 114–28
  graphs/tables, 118–22
  kurtosis, 123
  measures of central tendency, 115–16
  measures of relationship, 118
  measures of variability, 116–17
  skewness, 122–23
  transformed scores, 123–28
Developmental research, 95–96
  cross-sectional research, 96, 97
  longitudinal research, 95–96
Dewey, John, 194
Difference, tests for, 139–45, 150–52
Discourse on Method (Descartes), 8
Discussion section, research report, 257–58, 289, 300–302, 318, 333–34
Documentation, research report, 248–49
Double-blind procedure, 57
Duration, in reversal design, 89

E

Ecological validity, 47
Educational research, future view. (*See also* Research in schools)
  causal modeling, 353–56
  computer statistical packages, 350–51
  meta-analysis, 351–53
  path analysis, 356–60
Educational Resources Information Center (ERIC), 250, 251
  Current Index to Journals in Education, 252
Education Index, 252
Empiricism, 4–5, 8–9
Epistemology, 4–5
  meaning of, 4
Equivalent groups, 58–59
  by dependent selection, 59
  by independent selection, 59
  in sampling, 30
Error of affirming the consequent, 6
Ethical issues:
  APA guidelines, 168–69
  post-facto research, 73–74
  research in schools, 168–69
Ethnography, procedure in, 102–3
Evaluation studies, 103–6
  procedure in, 105–6
  process evaluation, 104–5
  product evaluation, 105
  purpose of, 104
Expectancy, effect on internal validity, 44

Experimental mortality, effect on internal
validity, 45
Experimental research, 56–71
after-only experimental design, 60–61
before-after experimental design, 61–65
control group in, 57, 58
dependent variable in, 58
design of, 57
equivalent groups, 58–59
experimental group in, 57, 58
external validity and, 58
hypothesis of difference and, 132–33
independent variable in, 57–58
matched-subjects experimental design, 65–
66
compared to post-facto research, 55–56, 75
quasi-experimental design, 68–71
repeated-measures experimental design, 63,
66–68
requirements for true experiment, 68
true experiment, example of, 275–89
External validity, 42, 46–48
importance of, 107
threats to, 47–48

F

Face validity, 38
Factorial ANOVA, 140–43
analysis of interaction in, 142–43
Factorial designs, 81–87
combination research, example of, 85–86
fully repeated measures design, 86
independent variables in, 81
interactions in, 81–84
main effects in, 81, 83
mixed designs, 86
post-facto factorial designs, 84–85
Solomon four-group design, 87
Field studies, 70
procedure in, 92–93
Formative evaluation, 104–5
F-ratio. (*See* Analysis of variance [ANOVA])
Frequency, in reversal design, 89
Frequency histogram, 119–20
Frequency polygon, 119, 120
Friedman ANOVA by ranks, 151–52
Fully repeated measures design, procedure
in, 86
Funnel organizational approach, research
report, 253–54

G

Galton, Sir Francis, 23
Generalizability issue, 330
Graphs/tables, 118–22
frequency histogram, 119–20

frequency polygon, 119, 120
horizontal histogram, 121
stem-and-leaf display, 121–22
Groups, differences between groups, 86

H

Hawthorn effect:
in before-after experimental design, 63–64
effect on internal validity, 44–45
Heterogenous tests, reliability of, 36
Histograms:
frequency histogram, 119–20
horizontal histogram, 121
Historical research, 96–97
procedure in, 96–97
History, effect on internal validity, 43
Homogeneous tests, reliability of, 36
Horizontal histogram, 121
Hume, David, 353
Hypothesis:
rival hypothesis, 42
in scientific method, 11
Hypothesis of association, 133–34, 308
Hypothesis of difference, 132–33, 308
experimental research and, 132–33
post-facto research and, 133
Hypothetico-deductive approach, 10

I

Independent group selection, in experimental
research, 59
Independent *t* test, 136, 137
procedure in, 137–39
Independent variables, 24–25
in experimental research, 57–58
in factorial designs, 81
in post-facto research, 71
types of, 25–27
Indexes, to publications, 252
Induction, 5, 7–8
in scientific method, 10–11
Inferential statistics, 128–34
alpha error, type 1 error, 130–31
alternative hypothesis, 130
beta error, type 2 error, 131
hypothesis of association, 133–34
hypothesis of difference, 132–33
measurement of scales and, 134
null hypothesis, 129–30, 131
significance, 132
standard deviation and, 128
Instrumentation, effect on internal validity,
43–44
Intact groups, comparison of, 69

Interactions:
  in factorial designs, 81–84
  between factors, effect on internal validity, 46
  of selection and experimental variable, 47
Internal consistency, in reliability of measurement, 36
Internal validity, 41–46
  confounding and, 42
  importance of, 107–8
  research in schools and, 164–65
  threats to, 43–46
Interrater reliability, 316
Interval-ratio tests of association, 147–49
  multiple *r*, 148–49
  Pearson *r*, 147–48
Interval-ratio tests of difference, 137
  analysis of covariance, (ANCOVA), 145–46
  analysis of variance (ANOVA), 139–45
  independent *t* test, 137–39
  multivariate analysis of covariance (MANCOVA), 146
  multivariate analysis of variance (MANOVA), 145
Interval scale, 32
Introduction, research report, 251–54

J

Journal article, example of, 260–69

K

Kant, Immanuel, 353
Kinsey studies, 93, 94
Kruskal-Wallis H test, 150
Kuder-Richardson formulas, 36
Kuhn, Thomas, 17
Kurtosis, 123
  leptokurtic shape, 123
  mesokurtic shape, 123
  platykurtic shape, 123

L

Leptokurtic shape, 123
Literature searches, computers, 343–44
Locke, John, 8–9
Longitudinal research, procedure in, 95–96

M

McNemar test, 154–55
Main effects, in factorial designs, 81, 83
Manipulated independent variable, in experimental research, 57–58

Mann-Whitney U test, 150
Matched group design, 69–70
  procedure in, 69–70
Matched-subjects experimental design, 65–66
  difficulty of, 66
  procedures in, 65
Maturation, effect on internal validity, 43
Mean, 115
Measurement, 31–40
  interval scale, 32
  measurement error, 32–33
  nominal scale, 31–32
  ordinal scale, 32
  ratio scale, 32
  reliability, 34–37
  validity, 37–40
Measurement scales, choice of statistical tests and, 134
Measures of central tendency, 115–16
  mean, 115
  median, 115
  mode, 115–16
Measures of relationship, 118
  negative correlation, 118
  positive correlation, 118
Measures of variability, 116–17
  range, 117
  standard deviation, 117
  variance, 117
Median, 115
Mesokurtic shape, 123
Meta-analysis, 109–10
  procedure in, 109–10
Method section, research report, 254–56, 286–88, 298–300, 315–16, 330–32
Minitabs, 342
Mixed designs, analysis of variance (ANOVA), 144–45
Mode, 115–16
Morgan's canon, 15
Multiple-baseline designs, procedure in, 90–91
Multiple comparison tests, 139
Multiple correlation, 148–49
Multiple *r*, 148–49
Multiple response measures, 106–7
  use of, 106–7
Multivariate analysis of covariance (MANCOVA), procedure in, 145–46
Multivariate analysis of variance (MANOVA), procedure in, 145
Multivariate studies, 106

N

Naturalistic observation, 97–98
  observer's role in, 98
  procedure in, 98

Negative correlation, 118
Nominal scale, 31–32
Nonparametric statistical tests, 149–56
  characteristics of, 149–50
  chi square, 153–54
  coefficient of contingency, 155–56
  Friedman ANOVA by ranks, 151–52
  Kruskal-Wallis H test, 150
  McNemar test, 154–55
  Mann-Whitney U test, 150
  Spearman r_s, 152
  Wilcoxon T test, 151
Nonreversal designs:
  AB design, 90
  procedure in, 90
Nonspuriousness, in causal modeling, 356,
    358–59
Normal curve, 124–26
  characteristics of, 124–25
  standard normal curve, 125–26
Null hypothesis, 129–30, 131

O

Observation, in scientific method, 10, 11–12,
    17
Occam's razor, 15
One-tail analysis, 138, 139
One-way ANOVA, 139–40
Open-ended questions, 317–18
Order effects, 66
Ordinal scale, 32
Outcome evaluation, 105

P

Paired *t* tests, 136
Parametric tests. (*See* Interval-ratio tests of
    difference)
Participant observation, procedure in, 103
Pass-fail grading:
  cause-and-effect trap, 54
  research example, 53–54
Path analysis:
  example of, 356–58
  history of, 356
Pearson *r*, 136, 137, 147–48
Percentile, 124
Permissions/cooperation, research in schools,
    170–71, 174
Pilot study, research in schools, 171
Plato, 5
Platykurtic shape, 123
Political polls, 94
Polling, 94
Polygon, frequency polygon, 119, 120

Population, in sampling, 27–28
Positive correlation, 118
Post-facto factorial designs, 84–85
Post-facto research, 42–43, 71–74
  compared to experimental research, 55–56,
    75
  dependent variable in, 71–72
  ethical issues, 73–74
  example of, 306–18
  hypothesis of difference and, 133
  independent variable in, 71
  predictive value of, 72–73
  problems of, 72
  usefulness of, 72
Post-hoc fallacy, 72
Post-hoc tests, 172
Power, increasing in statistical tests, 135–37
Prediction, post-facto research, 72–73
Predictive independent variables, 27
Predictive validity, 38–39
Pretesting, effect on external validity, 47–48,
    62
Primary variance, 217
Principles of Human Knowledge (Berkeley), 9
Process evaluation, 104–5
Product evaluation, 105
Product measures, in reversal design, 89
Product moment correlation, 147–48
Programming, computer, 348–49
Publications, research oriented, 250

Q

Qualitative research, 100–103
  data in, 100–101, 102
  ethnography, 102–3
  participant observation, 103
  compared to quantitative research, 101–2
  types of, 103
Quantitative research, compared to qualita-
    tive research, 101–2
Quartiles, 124
Quasi-experimental design, 68–71
  example of, 289–302
  intact groups, comparison of, 69
  matched group design, 69–70
  time series, 70–71
Questionnaires, 93

R

Random assignment, 30, 31, 65
  in experimental research, 59
Random sampling, 28–29, 31
Random selection, 47, 59
Range, 117
Rationalism, 4–5, 8

Ratio scale, 32
Reactive effects of experimental arrange-
    ments, effect on external validity, 47
References, research report, 258–59
Relationships, in causal modeling, 355–56,
    358
Reliability coefficient, in reliability of mea-
    surement, 34, 36
Reliability of measurement, 34–37
    alternate-form method, 35
    internal consistency, 36
    reliability coefficient, 34, 36
    split-half technique, 35–36
    test construction and, 36–37
    test-retest reliability, 34–35
Reliability of research, replications, 41
Repeated-measures experimental design, 63,
    66–68
    counterbalancing, 67–68
    sequencing effects, 66–67
Replications, and reliability of research, 41
Report, research in schools, 172–73 (*See also*
    Research report)
Research, basic rule of, 164–65
Research error, 40–48
    forms of, 40–41
    reliability of research, 41
    validity of search, 41–48
Research proposal, research in schools, 169–
    70
Research report:
    abstract, 251
    APA guidelines, 246
    appendix, 259
    authors, 250
    discussion section, 257–58, 289, 300–302,
        318, 333–34
    documentation, 248–49
    example of, journal article, 260–69
    funnel organizational approach, 253–54
    general mistakes to avoid, 246–48
    introduction, 251–54
    method section, 254–56, 286–88, 298–300,
        315–16, 330–32
    references, 258–59
    results section, 256–57, 288–89, 300–302,
        316–18, 332–33
    title, 250
Research review:
    meta-analysis, 109–10
    procedure in, 108–9
    weaknesses of, 109
Research in schools:
    basic rules, 164–65
    data gathering, 171
    ethical issues, 168–69
    examples of, research findings and altera-
        tion of teaching behavior, 175–90
    identification of problem, 167

independent/dependent variables, defini-
    tion of, 167–68
internal validity and, 164–65
literature review, 167
permissions/cooperation, 170–71, 174
pilot study, 171
planning project, 163–66, 173–75
report, 172–73
research proposal, 169–70
results/conclusions, 164, 172
statistical analysis, 171–72
Research simulations:
    checklist questions, 195–96
    critical decision points, 196–99
    examples of:
        business majors and future income,
            215–16
        effectiveness of comprehension instruc-
            tion methods, 210–11
        family size and IQ, 216
        financial aid and summer earnings, 215
        independence and type of education,
            214
        information processing at six months and
            IQ scores, 201–2
        in-service workshops and teacher com-
            petency test scores, 213
        instructor rating and student achieve-
            ment, 213
        listening and error identification, 210
        personality and academic performance,
            209
        personalized instruction and attitudes
            toward school, 212
        physical maturity and personality in
            teenage boys, 202–3
        popularity and academic performance,
            203–4
        positive reinforcement and learning,
            204–5
        preschool attendance and delinquent
            behavior, 199–200
        preschool attendance and social maturity,
            214
        racial identification and age, 200–201
        reading speed and extent of reading,
            216–17
        rehearsal technique with dyslexic/non-
            dyslexic children, 208
        relationship of competency test scores and
            classroom performance, 202
        salary/age relationship among teachers,
            211–12
        self-evaluation of special ed students, 204
        self-identity in college students, 207–8
        solutions to problems, 233–39
        spacing practice trials and retention
            scores, 200
        stages of moral growth, 206–7

teacher burn-out and number of years
teaching, 211
teaching style and learner performance,
205–6
Research strategies. (*See also* specific
methods)
action research, 99–100
combination research, 74–75
descriptive research, 98–99
developmental research, 95–96
evaluation studies, 103–6
experimental research, 56–71
factorial designs, 81–87
historical research, 96–97
meta-analysis, 109–10
multiple response measures, 106–7
naturalistic observation, 97–98
post-facto research, 71–74
qualitative research, 100–103
small sample designs, 87–93
survey research, 93–95
Resources in Education (RIE)
Annual Cumulative Abstracts, 252
Annual Cumulative Index, 252
document section, 251–52
index section, 252
Results/conclusions:
research report, 256–57, 288–89, 300–302,
316–18, 332–33
research in schools, 164, 172
Reversal designs:
ABA design, 89
procedure in, 88–90
variations of, 89–90
Rival hypothesis, 42
Rosenthal effect, 44
R/R research. (*See* Post-facto research)

S

Samples, small versus large, 87–88
Sampling, 27–31
bias in, 29–30
equivalent groups in, 30
populations in, 27–28
random assignment, 30, 31
random sampling, 28–29, 31
sample in, 28
stratified sampling, 29
with subject independent variables, 31
Science, meaning of, 4
Scientific method, 9–17
example of use, 12–13
history of, 4–9
law of parsimony, 15–16
operational definitions in, 14–15
proof in, 16
steps in, 10–12

as survival technique, 13
and truth, 13–14
Scientific theory, shifting theories, examples
of, 16–17
Secondary variance, 217
Selection, effect on internal validity, 46
Selection bias, effect on external validity, 47
Sequencing effects, 66–67
carryover effects, 66, 67
order effects, 66
Significance:
statistical tests, 132
tests of, 149–56
Simulations, computer, 348
Single-subject research:
compared to case studies, 319
example of, 320–34
Skewness, 122–23
Small-N research, 88–91
multiple-baseline designs, 90–91
nonreversal designs, 90
reversal designs, 88–90
Small sample designs, 87–93
case studies, 91–92
field studies, 92–93
small-N research, 88–91
Solomon four-group design, procedure in, 87
Spearman-Brown formula, 36
Spearman r_s, 136, 152
Split-half technique, in reliability of measure-
ment, 35–36
Split-plot designs, 144
S/R research. (*See* Experimental research)
Standard deviation, 117
inferential statistics and, 128
Standard normal curve, 125–26
Stanines, 127–28
Statistical analysis, research in schools, 171–72
Statistical Analysis System (SAS), 342–43
Statistical decision, 130
Statistical Package for Social Sciences (SPSS),
341–42
Statistical regression:
cause of, 45
effect on internal validity, 45–46
Statistical tests. (*See also* specific tests)
increasing power:
increasing alpha error, 135
increasing sample size, 135
statistical test and research design, 136–37
use of information, 136
interval-ratio tests of association, 147–49
interval-ratio tests of difference, 137
methodology, importance of, 156
nonparametric statistical tests, 149–56
power and, 134–37
Statistics. (*See also* individual topics)
descriptive statistics, 114–28
inferential statistics, 128–34

Stem-and-leaf display, 121–22
Stratified sampling, 29, 315
Subject independent variables, 26–27, 54
  in sampling, 31
Subsequent tests, 172
Summative evaluation, 105
Survey research, 93–95
  polling, 94
  purpose of, 93
  questionnaires, 93
  relationships examined in, 94–95
Systematic replications, 41

T

Tabula rasa, 9
Teaching practices, effects of research find-
    ings on, research example, 175–90
Terman studies, 96
Testing, effect on internal validity, 43
Test-retest reliability, 34–35
Theory, in scientific method, 11
Time precedence, in causal modeling, 355,
    358
Time sampling, in reversal design, 89
Time series, 70–71
  procedure in, 70–71
Time validity, effect on external validity, 48
Title, research report, 250
Transformed scores, 123–28
  deciles, 124
  normal curve, 124–26
  percentile, 124
  quartiles, 124
  stanines, 127–28
  t scores, 127
  z scores, 126–27
Treatment variables, 26
T scores, 127
T-tests:
  equation for, 136
  independent *t* test, 136, 137
  paired *t* tests, 136
Two-tail analysis, 138–39

U

U test, 150

V

Validity of measurement, 37–40
  concurrent validity, 39
  construct validity, 39–40
  content validity, 37–38, 40
  criterion-related validity, 38, 40
  face validity, 38
  predictive validity, 38–39
Validity of research, 41–48
  external validity, 42, 46–48
  internal validity, 41–46
Variables, 10, 11, 23–27
  active independent variables, 25–26
  assigned independent variables, 27
  cause and effect trap, 27
  classification independent variables, 27
  confounding variables, 24
  dependent variables, 25
  independent variables, 24–25
  manipulated independent variables, 25–26
  meaning of, 23
  predictive independent variables, 27
  subject independent variables, 26–27
  treatment variables, 26
Variance, 117

W

Wilcoxon T test, 151
Within-subject comparisons, 55
Within-subjects ANOVA, 144
Word processing, computers, 344

Z

Z scores, 126–27